REA: THE TEST PREP AP TEACHERS RECOMMEND

AP PHYSICS B & C

6th Edition

TestWare® Edition

David S. Jones
Physics Instructor
Florida International University
Miami, Florida

Edited by
John Kinard
AP Physics Teacher
Greenwood High School
Greenwood, South Carolina

Research & Education Association
Visit our website at: www.rea.com

Planet Friendly Publishing
✔ Made in the United States
✔ Printed on Recycled Paper
Text: 10% Cover: 10%
Learn more: www.greenedition.org

At REA we're committed to producing books in an Earth-friendly manner and to helping our customers make greener choices.

Manufacturing books in the United States ensures compliance with strict environmental laws and eliminates the need for international freight shipping, a major contributor to global air pollution.

And printing on recycled paper helps minimize our consumption of trees, water and fossil fuels. This book was printed on paper made with **10% post-consumer waste.** According to Environmental Defense's Paper Calculator, by using this innovative paper instead of conventional papers, we achieved the following environmental benefits:

Trees Saved: 4 • Air Emissions Eliminated: 837 pounds
Water Saved: 760 gallons • Solid Waste Eliminated: 247 pounds

For more information on our environmental practices, please visit us online at **www.rea.com/green**

Research & Education Association
61 Ethel Road West
Piscataway, New Jersey 08854
E-mail: info@rea.com

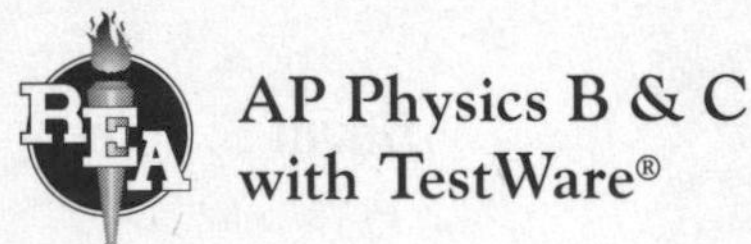

Published 2011

Printed in the United States of America

Library of Congress Control Number 2008942818

ISBN-13: 978-0-7386-0623-1
ISBN-10: 0-7386-0623-5

J10-0101

CONTENTS

ABOUT RESEARCH & EDUCATION ASSOCIATION

Founded in 1959, Research & Education Association (REA) is dedicated to publishing the finest and most effective educational materials—including software, study guides, and test preps—for students in middle school, high school, college, graduate school, and beyond.

Today, REA's wide-ranging catalog is a leading resource for teachers, students, and professionals.

We invite you to visit us at *www.rea.com* to find out how "REA is making the world smarter."

ACKNOWLEDGMENTS

In addition to our author, we would like to thank Larry B. Kling, Vice President, Editorial, for his overall guidance, which brought this publication to completion; Pam Weston, Publisher, for setting the quality standards for production integrity and managing the publication to completion; John Cording, Vice President, Technology, for coordinating the design and development of REA's TestWare® software; Diane Goldschmidt, Senior Editor, for editorial project management; Alice Leonard and Kathleen Casey, Senior Editors, for preflight editorial review; Heena Patel and Amy Jamison, Technology Project Managers, for their design contributions and software testing efforts; and Christine Saul, Graphic Designer, for designing our cover.

We also gratefully acknowledge John Kinard for his technical review of the manuscript, Barbara McGowran for copyediting, Ellen Gong for proofreading, and the team at Aquent Publishing Services for typesetting this edition.

ABOUT OUR AUTHOR

David Jones taught all levels of high school physics for 19 years in the Miami Dade County Public School system. Currently, he is teaching Physics I and II at Florida International University. Mr. Jones graduated from the University of Rochester, Rochester, N.Y. with a BA in Physics. He has served as an AP Physics Reader and an AP Physics Workshop Consultant for the College Board.

Mr. Jones was named Miami Dade County Science Teacher of the Year in 1996 and again, in 2006. Along with his teaching responsibilities, he is an assistant coach for the U.S. Physics Olympiad Team, which represents the United States at the annual International Physics Olympiad Competition.

A NOTE FROM THE AUTHOR

This review guide to AP Physics places emphasis on two very important aspects of learning physics that will improve your ability to solve physics problems. Namely, this book focuses on problem-solving techniques and conceptual understanding. Each chapter will provide insight into problem solving and provide the student with a foundation for the major concepts that are at the core of each unit in AP Physics.

This review guide is *not a textbook*! However, it will work well with your textbook by emphasizing important topics and providing you with enhanced learning opportunities in the form of extra problems sprinkled throughout each chapter. Each chapter focuses on the important topics that tend to be points of emphasis each year in the AP Physics curriculum. The practice sessions at the end of each chapter have a good mix of multiple-choice and free-response practice questions complete with answers. Each question in the guide was developed to address only AP Physics objectives. Note that questions marked with an asterisk (*) are considered to be more appropriate for the AP Physics C exam.

The sample practice tests reflect the current AP objectives and curriculum. All of the questions are relevant and correspond to the College Board's standards, and are at the appropriate difficulty level for AP Physics.

Good luck with your AP Physics exam!

David Jones

INDEPENDENT STUDY SCHEDULE

AP PHYSICS B

This study schedule allows for thorough preparation for the AP Physics B exam. Although it is designed to allow you to pace yourself comfortably over an eight-week preparation period, it can be condensed by collapsing each two-week period into one. Be sure to set aside enough time—at least two hours each day—to study. No matter which study schedule works best for you, however, the more time you spend acquainting yourself with the subject matter and the test, the more prepared and relaxed you will feel on the day of the exam.

Week	Activity
1	Acquaint yourself with the AP Physics exams by reading Chapter 1, "Excelling on the AP Physics B & C Exams." You will be introduced to key aspects of the exam and be given tips for success on the exam. Also, read and study Chapters 2 and 3. Use the Practice Session Problems at the end of each chapter to be certain you understand the content of the chapters.
2	Carefully read and study Chapters 4, 5, and 6 in this book. Be sure to use the Practice Session Problems at the end of each chapter to ascertain your test-readiness.
3	Carefully read and study Chapters 7, 8, and 9 in this book. Use the Practice Session Problems at the end of each chapter to be certain you understand the content of the chapters.
4	Carefully read and study Chapters 10, 11, and 12 in this book and use the Practice Session Problems to evaluate your understanding of the content.
5	Carefully read and study Chapters 13 and 14 in this book and answer the Practice Session Problems found in each chapter.
6	Carefully read and study Chapter 15 in this book. When finished, take Practice Exam 1 for the Physics B exam on CD-ROM, and after scoring your exam, carefully review all the answer explanations for the questions you answered incorrectly. If there are any types of questions or particular subjects that seem difficult to you, review those subjects by going over the appropriate sections of the AP Physics review chapters in this book.

7	Take Practice Exam 2 for the Physics B exam on CD-ROM. After scoring your exam, carefully review all the answer explanations for the questions you answered incorrectly. If there are any types of questions or particular subjects that seem difficult to you, review those subjects by going over the appropriate sections of the AP Physics review chapters.
8	This is the week you'll consolidate your gains and eliminate any continuing subject-matter weaknesses. Retake one or more of the practice tests printed in this book (as you deem necessary), paying particular attention to the questions with which you had difficulty the first time around. Going through the practice tests once again will put you on completely familiar terms with the subject matter and the AP exam itself.

INDEPENDENT STUDY SCHEDULE

AP PHYSICS C

This study schedule allows for thorough preparation for the AP Physics C exam. Although it is designed to allow you to pace yourself comfortably over an eight-week preparation period, it can be condensed by collapsing each two-week period into one. Be sure to set aside enough time—at least two hours each day—to study. No matter which study schedule works best for you, however, the more time you spend acquainting yourself with the subject matter and the test, the more prepared and relaxed you will feel on the day of the exam.

Week	Activity
1	Acquaint yourself with the AP Physics exams by reading Chapter 1, "Excelling on the AP Physics B & C Exams." You will be introduced to key aspects of the exam and be given tips for success on the exam. Also, read and study Chapters 2 and 3. Use the Practice Session Problems at the end of each chapter to be certain you understand the content of the chapters.
2	Carefully read and study Chapters 4 and 5 in this book. Be sure to use the Practice Session Problems at the end of each chapter to ascertain your test-readiness.
3	Carefully read and study Chapters 6 and 7 in this book. Use the Practice Session Problems at the end of each chapter to be certain you understand the content of the chapters.
4	Carefully read and study Chapters 10 and 11 in this book and use the Practice Session Problems to evaluate your understanding of the content.
5	Carefully read and study Chapters 12 and 13 in this book and answer the Practice Session Problems found in each chapter.
6	If taking the AP Physics C exam in Mechanics, carefully read and study Chapters 16 and 17 in this book. When finished, take Practice Exam 3 for the Physics C – Mechanics exam in this book, and after scoring your exam, carefully review all the answer explanations for the questions you answered incorrectly. If there are any types of questions or particular subjects that seem difficult to you, review those subjects by going over the appropriate sections of the AP Physics review chapters in this book.

7	For the Physics C – Electricity and Mechanics exam, read and study Chapter 18 in this book. When finished, take Practice Exam 4 in this book, and after scoring your exam, carefully review all the answer explanations for the questions you answered incorrectly. If there are any types of questions or particular subjects that seem difficult to you, review those subjects by going over the appropriate sections of the AP Physics review chapters.
8	This is the week you'll consolidate your gains and eliminate any continuing subject-matter weaknesses. Retake one or more of the practice tests (as you deem necessary), paying particular attention to the questions with which you had difficulty the first time around. Going through the practice tests once again will put you on completely familiar terms with the subject matter and the AP exam itself.

Note: The material covered in Chapters 8, 9, 14, and 15 in this book applies to the Physics B exam only.

INTRODUCTION

AP Physics B & C

Chapter 1

Excelling on the AP Physics B & C Exams

ABOUT THIS BOOK AND TestWare®

This book, along with our companion TestWare® software, provides an accurate and complete representation of the Advanced Placement Examinations for Physics B and Physics C. Our book includes four complete practice exams, two for Physics B and two for Physics C. Our practice tests are based on the format of the most recently administered Advanced Placement Physics exams. Each model exam includes every type of question that you can expect to encounter on the real test. Following each of our practice tests is an answer key, complete with detailed explanations designed to clarify the material for you. By using the subject reviews, completing the practice tests for the exams you are taking (B or C), and studying the explanations that follow, you will pinpoint your strengths and weaknesses and, above all, put yourself in the best possible position to do well on the actual test.

Practice Tests 1 and 2 for the Physics B exam are included in two formats: in printed form in this book and in TestWare® format on the enclosed CD. The software provides the added benefits of automatic, accurate scoring and enforced time conditions, which makes it all the easier to pinpoint your strengths and weaknesses.

ABOUT THE EXAM

The Advanced Placement Physics B and C examinations are offered each May at participating schools and multi-school centers throughout the world.

The Advanced Placement Program is designed to allow high school students to pursue college-level studies while attending high school. The participating colleges, in turn, grant credit and/or advanced placement to students who do well on the examinations.

The Advanced Placement Physics courses are designed to be the equivalent of a college introductory Physics course, often taken by Physics majors in their first year of college.

AP PHYSICS B EXAM FORMAT AND CONTENT

The AP Physics B exam is approximately three hours long, contains a 70-question multiple-choice section and a free-response section requiring the student to answer six to seven questions. The two sections are equally weighted and one score is reported for the Physics B exam. The Physics B exam primarily tests mechanics, heat, kinetic theory and thermodynamics, and electricity and magnetism, as well as wave theory and atomic and nuclear physics. A working knowledge of algebra and trigonometry is essential.

AP PHYSICS C EXAM FORMAT AND CONTENT

The more difficult Physics C exam consists of two tests, and students have the choice of taking either or both exams. One exam concentrates on mechanics, and the other concentrates on electricity and magnetism. Both exams require a strong knowledge of calculus. Separate grades are reported for each. Each AP Physics C exam is 1 hour and 30 minutes long. The time on each exam is divided equally between a 35-question multiple-choice section and a free-response section that usually contains three questions.

You may find either of the AP Physics exams considerably more difficult than many classroom exams. In order to measure the full range of your ability in physics, the AP exams are designed to produce average scores of approximately 50% of the maximum possible score for the multiple-choice and essay sections. Therefore, you should not expect to attain a perfect or even near-perfect score.

COMPARISON OF TOPICS FOUND ON THE PHYSICS B AND PHYSICS C EXAMS

The following table shows the content of the Physics B and Physics C exams, including subtopics. Percentages are approximate.

Content	% on Physics B exam	% on Physics C exam
I. Newtonian Mechanics		
A. Kinematics (including vectors, vector algebra, components of vectors, coordinate systems, displacement, velocity, and acceleration) 1. Motion in one dimension 2. Motion in two dimensions including projectile motion	7%	9%
B. Newton's laws of motion 1. Static equilibrium (first law) 2. Dynamics of a single particle (second law) 3. Systems of two or more bodies (third law)	9%	10%
C. Work, energy, power 1. Work and work-energy theorem 2. Forces and potential energy 3. Conservation of energy 4. Power	5%	7%
D. Systems of particles, linear momentum 1. Center of mass* 2. Impulse and momentum 3. Conservation of linear momentum, collisions	4%	6%
E. Circular motion and rotation 1. Uniform circular motion 2. Torque and rotational statics 3. Rotational kinematics and dynamics* 4. Angular momentum and its conservation*	4%	9%
F. Oscillations and gravitation 1. Simple harmonic motion (dynamics and energy relationships) 2. Mass on a spring 3. Pendulum and other oscillations 4. Newton's law of gravity 5. Orbits of planets and satellites a. Circular b. General*	6%	9%

* Indicates subtopics covered in Physics C, but not Physics B.

(*Continued*)

Content	% on Physics B exam	% on Physics C exam
II. Fluid Mechanics and Thermal Physics		
A. Fluid Mechanics 1. Hydrostatic pressure 2. Buoyancy 3. Fluid flow continuity 4. Bernoulli's equation	6%	
B. Temperature and heat 1. Mechanical equivalent of heat 2. Heat transfer and thermal expansion	2%	
C. Kinetic theory and thermodynamics 1. Ideal gases a. Kinetic model b. Ideal gas law 2. Laws of thermodynamics a. First law (including processes on pV diagrams) b. Second law (including heat engines)	7%	
III. Electricity and Magnetism		
A. Electrostatics 1. Charge and Coulomb's law 2. Electric field and electric potential (including point charges) 3. Gauss's law* 4. Fields and potentials of other charge distributions*	5%	15%
B. Conductors, capacitors, dielectrics 1. Electrostatics with conductors 2. Capacitors a. Capacitance b. Parallel plate c. Spherical and cylindrical* 3. Dielectrics*	4%	7%
C. Electric circuits 1. Current, resistance, power 2. Steady-state direct current circuits with batteries and resistors only 3. Capacitors in circuits a. Steady state b. Transients in RC circuits*	7%	10%

* Indicates subtopics covered in Physics C, but not Physics B.

Content	% on Physics B exam	% on Physics C exam
D. Magnetic Fields 1. Forces on moving charges in magnetic fields 2. Forces on current-carrying wires in magnetic fields 3. Fields of long current-carrying wires 4. Biot-Savart's law and Ampere's law*	4%	10%
E. Electromagnetism 1. Electromagnetic induction (including Faraday's law and Lenz's law) 2. Inductance (including LR and LC circuits)* 3. Maxwell's equations*	5%	8%
IV. Waves and Optics		
A. Wave motion (including sound) 1. Traveling waves 2. Wave propagation 3. Standing waves 4. Superposition	5%	
B. Physical optics 1. Interference and diffraction 2. Dispersion of light and the electromagnetic spectrum	5%	
C. Geometric optics 1. Reflection and refraction 2. Mirrors 3. Lenses	5%	
V. Atomic and Nuclear Physics		
A. Atomic physics and quantum effects 1. Photons, the photoelectric effect, Compton scattering, *x*-rays 2. Atomic energy levels 3. Wave-particle duality	7%	
B. Nuclear physics 1. Nuclear reactions (including conservation of mass number and charge) 2. Mass-energy equivalence	3%	

* Indicates subtopics covered in Physics C, but not Physics B.

USE OF CALCULATORS

Calculators are NOT permitted on the multiple-choice sections of either exam, but are allowed on the free-response sections. A programmable or graphing calculator may be used and students will not be required to erase their calculator memories before and after the exam. Visit the College Board website (*www.collegeboard.com*) for more information on what calculators are allowed.

HOW TO USE THIS BOOK AND TestWare®

What do I study first?

To begin your studies, read over this introduction and the suggestions for test taking. If you are taking the AP Physics B exam, take Practice Exam 1 on CD-ROM to determine your strengths and weaknesses. Next, study the course review material focusing on your specific problem areas. Studying the reviews thoroughly will reinforce the basic skills you will need to do well on the exam and will familiarize you with the format and procedures involved when taking the actual exam. To complete your studies for the AP Physics B exam, take Practice Exam 2 on CD-ROM.

If you are taking an AP Physics C exam, study the appropriate review chapters in this book and take Practice Exam 3 and/or 4 printed in this book.

To best utilize your study time, follow the appropriate Independent Study Schedule, which you will find in the front of this book. The schedule is based on an eight-week program, but if necessary can be condensed to four weeks by combining each two-week program into one week.

When should I start studying?

It is never too early to start studying for the AP Physics examinations. The earlier you begin, the more time you will have to sharpen your skills. Do not procrastinate! Cramming is *not* an effective way to study, since it does not allow you the time needed to learn the test material. The sooner you learn the format of the exam, the more time you will have to familiarize yourself with it.

SSD accommodations for students with disabilities

Many students qualify for extra time to take the AP Exams and our TestWare® can be adapted to accommodate your time extension. This allows you to practice under the same extended time accommodations that you will receive on the actual test day. To customize your TestWare® to suit the most common extensions, visit our website at *www.rea.com/ssd*.

ABOUT OUR REVIEW SECTION

This book contains AP Physics B and C course review material that can be used as both a primer and as a quick reference while taking the practice exams. Our course review is meant to complement your AP Physics textbook and is by no means exhaustive. While AP Physics C is covered throughout all the chapters in this book, Chapters 16 through 18 are specially written for the Physics C exams in Mechanics and Electricity and Magnetism. In each chapter you'll find sample problems with solutions and, at the end of each chapter, there is a section for you to check your understanding of the topic by solving practice problems. Questions marked with an asterisk (*) are more suited to the Physics C exam. By studying our review along with your text, you will be well prepared for the exam.

SCORING THE OFFICIAL EXAMS

Weighted Multiple-Choice + Weighted Free-Response = Total Composite Score

The College Board creates a formula (which changes slightly every year) to convert raw scores into composite scores grouped into broad AP grade categories. The weights for the multiple-choice sections are determined by the Chief Reader, who uses a process called *equating*. This process compares the current year's exam performance on selected multiple-choice questions to that of a previous year, establishing a level of achievement for the current year's group and a degree of difficulty for the current exam. This data is combined with historical trends and the reader's professional evaluation to determine the weights and tables.

The AP free-response is graded by teacher volunteers, grouped at scoring tables, and led by a chief faculty consultant. The consultant sets the grading scale that translates the raw score into the composite score. Past grading illustrations are available to teachers from the College Board, and may be ordered using the contact information given in this chapter. These actual examples of student responses and a grade analysis can be of great assistance to both the student and the teacher as a learning or review tool.

When will I know my score?

In July, a grade report will be sent to you, your high school, and the college you chose to notify. The report will include scores for all the AP exams you have taken up to that point and will show a grade between 1 and 5. Normally, colleges participating in the Advanced Placement Program will recognize grades of 3 or better, but be sure to check with the colleges where you wish admission.

Your grade will be used by your college of choice to determine placement in its Physics program. This grade will vary in significance from college to college, and is used with other academic information to determine placement. Contact your college admissions office for more information regarding its use of AP grades.

STUDYING FOR YOUR EXAM

It is very important for you to choose the time and place for studying that works best for you. Some students may set aside a certain number of hours every morning, while others may choose to study at night before going to sleep. Other students may study during the day, while waiting in line, or even while eating lunch. Only you can determine when and where your study time will be most effective. But be consistent and use your time wisely. Work out a study routine and stick to it.

When you take the practice tests, create an environment as much like the actual testing environment as possible. Turn your television and radio off, and sit down at a quiet table free from distraction. Make sure to time yourself, breaking the test down by section.

As you complete each practice test, score your test and thoroughly review the explanations to the questions you answered incorrectly; however, do not review too much at one time. Concentrate on one problem area at a time by reviewing the question and explanation, and by studying our review until you are confident that you completely understand the material.

TEST-TAKING TIPS

Although you may not be familiar with standardized tests such as the AP Physics B and C examinations, there are many ways to acquaint yourself with this type of examination and help alleviate any test-taking anxieties. Listed below are ways to help you become accustomed to the AP exams, some of which may be applied to other standardized tests as well.

Become comfortable with the format of the exam. Stay calm and pace yourself. After simulating the test a couple of times, you will boost your chances of doing well, and you will be able to sit down for the actual exam with more confidence.

Read all of the possible answers. Just because you think you have found the correct response, do not automatically assume that it is the best answer. Read through each choice to be sure that you are not making a mistake by jumping to conclusions.

Use the process of elimination. Go through each answer to a question and eliminate as many of the answer choices as possible. By eliminating just two answer choices, you give yourself a better chance of getting the item correct, since there will only be three choices left from which to make your guess.

Work quickly and steadily. Work quickly and steadily to avoid focusing on any one question too long. Remember, your time is limited. Taking the practice tests in this book will help you learn to budget your time.

Beware of test vocabulary. Words such as *always*, *every*, *none*, *only*, and *never* indicate there should be no exceptions to the answer you choose. Words like *generally*, *usually*, *sometimes*, *seldom*, *rarely*, and *often* indicate there may be exceptions to your answer.

Learn the directions and format for each section of the test. Familiarizing yourself with the directions and format of the exam will save you valuable time on the day of the actual test.

THE DAY OF THE EXAM

Before the exam

On the day of the test, you should wake up early (preferably after a good night's rest) and have a good breakfast. Make sure to dress comfortably, so that you are not distracted by being too hot or too cold while taking the test. Also plan to arrive at the test center early. This will allow you to collect your thoughts and relax before the test, and will also spare you the anxiety that comes with being late.

Before you leave for the test center, make sure that you have your admission form, social security number, and another form of identification, which must contain a recent photograph, your name, and signature (i.e., driver's license, student identification card, or current alien registration card). You will not be allowed to take the test if you do not have proper identification. You will also need to bring your school code. Also, bring several sharpened No. 2 pencils with erasers for the multiple-choice questions and black or blue pens for the free-response questions.

You may wear a watch, but only one without a beep or alarm. No dictionaries, textbooks, notebooks, compasses, correction fluid, highlighters, rulers, computers, cell phones, beepers, PDAs, scratch paper, listening and recording devices, briefcases, or packages will be permitted, and drinking, smoking, and eating are prohibited while taking the test.

During the exam

Once you enter the test center, follow all of the rules and instructions given by the test supervisor. If you do not, you risk being dismissed from the test and having your scores canceled.

After the exam

You may immediately register when taking the exam to have your score sent to the college of your choice; you may also wait and later request to have your AP score reported to the college of your choice.

CONTACTING THE AP PROGRAM

For registration bulletins or more information about the AP Physics B and Physics C exams, contact:

AP Services
Educational Testing Service
P.O. Box 6671
Princeton, NJ 08541-6671
Phone: (609) 771-7300 or (888) 225-5427
E-mail: apexams@ets.org
Website: *www.collegeboard.com*

COURSE REVIEW

AP Physics B & C

Chapter 2

Data Analysis and Interpreting Graphs

EXAM OVERVIEW

Since the late 1990s, the Advanced Placement Physics exam has placed an increased emphasis on physics laboratory experience, interpreting laboratory investigations, and interpreting graphs that accompany a laboratory experience. Questions appear every year in the AP Physics B and C exams, usually centering on a laboratory experience like determining gravity or making sense of data on position versus time or index of refraction. Occasionally, an AP exam has included a question asking the student to create or devise an experiment that incorporates certain equipment. Unfortunately, a review book cannot help you with that type of question. If you have not performed experiments in your high school course, you have missed an important learning experience. If your course is lacking in this area, the laboratory-focused questions on the AP Physics exam may be difficult for you.

However, this book can help you review how to work with data and how to interpret graphs in a physics class. So even if your AP Physics class lacks a strong experimentation component, you can improve your ability to interpret data gathered from experiments.

GRAPHING DATA CORRECTLY

The goal of a physics experiment is to determine how two sets of measurements are related to each other. In some physics experiments, you do not have clearly defined independent and dependent variables. Instead, your focus is understanding the two things you are measuring and why you need to measure them. Once you have the two sets of measurements, your next step is to create a graph. If your physics teacher has told you what the title of your graph is to be, you have a clue about how to begin. For example, if your graph is titled "Position vs. time," that tells you the position data are on the vertical axis and the time data are on the horizontal axis.

When graphing on your own, try using graph paper and a straight edge as well as a graphing software program like Microsoft Excel or Graphical Analysis by Vernier. On the AP Physics exam, you will have to do your graphing by hand on paper.

But the best way to understand graphing is to look at an example. So let's do that.

A GENERAL APPROACH TO LINEAR GRAPHING

Let's say we are in a physics class and we need to determine the spring constant for a linear spring. Recall that the spring constant is a measure of the stiffness or strength of a spring. To find the spring constant, we need to set up an experiment with a spring loaded with various weights. The spring stretches different amounts when we add different weights to it. During this experiment, we measure two quantities: the amount of weight (or force) in newtons and the stretch in meters. The weights represent both the force exerted on the spring and the force exerted by the spring. The following table shows the data we obtain from our experiment:

Force (N)	Stretch (m)
0.2	0.015
0.4	0.035
0.6	0.065
0.8	0.075
1.1	0.130
1.5	0.160
2.0	0.210

The graph of the data looks like this:

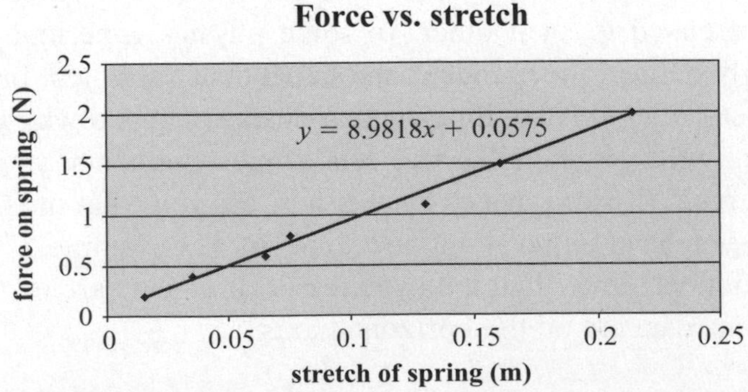

This is a typical graph of a physics experiment. The data clearly show a relationship between the two sets of measurements. In this case, it is a **linear relationship**. The line is called a **trend line**. (All the data do not fall on the line, but that is to be expected when we are dealing with real data.) We can use this linear relationship to understand how the spring behaves. From the linear relationship of the graph, we can determine the equation for the spring.

The equation for the spring is the equation of the graph's trend line. This simply follows the form of a line, $y = mx + b$. We can present the physics relationship this way:

$$\text{Force spring exerts } (F) = 8.92 \text{ N/m}$$

where the slope of the line is 8.92 and the y-intercept is negligible (0.05). Realize, however, that not all y-intercepts are negligible. Sometimes they have a physical meaning, so don't be too quick to write off all y-intercepts as 0.

This follows the typical relationship in introductory physics for a linear spring:

$$\vec{F} = -k\overrightarrow{\Delta x}$$

The negative sign in this complete vector relationship indicates that the spring exerts a force in the opposite direction of the spring's stretch. The k represents the physical constant called the spring constant, which is typically measured in Newtons per meter (N/m). In this example, the spring constant is 8.92 N/m.

WHAT IF WE GET A CURVE?

Here is where the fun begins. When the relationship between physical quantities is linear, we can use the line of best fit to make a model for the relationship. But, if we get a nonlinear relationship between our physical quantities, we will need to investigate further to figure out the exact model for this relationship. This is a more sophisticated exercise than plotting linear data and learning this skill takes practice. Computer software programs (i.e., Excel) are able to perform this skill, and most students have seen their own graphing calculator perform this skill by pushing a few buttons. However, the AP exam will have questions that will test the ability of physics students to be able to "curve fit" by using graph paper. In other words, AP students will have to do this skill by hand on the test. So, get used to using graph paper, pencil, and a straight edge to make this happen. This skill is addressed in the following section.

GENERAL APPROACH TO GRAPHING NONLINEAR DATA

Here is a sample set of position-versus-time data for an object accelerating at a constant rate:

Position (m)	Time (s)
5	0
10	1.0
16	1.5
26	2.0
36	2.5
51	3.0

Here is the accompanying graph for the data:

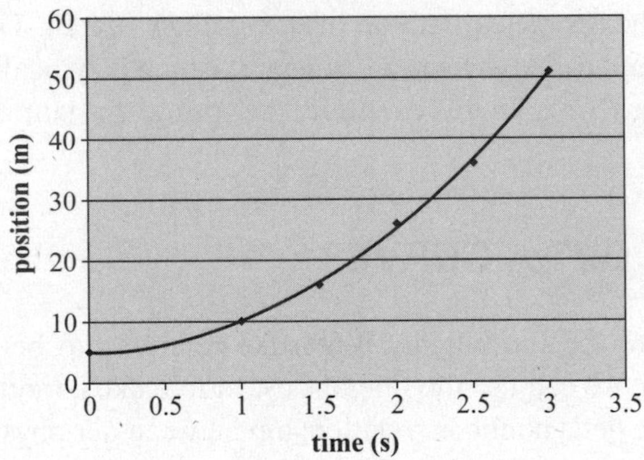

Looking at this graph, we might guess that the relationship between position and time is **quadratic**, meaning that position varies directly with time (t) squared. The equation for a quadratic relationship is

$$x(t) \propto kt^2.$$

To verify that our guess is correct, we need to create a second table and graph that plots position versus time squared:

Position (m)	Time^2 (s^2)
5	0
10	1.0
16	2.2
26	4.0
36	6.3
51	9.0

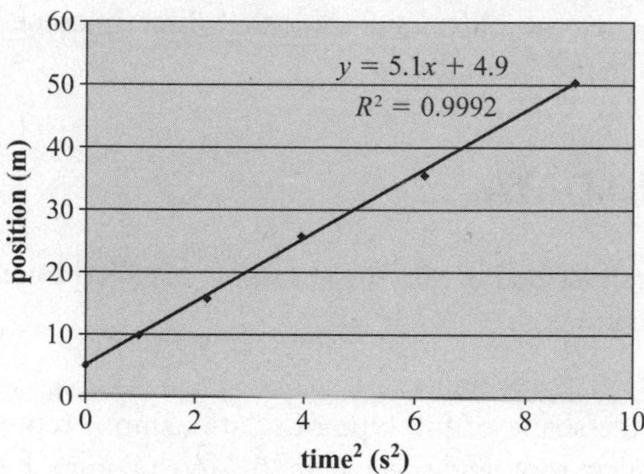

The linearity of this graph verifies our guess of a quadratic relationship. Now that we have a straight line, we can write an equation for the relationship n in standard slope-intercept form: $y = mx + b$. Our graph, with its x-axis being time squared and its y-axis position results in the equation

$$x(t) = 5.1t^2 + 4.9.$$

Add units for the axes, and the relationship makes even more sense:

$$x(t) = 5.1\ (\text{m/s}^2)t^2 + 4.9\ \text{m}$$

The term 5.1 m/s^2 has units of acceleration, and the term 4.9 m has units of position. The 4.9 value is the starting point for this object. If we think about kinematic relationships for constant acceleration, $\Delta x(t) = v_o t + \frac{1}{2}at^2$, we can see that our graphical relationship is exactly that equation without the initial velocity term. Therefore, the value of $5.1t^2$ is the term $\frac{1}{2}at^2$, meaning that

$$5.1 = \frac{1}{2}a$$

$$a = 10.2\ \text{m/s}^2$$

From our data and analysis, we were able to figure out the exact relationship between position and time. We could even determine the acceleration value from our analysis. Remember, the point of the graph is to find an "average" for our data. If we had to determine an average acceleration value for the experiment (position versus time data, in this example), we would use the 10.2 m/s^2 value.

You should avoid determining average values from data by using only one point of data. That is incorrect and makes the point of graphing irrelevant. Thus, do not compute acceleration by algebraically solving for acceleration from one point of data. That will get you into trouble when you do real laboratory work, and it will also get you into trouble on the AP exam. The purpose of graphing is to understand the relationship between two physical quantities. Therefore, use your graphs to determine other quantities that directly come from the graphs (i.e., acceleration in the example).

LINEARIZING DATA

The process described in previous example is called **linearizing** data. It is a simple five-step process:

1. Graph the original data.
2. Look at the shape of the type of relationship it represents (quadratic, cubic, square root, and inverse are the most common types).
3. Create a second set of data for the type of relationship you determined your graph represents. These data will have different x values. In the previous example, x changed from time to time squared. If the graphed shape had been a square root curve, the altered x would have been the square root of x.
4. Create a graph using your new data.
5. Use the slope-intercept form of the line to create the exact relationship for your data. You can see why this process is called linearizing the data.

This is the most important data analysis skill you will learn in your AP Physics course. You should practice it by working with graphs that present you with interesting relationships. The following are the most common relationships:

$$y = kx$$

$$y = kx^2$$

$$y = \frac{k}{x}$$

$$y = \frac{k}{x^2}$$

$$y = k\sqrt{x}$$

$$\frac{1}{y} = \frac{k}{x}$$

$$k_1 \sin y = k_2 \sin x$$

The last two relationships in this list come up in geometrical optics and have made their way onto the AP Physics exams over the years. Thus, it is important that you get experience in graphing all these types of relationships. Let's work through another problem before you try independently working the Practice Session.

Our physics class is now studying **simple harmonic motion**. We are conducting an experiment in which we put a series of masses on a spring and then set the spring/mass system into motion. The resulting motion is called simple harmonic motion. We measure each mass we place on the spring and the period of the simple harmonic motion. The period is always constant for any one mass. Here is a table of the data set we gather:

Mass (kg)	Period (s)
0.1	0.60
0.2	0.84
0.3	1.02
0.4	1.20
0.5	1.38
0.8	1.68
1.0	1.98

The graph we create for this set of data looks like this:

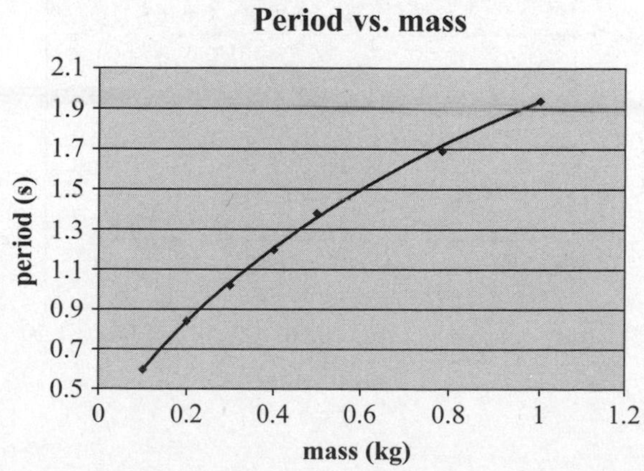

This graph shows more of a curve than a line. The ability to determine the type of curve takes practice and experience. The square root function can look very linear in a graph of experimental data. If there is not a good spread of data in the independent variable, the square root curve could look more like a line. A good rule of thumb in the physics lab is to have the minimum and maximum values of the independent variable differ by a factor of 10. This rule of thumb is useful in graphing and determining relationships. In our experiment, the data go from a minimum of 0.1 kg to 1.0 kg, which differ by a factor of 10 and thus produce a distinct curve.

Once we have made an intelligent guess that the curve is a square root curve, we need to test our hypothesis. We take the square root of the mass data and then make a new graph of period versus the square root of mass ($mass^{1/2}$). Our altered data are as follows:

Mass^{½} (Kg^{½})	**Period (s)**
0.32	0.60
0.45	0.84
0.55	1.02
0.63	1.20
0.71	1.38
0.89	1.68
1.00	1.98

And here is the graph for our new data:

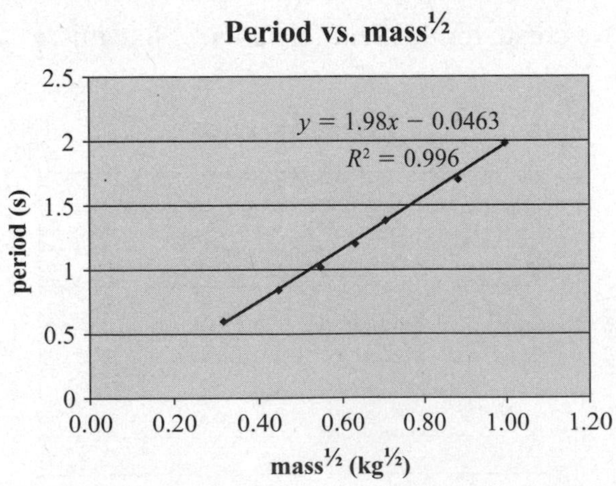

The graph is a line, and the relationship is given by the slope-intercept equation. Because the intercept is negligible, we can ignore it when writing the relationship. The relationship is

$$T = 1.98\ (\text{sec/kg}^{1/2})\ \text{m}^{1/2}.$$

We can also linearize the square root relationship by altering the *y*-axis. The square root function is the inverse function of the square. Thus, changing from period to period squared should linearize the data. Let's try it.

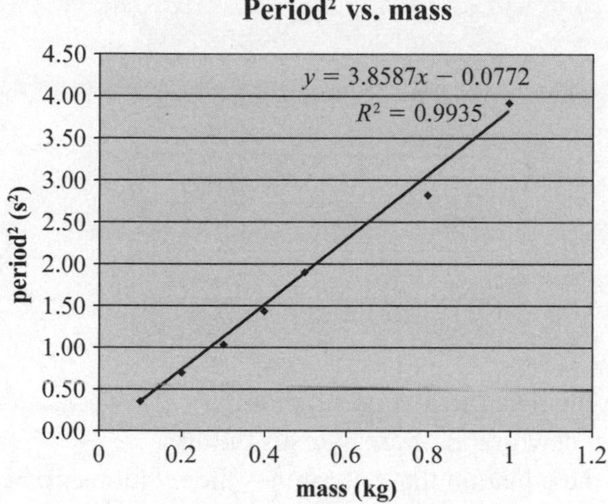

Another straight line. It is the same relationship you determined earlier, just presented in a different way. The relationship that this line gives is

$$T^2 = 3.86\ (\text{s}^2/\text{kg})\ \text{m}.$$

You should verify for yourself that this is the same relationship as $T = 1.98\ (\text{sec/kg}^{1/2})\ \text{m}^{1/2}$.

Practice Session Problems

To solve the following problems, use either a graphing software program or a sheet of graph paper.

1. Physics students perform an experiment in which they measure the radii and area of various disks. Here is a table of the data they obtained:

Area (m^2)	Radius (m)
0.1	0.2
0.5	0.4
1.1	0.6
2.1	0.8
3.1	1.0
4.5	1.2

   a. Graph the data (area versus radius).
   b. Make a new graph of area versus radius^2.
   c. Write the equation that determines the relationship between area and radius. What does the slope represent?

2. Physics students are doing an experiment with a pendulum. The teacher asks the students to measure the period of the pendulum at various lengths of the pendulum. Here is the set of data that the students obtained:

Period (s)	Length (m)
0.62	0.1
1.1	0.3
1.4	0.5
1.7	0.7
1.9	0.9
2.1	1.1
2.5	1.5

   a. Graph period versus length.
   b. Determine the equation for this set of data. Use the symbol T for period and l for length in your equation.

3. Physics students are measuring the intensity of light that falls on a screen from a light source on the lab table. The students gradually move the screen closer to the light source, measuring the new intensity after each move. The quantities measured by the students are intensity (W/m^2) and distance (m). Here is the data table the students make:

Intensity (W/m^2)	Distance (m)
2,500	0.1
625	0.2
280	0.3
102	0.5
69	0.6
39	0.8
17	1.2

a. Graph intensity versus distance.
b. Graph intensity versus the inverse of distance squared ($1/d^2$).
c. Write the equation for the relationship between intensity and distance.

Solutions

1. a. Area versus radius is parabolic, concave up.
   b. Area versus radius squared is linear with a positive slope.
   c. $A = (3.14)r^2$.

2. a. Period (T) versus length is a curve.

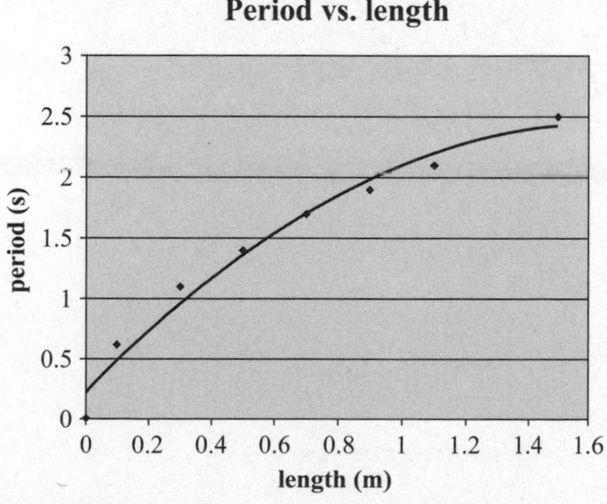

b. $T = 2\sqrt{l}$.

3. a.

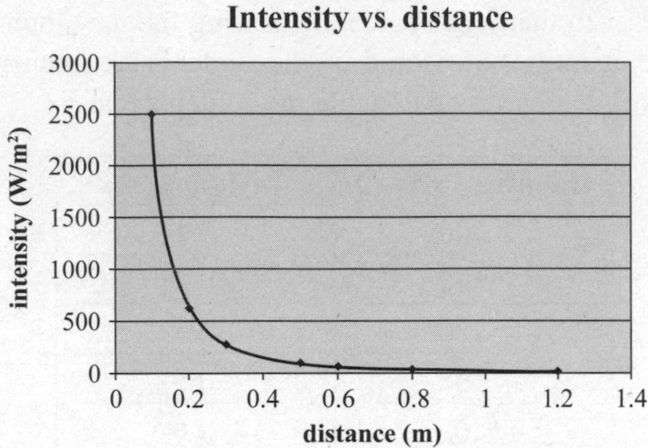

b.

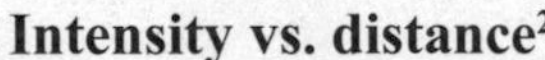

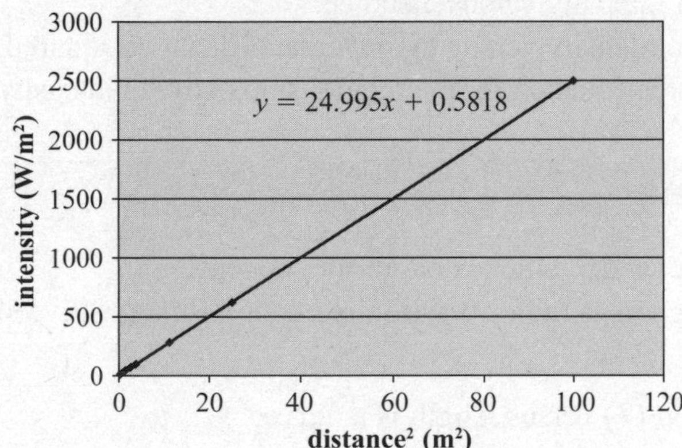

c. $I = \dfrac{25}{d^2}$.

Chapter 3

Kinematics: One- and Two-Dimensional Motion

EXAM OVERVIEW

Kinematics—which deals with the motion of a body or system without reference to force and mass—is a branch of physics you probably studied in the first weeks of your introductory course. And because it reappears at all levels of physics, it is a topic you need to master. Having a thorough understanding of kinematics gives you the confidence you need to continue studying physics at deeper levels.

But there is another reason to master kinematics. Once again, it has to do with confidence—the confidence you need to succeed on the AP Physics exam. You can count on 7 percent to 10 percent of the questions on the exam to be based on kinematics.

This chapter focuses on the concepts of kinematics you are likely to see on the exam. Some of the most common trouble spots for students are addressed in the Sample Problem and Practice Session sections. Reading the review and working the problems should help you master the ideas you may have missed in your physics course, raising your confidence to new heights.

ONE-DIMENSIONAL MOTION

The major areas of one-dimensional motion stressed on the AP Physics exam are the following:

- Understanding average velocity versus instantaneous velocity and the ability to describe these two ideas graphically
- Understanding velocity, acceleration, and displacement as vectors
- Graphically relating the relationships between velocity, acceleration, and displacement
- Qualitatively and graphically understanding uniformly accelerated motion

- Applying the relationships of uniform acceleration to physical situations
- Applying all these characteristics to "free fall" problems

The "Big Five" Relationships

The following equations represent the "Big Five" relationships. These relationships are valid only under the constraint of uniform acceleration. Therefore, it is imperative that you recognize when and where to apply each of the Big Five equations.

$$a_{avg} = \frac{\Delta\vec{v}}{\Delta t}$$

$$v_{avg} = \frac{\vec{v}_o + \vec{v}_f}{2}$$

$$v_f = v_o + at$$

$$v_f^2 = v_o^2 + 2a\Delta x$$

$$\Delta x = v_o t + \frac{1}{2}at^2$$

Keep in mind that all kinematic quantities are vectors. In this chapter, not all are marked with the vector symbol; therefore, in one-dimensional motion, velocity or acceleration can either be positively or negatively directed. The full vector notation will be addressed in the section on two-dimensional motion and in other chapters of this review.

The definition of **average velocity** must be used whenever the acceleration is either 0 or not uniform:

$$\vec{v}_{avg} = \frac{\Delta\vec{x}}{\Delta t}$$

One way of interpreting motion of objects is to use graphs or sketches of the objects in motion, sometimes called **motion maps**. A motion map can give you an overview as well as the details of an object's motion. There are graphical connections among the graphs of displacement versus time, velocity versus time, and accelerations versus time. The connections between the *x-t*, *v-t*, and *a-t* graphs make this topic a point of emphasis on the AP Physics exam.

Let's start our practice review by graphically analyzing one of the most classic one-dimensional physics problems.

Sample Problem 1

A baseball is thrown upward with a launch speed of 25 m/s. Use gravity = 10 m/s^2 to do the following:

- Graph position versus time.
- Graph velocity versus time.
- Determine the maximum height obtained by the ball.

Solution

The following two graphs are very common ways to depict the motion of a ball projected upward:

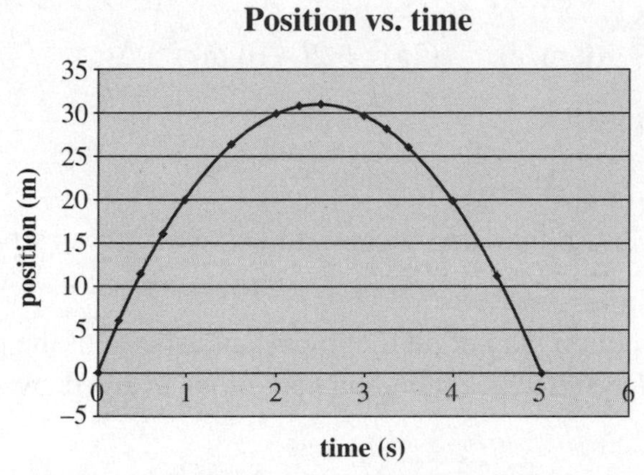

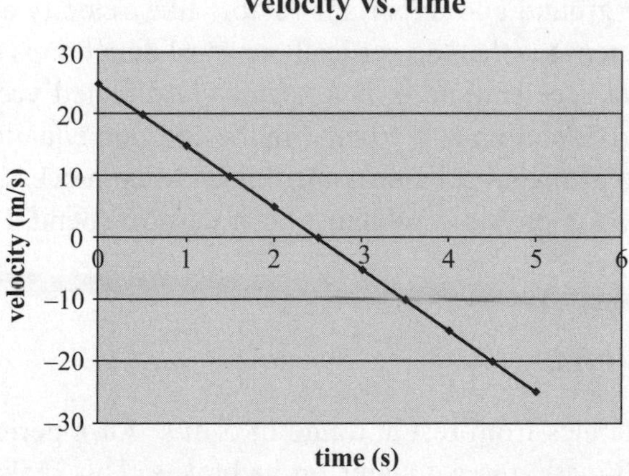

The maximum height of the ball can be shown graphically or calculated mathematically. Graphically, the maximum height is the area under the velocity-versus-time curve between the times of 0 and 2.5 seconds. That area is a triangle with a height of 25 m/s and a base of 2.5 seconds. The area of the triangle is

$$\text{Area} = \frac{1}{2}(25 \text{ m/s})(2.5 \text{ s}) = 31.25 \text{ m}$$

Thus, the maximum height of the ball is 31.25 m. Remember that the area under a velocity-versus-time curve is equal to the displacement of the projectile up to that point in time.

The other method to determine maximum height is to simply apply one of the Big Five equations. When an object reaches a velocity of 0 at the top of its trajectory, the object has reached its maximum height.

$$v_f^2 = v_o^2 + 2a\Delta y$$

$$(0 \text{ m/s})^2 = (25)^2 + 2(-10 \text{ m/s}^2)\ \Delta y_{max}$$

Solving for y_{max} gives

$$\Delta y_{max} = 31.25 \text{ m}.$$

You should use a two-step process to solve all physics problems of this type:

1. Draw a motion map of all the important aspects of the problem.
2. Name all the reference frames in your problem and draw all the important vectors.

A motion map of this example would include the object traveling vertically upward from the ground and important vectors like velocity and acceleration. The frame of reference is that the vertically upward direction is considered positive. Gravitational acceleration, g, is a negatively directed vector at all times. That is why the acceleration is -10 m/s^2 in the solution equation.

If you fail to plan your solution using this two-step process, you will always struggle with solving physics problems. So it pays to spend a few minutes on planning.

Sample Problem 2

A car accelerates from rest at a rate of 5 m/s^2 for a period of 8 seconds. At the 10-second mark, the car slams on its brakes. This braking produces an acceleration in the negative direction of -8.0 m/s^2. The car brakes uniformly until it comes to a complete rest. Determine the following:

- Distance traveled by the car at the 10-second mark
- Total time that the car was in motion
- Total distance traveled by the car

Solution

Before attempting to crunch any numbers, we need to draw a motion map on some scratch paper and continue drawing as we proceed through the problem.

The car will travel forward in the first 10 seconds. To determine how far it travels, we solve the constant acceleration relationship:

$$\Delta x = v_o t + \frac{1}{2}at^2$$

$$v_o = 0 \text{ m/s}$$

$$\Delta x = \frac{1}{2}(5 \text{ m/s}^2)(8)^2 = 160 \text{ m}$$

The car is traveling 160 m at the 8-second mark when the driver is about to slam on the brakes (instantaneously, of course). Therefore, we need to determine the car's instantaneous velocity at the 8-second mark:

$$v_f = v_o + at$$

$$v_f = (0 \text{ m/s}) + (5 \text{ m/s}^2)(8 \text{ s}) = 40 \text{ m/s}$$

When the car slams on its brakes ($a = -8 \text{ m/s}^2$), its speed is 40 m/s. To determine the time to stop, we need to determine the time for the car to go from a speed of 40 m/s to 0 m/s:

$$v_f = v_o + at$$

$$(0 \text{ m/s}) = (40 \text{ m/s}) + (-8 \text{ m/s}^2)(t)$$

$$\therefore t = 5 \text{ s}$$

Thus, the car was in motion for a total of 8 seconds + 5 seconds = 13 seconds.

To answer the third part, we must solve for the distance traveled by the car during the time the driver is braking. The car begins with a velocity of 40 m/s. It starts decreasing uniformly until it stops in 5 seconds. We can find the distance in several ways, but the most efficient way is to use the following relationship:

$$v_f^2 = v_o^2 + 2a\Delta x$$

$$(0 \text{ m/s})^2 = (40 \text{ m/s})^2 + 2(-8 \text{ m/s}^2)\,\Delta x$$

$$\therefore \Delta x_{stop} = 100 \text{ m}$$

We add 100 m to the initial distance of 160 m to get a total distance traveled during the acceleration and deceleration of 260 m.

TWO-DIMENSIONAL (PROJECTILE) MOTION

The physics of **projectile motion** applies the laws of kinematics to projectiles launched on the Earth in two dimensions, like a football kicked for a field goal or a basketball shot for a two-point score. The importance of understanding vectors becomes even more significant with two-dimensional motion that it was with one-dimensional motion.

The major ideas in projectile motion are as follows:

- Gravitational acceleration is only acting in the vertical direction.
- The horizontal and vertical motions of a projectile are completely independent of one another.
- The velocity vector of a projectile is always tangent to the projectile's path (trajectory).
- Frame of reference is a very important idea in solving advanced projectile problems.

To understand projectile motion, we start by diagramming the motion. In the top figure shown here, the horizontal and vertical components are drawn on the trajectory at several points. The bottom figure is an example with the components labeled.

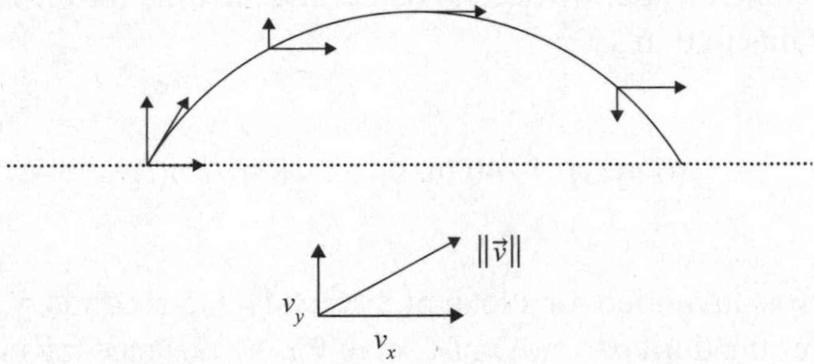

Notice that projectile motion is essentially the motion of a vertically launched object, combined with the motion of a constant horizontal velocity. Two separate motions at each point of the object's motion result in the parabolic trajectory. To understand what these two figures are telling us, we need to consider the following:

Q. During the motion of the object, where is acceleration equal to 0?

A. At no point is acceleration 0. The acceleration acting on the projectile is gravitational acceleration during all moments in time.

Q. Where does the moving object have a "speed" of 0?
A. The object never has a speed of 0. It has a vertical velocity component that is 0 m/s at the top of the trajectory, but the object has a speed at that point because it always has a horizontal velocity.

Q. What is the speed of the object at any point along the trajectory?
A. The speed of the object at any point along the trajectory is equal to the magnitude of the velocity vector. This is represented mathematically by

$$\|\vec{v}\| = \sqrt{(v_x^2 + v_y^2)}.$$

One important technique to solving two-dimensional motion problems is to write all the kinematic relationships in each direction. That is, write out the displacement relationship in the y direction like this:

$$\Delta y = v_{oy}t + \frac{1}{2}a_y t^2$$

Notice that all the characteristics are expressed in their correct directions.

Another important aspect of solving problems in two dimensions is that the time constraint is determined by the y direction. In other words, the projectile's time in motion ends when it strikes the Earth. The x direction of motion has no bearing on the object returning to the Earth.

The most common example of that idea is the object being propelled horizontally from a table, as shown in the following diagram. The diagram also shows the velocity components at a point along the trajectory.

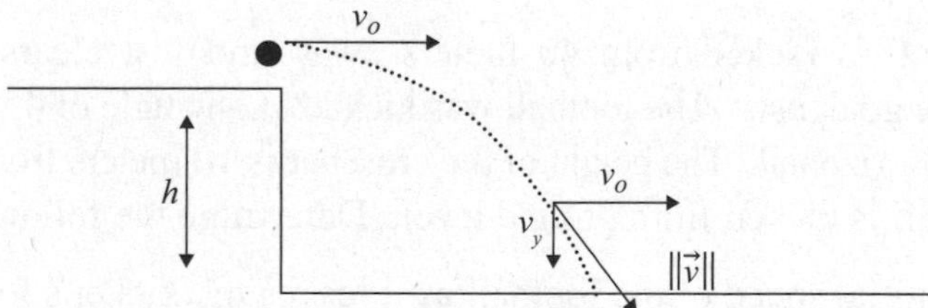

The time for the object to hit the ground would be identical to the time for a dropped object from a height of h to hit the ground. That might seem incorrect, but a quick demonstration in a physics laboratory shows it is true. Suppose an object propelled horizontally has a vertical velocity of 0 m/s at launch. The time to hit the ground is determined in the same way as for a one-dimensional problem of a projectile dropped from height h:

$$\Delta y = v_{oy}t + \frac{1}{2}a_y t^2$$

$$h = (0 \text{ m/s})t + \frac{1}{2}gt^2$$

$$\therefore t = \sqrt{\frac{2h}{g}}$$

Here's another question you might find more interesting: What is the speed at the impact point of the projectile shown in the diagram? Remember that the projectile is traveling in two dimensions, so it picks up a vertical velocity component directed downward, because gravity is acting vertically, and it has a constant horizontal velocity component while it is in motion. Therefore, the speed of the object looks like this:

$$v_{fy} = v_{oy} + a_y t$$

$$v_{fy} = (0 \text{ m/s}) + g\left(\sqrt{\frac{2h}{g}}\right) = \sqrt{2hg}$$

$$\|\vec{v}\| = \sqrt{(v_o)^2 + (v_{fy})^2}$$

$$\|\vec{v}\| = \sqrt{(v_o)^2 + (\sqrt{2hg})^2}$$

Sample Problem 3

A football is kicked from 40 meters away and just clears the football crossbar of the goalposts. The football was kicked at an angle of 45 degrees with respect to the horizontal. The height of the crossbar is 10 meters from the ground, and the football is kicked from ground level. Determine the following:

i) The initial speed of the football as it leaves the kicker's foot
ii) The speed of the football as it passes the crossbar

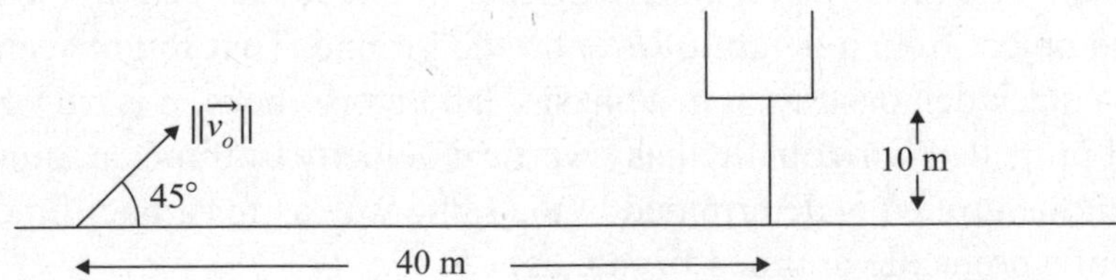

Solution

First we must set up two equations that contain the two unknowns of time and initial velocity. One equation will be the displacement of the football in the y-direction and the other equation will be the displacement of the football in the x-direction. The problem is solved from a standard reference frame of vertical y direction is the positive direction. This makes our value of gravity a -10 m/s^2 for the entire problem. Here are the two equations:

$$\Delta y = v_{oy}t - \frac{1}{2}gt^2$$

$$\Delta x = v_{ox}t$$

Also, both $v_{ox} = v_{oy} = v_o \cdot \sin 45 = v_o \cdot \frac{\sqrt{2}}{2}$.
Now, we will put in all the values into the equation:

$$\Delta x = v_{ox}t \Rightarrow 40 = v_o \cdot \frac{\sqrt{2}}{2}t$$

$$\Delta y = v_{oy}t - \frac{1}{2}gt^2 \Rightarrow 10 = v_o \cdot \frac{\sqrt{2}}{2} - \frac{1}{2}(10\ \text{m/s}^2)t^2$$

From the x-displacement equation we get an expression for time, $t = \frac{80}{\sqrt{2} \cdot v_o}$. Substitute this expression for time into the y displacement equation.

$$10 = v_o \cdot \frac{\sqrt{2}}{2} \cdot \left(\frac{80}{\sqrt{2} \cdot v_o}\right) - \frac{1}{2}(10)\left(\frac{80}{\sqrt{2} \cdot v_o}\right)^2$$

$$10 = 40 - \frac{16000}{v_o^2} \Rightarrow v_o^2 = \frac{16000}{30} \Rightarrow v_o = 23.1\ \text{m/s}$$

This is the answer for part one. The football has an initial speed of 23.1 m/s.

To determine the speed as it crosses the goalposts, we will need to determine the components of the velocity at that point in time. We will determine the time from the above equation and the newly found initial velocity value:

$$t = \frac{80}{\sqrt{2} \cdot v_o} = \frac{80\ \text{m}}{\left(\sqrt{2}\right) \cdot (23.1\ \text{m/s})} = 2.45\ \text{s} \approx 2.5\ \text{s}$$

Now, we will concentrate on determining the velocity components at this point in time. Remember that in projectile motion the x-component of the velocity is a constant throughout the motion, so v_{ox} is simply

$$v_{ox} = v_o \cdot \cos 45 = (23.1\text{ m/s})\left(\frac{\sqrt{2}}{2}\right) = 16.3\text{ m/s}$$

The y-component of the velocity can be determined by applying the velocity vs. time relationship

$$v_y = v_{oy} - gt = v_o \sin 45 - (10\text{ m/s}^2)t$$

$$= (23.1\text{ m/s})\left(\frac{\sqrt{2}}{2}\right) - (10\text{ m/s}^2)(2.5\text{ s})$$

$$v_y = -8.7\text{ m/s}$$

The negative sign in the y-component of the velocity means that the football is heading in the downward direction. The speed of the football can now be computed since we have both components of the velocity vector.

$$\|v\| = \sqrt{v_x^2 + v_y^2} = \sqrt{(16.3\text{ m/s})^2 + (-8.7\text{ m/s})^2} = 18.5\text{ m/s}$$

So as the football is crossing the bar, it has a speed of 18.5 m/s and is heading in the downward direction.

The following three projectile motion equations are very useful in problem solving. They are valid only for a projectile that is launched from ground level and lands at that same ground level:

$$Range = \frac{v_o^2 \sin(2\theta)}{g}$$

$$time_{flight} = \frac{2v_o \sin\theta}{g}$$

$$y_{maxheight} = \frac{v_o^2 \sin^2(\theta)}{2g}$$

You should memorize these equations because they will help you quite a bit on the multiple-choice section of the AP Physics exam.

All right, enough review. It's time for some practice.

Practice Session Problems

Multiple Choice

1. Which expression determines the range of a projectile that is projected from ground level?

(A) $R = \dfrac{v_o^2 \sin^2(\theta)}{g}$

(B) $R = \dfrac{v_o^2 \sin^2(\theta)}{2g}$

(C) $R = \dfrac{v_o^2 \sin(2\theta)}{2g}$

(D) $R = \dfrac{v_o^2 \sin(2\theta)}{g}$

(E) $R = \dfrac{2v_o^2 \sin^2(\theta)}{g}$

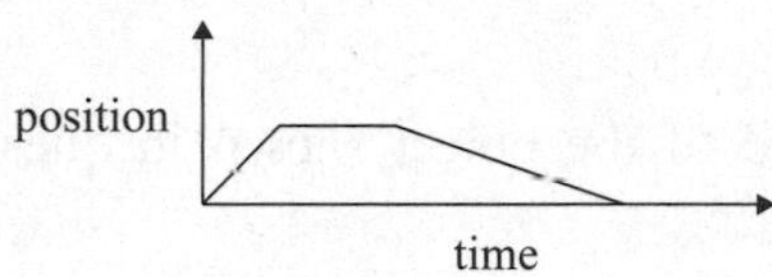

2. An object travels with the following position-versus-time graph shown above. Which of the following *velocity-versus-time* graphs would correspond to this motion?

(A) 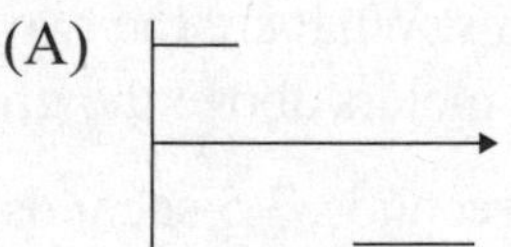

(B) 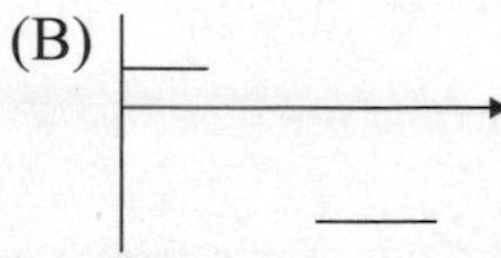

(C) 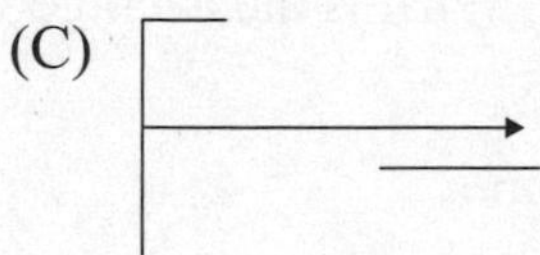

(D) 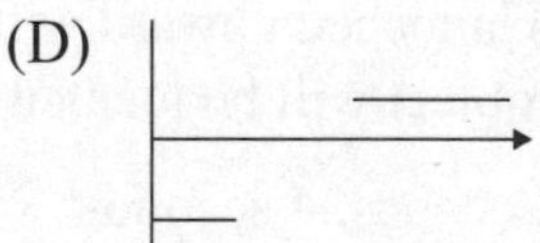

(E) 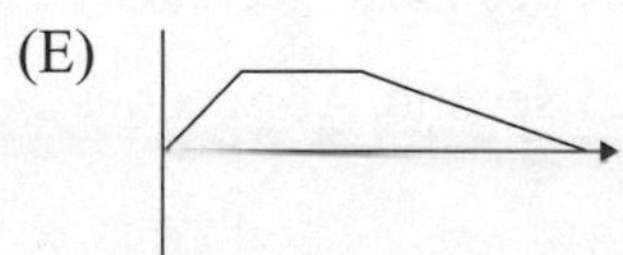

3. An object is launched horizontally from a building that is 250 meters high, as shown in the following diagram. The object's speed at launch is 15 m/s. The object strikes the ground at some horizontal distance from the ledge.

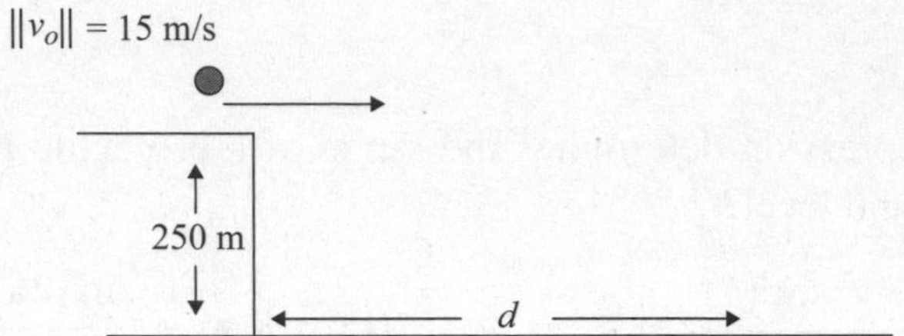

What is the distance d?

(A) 750 m
(B) 375 m
(C) 105 m
(D) 210 m
(E) 150 m

4. What is the speed of the object shown in question 3 when it hits the ground?

(A) 72 m/s
(B) 15 m/s
(C) 150 m/s
(D) 70 m/s
(E) 21 m/s

5. A ball is launched upward with a speed of 20 m/s. What are the two times that the object will be located at a height of 15 meters above the ground?

(A) 2 seconds, 4 seconds
(B) 1 second, 3 seconds
(C) 1 second, 2.5 seconds
(D) 1.5 seconds, 3.5 seconds
(E) 1.5 seconds, 3 seconds

6. A car accelerates at a constant rate of 6 m/s^2. The car starts from rest and accelerates at that constant rate for 10 seconds. What is the average velocity of the car during those 10 seconds?

(A) 6 m/s
(B) 60 m/s
(C) 30 m/s
(D) 10 m/s
(E) 40 m/s

7. A projectile's trajectory is shown in the following diagram:

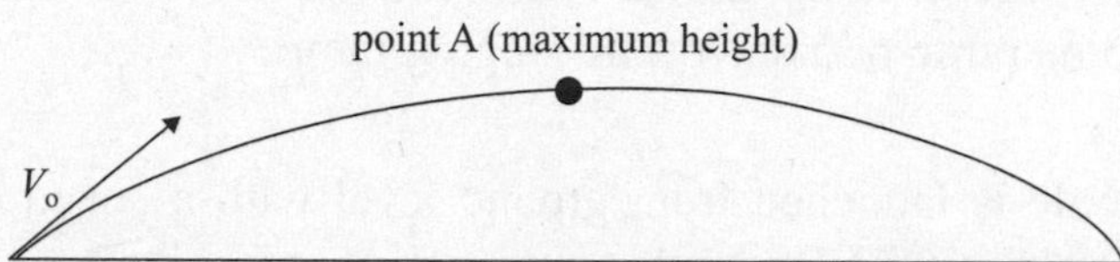

What is the direction of the acceleration vector and the velocity vector at point A? (Acceleration vector is shown first, velocity is shown second.)

(A) 0 m/s² and 0 m/s

(B) ↓ ↓

(C) ↓ →

(D) → ↓

(E) ↓ and no velocity vector

Free Response

1. The following is a velocity-versus-time graph of a metal ball moving in one dimension on a set of *frictionless* tracks and ramps. The metal ball is moving with a constant speed on a straight, level section of the track and then encounters an incline in the track that takes it to another straight level section of the track.

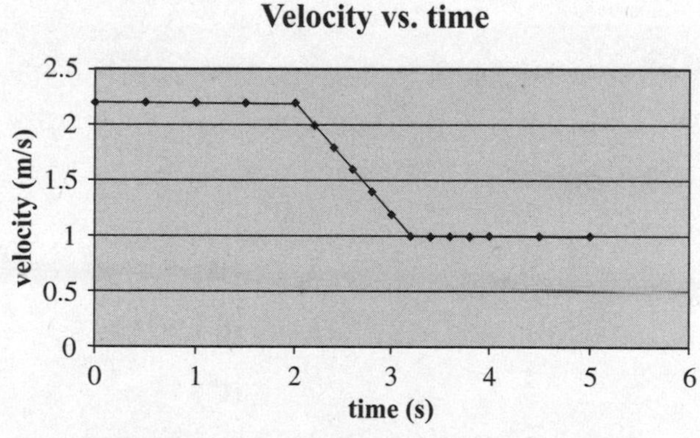

a. Determine the acceleration of the ball during the interval of time 2.0 seconds $< t <$ 3.2 seconds.

b. Determine the distance traveled by the ball during the same interval of time.

c. Determine the average velocity for the 5-second period.
d. What type of ramp did the ball encounter at 2.0 seconds, an upward sloping ramp or a downward sloping ramp?

*2. A projectile is launched from ground level with a speed of $\|\vec{v}_o\|$ and a launch angle of θ. Do the following in terms of v_o, g, θ:
a. Determine the ratio of the two times that the projectile is at the position of half of its maximum height. Express your ratio as a number greater than 1.
b. Write an expression for the projectile's vertical position (y) in terms of the horizontal position (x) and other constants.
c. Write an expression for the time it takes for the projectile to reach height h. This expression for time should be expressed in terms of v_o, g, θ.

*3. A ball is dropped from rest from the top of a tall building. The building's height is 500 m. A physics student on the ground simultaneously launches a ball upward with a speed of 75 m/s. The balls are traveling in the same vertical plane and eventually will collide when they are at the same position. Determine the following for this situation:
a. The height of the collision. Give your answer in terms of height above the ground.
b. The *velocity* of each ball at the point of collision.

Solutions

Multiple Choice

1. (D)
2. (C)
3. (C)
4. (A)
5. (B)
6. (C)
7. (C)

Free Response

1. a. $a = -1.0 \text{ m/s}^2$
   b. $\Delta x = 1.92 \text{ m}$
   c. $v_{avg} = 1.6 \text{ m/s}$
   d. An upward-sloping ramp

2. a. $\dfrac{t_2}{t_1} = 1 + 2\sqrt{2}$

   b. $y = x \tan\theta - \dfrac{gx^2 \, s^2\theta}{2v_o^2}$

   c. $t = \dfrac{v_o \sin\theta \pm \sqrt{v_o^2 \sin^2\theta - 2gh}}{g}$

3. a. Collision height = 277.8 m

   First, set up a common reference frame for both balls. Set the ground at $y = 0$ and upward as positive. Then write out the position-versus-time relationship for each ball:

$$y_{droppedball} = 500 - \frac{1}{2}gt^2$$

$$y_{projectedball} = 75t - \frac{1}{2}gt^2$$

   The two balls will collide when their positions are the same in the common frame of reference, so set those two equal and solve for t:

$$y_{droppedball} = y_{projectedball}$$

$$500 - \frac{1}{2}gt^2 = 75t - \frac{1}{2}gt^2$$

$$75t = 500$$

$$t = \frac{20}{3} \text{ s}$$

   Now, substitute in this time to find the collision height:

$$y_{dropped} = 500 - \frac{1}{2}(10 \text{ m/s}^2)\left(\frac{20}{3}\right)^2$$

$$y = 500 - 222.2 = 277.8 \text{ m}$$

b. $v_{drop} = -66.7\text{ m/s, down}$

$$v_{projected} = +8.33\text{ m/s, down}$$

$$v_{dropped} = v_o + at = (0\text{ m/s}) + (-10\text{ m/s}^2)\left(\frac{20}{3}\text{ s}\right)$$

$$= -66.67\text{ m/s, downwards}$$

$$v_{projected} = v_o + at = 75\text{ m/s} + (-10\text{ m/s}^2)\left(\frac{20}{3}\text{ s}\right)$$

$$= +8.33\text{ m/s, upwards}$$

Chapter 4

Applying Newton's Laws

EXAM OVERVIEW

The correct application of Newton's laws is the foundation of physics problem solving. Practice is essential not only for your success on the AP Physics exam but also for your continuing physics studies.

NEWTON'S LAWS

Newton's laws are relatively simple on their face:

Newton's first law: An object in a state of motion will remain in that state until acted on by a net force. Also called the law of inertia.

Newton's second law: $\Sigma \vec{F} = m\vec{a}$.

Newton's third law: Forces occur from mutual interactions between two systems. These forces always occur in pairs: one force caused by object 1 and acting on object 2, and the other force caused by object 2 and acting on object 1. These two forces are always equal in magnitude and opposite in direction: $\left\| \vec{F}_{1on2} \right\| = -\left\| \vec{F}_{2on1} \right\|$.

Like most physics students, you probably memorized Newton's laws in seventh grade science class and are still familiar with them. Where you're likely to fall short is in properly applying the laws to unique mechanical situations. A mastery of Newton's laws is crucial to solving mechanics problems.

Also, you must have a firm grasp on vector addition and trigonometry. Although this book includes many problems involving the application of those skills, they are not the focus of a separate chapter. If your skills in vector addition and trigonometry are weak, you probably have already found your physics course to be difficult. Before continuing with this chapter, you should review both skills in the appropriate textbook until you have mastered them.

These are the major ideas that the AP Physics exam will focus on in the area of Newton's laws:

- The nature of forces and the definition of force
- The idea of mass as an inertial measurement

- The types of forces that exist in the physical world: gravitational, frictional, normal, tension, spring, and others
- Free-body diagramming
- The nature of friction and the coefficient of friction

You can expect the AP Physics exam to ask you to solve

- equilibrium and accelerated system problems;
- multimass problems; and
- problems requiring rotation of the frame of reference.

This is obviously a lot of physics. If you know you are weak in certain areas, focus on them both in this review and while rereading your textbook. This chapter contains some problems that have appeared in AP Physics exams over the years. However, students who truly want to learn physics must not attempt to memorize problems or try to make problems fit a pattern. Successful test taking requires practice, practice, and more practice on unique problems. That is the whole point of applying Newton's laws. Mastering the laws will enable you to apply them correctly to any new mechanical system.

DEFINING FORCES

All forces are caused by two systems interacting with each other—a table acting on a mass and the mass acting on the table; the friction of the table acting on the mass and the friction of the mass acting on the table; tension on a cord attached to a mass and the mass acting on the cord; the Earth acting on a mass and the mass acting on the Earth and so on. In any physics problem, you should be able to name the object causing the force and the object receiving the force. The notation used to indicate the force of object 1 acting on object 2 is F_{1on2}, which is usually shortened to F_{12} (which is read "Force of 1 acting on 2," not "Force 12").

The following are the most significant forces you will deal with in the AP Physics exam:

- **Weight (W):** This force is defined as the gravitational force of attraction between the Earth and a mass. The equation for weight is $W = mg$.
- **Friction:** The two types of friction are static and kinetic. Two types of coefficients of friction correspond to the two types of friction. The coefficients (μ_k, μ_s) are both constants for each pair of surface materials. In general, $\mu_s > \mu_k$. Friction always opposes the direction of relative motion or, in the case of static friction, the direction of intended relative motion. Friction has the following relationship:

$\|f_k\| = \mu_k N$
(where "f" is frictional force and "N" is normal force)
$\|f_s\| \leq \mu_s N$

- **Spring force:** Spring force acts in opposition to the force acting on the spring. The definition of spring force is $\overrightarrow{F}_{spring} = -k\overrightarrow{\Delta x}$.

Other forces of contact have no defined relationship. They are forces that arise out of the interactions in the system:

- **Normal forces (N):** These forces result from contact between any two surfaces. A normal force always occurs perpendicular to two surfaces.
- **Tension forces (T):** Tension forces occur in strings, cords, wire, and the like. The magnitude of the tension depends on all the interactions occurring on any mass. To determine the value of a tension force, you need to know the value of the other forces resulting from those interactions.
- **Applied forces:** These are forces applied from external sources, either a person or an object.

FREE-BODY DIAGRAMS

Probably the most important skill covered in this chapter is creating **free-body diagrams (FBDs)**. This is the skill of analyzing a mechanical system and drawing all the forces acting on the mass.

Free-body drawing can get very interesting when there are multiple masses and multiple interactions among the masses. If a problem has multiple masses, each mass receives a separate FBD. You have to make sure you draw the FBD of each mass in isolation from those of the other masses.

For example, the following figure illustrates the simple problem of an applied force pushing a two-mass system. The surface is frictionless for this example.

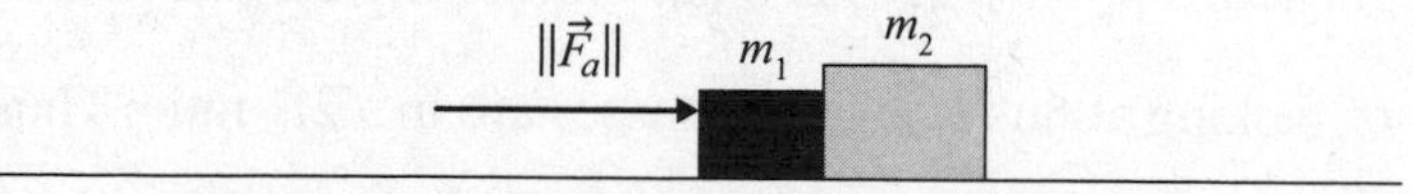

In this type of problem, you need to draw two separate FBDs: one for mass 1 (m_1) and another for mass 2 (m_2). The FBDs would look like this:

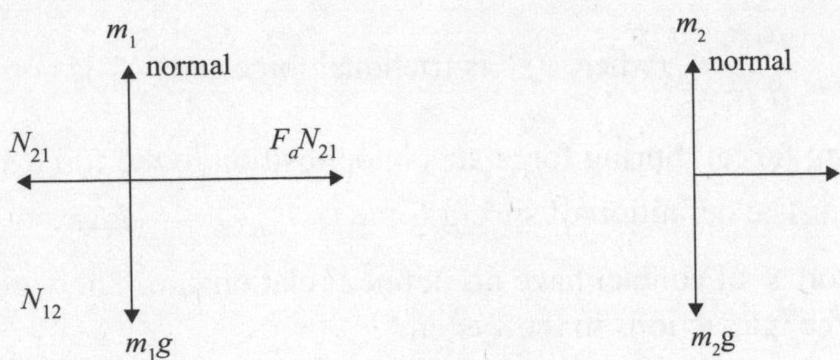

Note that $\|N_{12}\| = \|N_{21}\|$ is the action–reaction pair of Newton's third law. Also note that the applied force F_a is only applied to m_1. Avoid the common mistake of incorrectly drawing F_a acting on m_2 as well. Remember, it is the normal force of contact between m_1 and m_2 that causes m_2 to accelerate.

The net result of this applied force is that both masses accelerate to the right with the same value of acceleration—as long as the two masses remain in contact.

Let's add numbers to this example: $F_a = 12$ Newtons (N), $m_1 = 1$ kg, and $m_2 = 2$ kg. Now we can determine the value of the contact force between the two blocks.

The entire system has 3 kg of mass. The net external force on the two-mass system is 12 N. The net acceleration of the two-mass system is $a = \dfrac{\Sigma F}{m_{total}} = \dfrac{12\text{ N}}{3\text{ kg}} = 4\text{ m/s}^2$.

Applying Newton's second law to each mass gives us the following:

$$\text{Mass 1: } \Sigma\vec{F}_{m1} = m_1\vec{a} = F_a - N_{21}$$

$$\Sigma\vec{F} = (1\text{ kg})(4\text{ m/s}^2) = 12 - N_{21}$$

$$\therefore N_{21} = 8\text{ N}$$

$$\text{Mass 2: } \Sigma\vec{F}_{m2} = m_2\vec{a} = N_{12}$$

$$\Sigma\vec{F}_{m2} = (2\text{ kg})(4\text{ m/s}^2) = N_{12}$$

$$\therefore N_{12} = 8\text{ N}$$

Both applications prove that the contact force between the masses is 8 N. Another way of looking at this is that the masses are in a 2:1 ratio. Thus, the net force on each mass is also in a 2:1 ratio. Mass 2 has a net force of 8 N and mass 1 has a net force of 4 N. The more massive mass (2 kg) required two-thirds of the applied force $\left(\dfrac{8\text{ N}}{12\text{ N}}\right)$, while the less massive mass (1 kg) only required one-third of the applied force $\left(\dfrac{4\text{ N}}{12\text{ N}}\right)$. The vertical direction of the problem was ignored because it did not contribute to the solution of the problem. Basically, nothing interesting was going on in the vertical direction, and $\Sigma F_y = 0$ in both cases.

The preceding problem-solving strategy centered on creating an FBD for each mass to create the statement of Newton's second law for each mass. You can use this approach to solve similar mechanics problems. Let's work through a few trickier examples.

First, here is a block being held to a vertical wall by an applied force:

This problem could become very interesting. If the applied force is large enough, it is possible for the friction (static) to switch to the opposite direction. Think about that and convince yourself that it is true. In any case, if the block stays at rest relative to the wall, then forces in each direction will add to 0. Of course, the angle of the applied force would come into play, and its components would have to be determined.

Now consider a hanging mass attached via a pulley or string to a mass on a horizontal surface. The two-mass system is at rest relative to each other and the table, as shown here:

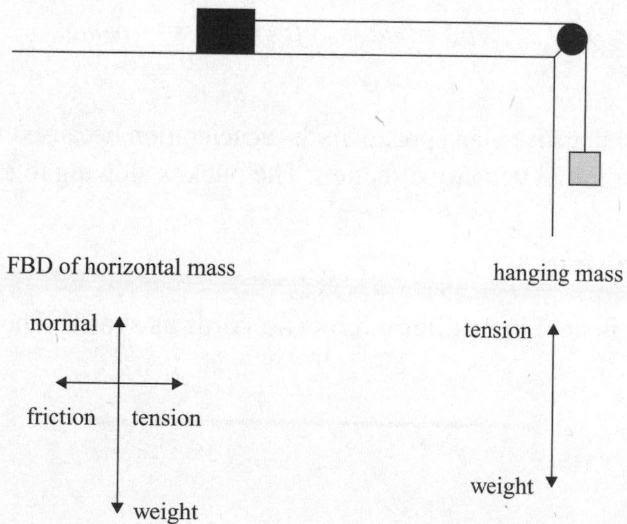

(Note: The pulley is an "ideal pulley" and only serves to change the direction of the force. We will look at a pulley with inertia in Chapter 17.)

Under Newton's third law, the tension acting on the horizontal mass is the same magnitude as the tension acting on the hanging mass.

This diagram shows a sliding hockey puck on a surface with some friction:

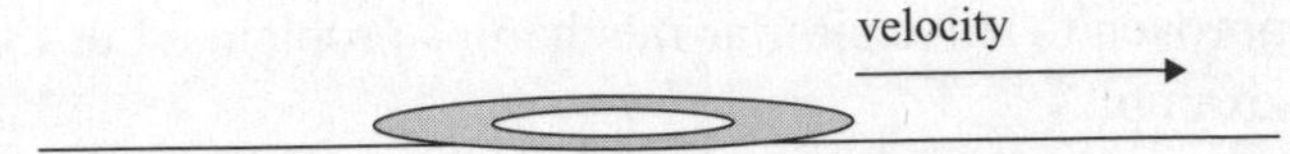

The FBD looks like this:

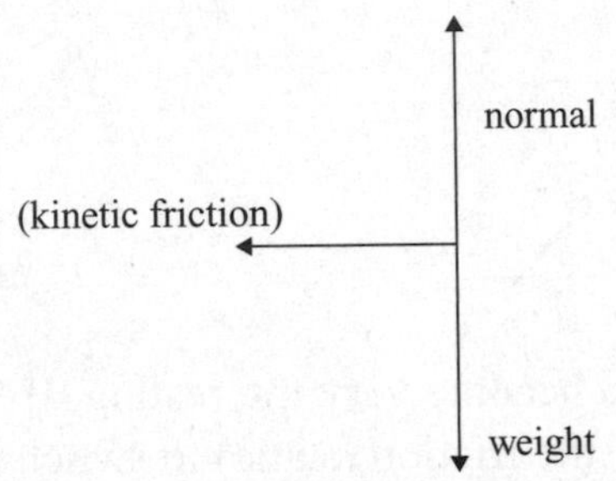

The analysis of this event in symbols is as follows:

$$\Sigma F_x = ma = -f_k$$

$$\Sigma F_y = 0 = N - mg \Rightarrow N = mg$$

and friction is related by the coefficient:

$$f_k = \mu_k N = \mu_k(mg) = \mu_k mg$$

$$\therefore \Sigma F_x = ma = -f_k \Rightarrow ma = -\mu_k mg$$

$$a = -\mu_k g$$

Notice that the negative sign appears in the acceleration because the acceleration is opposite the initial velocity direction. The puck is slowing to a stop.

Sample Problem 1

A block is held in equilibrium by two cords as shown. The weight of the block is 50 N.

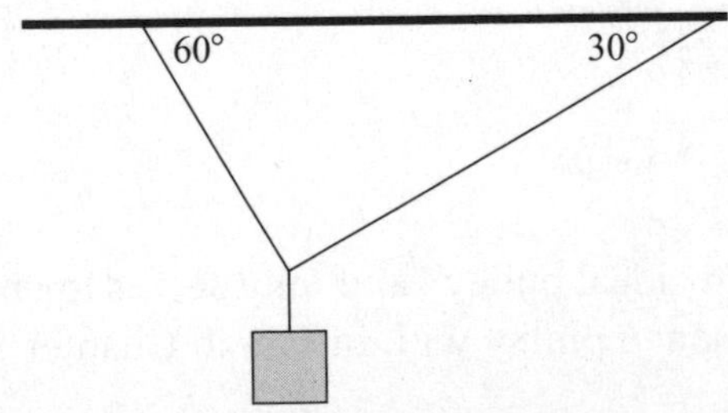

The FBD from the point where all three cords intersect looks like this:

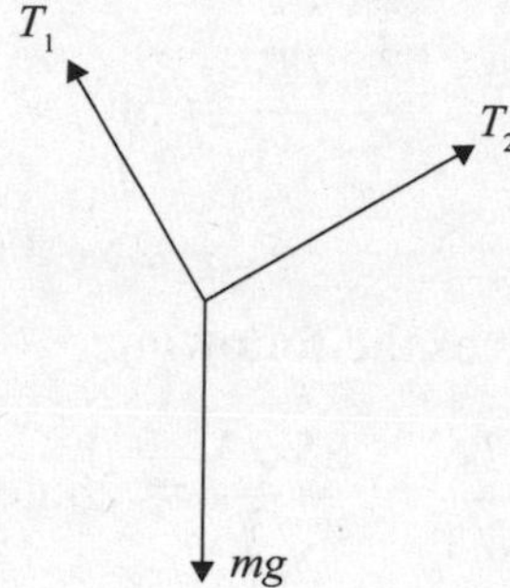

The analysis of this event in symbols is as follows:

$$T_{1x} = \|T_1\| \cos 60$$
$$T_{1y} = \|T_1\| \sin 60$$
$$T_{2x} = \|T_2\| \cos 30$$
$$T_{2y} = \|T_2\| \sin 30$$

Based on the diagram and equations, do the following:

- Draw the vertical and horizontal components of T_1 and T_2.
- Write equilibrium statements in both directions.
- Substitute in the components and solve.

Solution

$$T_2 \cos 30 = T_1 \cos 60$$

$$\therefore T_2 = T_1 \left(\frac{\frac{1}{2}}{\frac{\sqrt{3}}{2}} \right) = \frac{T_1}{\sqrt{3}}$$

and

$$T_1 \sin 60 + T_2 \sin 30 = 50$$

$$T_1 \left(\frac{\sqrt{3}}{2} \right) + T_2 \left(\frac{1}{2} \right) = 50$$

sub in T_2

$$T_1 \left(\frac{\sqrt{3}}{2} \right) + \left(\frac{T_1}{\sqrt{3}} \right) \left(\frac{1}{2} \right) = 50$$

$$T_1\left(\frac{3}{2\sqrt{3}}\right) + T_1\left(\frac{1}{2\sqrt{3}}\right) = 50$$

$$\frac{2T_1}{\sqrt{3}} = 50$$

$$T_1 = 25\sqrt{3} \approx 43 \text{ newtons}$$

Substituting back in for T_2 gives the following:

$$T_2 = \frac{T_1}{\sqrt{3}} = \frac{25\sqrt{3}}{\sqrt{3}} = 25 \text{ newtons}$$

We could also solve this problem by noticing that the two cords have a 90-degree angle between them. We could rotate the frame of reference to match the two cords and essentially solve the problem in two lines of mathematics as follows:

$$\Sigma F_y = 0 = T_1 - mg\cos 30 \Rightarrow T_1 = mg\cos 30 = 43 \text{ N}$$

$$\Sigma F_x = 0 = T_2 - mg\sin 30 \Rightarrow T_2 = mg\sin 30 = 25 \text{ N}$$

With a little cleverness, we could solve this problem with much less algebra:

$$\Sigma F_y = 0 = T_{1y} + T_{2y} - mg = 0$$

$$\Sigma F_x = 0 = T_{2x} - T_{1x} = 0$$

Sample Problem 2

The following diagram illustrates the Atwood machine. Two masses (M_1 and M_2) are attached by a frictionless pulley and a string of negligible mass.

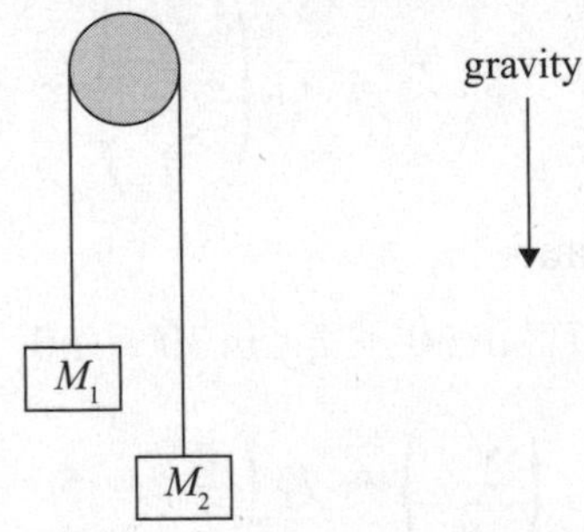

$M_2 > M_1$

- Determine the acceleration of the system. Answer in terms of M_1, M_2, and g (gravity).
- Determine the value of the tension in the string supporting the masses.

Solution

First, we draw the FBD on *each* mass:

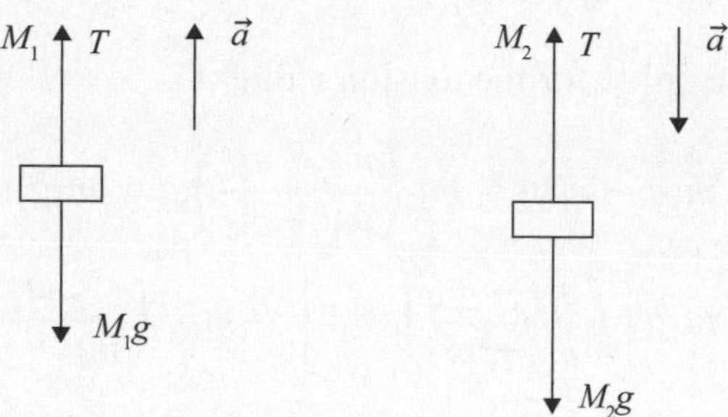

Notice in these FBDs that the vector that represents the weight of mass 2 is the largest of the vectors. The heavier weight creates the acceleration of the two masses. If a problem has two different masses accelerating, we need to write two different statements of Newton's second law.

We could not simply write that the tension force is equal to the weight of the hanging mass. That is true only in a state of equilibrium. The best way to avoid this mistake is to isolate masses, label forces correctly, and then draw the corresponding FBDs. Two strategies to keep in mind here are: (1) the acceleration of the system is the same value for both masses (just directed differently), and (2) the values of the tensions are the same (just directed differently) because of Newton's third law.

Here are the second-law statements for each mass:

$$\Sigma F_{m_1} = M_1 a = T - M_1 g \tag{1}$$

$$\Sigma F_{m_2} = M_2 a = M_2 g - T \tag{2}$$

Writing from the frame of reference of the direction of the acceleration avoids the problem of unnecessary negative signs. In other words, we let the acceleration vector determine the positive direction for our second-law statement. That is the convention that was used in equations 1 and 2.

Here is how to solve for acceleration:

From Eq. 1

$$T = m_1 a + m_1 g$$

substitute in to Eq. 2

$$m_2 a = m_2 g - (m_1 a + m_1 g) \Rightarrow$$

$$(m_1 + m_2)a = (m_2 - m_1)g$$

$$a = \frac{(m_2 - m_1)}{(m_1 + m_2)}g$$

If $M_1 = 10$ kg and $M_2 = 15$ kg, the acceleration is

$$\frac{15-10}{15+10}g = \frac{1}{5}g \approx 2\ \text{m/s}^2.$$

Here is how to solve for the tension value:

$$T = m_1 a + m_1 g = m_1\left(\frac{m_2 - m_1}{m_1 + m_2}\right)g + m_1 g$$

$$T = m_1 g\left[\left(\frac{m_2 - m_1}{m_1 + m_2}\right) + 1\right] = m_1 g\left(\frac{2m_2}{m_1 + m_2}\right)$$

Now evaluate this with the mass values of 10 kg and 15 kg:

$$T = (10)g\left(\frac{2(15)}{25}\right) = \frac{300}{25}g = 12\,g \approx 120\ \text{N}$$

Sample Problem 3

A block with mass $m = 2$ kg is resting on a moveable incline. The mass and the incline are both made of wood and have a coefficient of static friction of $\mu_s = 0.4$. The incline is raised slowly from the horizontal position to an angle at which the block starts to slip down the incline, as shown here:

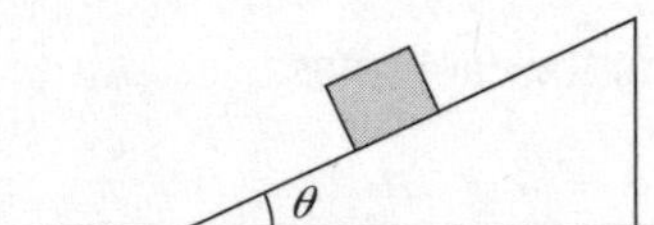

- Determine the angle at which the block starts to slip.
- Once the block has slipped, it has only kinetic friction acting between the block and the incline. The coefficient of friction is $\mu_k = 0.3$. Determine the acceleration of the block down the incline once it slips and begins to "slide" down with acceleration.

Solution

First, we draw the FBD for the mass at rest on the incline. The angle is the angle at which the mass is just about to slip, which means that static friction has reached its maximum value, and we can use the maximum static friction relationship.

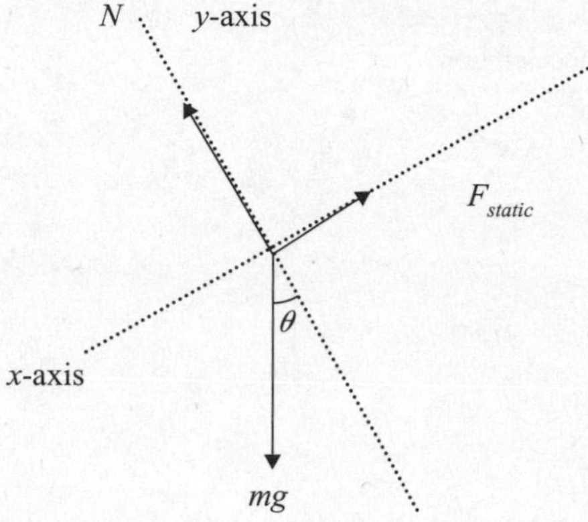

Now we write out the statements of equilibrium. Notice the frame of reference has been rotated to match the geometry of the problem. Remember, in equilibrium problems, the forces add to 0 in any frame of reference. So we have the choice to put our coordinate frame into the most convenient orientation possible.

$$\Sigma F_x = 0 = mg\sin\theta - f_{static}$$
$$\Sigma F_y = 0 = N - mg\cos\theta$$

and, $f_s \leq \mu_s N$

so,

$$f_s = mg\sin\theta$$
$$N = mg\cos\theta$$

and $\mu_s = \dfrac{f_s}{N} = \dfrac{mg\sin\theta}{mg\cos\theta} = \tan\theta$

Solve:

$$\mu_s = \tan\theta \Rightarrow \tan\theta = 0.4 \Rightarrow \theta = \tan^{-1}(0.4) = 21.8° \approx 22°$$

The tangent of the slip angle is equal to the coefficient of static friction. This is true in all cases.

Since the block has slipped, it is sliding with the kinetic friction force acting on it. Remember that kinetic friction is less than the maximum value of static friction. Thus, the block will *accelerate* down the incline.

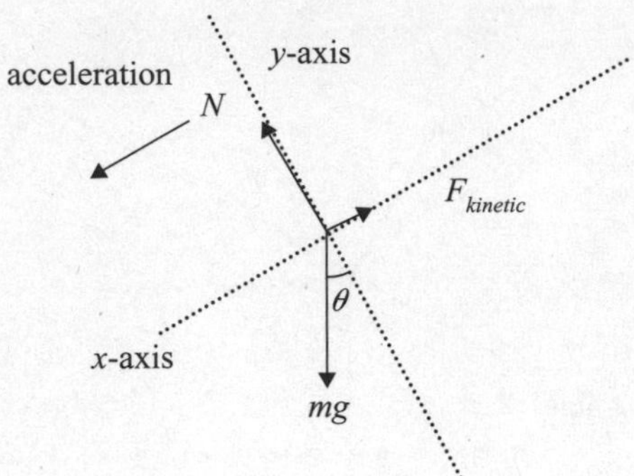

The second-law statement is written with the acceleration direction down the incline as shown in the FBD:

$$\Sigma F_x = ma = mg\sin\theta - f_k$$
$$N = mg\cos\theta$$
$$f_k = \mu_k N$$

Substitute in and evaluate using the angle and the coefficient value.

$$\Sigma F_x = ma = mg\sin\theta - \mu_k mg\cos\theta$$
$$\Rightarrow a = g\sin\theta - \mu_k g\cos\theta$$
$$a = (10\ \text{m/s}^2)\sin(21.8) - (.3)(10\ \text{m/s}^2)\cos(21.8)$$
$$a = 0.93\ \text{m/s}^2$$

Practice Session Problems

Multiple Choice

1. A person is standing on a scale inside of an elevator that is accelerating upward. The weight of the person is 500 N. The acceleration of the elevator is 2 m/s^2. What does the scale read?

   (A) 500 N
   (B) 100 N
   (C) 600 N
   (D) 400 N
   (E) Cannot be determined

2. A box is being dragged at a constant velocity as shown in the following diagram. The box has a mass of *m*.

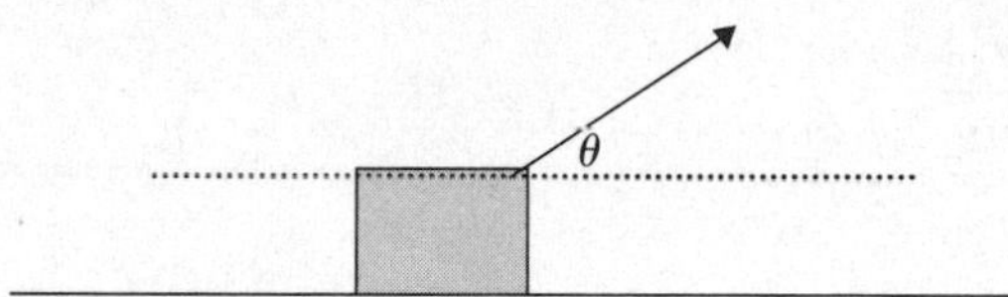

   What is the value of the normal force?

   (A) mg
   (B) $mg \cos \theta$
   (C) $mg - F \sin \theta$
   (D) $\mu mg \cos \theta$
   (E) $F \sin \theta + mg$

3. What is the value of the magnitude of the kinetic frictional force?

   (A) $F \cos \theta$
   (B) $mg \sin \theta$
   (C) $\mu mg \cos \theta$
   (D) $mg \cos \theta$
   (E) F

4. A set of blocks is dragged on a frictionless floor by a 30-N force as shown in the following diagram:

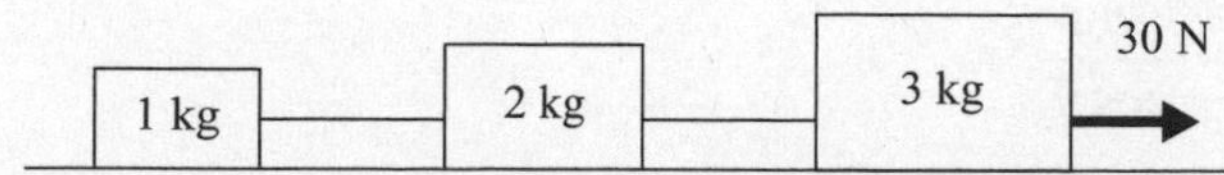

What is the value of the tension between the 1-kg and the 2-kg blocks?

(A) 30 N
(B) 25 N
(C) 15 N
(D) 10 N
(E) 5 N

5. A block is held to a vertical wall by a force $\|F\|$ as shown. What the minimum value of μ_s such that the block will not slip. The block has mass m?

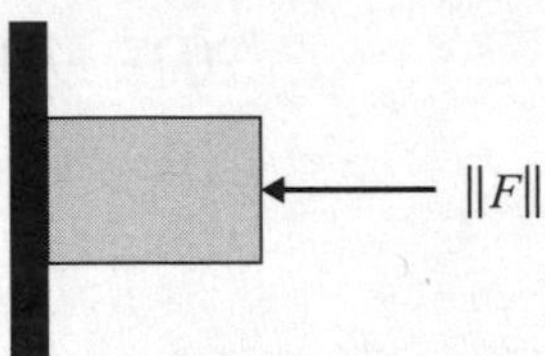

(A) $\mu_s = \dfrac{mg}{\|F\|}$
(B) $\mu_s = \dfrac{\|F\|}{mg}$
(C) $\mu_s = mg$
(D) $\mu_s = \dfrac{g}{\|F\|}$
(E) $\mu_s = 1$

6. Two cords support a mass m, as shown in the following diagram:

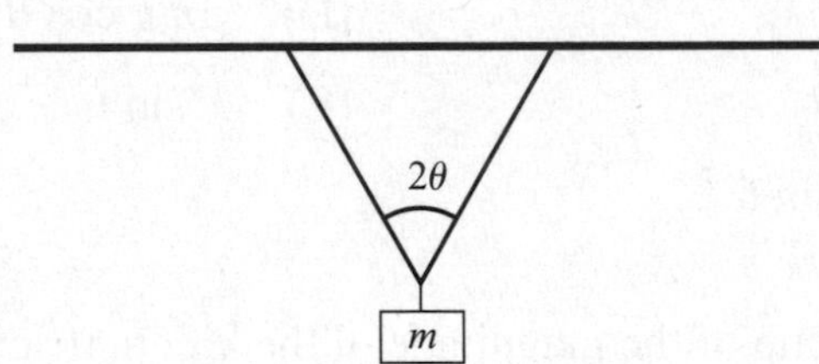

Notice that the angle between the two cords is 2θ. Which of the following is the correct expression for the magnitude of the tension in each cord?

(A) $T = \dfrac{mg}{\cos\theta}$
(B) $T = \dfrac{mg}{2\sin\theta}$
(C) $T = \dfrac{mg}{\cos\theta}$
(D) $T = \dfrac{mg}{2\cos\theta}$
(E) $T = \dfrac{\sin\theta}{mg}$

Free Response

For the following questions, use $g = 10\ \text{m/s}^2$.

1. A 0.5-kg ball is thrown upward from ground level through the air. The air resistance that the ball encounters has a constant magnitude of $\|F_{air}\| = 1.0$ N. The ball is propelled upward with an initial velocity of $v_o = 24$ m/s.

   a. Draw the FBD of the ball on its way up and on its way down.
   b. How much time does it take to reach its maximum height?
   c. What is the speed of the ball when it reaches ground level again?

2. The hanging block (m) causes the entire system to accelerate. The hanging block moves downward and hits the ground in time t_o. The mass on the incline (m) is attached to the hanging mass with a light string around a frictionless pulley. The incline is also frictionless. The angle θ is 37 degrees.

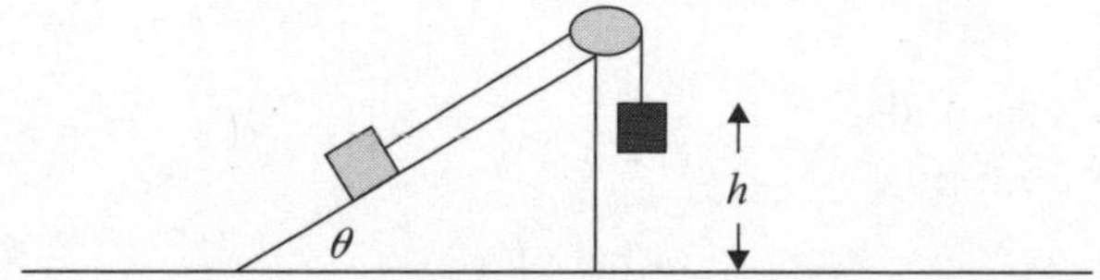

Using sin 37 = 0.6 and cos 37 = 0.8, determine the distance h in terms of m, g, and t_o.

*3. A block is dragged along the top of another block by an applied force of 8 N, as shown in the diagram. The friction between the blocks has a magnitude of 2 N. There is no friction between the bottom block and the table's surface. The top block's mass is 1.0 kg. The bottom block's mass is 2.0 kg. The length of the bottom block L is 0.5 m.

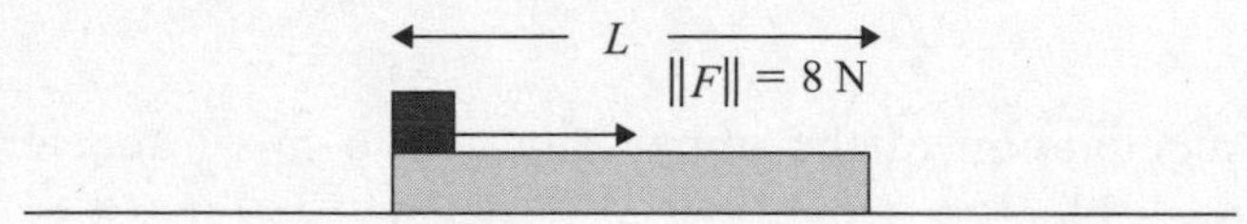

a. Draw the FBD for each mass.
b. Determine the acceleration of each mass.
c. How long does it take for the top block to fall off the bottom block?

Solutions

Multiple Choice

1.	(C)	4.	(E)
2.	(C)	5.	(A)
3.	(A)	6.	(D)

Free Response

1. a. Upward:  Downward: 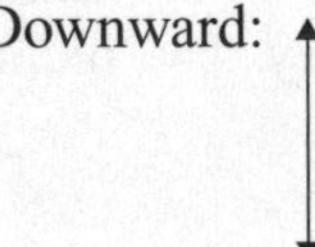

   b. $t = 2$ seconds
   c. $v = 19.6$ m/s

2. $h = (0.1)(g)t_o^2 = (1\ \text{m/s}^2)t_o^2 = t_o^2$

3. a. Upper block:

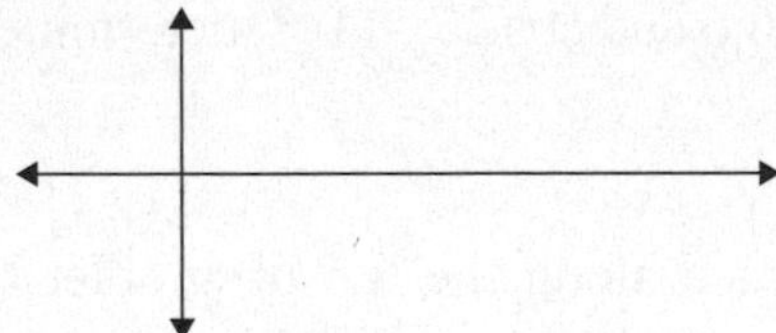

   Lower block:

   b. Acceleration of the upper block = 6 m/s^2; acceleration of the lower block = 1 m/s^2
   c. Time to fall off the lower block = 0.63 seconds

Chapter 5

Circular Motion

EXAM OVERVIEW

The concept of circular motion appears frequently on the AP Physics exam. Unfortunately, it is also a topic that gives many physics students trouble.

Two types of circular motion may occur: uniform and non-uniform. **Uniform circular motion** is the most common type of motion you will be asked to analyze. It can be any circular motion in which the object moves with a constant speed. Usually, the plane of motion is in the horizontal plane so that gravity is not acting to speed up the object and make the motion non-uniform. If you confront a problem involving vertical circular motion at a constant speed (e.g., a ride at an amusement park), then it fits into the "uniform circular motion." If you encounter a problem with vertical circular motion with changing speed (non-uniform circular motion), then your approach would be to use energy conservation. That topic is explored in Chapter 6.

THE BASICS

Solving circular motion problems can be simple. They are additional applications of Newton's second law. The approach is the same: analyze the forces, draw a free-body diagram (FBD), set up a frame of reference, solve for unknowns, and so forth. But to solve circular motion problems, you need to consider another factor: the direction of acceleration.

Centripetal acceleration is center-directed acceleration. This type of acceleration occurs when a velocity vector is changing direction. An object in circular motion can have a constant speed but constantly change direction. For any object traveling in uniform circular motion, the acceleration vector is always centripetal (i.e., along the radial direction), and the velocity vector is always tangent to the circular path.

In the following diagram, the acceleration vector is pointing toward the center of the circle, and the velocity vector is tangent to the path of the circle.

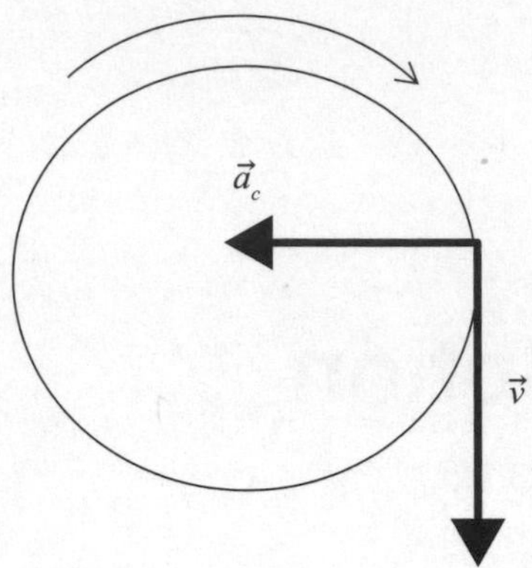

The definition of centripetal acceleration is $a_c = \frac{v^2}{r}$.

Let's analyze a couple of circular motion problems. The simplest starting point is to attach a small object to a light string and whirl it around in circular motion in the horizontal plane. For the sake of simplicity, we will disregard gravity for the moment. If we whirl a 1-kg mass in a circle of radius 0.5 m for a period of 2 seconds, what will the physics look like? The FBD of the mass while in circular motion is simply a radially directed tension force along the string. No appreciable tangential forces exist, and remember that we are ignoring gravity for the moment. The tension is directed radially and so is the acceleration, because it is a centripetal acceleration.

A setup of Newton's second law looks like this:

$$\Sigma F_{centripetal} = ma_c = Tension$$

$$\Rightarrow m\frac{v^2}{r} = T$$

Remember to identify the acceleration as centripetal. To determine the speed of the object, we simply use the fact that

$$\|v\| = \frac{2\pi r}{T} = \frac{2\pi(.5\text{ m})}{2\text{ sec}} = \frac{\pi}{2} \approx 1.57\text{ m/s}.$$

We can find the tension (T) in the string using this formula:

$$T = m\frac{v^2}{r} = (1\text{ kg})\frac{(1.57\text{ m/s})^2}{0.5\text{ m}} \approx 5\text{ N}$$

One mistake made by physics students is to ascribe all circular motion to some "centripetal force." This can be problematic. Centripetal force is not a type of force in the same way tension and weight are types of forces. Rather, a force acting on an object can act in the radial or centripetal direction, thereby producing an acceleration in that direction. In a more complicated motion problem, two forces or two components may both act in the centripetal direction and produce a net acceleration in the centripetal direction. Thus, it would be wrong to say that a "centripetal force" is the force causing the circular motion.

Let's try a fairly typical circular motion problem.

Sample Problem 1

An object $m = 1.5$ kg at the end of a string is whirled around in a vertical circle. The circular motion has a radius of $r = 0.75$ m. Answer the following questions:

- If the speed of the object is 5 m/s at the bottom of the circle (point A in the following diagram), what is the tension in the string at that point?

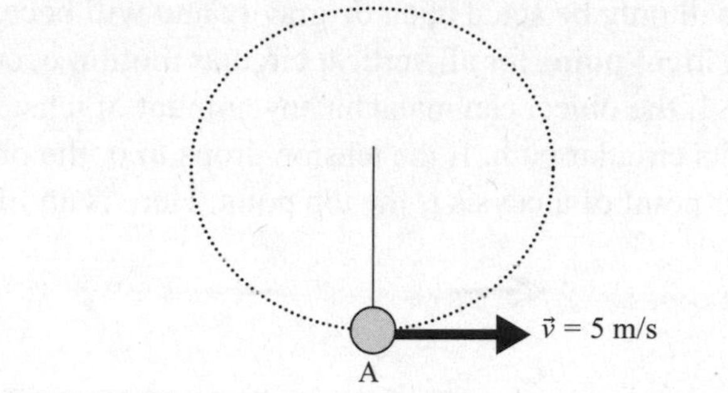

- What is the minimum speed necessary for the object to maintain circular motion?

Solution

As in all dynamics problems, we will start with an FBD. Here is what it looks like:

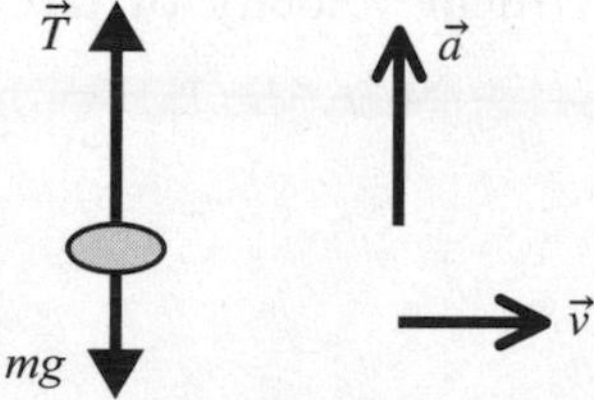

Then we set up a Newton's second law statement for that point.

$$\Sigma F_c = ma_c = T - mg$$

$$\therefore T = ma_c + mg = m\frac{v^2}{r} + mg$$

$$T = (1.5\text{ kg})\frac{(5\text{ m/s})^2}{0.75\text{ m}} + (1.5\text{ kg})(10\text{ m/s}^2) = 48.3\text{ N}$$

The value of the tension is about three times that of the weight of the actual mass.

To answer the second question, we must think about what it means to maintain circular motion. Getting the mass to the top of the circle with enough speed to allow it to complete the circular motion requires some amount of tension in the string. In other words, as long as the string is tugging inward on the mass, the mass will remain in the circular path. If the string ever becomes slack, the mass will only be acted upon by gravity and will become a projectile. Therefore, the **critical point** for all vertical circular motion occurs at the top of the circular path. If the object can maintain any amount of tension on the string, it can complete its circular path. If the tension drops to 0, the object becomes a projectile. So our point of analysis is the top point. Here is an FBD for the top:

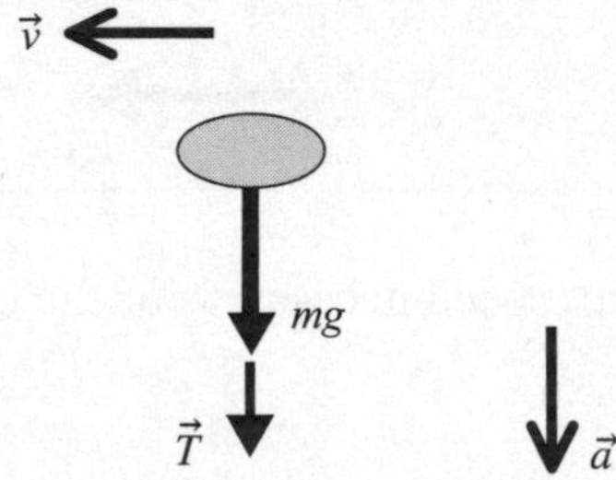

The trick then is to take the tension value to 0. That is the critical point. The speed required to make the tension yet maintain a circular radius at that point is the minimum speed necessary to maintain circular motion. Some physics textbooks call this critical velocity of circular motion. Here is the physics:

$$\Sigma F_{c,top} = ma_c = T + mg$$

Let $T \to 0$

$$\Sigma F_{c,top} = ma_c = mg$$

$$m\frac{v^2}{r} = mg$$

$$\frac{v^2}{r} = g \Rightarrow v_{critical} = \sqrt{rg} = \sqrt{(0.75\text{ m})(10\text{ m/s}^2)} = 2.73\text{ m/s}$$

Sample Problem 2

A car is making a turn on a level road. The mass of the car is 1,200 kg. The radius of the turn is 50 m. The car is moving at 40 mph (18 m/s) at one moment in the turn.

- Draw an FBD.
- Determine a value for friction.
- Determine a minimum value for the coefficient of static friction such that the car will not slip off the road.

Solution

Here is our FBD (viewed head-on toward the car, with the velocity of the car coming out of the page).

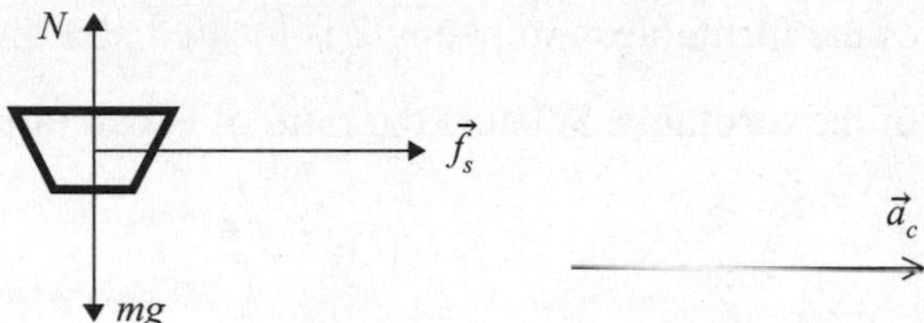

Solving for the value of the frictional force (f_s), we get

$$\Sigma F_c = ma_c = f_s$$

$$f_s = ma_c = m\frac{v^2}{r} = (1200\text{ kg})\frac{(18\text{ m/s})^2}{50\text{ m}} = 7776\text{ N}$$

Now let's analyze the frictional aspect. If we need the minimum coefficient of static friction, we must be at the point where the frictional force is at its maximum value:

$$f_s \leq \mu_s N = \mu_s mg$$

$$\therefore \mu_s = \frac{f_s}{mg} = \frac{7776\text{ N}}{(1200\text{ kg})(10\text{ m/s}^2)} = 0.648$$

Practice Session Problems

Multiple Choice

1. A physics student is standing on a rotating merry-go-round without slipping. Which force provides the student's centripetal acceleration?

(A) Normal force
(B) Weight
(C) Friction on feet
(D) Centrifugal force
(E) None

2. Two pennies lay on a spinning turntable. Penny 1 is at a distance $R/2$ from the center of the turntable, and penny 2 is located at a distance of R from the center of the turntable. What is the ratio of accelerations $\left(\frac{a_1}{a_2}\right)$?

(A) $\frac{2}{1}$
(B) $\frac{1}{2}$
(C) $\frac{1}{1}$
(D) $\frac{\sqrt{2}}{1}$
(E) $\frac{1}{\sqrt{2}}$

3. What is the centripetal acceleration of the Earth around the sun in m/s^2?

(A) 5.95×10^{-3} m/s^2
(B) 5.95×10^{3} m/s^2
(C) 5.95×10^{11} m/s^2
(D) 5.95×10^{-11} m/s^2
(E) 3.3×10^{-2} m/s^2

A pendulum swings through its arc as shown in the following diagram. Points A and C are the points of maximum displacement for the pendulum.

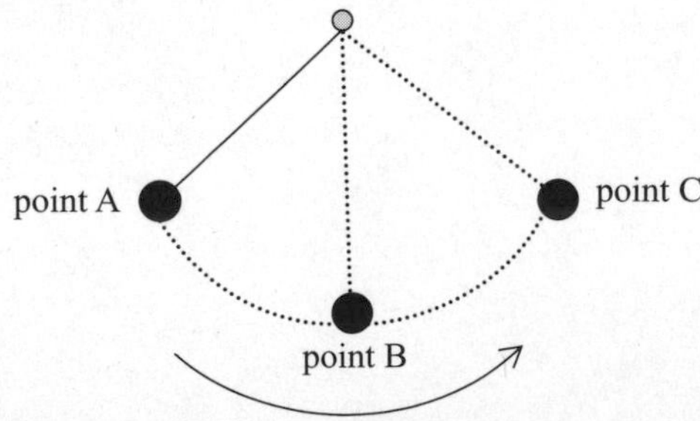

For questions 4 through 6, use the following choices for your answers:

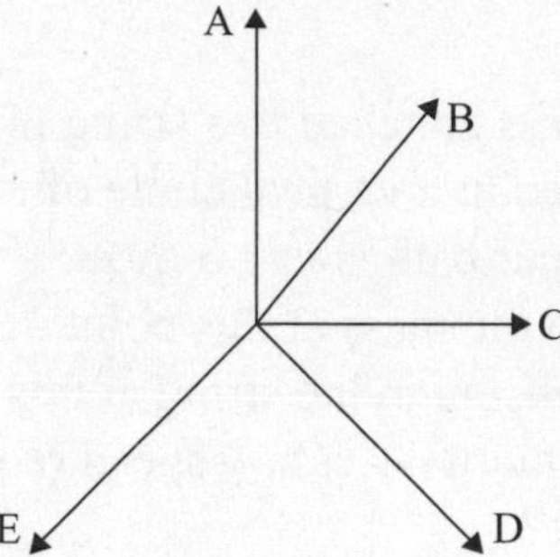

4. What is the direction of the acceleration of the pendulum bob at point A?

5. What is the direction of the acceleration at point B?

6. What is the direction of the velocity vector at point C?

Free Response

1. A conical pendulum of length L is rotating as shown in the following diagram. Determine the period of circular motion for this conical pendulum in terms of L, g, θ, and other constants.

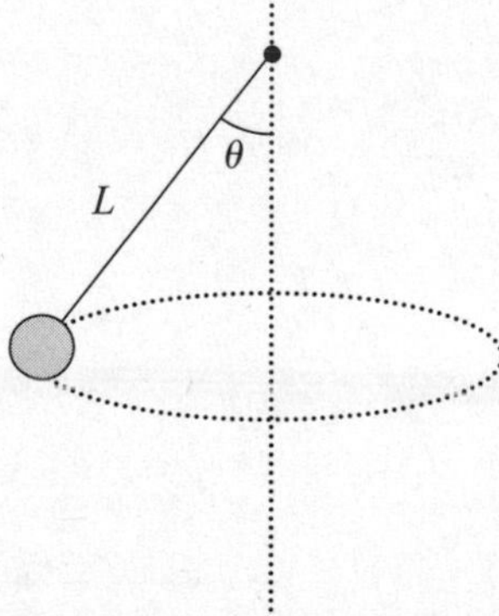

2. A car is traveling in circular motion on an exit ramp. The road is slightly banked at a subtle angle of 8 degrees.
   a. Determine the maximum speed that the car can have without using friction as it is making this circle arc of radius 100 m.

b. If the car exceeds the maximum speed found in part a, draw the new FBD for the car traveling around the banked turn.

3. A student whirls a mass attached to a string in a vertical circle. The mass is 0.2 kg and is whirled in a vertical circle of radius $r = 0.5$ m. The speed at the top of the circular path is $v = 3$ m/s.

   a. Draw an FBD on the mass at this point.
   b. Determine the tension in the string at this point.
   c. What is the minimum necessary speed required for the mass to make a complete circle?

Solutions

Multiple Choice

1.	(C)	4.	(D)
2.	(B)	5.	(A)
3.	(A)	6.	(E)

Free Response

1. $T = 2\pi\sqrt{\dfrac{L\cos\theta}{g}}$

   The FBD is as follows:

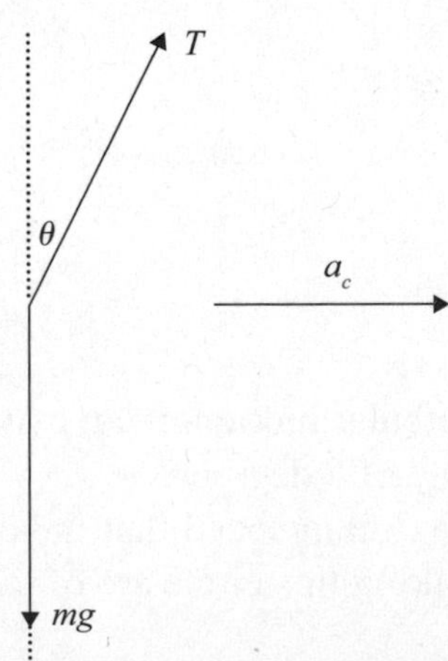

The solution is as follows:

$$\Sigma F_y = 0 = T_y - mg$$

$$\Sigma F_y = 0 = T\cos\theta - mg$$

$$\Rightarrow T = \frac{mg}{\cos\theta}$$

$$\Sigma F_c = ma_c = T_c$$

$$\Sigma F_c = ma_c = T\sin\theta$$

$$\Rightarrow m\frac{v^2}{r} = T\sin\theta$$

Substitute in T:

$$m\frac{v^2}{r} = \left(\frac{mg}{\cos\theta}\right)\sin\theta = mg\tan\theta$$

$$\Rightarrow v = \sqrt{rg\tan\theta}$$

Now, notice that "r" is actually $L\sin\theta$.
So...

$$v = \sqrt{rg\tan\theta} = \sqrt{L\sin\theta \cdot g\tan\theta}$$

$$\text{and, } T = \frac{2\pi r}{v} = \frac{2\pi L\sin\theta}{\sqrt{L\sin\theta \cdot g\tan\theta}} = 2\pi\sqrt{\frac{L\cos\theta}{g}}$$

2. a. 11.7 m/s
   b. The FBD is as follows:

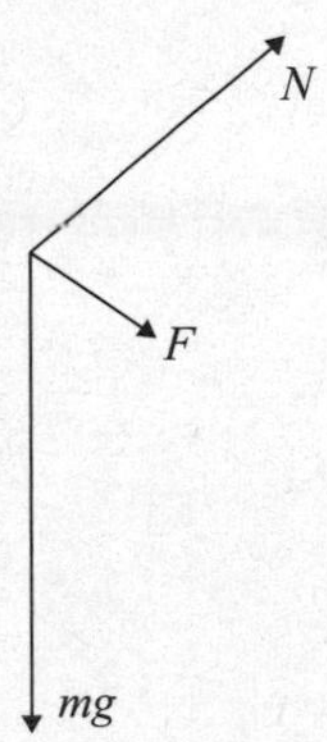

3. a. The FBD is as follows:

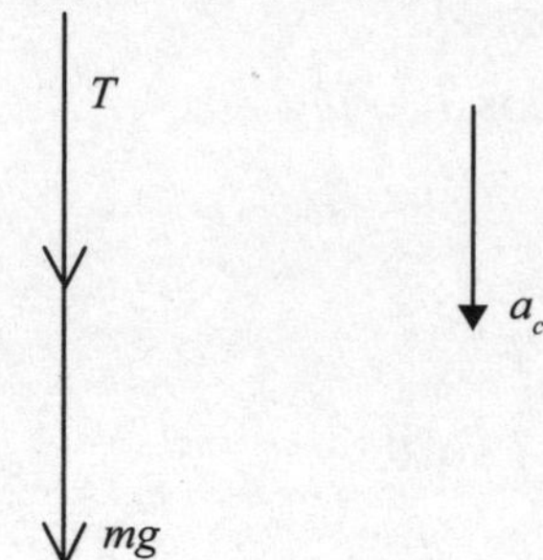

b. $T = 1.6$ N
c. $v = 2.2$ m/s

Chapter 6

Work and Conservation of Energy

EXAM OVERVIEW

It is often said that you can solve most physics problems if you understand the concepts of work and energy. That may be an oversimplification, but if you look at any of the past AP Physics exams, you will see that many problems have work and energy concepts built into either the solutions or the frameworks of the questions. Energy appears throughout the physics curriculum: mechanics, fluids, thermodynamics, electricity and magnetism, and modern physics. Therefore, this chapter is critical for all physics students. Let's take a look at some of the important ideas in work and energy.

DEFINITIONS OF WORK AND ENERGY, AND THE WORK–ENERGY THEOREM

An object or a system with mass in motion at velocity v is defined as having energy resulting from its motion. That energy is called **kinetic energy** and is expressed as $KE = \frac{1}{2}mv^2$. An object that has some height h above the ground (in the Earth's gravitational field) is defined as having a **gravitational potential energy** expressed as $U_g = mgh$. Another type of mechanical energy is defined as a spring or elastic system having an **elastic potential energy** expressed as $U_{spring} = \frac{1}{2}k(\Delta x)^2$. These three energies together are called the **total mechanical energy of a system** (TE). Most physical systems will have two of the three energies involved, but sometimes all three energies come into play—for example, when you have an oscillating mass (with a spring system) on an inclined track.

Let's use the definitions in a few examples. A projectile at some instant in time has a velocity of 5 m/s and a height above the ground of 8.0 m. The projectile has a mass $m = 0.2$ kg. We would define the energies of this system as follows:

$$KE = \frac{1}{2}mv^2 = \frac{1}{2}(0.2\text{ kg})(5\text{ m/s})^2 = 2.5\text{ joules}$$

$$U_g = mgh = (0.2\text{ kg})(10\text{ m/s}^2)(8\text{ m}) = 16\text{ joules}$$

$$TE = U_g + KE = 2.5 + 16 = 18.5\text{ joules}$$

The unit of energy and work is the joule, which is defined as follows:

$$1\text{ J} = \text{N} \cdot \text{m} = \text{kg} \cdot \frac{\text{m}^2}{\text{s}^2}.$$

Work is defined as the product of force times displacement (or the component of the force in the direction of displacement times displacement). The formal definition is $W = \left\|\vec{F}\right\| \left\|\vec{\Delta x}\right\| \cdot \cos\theta$. The angle θ is defined as the angle between the two vectors when drawn from a common origin. Here is a picture of that:

A vector diagram showing the force vector and the displacement vector is shown here:

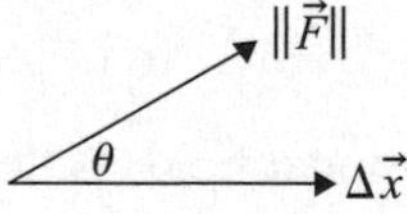

Combining the two definitions gives you the **work–energy theorem**, which states $Work_{system} = \Delta Energy_{system}$. Work can be a positive or negative value, just as the energy change can be a positive or negative value.

The work–energy theorem is simple yet powerful. It is a very powerful problem-solving tool. If you use the work–energy theorem to solve a problem, you usually only need information about the beginning state and the ending state. Typically, work and energy analysis does not involve time, only the various states of the mechanics.

Another way that work is represented in physics problems is through the use of a graph in the form shown here:

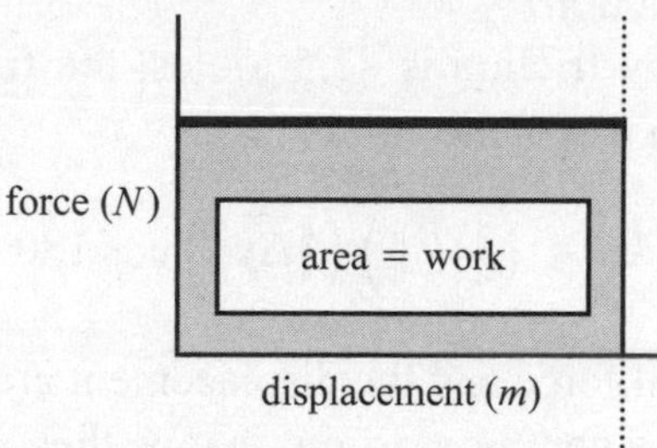

If you have information about force and displacement that you can put in graphical format, then you can use the graph to compute work simply. Work is the area of a force-versus-displacement graph (if both are in the same direction).

Let's revisit a familiar physics problem, this time analyzing work and energy.

Sample Problem 1

A physics book of mass 0.2 kg slides across the floor and eventually comes to a stop after sliding 8 m. The book was initially launched across the floor at a speed of 5 m/s. Determine the work done by friction in this situation.

Solution

At first we might consider drawing FBDs, computing friction, and applying the definition of work. That could be a valid approach. However, because we know the initial condition of the book, we know the initial energy. From that information, we can determine work done by friction.

The initial energy of the book is

$$E_o = KE_o = \frac{1}{2}mv^2 = \frac{1}{2}(0.2\text{ kg})(5\text{ m/s})^2 = 2.5\text{ J}.$$

By the work–energy theorem, work done by friction is equal to the energy change. In this problem, the only force doing work is friction. The normal force and the weight are perpendicular to the displacement of the book and thus do no work on the book. Therefore, we can calculate work as follows:

$$W_{friction} = \Delta KE_{book}$$
$$W_{friction} = KE_f - KE_o = 0 - 2.5 \text{ J}$$
$$W_{friction} = -2.5 \text{ J}$$

Now let's go a little further with this problem. What is the frictional force and the coefficient of friction?

If the work done by friction is –2.5 joules, the frictional force times the displacement is equal to that same value:

$$W_f = \left(\|\vec{f}\|\right)\left(\|\vec{\Delta x}\|\right)\cos 180$$

Remember that frictional force and the displacement are 180 degrees from each other when drawn from a common origin; that is, they are opposite:

$$W_f = \left(\|\vec{f}\|\right)(8 \text{ m})\cos 180 = -2.5$$
$$\text{So,} \Rightarrow -(8 \text{ m})(\|f\|) = -2.5 \text{ J}$$
$$\Rightarrow \|f\| = \frac{2.5 \text{ J}}{8 \text{ m}} = \frac{5}{16} \text{ Newtons} \approx .31 \text{ N}$$

We can now solve for the coefficient of sliding friction between the book and the floor:

$$\mu_k = \frac{f_k}{N} = \frac{0.31}{(0.2 \text{ kg})(10 \text{ m/s}^2)} = 0.15$$

DEFINITIONS OF CONSERVATIVE FORCES AND POTENTIAL ENERGY

Two types of forces are discussed in the area of work and energy: dissipative forces and conservative forces. **Dissipative forces** are forces that dissipate energy out of the system. The most common dissipative force in mechanics is friction. Friction usually takes energy from the system, which is why work done by friction is negative. This negative work can never be recovered and is lost to the larger system of the surroundings (e.g., the Earth). Dissipative forces also include air resistance, applied forces, and various resistive forces, among others.

Conservative forces are forces that return to the system all the energy it gained from an outside source. The three conservative forces typically covered in the AP Physics exam are gravitational, elastic (spring), and electrostatic. All three forces have a potential energy function associated with them. The precise definition of a conservative force involves its potential energy function:

$$W_{conservativeforce} = -\ \Delta U_{conservativeforce}$$

The negative sign may seem odd at first, but it is important. It is saying that when the conservative force is doing negative work on the system, the system gains potential energy. For example, when an object is lifted upward in a gravitational field, the conservative force—gravity—does negative work, but the system gains potential energy. The energy is put into the system by the outside force that lifts the block and therefore does positive work.

The opposite situation—when the conservative force does positive work on the system—results in the system losing potential energy. For example, when an object begins to freely fall under the influence of gravity, the work done by the gravitational force is positive and the potential energy of the block begins to decrease. It is very important to see the significance of the negative sign in this definition. It is a subtle but important point on which the AP Physics exam will test you.

CONSERVATION OF TOTAL MECHANICAL ENERGY

Technically, the conservation of mechanical energy is an idealization of real-world physics, because all systems lose mechanical energy to frictional effects. But it is a simple and fun problem-solving tool with many interesting applications. The main examples usually used in the AP Physics exam are

- the pendulum;
- the projectile or an object sliding on a pathway without friction but in a gravitational field; and
- a perfectly linear elastic spring.

If you understand these three problem types, you should be ready to handle any problem involving conservation of energy on the AP Physics exam.

It is important to know when to apply the principle of the conservation of total mechanical energy. Although you can apply the principle when only a conservative force is doing *work* on a system, you need to remember that in many problems, other forces are acting in the system that are not doing work. For example, consider the pendulum. Clearly, two forces act on a pendulum: tension and weight. Tension does not do any work because it is perpendicular to the displacement of the pendulum at any point in time.

In general, centripetal forces do not do work on a system. They never change the energy of a system; they only change the direction of the velocity. This is an important point to understand in conservation of energy problems.

Here is a look at a typical conservation of energy problem.

Sample Problem 2

A projectile is launched at a speed of 20 m/s at an angle of 60 degrees. Determine the projectile's maximum height using energy methods.

Solution

Of course, we could solve this problem with a projectile motion equation, but it is a useful exercise to employ energy principles instead. The solution is very simple. Because the only force acting on a projectile in free fall is gravity (disregarding air resistance, of course), the total mechanical energy will be conserved. The energies involved in the system are gravity (U_g) and kinetic energy (KE). Determine the total energy (TE) at the launch and compare it to the total energy at the maximum height.

$$TE_{launch} = U_g + KE$$

Set $U_g = 0$, at launch point.

$$TE_{launch} = U_g + KE = (0 \text{ J}) + \frac{1}{2}mv^2$$

$$TE = \frac{1}{2}\text{m}(20 \text{ m/s})^2 = 200 \text{ m}$$

Now compare this to the total energy at the maximum height. Remember, when making comparisons with energy, do not make the mistake of assuming that all the energy at the peak point is potential energy. Rather, you need to include the kinetic energy of the projectile at the maximum height because the projectile has its horizontal velocity at that point.

$$v_{ox} = v_x = (20 \text{ m/s}) \cos 60 = 10 \text{ m/s}$$

$$KE_{top} = \frac{1}{2}mv_x^2 = \frac{1}{2}\text{m}(10 \text{ m/s})^2 = 50 \text{ m}$$

$$U_{top} = mgh_{max}$$

$$\Rightarrow \therefore TE_{launch} = TE_{top}$$

$$200 \text{ m} = 50 \text{ m} + mgh_{max}$$

$$mgh = 150 \text{ m}$$

$$gh = 150$$

$$h = \frac{150}{g} \approx 10 \text{ meters}$$

You could obtain the same solution by using projectile motion. Try it.

Another important concept is power. **Power** is the rate of energy change or energy consumption. It can also be the rate at which work is performed. The concept of power being a rate is a source of confusion for many physics students. The formal definition of power is

$$power = \frac{\Delta\ Energy}{\Delta\ time} \text{ or } \frac{Work}{\Delta\ time}.$$

The unit for power is joules/second, which equals a watt.

Another way to define power is as the product of force times velocity:

$$P = \|\vec{F}\| \cdot \|\vec{v}\|.$$

This is useful when an object is being lifted in equilibrium.

Practice Session Problems

Multiple Choice

1. A box of mass m is pushed up an incline of 5 m. The mass is pushed up the incline in equilibrium. The incline makes a 37-degree angle as shown. The incline has no friction. What is the amount of work necessary to lift the mass to the top of the incline if it starts at the bottom?

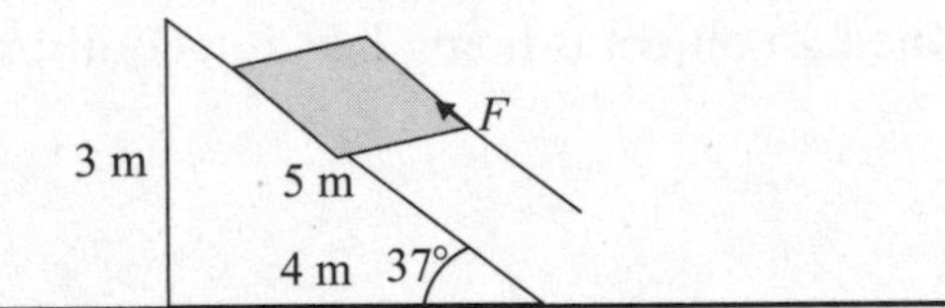

(A) 5 mg

(B) (3 mg)(sin 37)

(C) 3 mg

(D) 5 mg/(sin 37)

(E) 4 mg

2. A mass of 2 kg is pushed along a frictionless floor by an outside force of 5 N. The mass is pushed along at a constant velocity of 2 m/s. What is the amount of power developed by the 5-N force?

(A) 10 watts

(B) 4 watts

(C) 40 watts

(D) 100 watts

(E) 0 watts

3. A projectile is launched vertically into the air by a spring-loaded gun. The projectile has a launch speed of v_0 and an initial launch energy of E_0. The next time the projectile is launched, the spring is loaded such that it gives the projectile a launch speed of $2v_0$. What is the launch energy of the second launch?

(A) E_o

(B) $2E_o$

(C) $4E_o$

(D) $8E_o$

(E) $16E_o$

4. A frictionless ball-and-track system is set up in three ways as shown in the following diagrams. The ball is started at the top of the track and slides down to the bottom. Which of the following correctly compares the speeds of the ball at the bottom of the tracks in all three situations? (Note: All three tracks have the same starting height.)

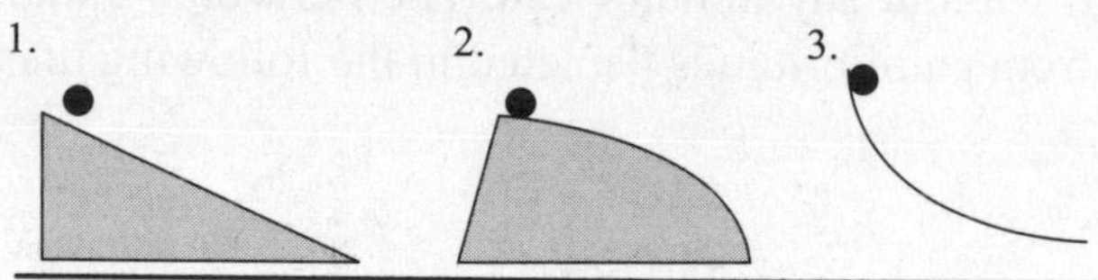

(A) $v_1 > v_2 > v_3$

(B) $v_1 > v_3 > v_2$

(C) $v_3 > v_1 > v_2$

(D) $v_3 > v_1 = v_2$

(E) $v_1 = v_2 = v_3$

5. A ball is whirled in a vertical circle of radius r. The only forces acting on the ball are gravity and the tension in the string. The ball has the exact critical velocity for a ball in a vertical circle at the top: $v_c = \sqrt{gr}$. What is the speed of the ball (v_b) at the bottom of the vertical circle?

(A) $v_b = 2\sqrt{gr}$

(B) $v_b = \sqrt{2gr}$

(C) $v_b = \sqrt{\frac{5}{2}gr}$

(D) $v_b = \sqrt{5gr}$

(E) $v_b = \sqrt{gr}$

6. A bullet with a mass of 2 g impinges into a wooden board that is deep enough to hold the bullet. The bullet is traveling at a speed of 400 m/s when it hits the board. The board exerts a constant stopping force of 1,000 N while the bullet moves through the board. How far does the bullet bore through the board?

(A) 160 m

(B) 16 m

(C) 1.6 m

(D) 0.16 m

(E) 0.016 m

Free Response

1. A mass of 0.1 kg is oscillating back and forth on a linear spring. There is no frictional loss in the system. The mass is pulled out to $x = -0.5$ m and let go without any initial speed. The mass's potential energy versus distance from equilibrium is depicted in the following diagram.

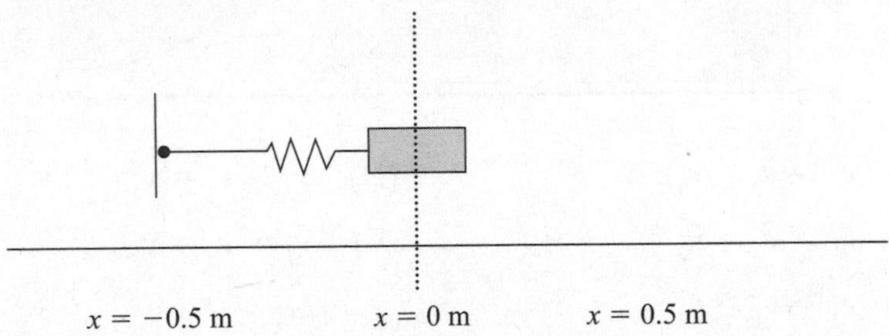

Here is a graph of the potential energy function versus displacement.

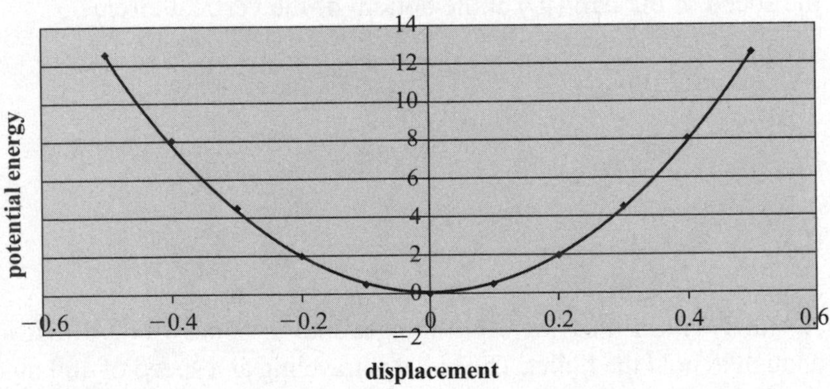

a. On the graph, sketch in the following: kinetic energy versus displacement and total energy versus displacement.
b. From the graph, determine the value of the kinetic energy of the mass at a distance of 0.2 m from the equilibrium point ($x = 0$).
c. Determine the spring constant of the spring.

*2. A pendulum of mass m is started from a horizontal position, as shown in the following diagram. The pendulum swings, passing through points A and B. Answer the following questions in terms of m, g, L, and θ.

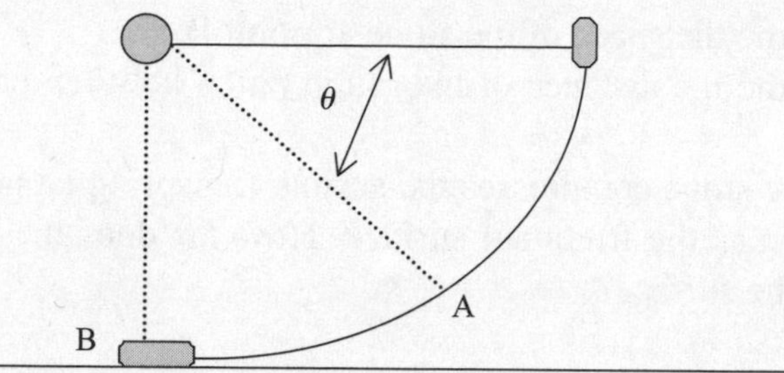

a. What is the total energy of the pendulum at the starting point? (Use a potential energy of 0 at the lowest point of the pendulum's swing, point B.)
b. What is the velocity of the pendulum at point A?
c. What is the tension in the cord at point A?
d. What is the tension in the cord at point B?

3. A stone of mass $m = 5$ kg is sitting at rest on a hill (height of 20 m) at point A, as shown in the following diagram:

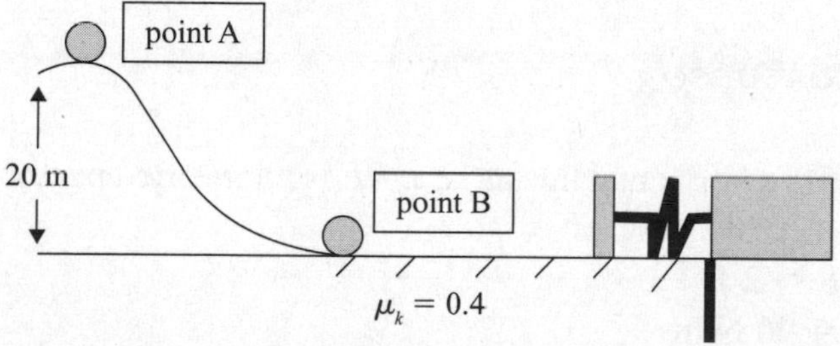

The stone begins to slide down this frictionless hill until it reaches point B; then it runs into friction. The coefficient of friction between the stone and the horizontal rough patch of ground is $\mu_k = 0.4$. The spring constant for the spring is $k = 10{,}000$ N/m. The stone slides along the rough patch and hits the spring and compresses the spring in a distance of 0.2 m before coming to a stop. You may use gravity as $g = 10$ m/s^2 and consider the 0.2-m distance stretched by the spring does not count in the frictional loss of energy of the stone.

a. Determine the speed of the stone at point B.
b. Determine the distance of the rough patch between point B and the spring.
c. After the stone compresses the spring, the spring launches the stone back across the frictional surface. How far does the stone make it across the surface?

Solutions

Multiple Choice

1. (C)
2. (A)
3. (C)
4. (E)
5. (D)
6. (D)

Free Response

1. a. *TE* is a horizontal line at 12 J. *KE* is an inverted parabola with vertex at 12 J, 0.
   b. $KE = 2$ J
   c. $k = 96$ N/m
2. a. $U_{top} = mgL$
   b. Speed at point A: $v_a = \sqrt{2gL\,(1 - \sin\theta)}$. The height of the pendulum above point B is $h = L\sin\theta$. Thus, energy is conserved from the top to point B.

$$\Rightarrow U_{top} - U_a = KE_a$$

$$\Rightarrow mgL\sin\theta - 0 = \frac{1}{2}mv_a^2$$

$$mgL(\sin\theta) = \frac{1}{2}mv_a^2$$

$$v_a = \sqrt{2gL\sin\theta}$$

c. Solving for tension at this point results in the following FBD and equations:

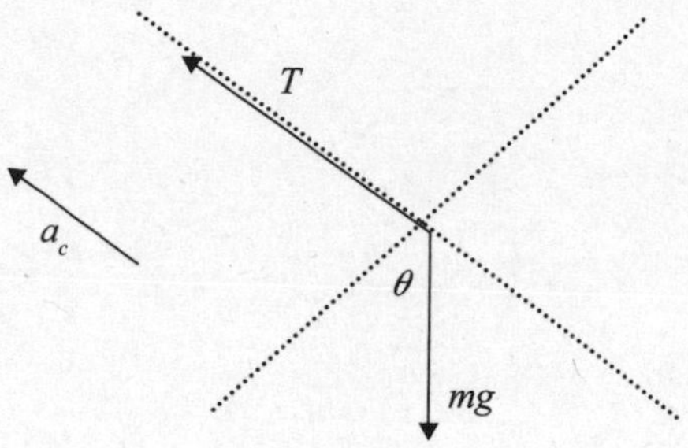

$\Sigma F_c = ma_c = T - mg \sin\theta$

Substitute, a_c

$$a_c = \frac{v^2}{r} = \frac{\left(\sqrt{2gL\sin\theta}\right)^2}{L} = 2g\sin\theta$$

$\Rightarrow T = ma_c + mg\sin\theta = m2g\sin\theta + mg\sin\theta$

$\therefore T = 3mg\sin\theta$

d. $T = 3mg$ at the bottom (you can use the expression from part c).

3. a. $v_b = 20$ m/s
   b. $\Delta x = 40$ m
   c. $\Delta x = 10$ m

Chapter 7

Momentum and Impulse

EXAM OVERVIEW

The concepts of momentum and impulse are fairly intuitive, and most physics students enjoy experimenting with them in their physics courses. The law of conservation of momentum is really a restatement of Newton's first and third laws. Impulse is simply another way to describe Newton's second law. Realizing that the concepts provide another way to describe Newton's laws and dynamics, many students are comfortable working with them. However, some students confuse the two conservation laws and confuse the definitions of work and impulse. This chapter gives you a close look at these ideas and offers a warning about common mistakes that students make as they apply the new concepts to those discussed in previous chapters.

DEFINITIONS

The definition of **momentum** is $\vec{p} = m\vec{v}$. Essentially, any object with mass that is moving in any direction will have a measurable value of momentum. The units of momentum are kilogram times second (kg · m/s). Thus, another way to think of momentum is the inertia of an object in motion. To stop an object that has momentum, an *impulse* will have to act on the object to change its state of motion. Thinking about momentum in this way makes it easy to understand why Newton preferred working with momentum.

Impulse is the net force acting on an object over an interval of time. An impulse can occur in a very small period (like a bat hitting a baseball) or over an extended period (like gravity acting on a freely falling object for 4 seconds). The definition for AP Physics B is impulse $= \vec{J} = \vec{F}\Delta t$. The units for impulse are Newton times second $(\mathrm{N \cdot s})$. Impulse is connected to momentum by the relationship $\vec{F}\Delta t = \Delta\vec{p}$, which is simply another way to state Newton's second law:

$$\vec{F}\Delta t = \Delta\vec{p} \Rightarrow \vec{F} = \frac{\Delta\vec{p}}{\Delta t} \Rightarrow \vec{F} = \frac{\Delta(m\vec{v})}{\Delta t} = m\vec{a}$$

CONSERVATION OF MOMENTUM

Now let's look at the next conservation law in physics—the conservation of linear momentum. This law is frequently used in solving collision problems or problems involving a system that is not acted on by outside forces. The law states that, in the absence of outside or external forces, the total momentum in a system is conserved. In physics language, that is stated as

$$\text{If, } F\Delta t = 0 \Rightarrow \Delta\vec{p} = 0.$$

Thus, the total momentum in the system does not change over time. A collision involves internal forces in the system, and of course internal forces do not count as outside forces. The momentum of each component of the system could change as a result of the system, but the law of conservation of momentum states that the total momentum must remain constant. Because momentum is a vector measurement, some collision problems can involve two dimensions. These types of problems bring vector addition into the solution.

Many physics students mix up the ideas of momentum and energy. And because each concept has its own conservation law, that confusion can lead to applying the incorrect law to a problem. The law of conservation of momentum is only applicable in the absence of outside forces—a rare occurrence in the real world. Therefore, physics books have to be creative in writing problems in which momentum is conserved. Usually these problems involve a "frictionless" object, like an air table or cart. On the other hand, energy conservation can occur with outside forces, like a spring or gravity. Be sure you apply the conservation laws correctly.

You also need to be sure you understand the difference between the definition of *work* and the definition of *impulse*. It might help you to think of these two concepts in this way: work is the cumulative effect of force over distance, and impulse is the cumulative effect of force over time. That is why the area of a force-versus-displacement graph is equal to work, and the area of a force-versus-time graph is equal to impulse, or change in momentum.

Energy and momentum can be connected. Often a textbook will ask students to find the "energy change" or "energy loss" in some "inelastic collision." This is a typical way of testing the two concepts together. An **inelastic collision** has a net loss of energy as a result of the collision. In the real world of measurement, all collisions are truly inelastic. In the world of fun physics textbook problems, there is also the **elastic collision**, in which no energy is lost. This is an idealized type of problem on which many physics textbooks and the AP Physics exam like to test students. To solve this type of problem, students must correctly apply two laws of physics.

Now let's take a look at some practice problems in the area of momentum and impulse and the conservation of momentum.

Sample Problem 1

An asteroid of mass m = 1,000 kg is moving through space at a speed of 100 m/s. Compute the kinetic energy and the momentum of the asteroid.

Solution

$$KE = \frac{1}{2}mv^2 = \frac{1}{2}(1000\text{ kg})(100\text{ m/s})^2 = 5 \times 10^6\text{ J}$$

$$\vec{p} = m\vec{v} = (1000\text{ kg})(100\text{ m/s}) = 1 \times 10^5\text{ kg}\cdot\text{m/s}$$

Sample Problem 2

A baseball of mass m = 0.25 kg is moving at a speed of 40 m/s toward a batter. The batter strikes the ball, applying an impulse to the ball. The average force applied to the ball during the contact with the bat is F_{avg} = 1,000 N. The ball leaves the bat at a speed of 60 m/s, in the opposite direction of the incoming speed. Determine the amount of time the bat was in contact with the ball.

Solution

This is an application of the rule that impulse equals change in momentum. First, we compute the change in momentum of the ball:

$$\Delta\vec{p} = m\vec{v}_f - m\vec{v}_o = m(\vec{v}_f - \vec{v}_o) = 0.25\text{ kg}(-60\text{ m/s} - 40\text{ m/s})$$
$$= -25\text{ kg}\cdot\text{m/s}$$

We need to keep in mind that the negative sign simply means the direction of the momentum change and the direction of the applied impulse and force, which would be opposite of the incoming baseball.

Now we take the momentum change and equate it to the impulse:

$$\vec{F}\Delta t = \Delta\vec{p}$$

$$\Delta t = \frac{\Delta\vec{p}}{\vec{F}} = \frac{-25\text{ kg}\cdot\text{m/s}}{-1000\text{ N}} = 0.025\text{ sec}$$

Therefore, the bat is in contact with the ball for 25 milliseconds.

Sample Problem 3

A collision between two railroad cars occurs on a track (assume it is frictionless). One cart with a mass of 1,000 kg smashes into a stationary car with a mass of 500 kg. The 1,000-kg cart had a speed of 10 m/s at the moment of impact. The two cars couple together after the collision and move off as one massive car. Use this information to answer the following questions:

- What is the speed of the coupled cars?
- What is the loss of energy in the collision?
- Can you account for this missing energy?

Solution

This type of collision—one object collides into another object and they become one mass—is called **totally inelastic**. It represents the maximum loss of energy of any collision type.

The momentum before the collision must equal the momentum after the collision:

$$\vec{p}_{before} = \vec{p}_{after}$$

$$p_{before} = p_{1000\text{ kg}} + p_{500} = (1000\text{ kg})(10\text{ m/s}) + (0\text{ kg} \cdot \text{m/s})$$

$$p_{after} = (m_{1000} + m_{500})v_{combinedmass}$$

$$p_{after} = (1500\text{ kg})v_{comb}$$

$$\therefore 1500v_{comb} = 10{,}000\text{ kg} \cdot \text{m/s}$$

$$v_{combined} = 6.7\text{ m/s}$$

The loss of kinetic energy from the collision is very simple to compute:

$$KE_{after} = \frac{1}{2}m_{total}v_{comb}^2 = \frac{1}{2}(1500\text{ kg})(6.7\text{ m/s})^2 = 3.33 \times 10^4\text{ J}$$

$$KE_{before} = \frac{1}{2}mv^2 = \frac{1}{2}(1000\text{ kg})(10)^2 = 5 \times 10^4\text{ J}$$

$$\Delta KE = KE_f - KE_o = 3.33 \times 10^4 - 5.0 \times 10^4 = -1.67 \times 10^4\text{ J}$$

Energy is lost through the heat generated from the metal deforming, the sound, and the inelastic properties of the metal.

Sample Problem 4

A bullet of mass m is shot into a block of mass $99m$, as shown in the diagram. The mass of the block and bullet combined then begins to rise up to a height of h_o. Determine the speed of the bullet before entry into the block in terms of m, g, and h_o.

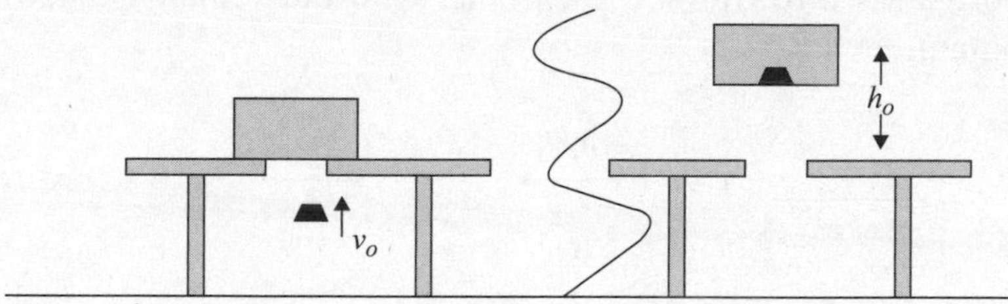

Solution

First, we must realize that energy is conserved in the block's rise to height h_o. So the speed of the block and bullet combination can be determined at the collision impact, because the energy at that point must equal the energy at height h_o:

$$U_{g,top} = (100m)gh_o$$

$$KE_{impact} = \frac{1}{2}(100m)v^2_{block/bullet}$$

$$\Rightarrow v_{block/bullet} = \sqrt{2gh_o}$$

Now that we have the speed of the combined mass, we can determine the bullets' original speed from conservation of momentum:

$$\vec{p}_{before} = \vec{p}_{after}$$

$$m_{bullet}v_{bullet} = (m_{bullet} + m_{block})v_{bullet/block}$$

$$mv_b = (100m)\sqrt{2gh_o}$$

$$v_{bullet} = 100\sqrt{2gh_o}$$

One idea evident in this problem is that the conservation of energy occurred after the collision, not before.

Practice Session Problems

Multiple Choice

1. Two masses travel toward each other with the velocities shown in the diagram.

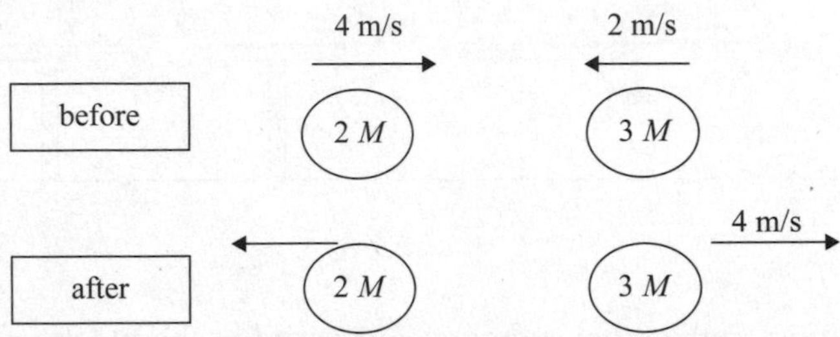

After the collision, the two masses rebound with different velocities in the opposite direction. Mass 3 M has a speed of 4 m/s after the collision. What is the speed of the mass 2 M after the collision?

(A) 1 m/s
(B) 2 m/s
(C) 3 m/s
(D) 4 m/s
(E) 5 m/s

2. Which of the following expressions is equivalent to the kinetic energy of a mass in terms of its momentum?

(A) $\frac{\|\vec{p}\|}{m}$

(B) $\frac{\|\vec{p}\|^2}{m}$

(C) $\frac{\|\vec{p}\|^2}{2m}$

(D) $\frac{\|\vec{p}\|^2}{m^2}$

(E) $\frac{\|\vec{p}\|^2}{2m^2}$

An exploding-cart system is set up on a frictionless track in a physics lab. Cart 1 has a mass of 3 M and cart 2 has a mass of 5 M. The two carts are initially at rest on the track and then are launched with a spring-loaded launcher set between them. Cart 1 moves away at a speed of 3 m/s. Cart 2 moves away at an unknown speed. Use this information and the following diagram to answer questions 3 and 4.

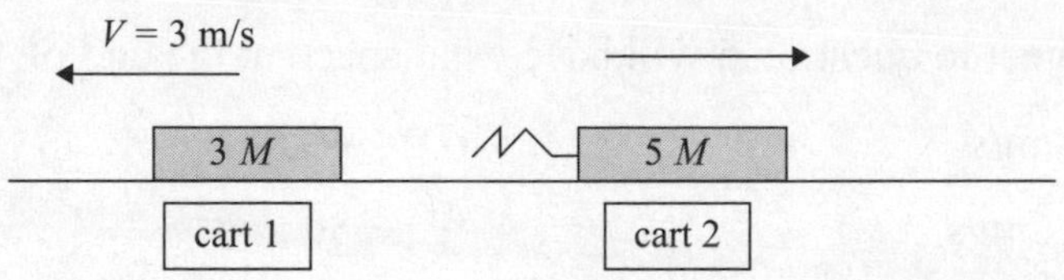

3. What is the speed of cart 2?

(A) 5 m/s
(B) 5/9 m/s
(C) 9/5 m/s
(D) 9 m/s
(E) 3 m/s

4. What is the total momentum of the two-cart system after the explosion?

(A) 18 M kg · m/s
(B) 9 M kg · m/s
(C) 0 kg · m/s
(D) 8 M kg · m/s
(E) 24 M kg · m/s

5. A free-falling body is acted on by gravity for exactly 4 seconds. The mass of the object is 2 kg, and the object begins its free fall from rest. What is the impulse on the object from the gravitational force?

(A) 8 N · s
(B) 80 N · s
(C) 16 N · s
(D) 64 N · s
(E) 800 N · s

6. The object in question 5 will have what value for momentum at the end of the 4 seconds?

(A) 8 kg · m/s
(B) 80 kg · m/s
(C) 16 kg · m/s
(D) 64 kg · m/s
(E) 800 kg · m/s

7. The object in question 5 will have what speed at the end of 4 seconds?

(A) 8 m/s
(B) 16 m/s
(C) 20 m/s
(D) 40 m/s
(E) 80 m/s

Free Response

1. Two carts collide on a frictionless track. A mass of M_1 and speed v_o collides with another mass M_2. M_2 is initially at rest. After the collision, both masses have coupled together, forming a total mass of $M_1 + M_2$. The new mass moves off with a new speed in the direction of v_o. Determine the following for this collision:
   a. Speed of the coupled mass
   b. Fractional loss of energy, $\dfrac{\Delta KE}{KE_o}$

2. A bullet is shot into a wood block. As shown in the following diagram, the bullet becomes embedded in the block, and they move off the ledge and land on the ground. The mass of the bullet is 2 g. The mass of the block is 98 g. The ledge height is 5 m. The block lands 10 m horizontally from the ledge. Determine the initial speed of the bullet.

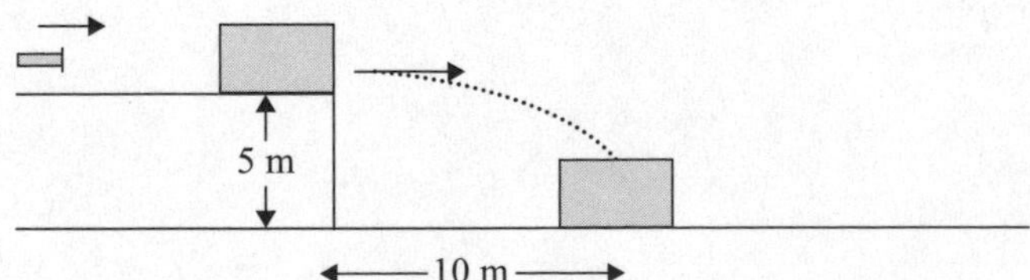

*3. Object 1 (O_1) is traveling along a frictionless table with a velocity $\vec{v}_o$ and momentum $\vec{p}$ and collides with object 2 (O_2), as shown in the following diagrams:

View from above, before the collision:

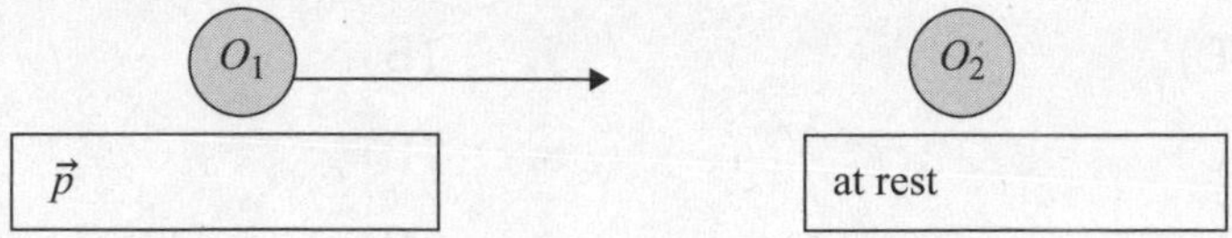

View from above, after the collision:

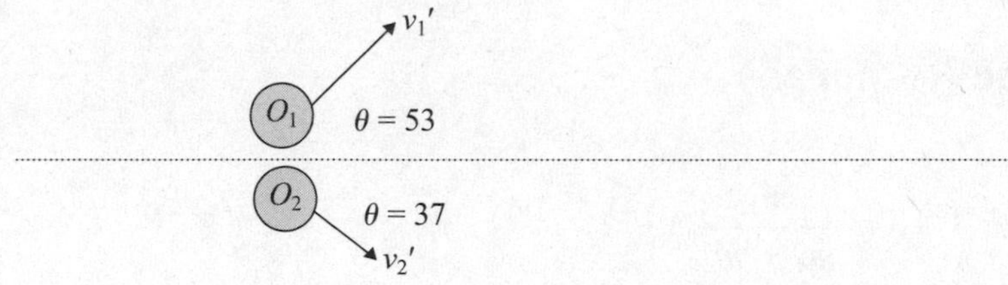

Object 2 is initially at rest and moves off at the angle indicated with a momentum of $\left\| \frac{\overrightarrow{4p}}{5} \right\|$. The mass of object 1 is M and the mass of object 2 is 2 M.

a. Determine the speeds of the objects after the collision. Give your answer in terms of the initial speed (v_o) of object 1.
b. Compare the initial velocity vector with the velocity vectors of the two objects after the collision. What do you notice about the two vectors? Do they add up (vector addition) to the initial velocity vector? Explain your answer, and explain whether it is valid based on conservation of momentum.

Solutions

Multiple Choice

1. (E)
2. (C)
3. (C)
4. (C)
5. (B)
6. (B)
7. (D)

Free Response

1. a. $v_{after} = \dfrac{m_1}{m_1 + m_2} v_o$

   b. $\dfrac{\Delta KE}{KE_o} = \dfrac{-m_2}{m_1 + m_2}$

2. $v_o = 500$ m/s

3. a. After the collision, the speed of object 1 is $\frac{3}{5}v_o$, and the speed of object 2 is $\frac{2}{5}v_o$.

   b. Using vector addition, the velocity vectors do not add up. This conclusion is consistent with momentum conservation because it is the momentum that is conserved, not the velocities.

Chapter 8

Thermodynamics

For Physics B Test Takers

EXAM OVERVIEW

Thermodynamic topics are covered only in AP Physics B and account for 9 percent of the AP Physics exam. Thermodynamics has taken a smaller role in the curriculum since 2002. For instance, many teachers and students assume that calorimetry problems will be included in the AP Physics B exam. However, calorimetry was removed from the exam in 2002. These are the topics in thermodynamics that the exam currently emphasizes:

- **Mechanical equivalent of heat**
- **Heat transfer and expansion**
- **Kinetic theory and the model of the internal energy of a gas**
- **Gas laws**
- **Thermodynamic processes: pressure–volume (PV) diagrams, Newton's first and second laws in cycles**

You should plan your studying around those topics. This review chapter points out the areas within these topics that typically cause the most trouble for students.

MECHANICAL EQUIVALENT OF HEAT AND HEAT TRANSFER

The **mechanical equivalent of heat** is a very simple topic. Most students intuitively understand the idea when they first approach it. The underlying concept implies that when mechanical work is done by friction, work appears in the system as increased heat. When a block slides to rest on a tabletop, both the tabletop and block heat up. The temperature change in the objects can be computed or measured. The law for this **heat exchange** is described by the following relationship:

$$\Delta Q = mc\Delta T,$$

where ΔQ is the heat gained or lost measured in joules (J), c is the specific heat of the material measured in J/kgC, and ΔT is the change in temperature of the material measured in C (or Kelvin).

A tricky concept in thermodynamics is the use of the correct temperature units. The unit for temperature is the Kelvin. However, a change in the Kelvin scale is equivalent to the change in the Celsius scale. For all quantities that involve a change in temperature, Celsius is the natural unit. When the gas law is used or an exact temperature value is necessary, the Kelvin scale *must* be used. This fact has caused many physics students over the years to kick themselves after taking their test on thermodynamics.

Heat transfer can result from conduction, radiation, or convection. Convection and radiation are too complex for inclusion on the AP Physics B exam. Thus, the only area of heat transfer that you should be concerned with is conduction.

Conduction occurs when one object comes in contact with another, causing one object to lose heat and the other to gain heat. It is expressed mathematically as $Q = mc\Delta T$.

The following mathematical model represents the power conducted through a medium:

$$\frac{\Delta Q}{\Delta t} = \frac{kA\Delta T}{d},$$

where k is the coefficient of conductivity, which is a property of the material; A is the surface area of contact between the two temperature differences; and d is the thickness (sometimes textbooks use t for thickness and *Power* for $\frac{\Delta Q}{\Delta t}$).

Sample Problem

A block of mass 500 g slides across a table with an initial speed of 5 m/s. The coefficient of friction is 0.4. The heat capacity of the block is $c = 200$ J/kgC. Determine the temperature change resulting from the block sliding across the surface. Assume the tabletop absorbs no heat.

Solution

The block's loss of kinetic energy (KE) will be converted completely into heating the block. Therefore, we calculate the loss of KE as follows:

$$\Delta KE = 0 - \frac{1}{2}(0.5\text{ kg})(5\text{ m/s})^2 = 6.25\text{ J}$$

$$\Rightarrow 6.25\text{ J} = \Delta Q$$

$$\Delta Q = mc\Delta T \Rightarrow \Delta T = \frac{\Delta Q}{mc} = \frac{6.25\text{ J}}{(0.5\text{ kg})(200\text{ J/kg}\cdot{}^\circ\text{C})} = 0.0625\ {}^\circ\text{C}$$

Typically, this type of problem does not involve a large temperature change.

THERMODYNAMIC LAWS AND PROCESSES

Kinetic theory is the foundation of the ideal gas law, the model of the internal energy of a gas, and the definition of the kinetic energy of molecules. The entire derivation of kinetic theory is beyond the scope of this review. However, it is a useful exercise for all physics students, so you should reread that part of your textbook and give it some attention.

Essentially, **kinetic theory** is the idea that molecules of a gas act like point particles as they bounce into each other and the walls of a container. Derived from the kinetic theory is the classic relationship of the **ideal gas law**. This is a state function that relates a gas's pressure and volume to the absolute temperature:

$$PV = nRT,$$

where P is the pressure measured in Pascals (N/m^2), V is the volume of the gas (usually contained in a container of volume, V), n is the number of moles (typically, 1), R is the gas constant $R = 8.31\frac{\text{J}}{\text{mole}\cdot\text{Kelvin}}$, and T is the temperature of the gas measured in Kelvin.

Under the ideal gas law, if the temperature of a gas in a container remains constant, the pressure and volume at two different states are related as follows:

$$P_1V_1 = P_2V_2$$

This is a simple but powerful relationship that can be used frequently in solving PV diagram problems.

Another important relationship in kinetic theory is the total internal energy of a gas, otherwise known as the average translational kinetic energy of the gas. It is given the symbol U in thermodynamics and is defined as follows:

$$U = \frac{3}{2}nRT = \frac{3}{2}NkT,$$

where k is Boltzman's constant, which is simply the ratio of the gas constant R to Avogadro's number:

$$k = \frac{R}{N_a} = 1.38 \times 10^{-23} \frac{\text{J}}{\text{molecule} \cdot \text{Kelvin}}$$

This relationship also gives rise to two other important relationships showing that the kinetic energy of a gas molecule is related to the temperature of the gas, not pressure or volume:

Average KE of a gas molecule

$$\Rightarrow \frac{1}{2}mv_{rms}^2 = \frac{3}{2}kT \qquad (1)$$

$$\Rightarrow v_{rms} = \sqrt{\frac{3kT}{m}}$$

where v_{rms}, the root mean squared speed, is the best of all the possible average velocities of the gas particles that we use in these relationships. The truth is that in a collection of gas affected by pressure, temperature, and other elements, molecular speeds are widely distributed because of all the collisions with walls and other molecules. The speeds of the molecules vary greatly from the minimum to the maximum. The mathematical model for this distribution is called the Maxwell Boltzman distribution. The mathematics of the distribution is beyond the scope of this course and certainly this review book. All you need to know is that the Boltzman distribution gives rise to several average speeds, but the one used in kinetic theory is the root mean squared speed.

Now on to our graphical interpretation of these ideas. The states of a particular gas undergoing different processes (heating, cooling, expanding, etc.) can be expressed succinctly using PV diagrams. Another useful aspect of a PV diagram is that the work done on or by a gas is equal to the area under the curve of the PV diagram. This makes the PV diagram and processes a favorite topic on the AP Physics exam.

The following figure represents a gas under pressure from a piston head:

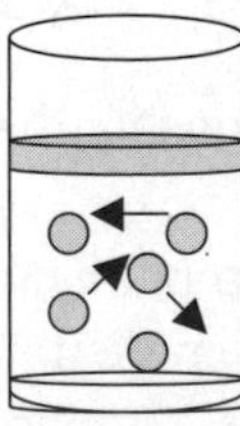

The gas particles are in constant motion, with kinetic energy represented by equation 1. The volume is represented by the volume of the enclosed container. Many PV diagram questions are based on this type of arrangement of a gas in a piston.

We can change the volume of this by one of several processes. For instance, we can physically change the volume by lifting the piston head. Or we can heat or cool the gas, thus changing the pressure of the gas, which in turn changes the volume (if the piston head is free to move).

Here is a typical PV curve for a constant temperature:

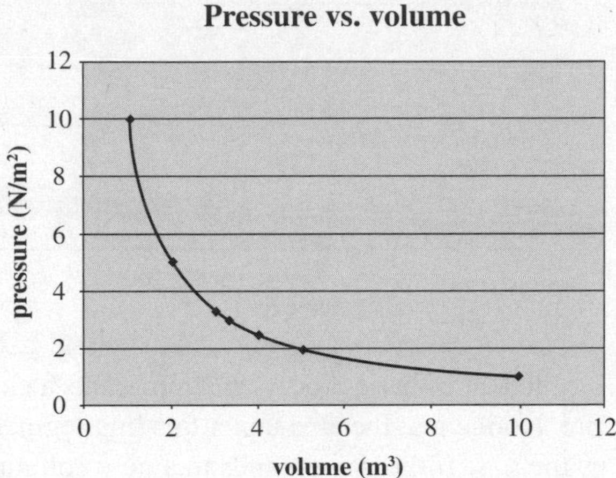

This is an inverse relationship and is a graphical interpretation of $P_1V_1 = P_2V_2$. It is only valid at one constant temperature for the gas. If the gas is heated to a new constant temperature, the curve shifts upward:

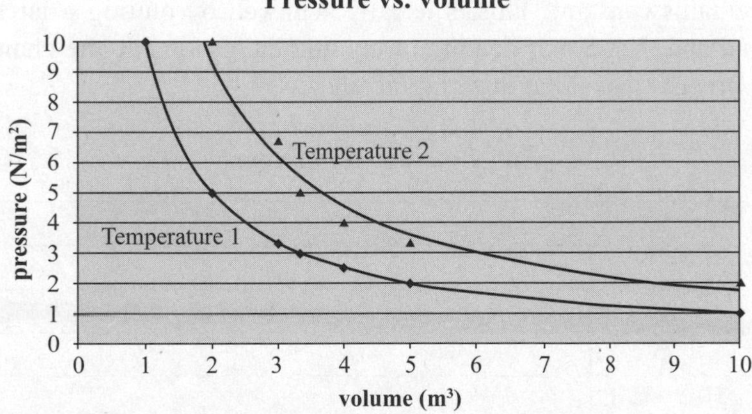

In this example, temperature 2 is greater than temperature 1. Notice that temperature 2 shifted to the right. This typical inverse curve is called an **isothermal** line. The prefix *iso* means "the same," and *thermal* refers to temperature.

Isobaric is another term identifying a type of pressure-versus-volume relationship. *Isobaric* means "the same pressure." Typically, a change in the volume of gas in a piston can occur while the pressure remains constant. Graphically, it will look like this:

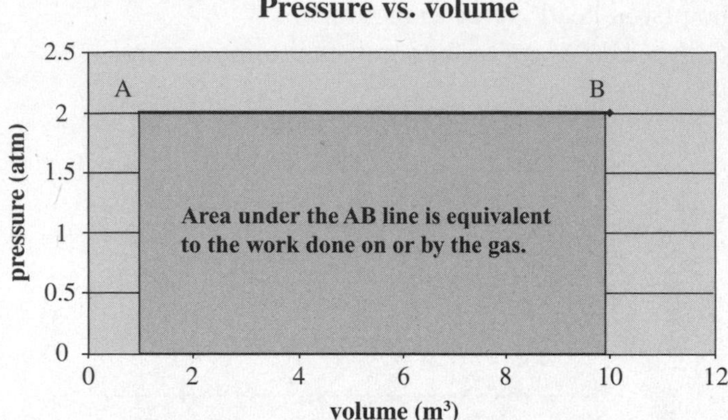

The line AB is called an isobaric process and represents a change in volume at a constant pressure. Notice that the area under this line segment is equivalent to the work done by the gas. If the gas expands to a new volume of 10 units, it does work to push the piston head upward against pressure. If the process had gone from B to A, the gas would have had work done on it by an outside force (pressure, in this case). The relationship for this is $Work = P\Delta V$. The unit of measure for the product of P (N/m^2) and V (m^3) is N-m, which is a joule.

In an **isochoric** process, the gas increases or decreases in pressure, while volume remains constant. This is usually achieved by putting a latch on the piston head and then either heating or cooling the gas inside the chamber. An isochoric process looks like this graphically:

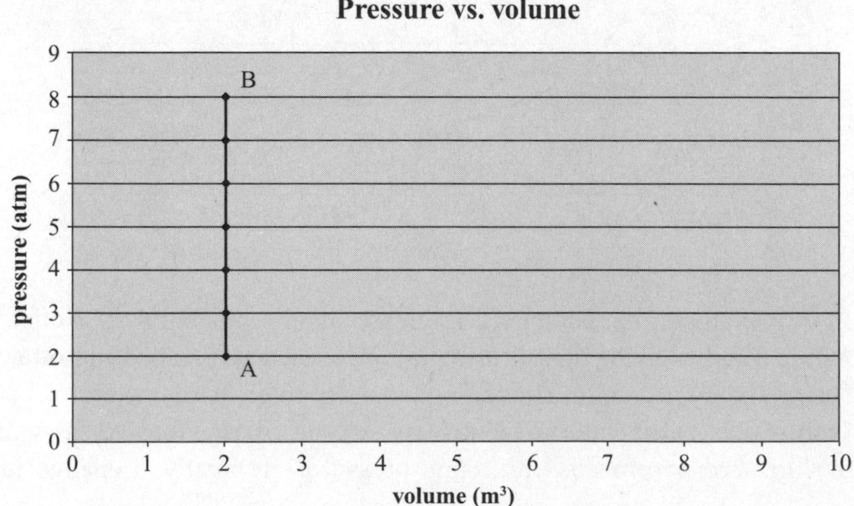

In this example, the gas goes from a state of 2 atmospheres of pressure to 8 atmospheres of pressure while keeping the volume of the gas constant. This causes a temperature change in the gas that increases the internal energy:

$$\Delta U = \frac{3}{2}Nk\Delta T$$

Another important aspect of the isochoric process is that during the raising or lowering of pressure, no work is done on or by the gas. Graphically, this is easy to see because no area under this curve can be obtained.

The final PV process that you should know is called **adiabatic**. In an adiabatic system, no heat flows in or out. Practically, it is the most difficult thermal process to achieve. It requires a container that is perfectly insulated, and no exchange of heat can occur in or out of the piston chamber. An adiabatic process looks similar to an isothermal process, and many students confuse the two curves. But there is a major difference in an adiabatic expansion or contraction: final states of the gas always end up with either higher or lower temperatures (and internal energy). Here is a graph of an adiabatic process:

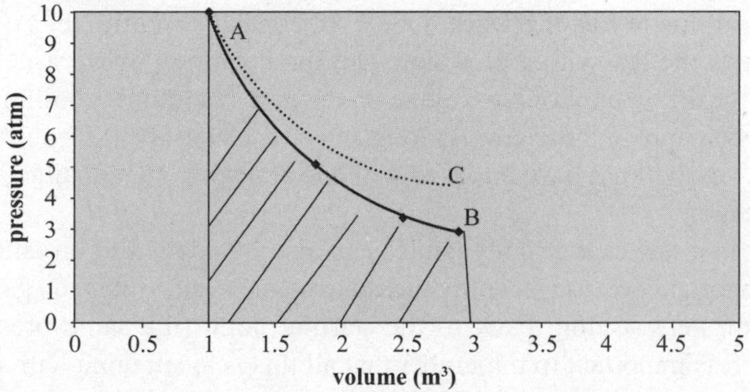

The shaded area of the graph represents the work done by the gas. This work was at the expense of a temperature and energy loss of the gas. Notice that point B is under point C. The process A to B represents the adiabatic process, and the process A to C represents an isothermal process. Because point B is under point C on the graph, the gas is at a lower temperature at point B than at point C. This differentiates the adiabatic curve from the isothermal curve.

UNDERSTANDING A COMPLETE THERMODYNAMIC CYCLE USING PV CURVES

Let's put these types of processes together and apply them to thermodynamic cycles. **Thermodynamic cycles** are meant to model the cycle of an engine. The models represent an ideal engine cycle in which no heat is lost to the surroundings and all processes performed are reversible. In other words, if we moved from point A to point B in a cycle, we should be able to move back from point B to point A, and the gas would have exactly the state properties it had when we started. In contrast, a real engine would lose energy and gain entropy. The study of the cycle is important in thermodynamics. The conservation of energy in disguise is called the **first law of thermodynamics**. This law states that the relationship for any process experienced by a gas in a piston is

$$\Delta U = \Delta Q - W.$$

That is, any increase in the internal energy of the gas will equal the heat gained by the gas (ΔQ) minus any work done by the gas.

Much has been written about the minus sign in the first law of thermodynamics. For more than a hundred years, physics textbooks have referred to the work in this law as the work done by the gas. Currently, the AP Physics exam writes the law with a plus sign. But the definition of work is reversed: it stands for the amount of work done on the gas. Therefore, you'll need to be careful when applying the law. As long as you are consistent throughout your problem, you will not have an issue with the annoying sign change in the AP Physics exam.

The first law of thermodynamics can also be applied to an entire cycle. This is important because an entire thermodynamic cycle brings the gas through a series of steps leading back to the starting point (the same pressure and volume). It is important to remember that all this is ideal, done without losing real heat and totally reversible. Therefore, when a cycle is complete, the total change in internal energy is 0. It is back at the same pressure and volume and, according to the ideal gas law, the same temperature. That means the net change in internal energy is 0. It can be concluded from the first law of thermodynamics that during one complete cycle, the heat added to the system equals the net work done by the system. The net work is represented by the area enclosed by the cycle. Here is a graphical example:

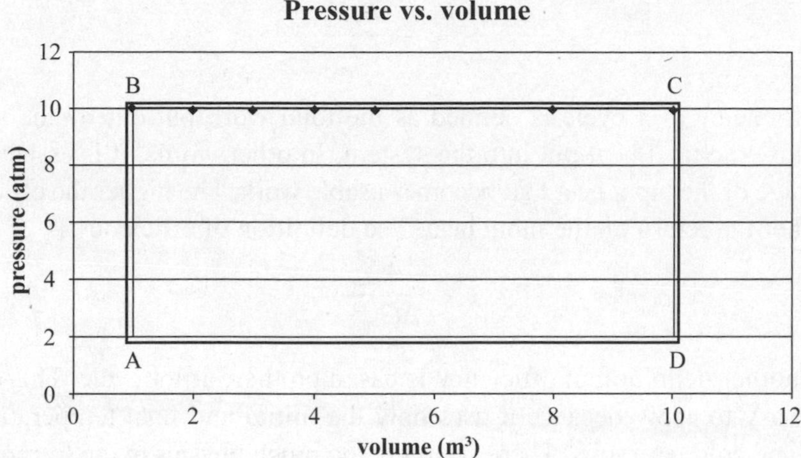

The cycle starts at A and ends at A, going around the rectangle ABCD as follows:

Process 1: from A to B at constant volume (isochoric); no work is done, and $\Delta U = \Delta Q$. This process is accomplished by adding heat to the gas.

Process 2: from B to C at a constant pressure. The area under the line BC to the axes equals the work done by the gas during this expansion. The internal energy also changes because the temperature increases. This is accomplished by adding more heat to the system.

Process 3: cooling of the gas. The gas is cooled while the piston chamber is locked at a certain volume. The gas loses energy and temperature. Because no work is done on or by the gas, $\Delta U = \Delta Q$, as in process 1.

Process 4: more cooling of the gas. The gas is further cooled by letting the volume of the chamber contract at a constant pressure. This brings the gas back to the initial state of pressure, volume, and temperature.

Therefore, in the entire cycle of ABCDA, the gas has a 0 change in internal energy. Because the work done on the gas in process 4 is the area under the curve of that line, an obvious rectangle is left enclosed by the cycle. That rectangle is the sum of the work done in process 2 and the work done in process 4. If we are given the initial temperature at point A, it is entirely possible to calculate all work, heat, and change in internal energy from the graph. If we know the initial temperature, we can get all of the other temperatures (T_b, T_c, and T_d) by the gas law:

$$\frac{P_1V_1}{T_1} = \frac{P_2V_2}{T_2}$$

Efficiency of a cycle is defined as the total work put out by the system divided by the total heat put into the system. In other words, it is essentially a percentage of the input heat that becomes usable work. The higher the efficiency, the higher the return on the input heat. The definition of efficiency is

$$e = \frac{W_{out}}{\Delta Q_{input}}.$$

Another definition of efficiency is based on the Carnot cycle. This definition is easy to apply because it uses only the initial and final temperatures of the hot and cold reservoirs. There is simply too much physics in the Carnot cycle to cover in this review, so refer to your textbook to properly understand it. The efficiency definition is as follows:

Carnot − efficiency

$$e = \frac{Q_{hot} - Q_{cold}}{Q_{hot}} = 1 - \frac{Q_{cold}}{Q_{hot}}$$

and since Q is proportional to temperature of the gas,

$$\Rightarrow e = \frac{T_{\text{hot}} - T_{cold}}{T_{hot}}$$

This definition can only be used if the engine cycle is stated as being a Carnot cycle.

Practice Session Problems

Multiple Choice

1. One mole of gas is in a closed container of volume V_o and pressure P_o. The initial temperature of the gas is T_o. The container of gas is heated up to a temperature of $3T_o$. Which of the following statements is (are) true about gas after it has reached this new temperature:

   I. The pressure of the gas increases to $3P_o$.

   II. The kinetic energy of the gas molecules increases by a factor of 3.

   III. The root mean squared speed of the gas molecules increases by a factor of 3.

   (A) I only

   (B) II only

   (C) I and II only

   (D) III only

   (E) I, II, and III

The following is a PV diagram showing an engine cycle labeled to indicate various endpoints of processes. The cycle starts at point A.

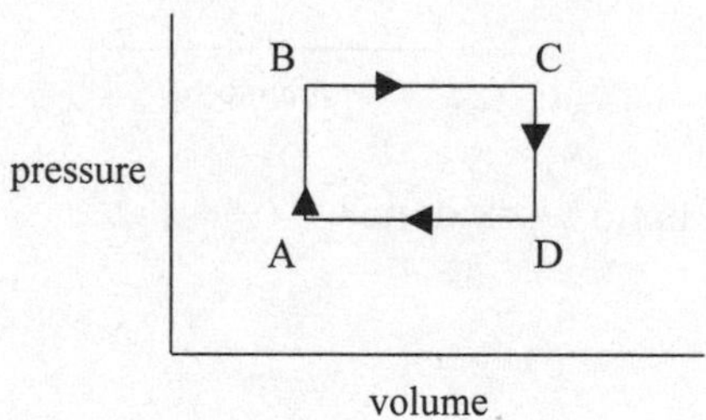

Use this diagram to answer questions 2 and 3.

2. At which of the points—A, B, C, or D—is the gas at the greatest temperature?

   (A) Point A

   (B) Point B

   (C) Point C

(D) Point D

(E) Gas is at the same temperature at all points.

3. In which of the following processes is the gas undergoing a cooling phase?

I. AB

II. BC

III. CD

IV. DA

(A) II only
(B) IV only
(C) III and IV
(D) II, III, and IV only
(E) I only

4. Three thermodynamic processes are shown in the following *PV* diagram:

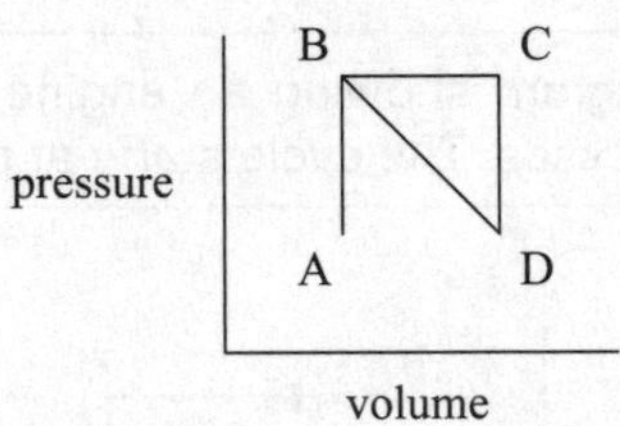

In which process is no work done?

I. AB

II. BC

III. BD

(A) I only
(B) II only
(C) III only
(D) I and III only
(E) II and III only

Free Response

For the following questions, use R = 8.31 J/mole Kelvin.

1. A mole of gas undergoes a complete cycle of thermodynamic processes, as shown in the following PV diagram:

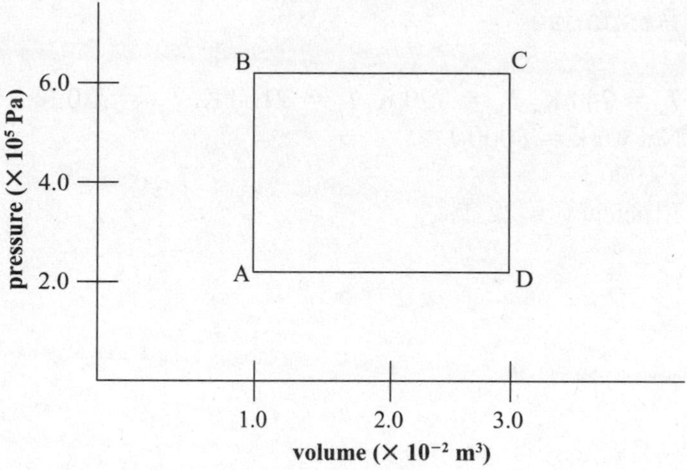

Each process is described here:

Process AB: The gas is heated while the container maintains a constant volume.

Process BC: More heat is added to the gas, but this time the pressure is kept constant and the volume is increased.

Process CD: The gas is cooled while keeping a constant volume, and pressure decreases.

Process DA: The gas is cooled again at a constant pressure, bringing the gas back to the original state and initial conditions.

a. Determine the temperature at all four points labeled in the diagram (T_a, T_b, T_c, and T_d).
b. Determine the net work done by the gas in the complete cycle.
c. How much heat was added to the system in process BC?
d. Determine the efficiency of this cycle.

Solutions

Multiple Choice

1. (C)
2. (C)
3. (C)
4. (A)

Free Response

1. a. $T_a = 240$ K, $T_b = 720$ K, $T_c = 2160$ K, $T_d = 720$ K
   b. Net work = 8000 J
   c. 29,900 J
   d. Efficiency = 22.2%

Chapter 9

Fluids

For Physics B Test Takers

EXAM OVERVIEW

Fluid mechanics was only recently added to the AP Physics B curriculum and makes up only 6 percent of the curriculum. For these reasons, some teachers ignore the topic. However, the concepts in fluid mechanics are relatively simple and can be learned quickly with some practice in the basics.

Your physics textbook may devote an entire chapter or two to the topics of fluid mechanics and may cover concepts beyond those necessary for the AP Physics B exam. These are the topics you need to focus on:

- **Definition of pressure and density**
- **Archimedes' law and buoyant force**
- **Pascal's law and pressure in a fluid**
- **The Bernoulli equation and fluid flow through a closed container**
- **The continuity relationship**

If you master these areas, you will be prepared for the fluid mechanics section of the AP Physics exam.

PRESSURE AND DENSITY DEFINED

The definition of density is $\rho = \frac{Mass}{Volume}$, and the correct unit is kg/m^3, not g/cm^3, as used in some textbooks. Most students recall from high school chemistry that the density of water is 1.0 g/cm^3. However, the meter-kilogram-second (mks) system is used in physics, and the density of water is expressed as 1,000 kg/m^3. Avoid errors by paying attention to the units and being careful with your work.

The definition of pressure is $p = \frac{Force}{Area}$, and the correct unit is N/m^2 (1 N/m^2 = 1 pascal [Pa], and 1 atmosphere [atm] = 1.01×10^5 Pa).

ARCHIMEDES' LAW

Probably the most important topic in fluid mechanics is the application of Archimedes' law. This basic principle explains the buoyant force of liquid. Although it is fairly simple, applying Archimedes' law to problem solving can be challenging.

An object placed in water will either sink or float. The point at which the object begins to sink can be determined by specific gravity. **Specific gravity** is the ratio of the density of an object to the density of water. For example, the specific gravity of wood with a density of 500 kg/m^3 is 0.5. Knowing the specific gravity value enables us to determine whether an object will float or sink. A specific gravity value less than 1.0 means that the object will float in water. Although specific gravity is considered an obsolete concept and is not included in most of the newer physics textbooks, it is still an important idea that can help you understand the proper scale of the values in problems involving fluids.

The force acting on an object while it is either submerged or partially submerged (floating) is called the **buoyant force**. It is the result of the pressure on the top of an object (in the fluid) being different from the pressure on the bottom of the object. This difference in pressure leads to a net upward pressure (pressure is greater at lower levels of a column of fluid). Archimedes' law gives the magnitude of the buoyant force:

> The magnitude of the buoyant force is equal to the weight of the amount of the liquid displaced by the object.

Therefore, to determine the magnitude of the buoyant force, we need to know the density of the liquid being used. Most likely, the fluid will be water, and the density of water is easy to remember: 1,000 kg/m^3.

As shown in the following free-body diagram, the buoyant force is always directed upward, and the net buoyant force acts at the geometric center of the object:

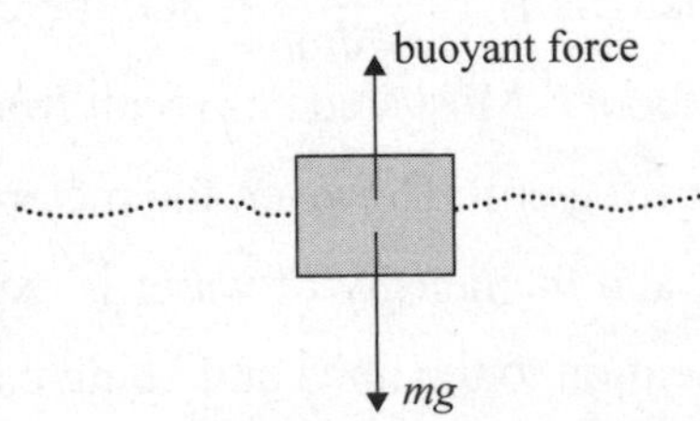

The buoyant force is equivalent to the weight of the object. In the case of a floating object, two force statements can be obtained: F_b = weight of the object, and F_b = weight of the liquid displaced by the water.

We can determine the weight of the liquid displaced by an object by using the density of the liquid and the volume of the object. If we know the volume of the object submerged under the water line, the buoyant force is $F_b = \rho_{liquid} V_{object} g$. Typically, problem solving with Archimedes' law involves connecting density and volume to solve for buoyant force.

Sample Problem 1

A cube made of wood (with a density equal to 0.7 times that of water) is floating in water. Determine what fraction of the cube is above the water line.

Solution

At first, we might think more information is necessary to solve this problem, but that is not the case. We can solve the problem by making the two basic connections: the buoyant force is equivalent to both the weight of the object and the weight of the water displaced. Let's draw a picture to show the significant quantities for our solution:

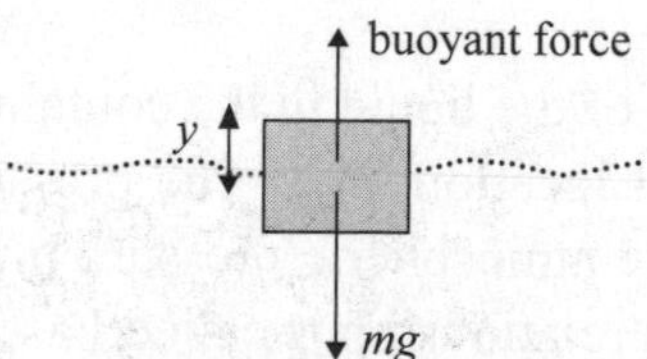

The portion of the cube above the water is y, and the length of one side of the cube is d. Therefore, the amount of cube below the water line is $d - y$.

We need to compute the volume of the object submerged underwater. Let's call the surface area of the cube A. The volume submerged is $V_{submerged} = A(d - y)$. We can use this value to compute the weight of the water displaced by the cube:

$$\textit{weight of water displaced} = \rho_{water} V_{sub} g$$

$$mg_{water} = \rho_{water} (A[d - y])g$$

Now we need to equate this value to the actual weight of the floating object. Not knowing the mass or weight of the object is not a problem. We know the density of the object, which is good enough in fluid mechanics. Thus, the weight of the object is

$$mg_{object} = \rho_{object} V_{object} g.$$

Then we equate the two relationships and solve for y:

$$F_b = mg_{object}$$

$$\rho_w V_{sub} g = \rho_{object} V_{object} g$$

$$A(d - y) = \left[\frac{\rho_{obj}}{\rho_{water}}\right](A \cdot d)$$

$$\left[\frac{\rho_{obj}}{\rho_{water}}\right] = 0.7$$

$$\Rightarrow \frac{d - y}{d} = 0.7 \Rightarrow y = 0.3d$$

Thus, 30 percent of the entire cube is above the water.

Using the same reasoning, we can determine how much of an ice cube is above the water line in a drink. The density of an ice cube is about 0.970 kg/m^3. Our reasoning method leads us to conclude that 3 percent of the ice cube is above the water line. Check the next time you are drinking a glass of water. Would it be the same for ice floating in soda?

PASCAL'S LAW

The pressure at the top of the liquid in the container is simply equal to the atmospheric pressure at that location, P_{atm}. The pressure at the bottom of the container is equivalent to the atmospheric pressure plus the average weight of the water over the area. This relationship is called Pascal's law:

$$P_h = P_{atm} + \rho g h,$$

where h is the depth below the surface of the liquid. The liquid must be of uniform density. The following diagram illustrates the principle:

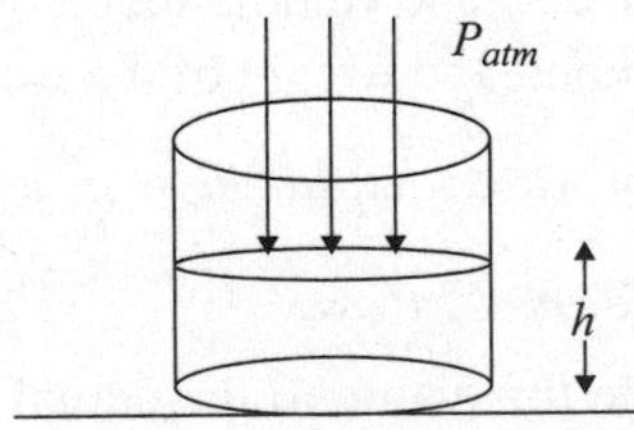

Pascal's law also governs how the pressure in a closed container behaves:

> If a liquid is in a closed container, the pressure applied to the enclosed fluid is transmitted undiminished to every part of the fluid and the walls of the container. If the atmospheric pressure is changed, the pressure at every part of the liquid increases or decreases by the amount of the change.

This brings into play the physics of a hydraulic lift. The hydraulic lift is basically a force-multiplying effect provided by the physics of Pascal's law. Car lifts, dentists' chairs, and elevators all use this principle. It implies that the pressure at one end of a lift is equivalent to the pressure at the other end of the lift. Because a lift is essentially a large reservoir of fluid, the pressure at both ends of the lift must be equal due to Pascal's law. If one end of the lift has a very small area (this is where the force from a human being would be applied) and the other end of the lift has a very large area, the force-multiplying effect can happen:

$$P_1 = P_2 \Rightarrow \frac{F_1}{A_1} = \frac{F_2}{A_2} \Rightarrow F_2 = F_1\frac{A_2}{A_1}$$

If the areas differ by a factor of 5, then we can multiply the input force (F_1) by a factor of 5.

ABSOLUTE AND GAUGE PRESSURE

Absolute pressure is the sum of all pressures acting at a given location. Thus, the absolute pressure 100 meters below the surface of the ocean is calculated as follows:

$$P_{absolute} = P_{atmosphere} + \rho gh = 1 \times 10^5 + (1000\text{ kg/m}^3)(10\text{ m/s}^2)(100\text{ m})$$

$$P_{absolute} = 1 \times 10^5\text{ Pa} + 1 \times 10^6 = 11 \times 10^5\text{ Pa} = 11\text{ atm}$$

The effect of the water depth is equivalent to 10 atm of pressure. If we took a pressure gauge and used it at that depth, it would read 10 atm, not 11 atm. The reason is that pressure gauges only measure the difference in pressure above the atmospheric pressure. For example, when you inflate a car tire to 32 pounds per square inch (psi), you have made the pressure in the tire 32 psi above the atmospheric pressure.

BERNOULLI EQUATION

The Bernoulli equation is a relationship that describes fluid flow through a pipe or other closed container. When applying the Bernoulli equation, we must use two assumptions: (1) the fluid has negligible "friction," or **viscosity**; and (2) the fluid is **incompressible**, meaning that no matter what the pressure, the fluid's properties will remain the same (constant density).

Another relationship that goes hand in hand with the Bernoulli equation is the equation of continuity. Underlying the equation of continuity is the principle that no matter what the size of the pipe opening, the amount of fluid passing a given point will be a constant. This becomes the following relationship:

$$A_1v_1 = A_2v_2,$$

where A is the cross-sectional area of the pipe (or container), and v is the velocity of the fluid at that location. You may have experienced this effect when you put your thumb over the opening of a hose: the closing of the effective cross-sectional area increases the velocity of the water coming out of the hose. The same amount of water is ejected per unit of time, but less water comes out with a faster velocity.

The Bernoulli equation is equivalent to the conservation of mechanical energy in a closed system with no outside forces (other than gravity) acting on it. If our fluid system is closed and only affected by gravitational force, the total energy in our system at any point in the system will be a constant. Thus, the Bernoulli equation is as follows:

$$P_1 + \rho g y_1 + \frac{1}{2}\rho v_1^2 = P_2 + \rho g y_2 + \frac{1}{2}\rho v_2^2 \,.$$

Notice the similarity to the conservation of energy in a system.

Sample Problem 2

A fluid is flowing through a horizontal pipe as shown in the following figure:

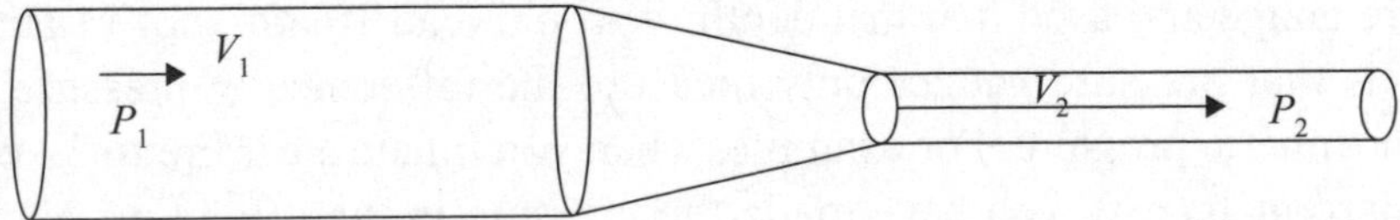

The cross-sectional area in the wide section of the pipe is 0.6 m^2. The cross-sectional area in the narrow section is 0.2 m^2. The speed of the fluid at the wide section is 2 m/s. Determine the following:

- The speed of the fluid in the narrow section
- The difference in pressure at point 1 and point 2

Solution

The speeds of the fluid at the two points are related by the continuity equation:

$$A_1 v_1 = A_2 v_2 \Rightarrow v_2 = v_1 \frac{A_1}{A_2} = (2\text{ m/s})\left(\frac{0.6}{0.2}\right) = 6\text{ m/s}$$

The difference in pressure can be computed using the Bernoulli equation. Because the fluid is at the same height vertically at both points, only the pressure and velocity contribute to the equation:

$$P_1 + \frac{1}{2}\rho v_1^2 = P_2 + \frac{1}{2}\rho v_2^2$$

$$P_1 - P_2 = \Delta P = \frac{1}{2}\rho v_2^2 - \frac{1}{2}\rho v_1^2$$

$$\Delta P = \frac{1}{2}(1000\text{ kg/m}^3)\left[v_2^2 - v_1^2\right] = 500\left(\left(v_1 \frac{A_1}{A_2}\right)^2 - v_1^2\right)$$

$$= 500 \cdot v_1^2\left(\frac{A_1^2}{A_2^2} - 1\right)$$

$$\Delta P = 500 \cdot (2\text{ m/s})^2\left(\frac{0.6^2}{0.2^2} - 1\right) = 500 \cdot 32 = 16{,}000\text{ Pa}$$

Therefore, the pressure at point 1 is higher than at point 2 by 16,000 Pa, or 0.16 atm.

Practice Session Problems

Free Response

1. A boat with an area of 1.0 m^2 and length of 3.0 m is floating on the water. The boat has a density of 500 kg/m^3. How many people, each with a mass of 100 kg, could the boat support before it would sink?

2. A mass of density $\rho = \frac{\rho_{water}}{4}$ is tied to the bottom of a container of water as shown in the following diagram:

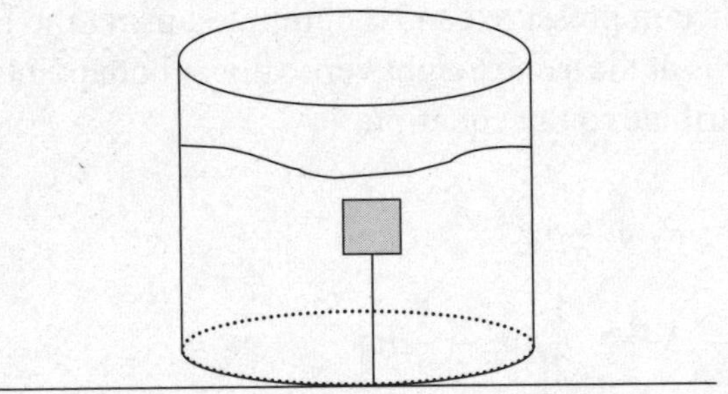

What is the tension in the cord that is attached to the mass?

Solutions

1. More than 15 people would sink the boat.
2. The tension in the cord is 3 times the weight of the mass.

Chapter 10

Electrostatics

EXAM OVERVIEW

With a firm understanding of electrostatics, you can master the more difficult aspects of electricity and magnetism that are coming in the later chapters. So don't take any shortcuts during the learning process. The extra time will pay off when we get to topics like circuits, capacitors, and magnetism.

CHARGE AND CHARGING OBJECTS

All matter is made up of atoms, and all atoms are composed of equal amounts of protons and electrons. In the world of physics, an object is considered "charged" when it has a **residual charge**. For instance, a wool cloth vigorously rubbed against a PVC pipe acquires a net charge. The wool readily gives up electrons to the PVC pipe, and the PVC pipe is a good insulator that readily keeps the charge on the surface. Therefore, the PVC pipe has an excess amount of negative charge. The friction provided by the rubbing causes the transfer of charge, and it took work for the event to happen.

Over time, the PVC pipe will discharge a bit of its charge because it sits in a humid environment, the air molecules interact with it, or some other reason. Most charged objects referred to in this review and in most AP Physics textbooks are conductive spheres or conductive rods. Insulators usually are similar shapes but made out of an insulating material like plastic, PVC, or glass.

Charge is a property of the electron and proton. Each has the same magnitude of charge. The magnitude of charge on the electron or proton is the smallest unit of charge. This value is called the charge on the electron:

$$e = 1.6 \times 10^{-19} \text{ Coulomb}$$

You should memorize this value so that you can make calculations quickly. The value is given on the constant sheet, but it is such an important constant that it should be memorized for quick access. The coulomb (C) is the unit of charge, and all charge must be measured in coulombs when we are computing electrostatic forces, fields, and potentials.

CONDUCTORS AND INSULATORS

Recognizing the properties of conductors and insulators is the first step in learning how charge behaves at the microscopic level. An **insulator** is a material with excess charge bound to it. The charge moves along the surface of the material. Plastic, glass, paper, and wood are all good electrical insulators. Any material that is a good insulator of heat is also a good electrical insulator. A **conductor**, on the other hand, is usually a metal material that allows charge to move (flow) along the surface of the conductor. A metal has the property of having extra valence electrons. Essentially, these electrons can move along the surface of the conductor. Any excess charge on the metal will move about like a "sea of charges" in motion on the surface of the metal. Because electrons are the "free charges" and the protons are bound in the atomic core, all exchange of charge is done by the transfer of electrons. If an object becomes positively charged, it has lost electrons. If an object becomes negatively charged, it has gained electrons.

INDUCED CHARGE ON CONDUCTORS

When a metal object has excess charge on the surface, the charge spreads uniformly across the surface, as shown in the following figure (the positive charges represent the excess charge):

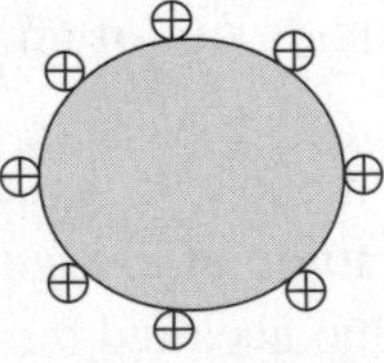

Likewise, when a charge is placed on a metal plate, it spreads uniformly across the surface (in reality, the charge would go to all sides of the plate; the figure shows only one side for simplicity):

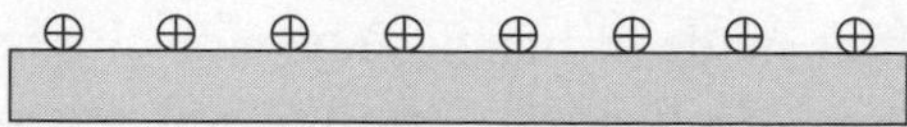

In contrast, a charge placed on a plastic plate, an insulator, stays at the point of placement, as show here:

What happens when a charged insulated rod gets near a metal plate? As the following figure shows, the side nearest the rod becomes negatively charged, and the side furthest from the rod becomes positively charged:

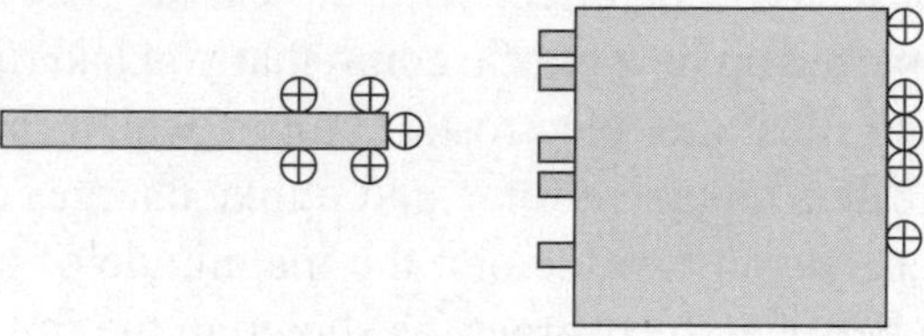

The metal plate is still electrically neutral (with equal positive and negative charges), but it is now a **polarized** conductor, with one side negative and the other side positive.

The metal plate has induced positive and negative charges on each side. The amount of the induced charge on the metal plate equals the magnitude of the charged region. Therefore, the magnitude of charge on the rod in the previous figure is the magnitude of the induced charge on each side of the metal plate.

POLARIZATION IN AN INSULATOR

If a charged insulated rod gets close to an insulator, the effect is similar to that on the metal plate, but not exactly the same. Because an insulator does not allow the charge to move on its surface, only one side becomes slightly more negative than the other; the atoms polarize only slightly. The following figure shows how a charge is distributed on an insulating object.

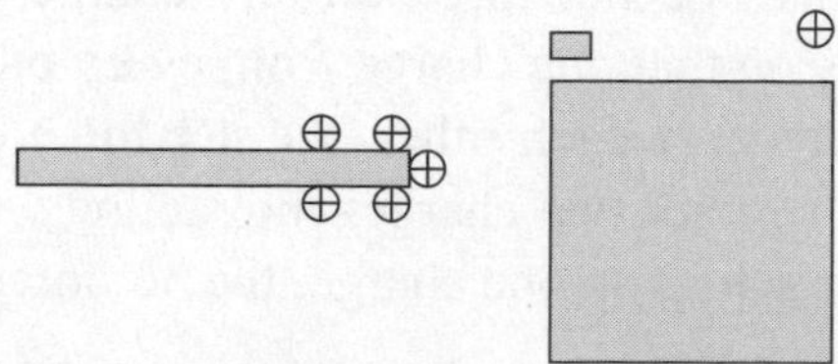

The object on the right is made of plastic. The side closest to the rod becomes slightly negative and the side furthest from the rod becomes slightly positive. The degree to which an insulator can become polarized has to do with a property called the **dielectric constant**.

ELECTROSTATIC FORCE

Whether polarization and induced charge occur on a conducting or insulating material, that material is attracted to the rod. For the metal, the attraction is relatively stronger, whereas for the insulator, the attraction is slightly weaker. You may have seen this effect with the classic demonstration of small bits of paper being picked up by a plastic comb that you had rubbed through your hair. That experiment illustrates electrostatic force, which follows the principle that like charges create a repulsive force and unlike charges create an attractive force. The force depends on two factors: the magnitude of charge and the distance of separation between the charges, as shown in the following equation:

$$\|F_E\| = \left\| \frac{kq_1q_2}{r^2} \right\|$$

$$k = 9.0 \times 10^9 \frac{\text{N} \cdot \text{m}^2}{\text{C}^2}$$

A classic use of this relationship is to calculate the amount of force between an electron and a proton separated by one atomic distance (1×10^{-10} m):

$$F_E = \frac{kq_1q_2}{r^2} = \frac{9 \times 10^9(1.6 \times 10^{-19}\ \text{C})(1.6 \times 10^{-19}\ \text{C})}{(1 \times 10^{-10}\ \text{m})^2} = 2.3 \times 10^{-8}\ \text{N}$$

This is a massive force to any charged particle. The mass of an electron is 9.1×10^{-31} kg, so a force of 10^{-8} N would be a massive force in the world of an electron.

TYPICAL FORCE PROBLEMS WITH CHARGE

Electrostatic force is interesting mathematically. The **principle of superposition** states that the net force on any charge is the sum of all the individual forces acting on that one charge from every other charge. Therefore, if three charges are very near each other, the net force of one charge will be the resultant force of the other two charges interacting with it. If you have 100 charges near each other acting on one charge, the net force will be the net effect of 100 separate forces, and the effect can extend to an infinite number of charges. Obviously, calculating the net force can become quite a time-consuming and tedious task. The electric field will be introduced in the next section to help make the task easier. Meanwhile, let's try a few problems that demonstrate the superposition principle and are typical of the problems found in textbooks and on the AP Physics exam.

First, it is important to note that in the typical electrostatic problem, the charges are held fixed and cannot move, are massless, and only experience the electrostatic force between all the other charges.

Sample Problem 1

Three charges are arranged in a line and are held fixed in space as shown here:

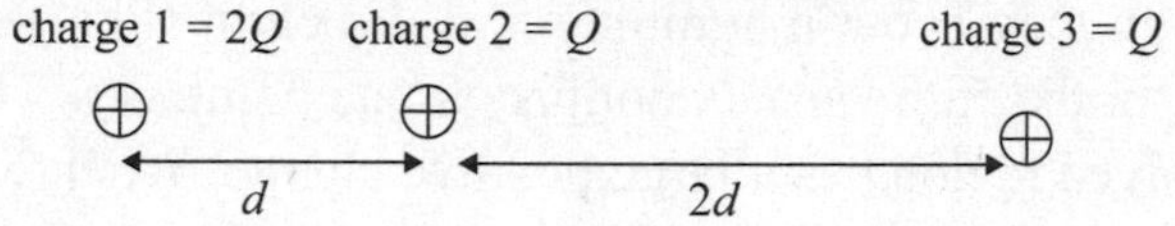

charge 1 = 2Q charge 2 = Q charge 3 = Q

d $2d$

Determine the net force on charge 3 resulting from the other two charges.

Solution

Charge 3 has two repulsive forces acting on it, as shown in the following free-body diagram (FBD):

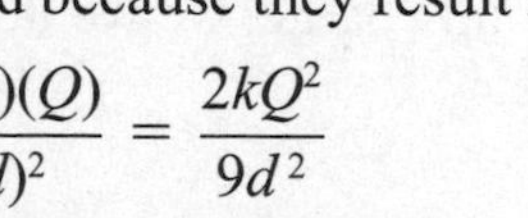

charge 3 = Q

F_{1on3} F_{2on3}

To determine the net force, we must first determine the two forces (F_{1on3} and F_{2on3}) and then add them together. (Note that the use of electron and proton charge magnitudes is avoided because they result in very small numbers.)

$$\|F_{1on3}\| = \frac{k(2Q)(Q)}{(3d)^2} = \frac{2kQ^2}{9d^2}$$

$$\|F_{2on3}\| = \frac{k(Q)(Q)}{(2d)^2} = \frac{kQ^2}{4d^2}$$

$$\|F_{net}\| = \|F_{1on3}\| + \|F_{2on3}\| = \frac{2kQ^2}{9d^2} + \frac{kQ^2}{4d^2} = \frac{17kQ^2}{36d^2}$$

This force is directed to the right, as shown in the previous FBD.

ELECTRIC FIELDS

An **electric field** is a region where a charged particle can experience an electric force. The field simply shows the effect of a charged region on the spaces surrounding it. The definition of the electric field is

$$\left\| \vec{E} \right\| = \frac{\left\| \vec{F_E} \right\|}{q'}.$$

The unit for electric fields is newtons/coulomb (N/C). The direction of the electric field vector is the direction that a positive charge takes when placed in that field.

To understand the concept of the electric field, let's consider a charged region and a positive **test charge** placed near that region. We can map the behavior of the test charge using the **electric field lines**. These lines are not vectors. Although they show magnitude and direction (like vectors), electric field lines do it for the entire space, not just at one point.

So our charged region has a large positive charge. When we place a small test charge at three points (A, B, and C) near that large charge, called the **point charge**, a force acting on the test charge is directed outward from each test charge, as shown in the following FBD:

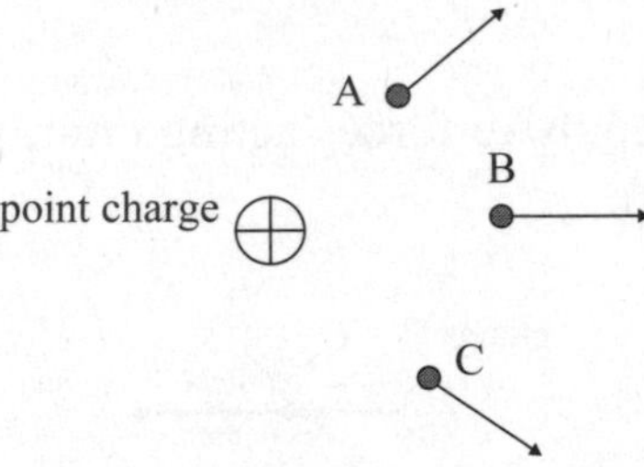

If we were to continue that process, we would find that all around the large positive point charge are points in space showing outward radial vectors. The vectors get smaller the further they are from the point charge. If we probed the entire space around the point charge, we would find a **radial field** around it that looked like this:

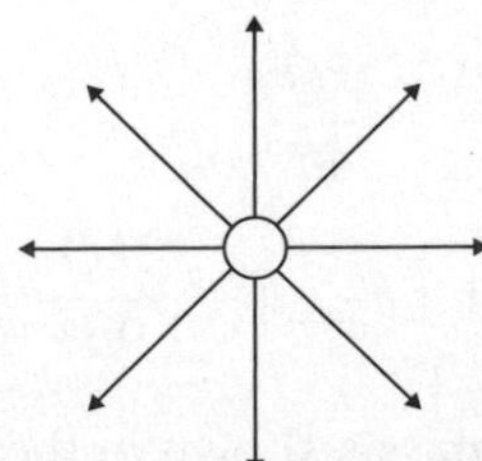

This is called the **field of a point charge**. Each line shows the direction that a positive charge would move if placed in the field. The magnitude of the field is represented by the density of the field lines. The more lines in an area, the higher its field strength. A negative charge would experience a force opposite the field line.

The field of a point charge (Q) is defined by applying Coulomb's law and then dividing the test charge (q) out of the expression, as shown here:

$$\left\|\vec{E}\right\| = \frac{\left\|\vec{F_E}\right\|}{q'} = \frac{\frac{kQq'}{r^2}}{q'} = \frac{kQ}{r^2}$$

Thus, the net field resulting from several point charges is the vector sum of all of the fields at that point:

$$\vec{E}_p = \vec{E}_1 + \vec{E}_2 + \vec{E}_3 + \ldots$$

This is the principle of superposition. Finding a net field created by a collection of point charges is a fairly typical problem in AP Physics textbooks. Here is an example.

Sample Problem 2

Two charges are stationary on the x-axis. One charge has a magnitude of $Q_1 = +2Q$ and is placed at the $x = -2$ coordinate. The other charge is $Q_2 = +3Q$ and is placed at the $x = +2$ coordinate. Find a location where the net electric field is 0.

Solution

First, we set up the diagram of the charge system and then identify some point P between the two charges, as shown here:

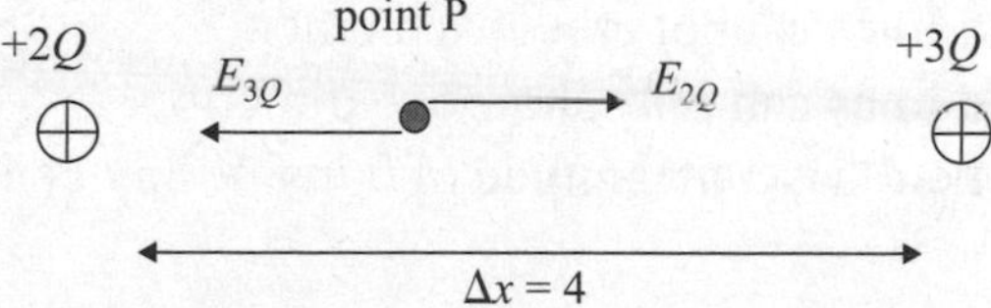

By inspection, we can conclude that point P must be closer to the $+2Q$ charge than the $+3Q$ charge. The question is how much closer?

At point P, we want the net field to be 0. The field caused by the $+3Q$ charge must equal the field caused by the $+2Q$ charge. If we identify the distance between $+2Q$ and point P as d, then the distance between the $+3Q$

charge and point P would be $4 - d$. Then we can set up the following expression for the field:

$$E_{2Q} = E_{3Q}$$

$$\frac{k(2Q)}{d^2} = \frac{k(3Q)}{(4-d)^2} \Rightarrow 3d^2 = 2(4-d)^2$$

$$3d^2 = 2\left(16 - 8d + d^2\right)$$

$$d^2 + 16d - 32 = 0$$

$$d = \frac{-16 \pm \sqrt{256 + 128}}{2} = \frac{-16 \pm 8\sqrt{6}}{2} = -8 \pm 4\sqrt{6}$$

$$d = 4\left(\sqrt{6} - 2\right) \approx 1.8$$

So the placement of point P to create a 0 field would be approximately 1.8 m from the $+2Q$ charge. This would put the point at $x = -0.2$ on the x-axis.

BASIC PRINCIPLES OF CONDUCTORS AND FIELDS

Before we delve further into electric fields, let's review a few principles of conductors and fields:

- In conductors, all charges reside on the surface of the conductor.
- The charges on the surface of a conductor are in electrostatic equilibrium, or **equipotential**. The charges do not move along the conductor once they have reached equilibrium. Therefore, there is no electric field tangential to a conductor with charge on it; if there were an electric field, the charges would no longer be in electrostatic equilibrium.
- The electric field outside any charged conductor is directed normally to the surface.
- Electric field lines cannot cross each other.
- Electric field lines can only show one direction.
- An electric field has a magnitude of 0 inside any conductor.

ELECTRIC FIELD OF A CHARGED METAL SPHERE

A sphere's field behaves just like a point charge outside the sphere. In fact, the entire charge on the sphere acts as if all the charge were concentrated at a point at the center of the sphere. However, as shown in the following diagram, because of the laws of conductors (and vector addition), the field inside the sphere is 0. (Convince yourself this is true by using vector addition of fields.)

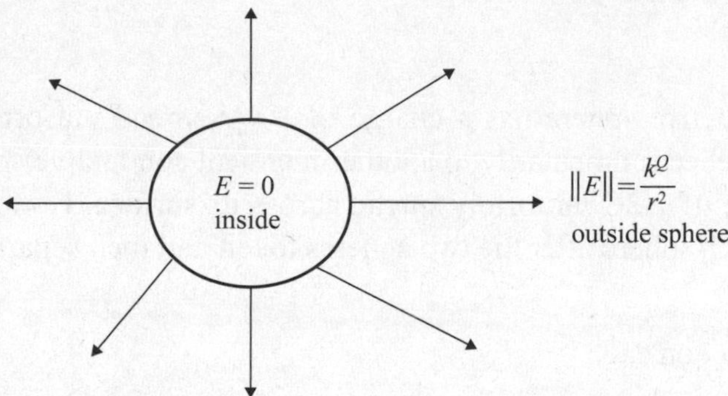

The type of electric field most often used in problems on the AP Physics B exam is the field of charged plates, because its uniform intensity makes the mathematics easier. It also simulates a constant field, which is just like our mechanical analogy of a constant gravitational field. Likewise, we can use the four equations for uniform acceleration to describe the behavior of motion in a constant electric field.

The following diagram shows two oppositely charged plates separated by a small distance. The field lines show uniform spacing and are representing a constant field between the plates. The electric field outside the plates is effectively 0.

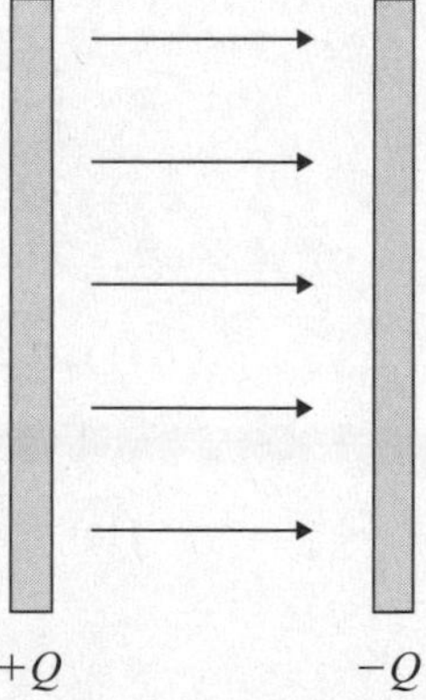

A positive test charge placed anywhere between the plates would experience a constant force at all points between the plates. This parallel plate setup is also the definition of a capacitor.

Practice Session Problems

Multiple Choice

1. A conductive sphere has a charge of $+4Q$ spread uniformly across it. It is touched momentarily to another identical conductive sphere that has a charge of $-2Q$ uniformly spread across its surface. How much charge is on each sphere after the two spheres touch and then separate from each other?

   (A) $+Q$ on each

   (B) $-Q$ on each

   (C) $+2Q$ on one sphere and 0 on the other

   (D) $+6Q$ on one and 0 on the other

   (E) No charge on either

2. What is the net force on the charge Q shown in the following diagram?

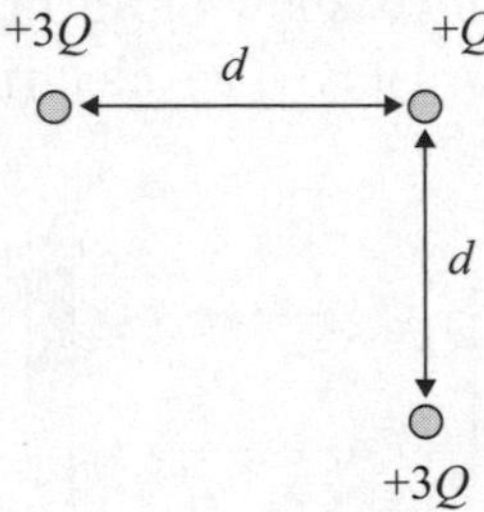

   (A) $\dfrac{3kQ^2}{d^2}$

   (B) $\dfrac{6kQ^2}{d^2}$

   (C) $\dfrac{3\sqrt{2}kQ^2}{d^2}$

   (D) $\dfrac{6kQ}{d^2}$

   (E) $\dfrac{3\sqrt{2}Q}{d^2}$

3. Four charges are placed in a square (sides of length d) as shown here:

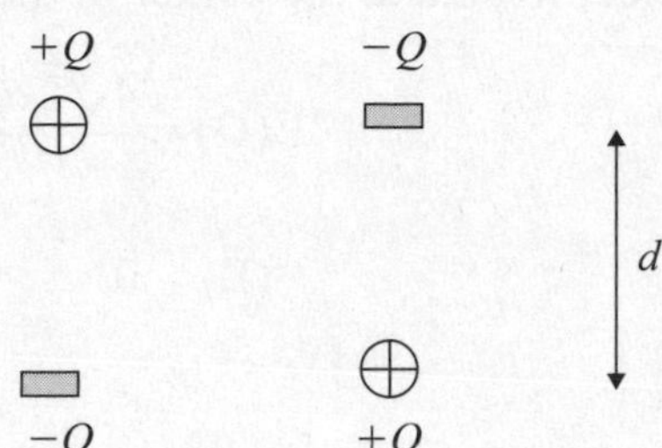

What is the magnitude of the net electric field at the center of the square?

(A) $\frac{8kQ}{d^2}$

(B) $\frac{2kQ}{d^2}$

(C) $\frac{4kQ}{d^2}$

(D) $\frac{4\sqrt{2}kQ}{d^2}$

(E) 0

4. The four charges have been rearranged in the same square of side d.

What is the direction of the net electric field at the center of the square?

(A) Zero field

(B) →

(C) ↑

(D) ↓

(E) ↘

5. Using the situation described and illustrated in question 4, what is the net magnitude of the electric field at the center of the square?

(A) $\frac{8kQ}{d^2}$

(B) $\frac{2kQ}{d^2}$

(C) $\frac{4kQ}{d^2}$

(D) $\frac{4\sqrt{2}kQ}{d^2}$

(E) 0

6. An electron is placed in a uniform field of $E = 300 \times 10^5$ N/C. What is the magnitude of force that the electron experiences?

(A) 4.8×10^{-12} N

(B) 5.33×10^{-22} N

(C) 5.33×10^{-27} N

(D) 4.8×10^{-17} N

(E) 1.6×10^{-19} N

7. In a uniform field between two charged plates, an electron is placed at the labeled points A, B, and C, as shown in the following diagram:

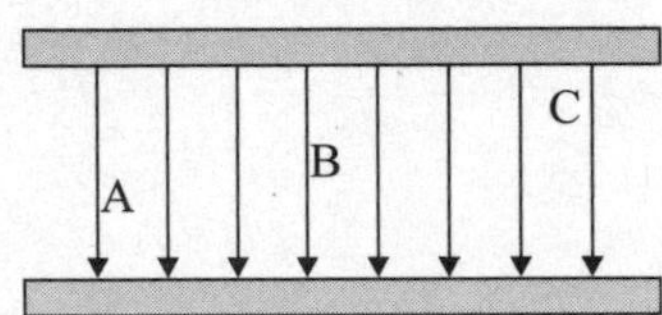

Rank the magnitude of the force on the electron when placed at each of the three points.

(A) $F_A > F_B > F_C$

(B) $F_C > F_B > F_A$

(C) $F_A = F_B = F_C$

(D) $F_B > F_A = F_C$

(E) $F_A = F_C > F_B$

Free Response

*1. Three charges are arranged as shown here:

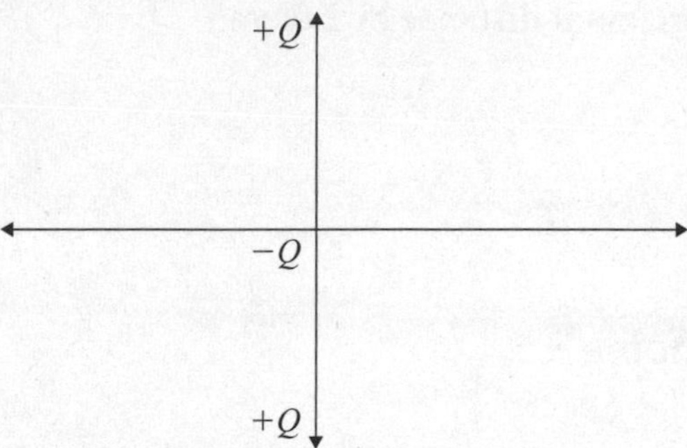

The $-Q$ charge is placed on the origin. The two $+Q$ charges are placed at the coordinates $(0, d)$ and $(0, -d)$. The $-Q$ charge will be moved in each part of the problem. The $+Q$ charges are stationary and do not move.

a. What is the net force on the $-Q$ charge in this setup?
b. If the $-Q$ charge moves to the coordinate $(0, y)$, where $0 < y < d$, what is the net force on the $-Q$ charge?
c. If the $-Q$ charge moves to another new location $(-x, 0)$, what is the net force on the $-Q$ charge?
d. Determine the electric field (magnitude and direction) at the coordinate $(-x, 0)$?
e. (AP Physics C only). In question c, the $-Q$ charge will exhibit simple harmonic motion as long as the x coordinate is small compared with d. If the $-Q$ charge has mass m and the distance x is $<< d$, (x is much, much smaller than d) what is the frequency of the simple harmonic motion?

2. An electron (e) is shot at a horizontal velocity into a uniform electric field (E), as shown in the following diagram:

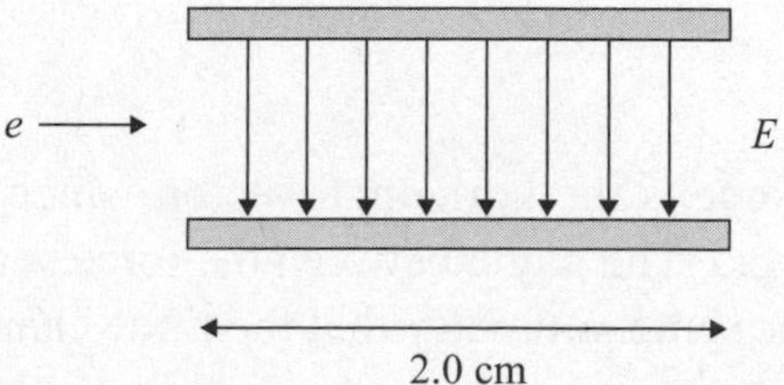

The electron has a velocity $v = 2.0 \times 10^6$ m/s in the positive x direction, and the electric field has a magnitude of 400 N/C in the $-y$ direction.

a. Draw the trajectory of the electron as it moves through the electronic field.

b. Determine the vertical displacement of the electron after traveling the entire horizontal distance of 2.0 cm.

Solutions

Multiple Choice

1. (A)
2. (C)
3. (E)
4. (D)
5. (D)
6. (A)
7. (C)

Free Response

1. a. The net force is 0.

b. The net force is $F_{net} = kQ^2\left[\frac{4dy}{(d^2 - y^2)^2}\right]$, directed in the positive y direction.

c. The net force is $F_{net} = 2kQ^2\frac{x}{(x^2 + d^2)^{\frac{3}{2}}}$, directed in the positive x direction. The solution requires the following process: First, you draw a free-body diagram on the $-Q$ charge at this new location:

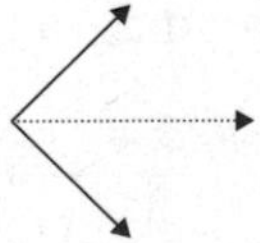

The net force is the horizontal vector, which is the sum of the two force vectors. The angle between the force vector and the horizontal creates the same geometry that the three charges created.

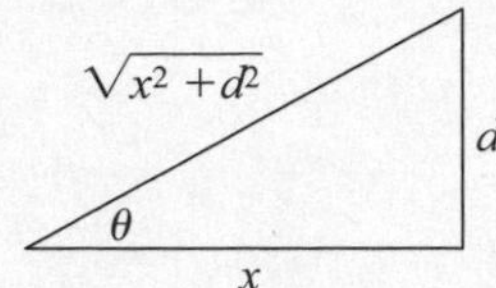

Thus, the cosine of the angle θ can be expressed using ratios:

$$\cos\theta = \frac{x}{\sqrt{x^2 + d^2}}$$

The net force comes from the sum of the two x components of the equal forces acting on $-Q$:

$$F_{net} = 2F_x = 2\,\|F\|\cos\theta = 2\,\|F\|\frac{x}{\sqrt{x^2 + d^2}}$$

$$\|F\| = \frac{kQ^2}{\left(\sqrt{x^2 + d^2}\right)^2}$$

$$F_{net} = \frac{kQ^2}{\left(\sqrt{x^2 + d^2}\right)^2} \cdot \frac{x}{\sqrt{x^2 + d^2}} = \frac{kQ^2 x}{(x^2 + d^2)^{\frac{3}{2}}}$$

d. The electric field at this point is $\left\|\vec{E}\right\| = \frac{kQx}{(x^2 + d^2)^{\frac{3}{2}}}$, directed in the $-x$ direction.

e. The frequency of simple harmonic motion is

$$\omega = \frac{1}{2\pi} \cdot \sqrt{\frac{2kQ^2}{md^3}}.$$

2. a. The motion is an upward parabola (like projectile motion) and looks like this:

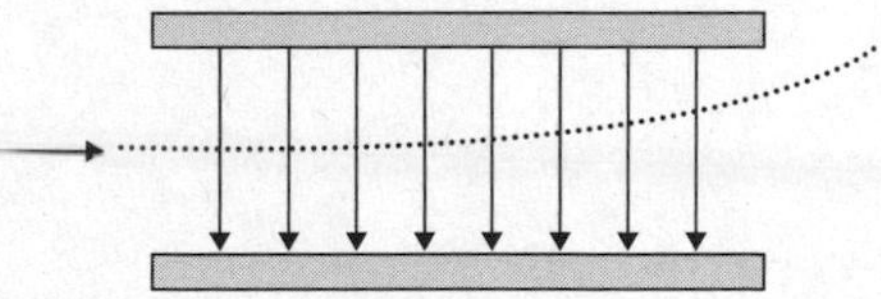

b. $\Delta y = 3.5 \times 10^{-3}$ m, above the starting position

Chapter 11

Electric Potential and Capacitance

EXAM OVERVIEW

Electric potential is a term that gets misused frequently in introductory physics. It is not a term for energy but rather a quantity that measures the ratio of energy to charge. It is more like a level of energy.

As in mechanics, the idea of an absolute energy level is only significant in relation to some standard reference level of energy. This is also the case with electric potential. It Is most important to know the change in electric potential between two points.

In AP Physics, students should have a working understanding of the electrostatic electric potential and be able to solve electric potential problems involving point charges, spheres, and parallel plates. AP Physics students should also understand the ideas of *equipotential and equipotential lines.* We touched on these points in the last chapter and will review them here. We will also cover the fundamentals of capacitance.

ELECTRIC POTENTIAL

The standard definition of electric potential is

$$\Delta V = V_b - V_a = \frac{\Delta U_E}{q'} = \frac{W_{a\to b}}{q'}.$$

The unit for electric potential is joules/coulomb (J/C), which is equivalent to a volt (V).

It takes work to move a charge around various areas of an electric field. If a positive test charge (q) is moved closer to a positive point charge (Q), the test charge gains electric potential energy (U_E), and it takes work from an external source to make that happen. If a test charge is repelled from a source charge without any other forces acting on the test charge, the test charge is losing electric potential energy but gaining kinetic energy. Thus, the electrostatic force is a *conservative* force, and all energy manipulation problems involve conservation of energy.

The mechanical analogy to electric potential is the idea that if you lift a mass in the gravitational field, you gain an amount of energy equal to mgh.

If you divide that increase in energy by the amount of mass lifted, you get a value that is totally independent of the amount of mass that experienced the increase in energy but totally dependent on the two things that created the energy: the Earth and the height. A mechanical gravitational potential would look something like this:

$$\frac{\Delta U_g}{m'} = \frac{m'gh}{m'} = gh$$

In the world of AP Physics B, you need to be concerned with three types of electric potential:

- Potential of a point charge
- Potential of a sphere
- Potential of parallel plates

You also should be familiar with practical uses of the idea of electric potential with respect to batteries, charged objects, and equipotential lines.

POINT CHARGES AND SPHERES

The electric potential of a point charge is a very simple expression:

$$V_p = \frac{kQ}{r},$$

where p represents a point P in space near the point charge, Q is the charge creating the electric field, and r is the position vector measured from the point charge to point P.

The equal level of energy that surrounds a point charge is the set of all points equidistant from the point charge—and that is the definition of a sphere. Thus, a circular line surrounding a point charge is a line of equal potential energy level, or **equipotential**. Here is what it would look like:

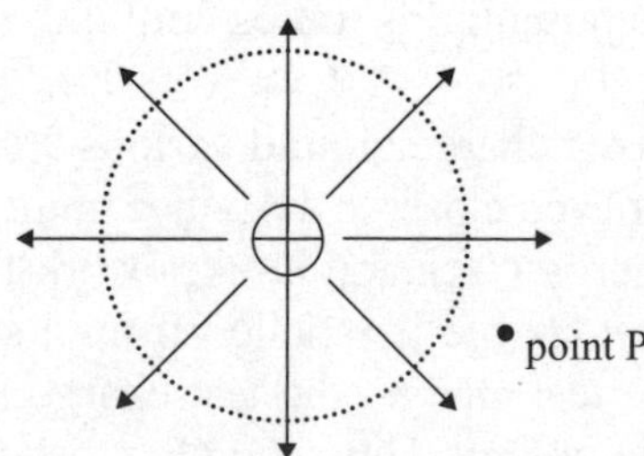

If point charge $Q = 2\ \mu C$, and point P is 5 cm away from the point charge, we can calculate the value of the electric field at point P as follows:

$$E = \frac{kQ}{r^2} = \frac{\left(9 \times 10^9 \frac{N \cdot m^2}{C^2}\right)(2 \times 10^{-6}\ C)}{(0.05\ m)^2} = 7.2 \times 10^6\ N/C$$

The electric potential at point P has a value of

$$V_p = \frac{kQ}{r} = \frac{\left(9 \times 10^9 \frac{N \cdot m^2}{C^2}\right)(2 \times 10^{-6}\ C)}{(0.05\ m)} = 3.6 \times 10^5\ \text{Volts}.$$

This value has meaning relative only to another value of potential. The standard reference level for potential for point charges is infinity. The value of electric potential for any point charge at infinity is 0.

Another way to think about the value of 3.6×10^5 volts of electric potential at point P is as follows: It takes 3.6×10^5 joules to move 1 coulomb of charge from infinity to point P. It takes that much work to move that charge of 1 coulomb against the E field of the point charge. As you move the test charge closer to the point charge, the test charge is gaining more electric potential energy. Electric potential describes how much energy a test charge would have available at some point outside the point charge.

If we had moved a proton from infinity to point P in our example, the electron would have gained the following:

$$\Delta V = \frac{\Delta U_E}{q'} \Rightarrow \Delta U_E = \Delta V q'$$

$$= (3.6 \times 10^5\ J/C)(1.6 \times 10^{-19}\ C) = 5.76 \times 10^{-14}\ \text{Joules}.$$

The concept of electric potential can be very useful. Here are some of its features:

- It is a scalar value.
- It can have a negative value.
- The value of the electric field at a point does not give you any information about the electric potential at that same point.
- The strength of the electric field is proportional to the change in electric potential over change in displacement:

$$E = -\frac{\Delta V}{\Delta x}$$

The negative sign is necessary because the electric field points away from increasing potential energy. This relationship also shows that the electric field can be measured in volts per meter.

MULTIPLE POINT CHARGES

In physics we often work with a set of charges. The electric potential at a point P resulting from multiple point charges is equal to the sum of the individual potentials at that point P. This is the principle of superposition again, except that electric potential is scalar. So we are only adding positive and negative values and not vectors. The formal definition looks like this:

$$V_p = \sum_i \frac{kQ_i}{r_i}$$

Let's start with a simple example of two point charges on the x-axis and explore the values of electric potential at various points.

Sample Problem

A negative point charge of $-2\ \mu C$ is placed at $x = -4$ m, and a positive point charge of $+2\ \mu C$ is placed at $x = +4$ meters, as shown in the following diagram:

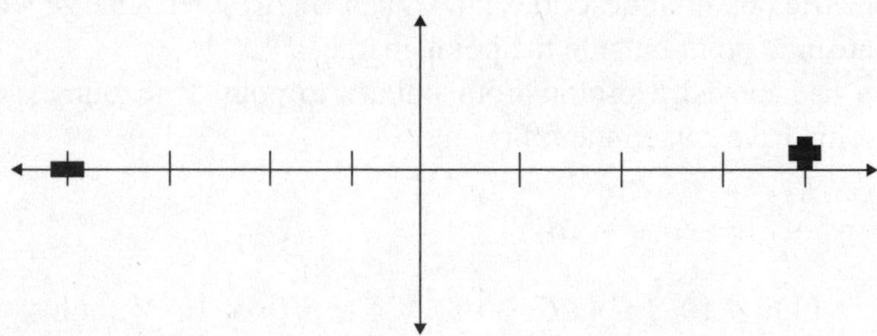

Determine the electric potential at the following points:

a. $x = -2$ m

b. $x = 0$ m

c. $x = +2$ m

d. The coordinate (0, 3) on the y-axis

Solution

a.

$$V_{-2m} = \sum \frac{kQ}{r} = \left(\frac{(9 \times 10^9)(-2 \times 10^{-6})}{2}\right) + \left(\frac{(9 \times 10^9)(2 \times 10^{-6})}{6}\right)$$

$$= (9 \times 10^9)(2 \times 10^{-6})\left(\frac{-1}{2} + \frac{1}{6}\right)$$

$$= -6000 \text{ Volts}$$

b.

$$V_0 = \sum_i \frac{kQ}{r} = \left(\frac{(9 \times 10^9)(-2 \times 10^{-6})}{4}\right) + \left(\frac{(9 \times 10^9)(2 \times 10^{-6})}{4}\right)$$

$$= 0 \text{ Volts}$$

c.

$$V_{+2m} = \sum \frac{kQ}{r} = \left(\frac{(9 \times 10^9)(-2 \times 10^{-6})}{6}\right) + \left(\frac{(9 \times 10^9)(2 \times 10^{-6})}{2}\right)$$

$$= (9 \times 10^9)(2 \times 10^{-6})\left(\frac{-1}{6} + \frac{1}{2}\right) = +6000 \text{ Volts}$$

d. The distance from each charge to the point (0, 3) on the y-axis is the same value: 5 m. This means the calculation will be similar to the answer in part b. Thus, the electric potential at this point on the y-axis will also be 0 volts. In fact, at any point on the y-axis, the potential value would be 0 volts, because it would be equidistant from each charge. Therefore, the y-axis is an **equipotential line**. Here the equipotential surface is a line, yet the other equipotentials look more like squashed circles around the charges. You can probably find a good diagram of this effect in your textbook.

ELECTRIC POTENTIAL OF SPHERES AND PLATES

A charged, conducting metal sphere is used in many textbook problems on electric potential. The charged metal sphere behaves exactly like a point charge, with all the charge concentrated at the center of the sphere. The electric field of a sphere charged to a magnitude of Q is the same as the electric field for a point charge of magnitude Q (for all values of r greater than the radius of the sphere). Inside the sphere, the electric field is 0. If the sphere's field mimics a point charge, then it makes sense that the potential of a point near a charged sphere would mimic the point charge as well—and it does.

The electric potential at a point P outside of a charged sphere is

$$V_p = \frac{kQ}{r}(r > R)$$

$$V_{sphere} = \frac{kQ}{R}$$

The electric potential at the sphere's surface is the second expression. The potential at any point inside the sphere is the same as any point on the sphere. The sphere itself is called an **equipotential surface**. Here is a graph of this relationship, with potential represented by V (volts) and the radial distance from the center of the sphere represented by R (meters):

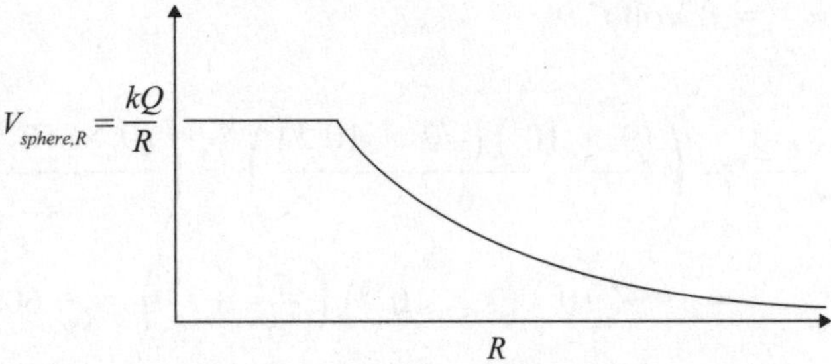

Note that the electric potential at the center of the sphere is the same as at the edge of the sphere. Thus, it takes the same amount of work to move a charge q against the sphere all the way up to the sphere's edge. It takes no more additional work to move it to the center of the sphere. So the cumulative amount of work to take a test charge to the edge of the sphere is the same as it is to take the test charge to the center of the sphere.

Parallel plates are often used in AP Physics B problems in electrostatics. Problems using parallel plates bring in the idea of a constant field between the plates. With that constant field comes a constant force. Because the force is constant across the distance of separation between the plates, it is easy to compute the work done in moving a charge through the field.

Given a constant field of magnitude E, a positive point charge q is moved from point B to point A, as shown in the following diagram:

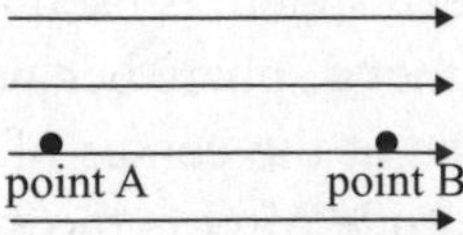

We can compute the work done in moving a charge q from point B to point A as follows:

$$Work = \|\vec{F}\| \cdot \|\Delta x\| = qE \cdot \Delta x$$

If we apply the definition of electric potential, we get the following computation:

$$V = \frac{W_{B \to A}}{q} = \frac{qE\Delta x}{q} = E\Delta x$$

Therefore, the potential between any two points in a uniform field is $E\Delta x$.

To have a difference in potential, we would have to move along the field lines. If two points lie on a line perpendicular to the field lines, as in the following diagram, there would be no difference in potential between the points. The dashed line in the figure is the equipotential line:

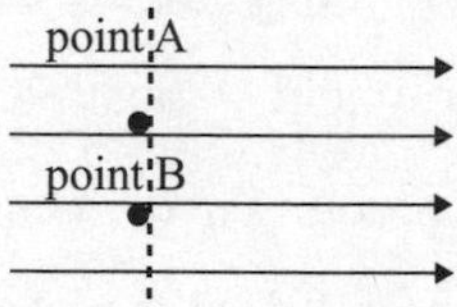

This time, point A and point B are directly above each other in the vertical direction, perpendicular to the field lines. The difference in potential between point A and point B is 0 in this case. In other words, it takes no work to move a point charge from point B to point A. Think about this. Can you understand how it makes sense?

Let's take this definition and apply it to parallel plates. If two plates have opposite charges and create a uniform field between them, the potential difference between the plates is $V = Ed$, where E is the electric field between the plates and d is the distance of separation between the plates.

In the following diagram of oppositely charged parallel plates, the field lines and equipotential lines have been drawn. The equipotential lines represent a level of equal potential everywhere on the line. The electric field lines are perpendicular to all equipotential lines.

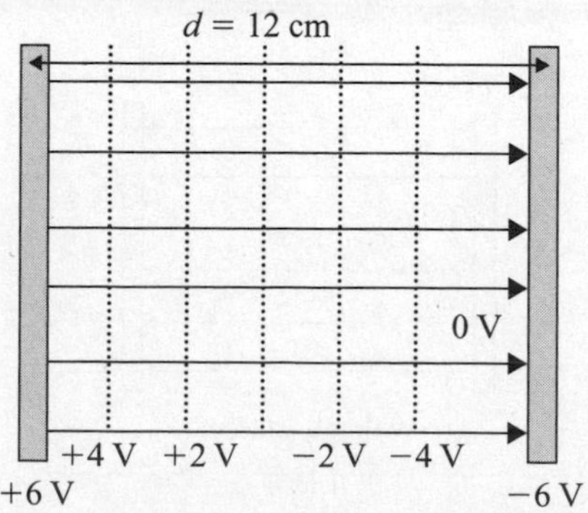

The **potential gradient** $\frac{\Delta V}{\Delta x}$ gives a value for the electric field strength between the plates. The equipotential lines are shown as dashed lines. The absolute value of the line is marked. The difference in potential between the plates is

$$6\text{ V} - (-6\text{ V}) = 12\text{ Volts}.$$

The electric field strength is

$$\frac{\Delta V}{\Delta x} = \frac{12\text{ V}}{0.12\text{ m}} = 100\ \frac{\text{V}}{\text{m}}.$$

And the gradient is the same value for any two lines chosen.

Notice that the equipotential lines and the direction of decreasing potential show the direction of the electric field. A positive charge located at any equipotential line will move in the direction of *decreasing* potential. This is the same as the direction of the electric field, and it is the reason that the definition of *electric field* in relation to potential gradient, $E = -\frac{\Delta V}{\Delta x}$, has a negative sign.

CAPACITANCE

A **capacitor** is an electrical device that stores charge and energy, usually in a very small space. The capacitor has two conductive plates placed very close together and separated by a dielectric (insulating material). A voltage (potential difference) is then applied across the two plates with a source of electrical energy. The two plates receive equal and opposite charges, and an electric field is maintained between the plates. The electrical energy stored in the field can be used by another part of the circuit. The following diagram is the standard model for a capacitor, with parallel charged plates separated by a distance *d*.

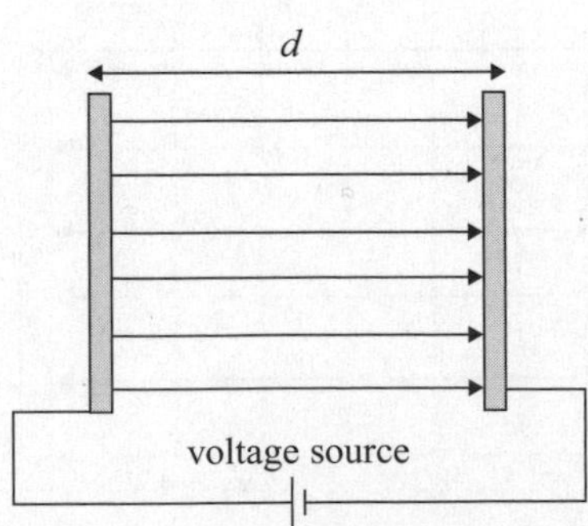

The definition of capacitance in terms of the electrical properties is $C = \frac{Q}{\Delta V}$. The units of capacitance are farads, where 1 farad $= \frac{\text{coulomb}^2}{\text{joule}}$.

A capacitor can be defined by its physical properties as well, so the amount of charge that can be squeezed onto the two plates at a given level of energy (potential difference) is proportional to the area of the plates and the distance of separation, which is the definition of capacitance:

$$C = \frac{\varepsilon_o A}{d},$$

where the permittivity of free space $\varepsilon_o = 8.85 \times 10^{-12} \frac{\text{C}^2}{\text{N} \cdot \text{m}^2}$, and Coulomb's constant $k = \frac{1}{4\pi\varepsilon_o}$.

Inserting an insulator between the metal plates increases the capacitance. This is typically done in the making of real capacitors. The new definition of the capacitor, including the dielectric, is $C = \frac{\kappa\varepsilon_o A}{d} = \kappa C_o$, where κ is the dielectric strength of the insulator. Thc higher the insulator's dielectric strength, the greater the capacitance becomes.

The properties of capacitors in circuits is discussed in the next chapter.

Practice Session Problems

Multiple Choice

1. Two positive charges are placed on the y-axis at the positions $y = +a$ and $y = -a$. These two charges are held fixed and stationary. What is the potential at a point on the x-axis $(a, 0)$?

(A) $V_{(a,0)} = \dfrac{2kQ}{a}$

(B) $V_{(a,0)} = \dfrac{\sqrt{2}kQ}{a}$

(C) $V_{(a,0)} = \dfrac{kQ}{a^2}$

(D) $V_{(a,0)} = \dfrac{2kQ}{a^2}$

(E) $V_{(a,0)} = \dfrac{\sqrt{2}kQ}{a^2}$

The following diagram shows lines of equipotential in a region of space that contains an electric field. Use this diagram to answer questions 2 through 4.

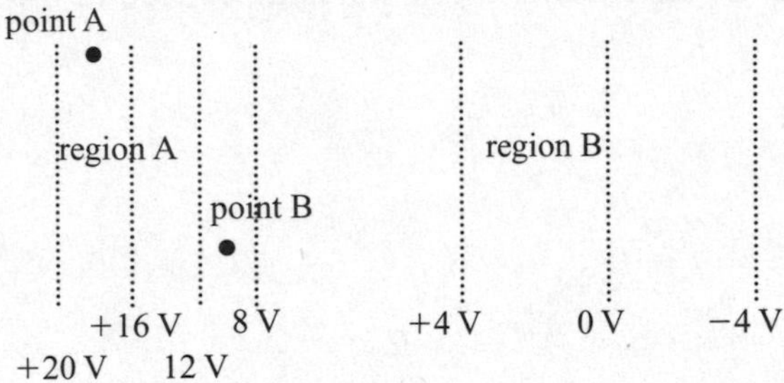

2. Which statement about the electric fields in regions A and B is correct?

(A) $\left\|\vec{E}_A\right\| > \left\|\vec{E}_B\right\|$

(B) $\left\|\vec{E}_A\right\| < \left\|\vec{E}_B\right\|$

(C) $\left\|\vec{E}_A\right\| = \left\|\vec{E}_B\right\|$

(D) Cannot determine from information given

3. The same charge is placed at point A and at point B. Which of the following correctly compares the magnitudes of the forces on the charges?

   (A) $\left\|\vec{F_A}\right\| = 1.5\left\|\vec{F_B}\right\|$

   (B) $\left\|\vec{F_A}\right\| = 2\left\|\vec{F_B}\right\|$

   (C) $\left\|\vec{F_A}\right\| = \frac{2}{3}\left\|\vec{F_B}\right\|$

   (D) $\left\|\vec{F_A}\right\| = \left\|\vec{F_B}\right\|$

   (E) $\left\|\vec{F_A}\right\| = \frac{1}{2}\left\|\vec{F_B}\right\|$

4. An electron is placed somewhere on the 0-V line. Which of the following statements best describes what will happen to the electron?

   (A) It will move vertically on the line.

   (B) It will move to the +4-V line.

   (C) It will move toward the −4-V line.

   (D) It will remain stationary.

   (E) It will move in a circular path.

A conducting metal sphere of radius a has charge Q spread over its surface. The following four graphs show electric potential or electric field versus radial distance from the center of the sphere. Use the graphs to answer questions 5 and 6.

I.

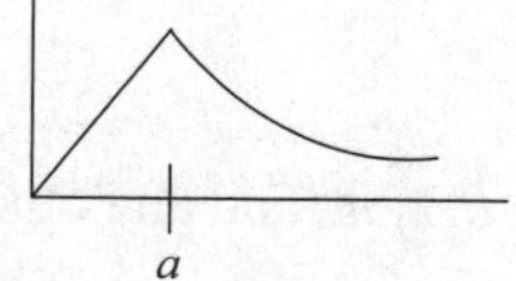

III.

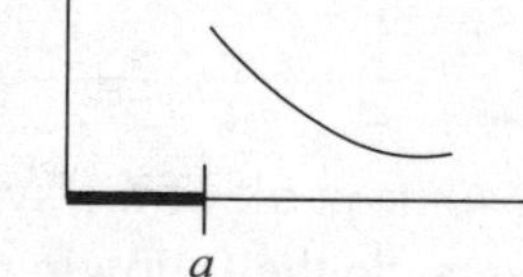

II.

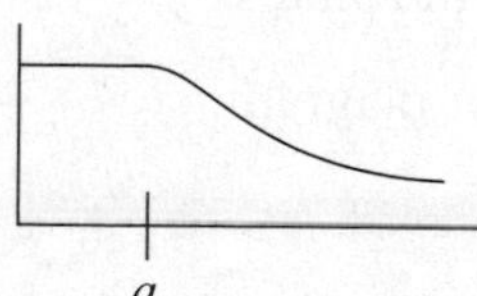

IV.

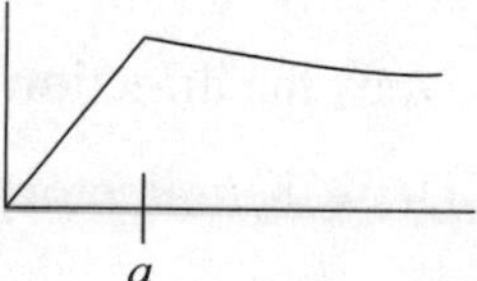

5. Which graph best represents the sphere's potential as a function of the radial distance from the sphere?

   (A) I

   (B) II

   (C) III

   (D) IV

   (E) None of the graphs

6. Which graph best represents the sphere's electric field as a function of the radial distance from the sphere?

(A) I

(B) II

(C) III

(D) IV

(E) None of the graphs

Free Response

1. An electron with charge e and mass m is shot horizontally into an electric field created by two parallel plates (oppositely charged), as shown in the following diagram. The electron eventually hits a large target wall. The electron's initial horizontal velocity is v_o. The voltage between the two plates is kept at V_o volts. The distance between the two plates is d. The length of the plates is L.

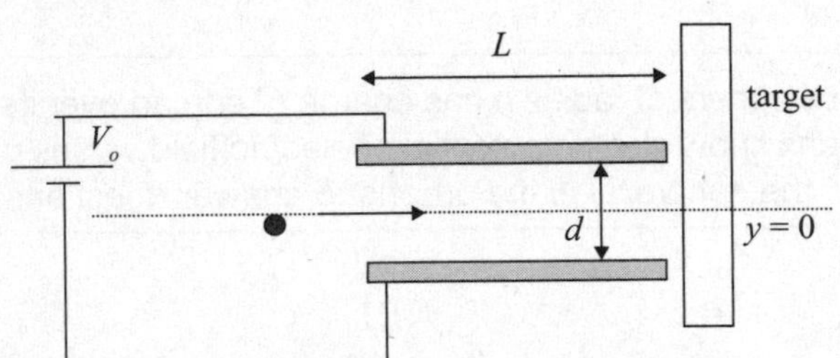

Using some or all of the symbols V_o, v_o, L, d, e, m, and any other physical constants, do the following:

a. Determine the electric field between the plates.

b. Draw the direction of the field in your diagram.

c. Draw the trajectory of the electron.

d. Determine the vertical position y as it hits the target.

2. Three point charges are arranged as shown in the diagram. Two $+Q$ charges are placed a distance d away from the origin (0, 0) at points (0, d) and (0, $-d$), and a third charge of $-2Q$ is placed on the x-axis at point ($-d$, 0).

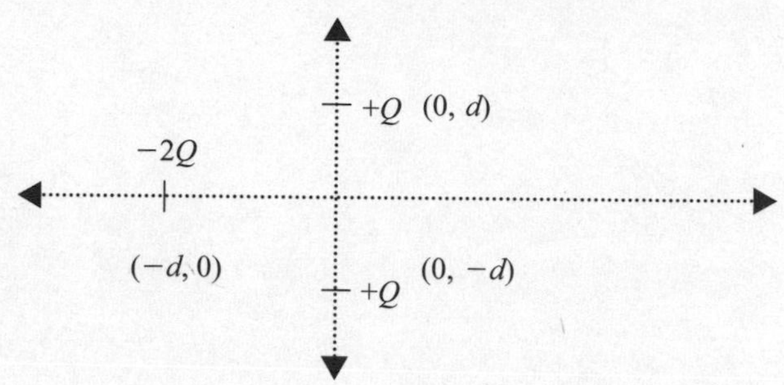

a. Determine the potential at the point $(+d, 0)$.

b. Determine the magnitude and direction of the electric field at the point $(+d, 0)$.

c. Determine the potential at the origin $(0, 0)$.

Solutions

Multiple Choice

1. (B)
2. (A)
3. (D)
4. (B)
5. (B)
6. (C)

Free Response

1. a. $E = \dfrac{V_o}{d}$

   b. The field is vertically downward and uniform.

   c. The trajectory is a parabola opening slightly upward.

   d. $y = \dfrac{eV_o}{2md} \cdot \dfrac{L^2}{v_o^2}$

2. a. $V_{(d,0)} = \dfrac{kQ}{d}\left(\sqrt{2} - 1\right)$

   b. $\left\| \vec{E} \right\| = \dfrac{kQ}{2d^2}\left(\sqrt{2} - 1\right)$, in the positive x direction

   c. $V_{(0,0)} = 0$

Chapter 12

Circuits

EXAM OVERVIEW

The study of circuits is usually one of the most interesting units for AP Physics students. The physics is fun and practical and the mathematics fairly simple. Understanding circuits correctly and avoiding common pitfalls is likely to improve your score on the AP Physics exam.

The circuitry topics emphasized on the exam include the following:

- Definition of current
- Definition of resistance
- Sources of electrical energy
- Ohm's law
- Circuit as a complete conductive loop
- Circuit analysis for series and parallel circuits
- Electrical energy and power in a circuit
- Capacitors in a static state in a circuit (the RC circuit in a transient state is covered only in Physics C)

CURRENT, RESISTANCE, AND OHM'S LAW

The definition of current is fairly simple. It is simply the number of charges that pass by a given point per unit time:

$$I = \frac{\Delta Q}{\Delta t}$$

The unit of current is the ampere (which is equivalent to 1 coulomb per second).

Make sure you can easily go back and forth between coulomb (C) and electron (e). Remember that the charge on electron is $e = 1.6 \times 10^{-19}$ C. Also, be aware that many physics problems use milliamperes or microamperes.

Resistance is the opposition electric charges meet as they attempt to move freely through conductors. The electrons that move through conductors encounter resistance in the form of collisions with atomic cores in the conductor. These collisions cause the electrons' movement to stop and start rather than flow smoothly.

The general definition of resistance in a conductor almost mirrors the relationship of heat conduction in thermodynamics:

$$R = \frac{\rho l}{A},$$

where ρ is the constant called **resistivity**, which essentially indicates how much resistance a particular conductor has, l is the length of the conductor, and A is the cross-sectional area of the conductor. This definition of resistance is used to compare conductors' abilities to carry a current.

Determining the resistance of a conductor, or a particular part of the circuit, using experimental measurements requires the application of **Ohm's law**: $V = IR$, where V is the potential difference between two points of interest in volts, I is the current in amperes, and R is a circuit parameter measured in ohms (which is equivalent to volts per ampere). Ohm's law is true for any part of a circuit, any branch in a circuit, or the entire circuit. It is easily the most used relationship in electronics. Essentially, with Ohm's law and its companion relationship, $P = VI$, an entire circuit can be thoroughly analyzed.

Before we can measure or talk about current and resistance, we need to define what is necessary to produce a current in a circuit. A complete **circuit pathway** or **conductive pathway** is necessary to produce a current in a circuit. The circuit pathway connects the positive side of a source of electric potential (a battery or power supply) to the negative side of the potential (a difference in potential). This potential difference sets up an electric field through the circuit pathway.

Without the circuit pathway, no current could be established. Thus, the field sets up around the circuit pathway and continuously pushes the charges in the conductor around the pathway in a continuous loop of energy conservation. If the path at some point is broken, the circuit becomes inoperable. However, if an electronic gizmo—for instance, a light, buzzer, or signal—is placed in the loop, the current established in the circuit can do work within that electric device and make it operate.

A typical circuit pathway looks like this:

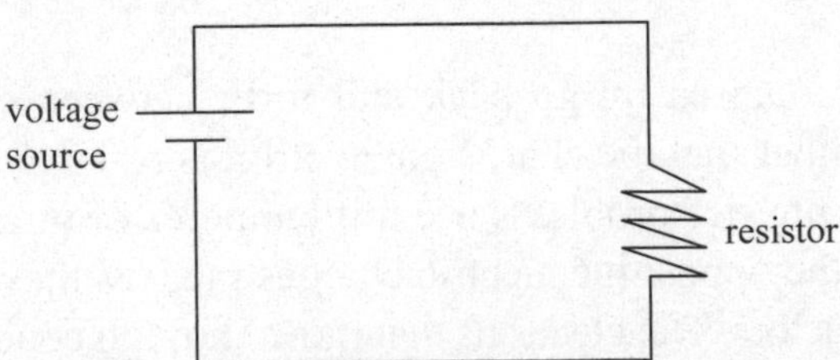

Note the typical jagged-line depiction of a resistor in the diagram. Typically, a circuit has resistors in place for certain reasons. However, all conductors have resistance (even connecting wires in a circuit). Sometimes the depiction of a resistor in a physics problem diagram represents all possible resistance in the circuit, including the resistance in the conductors. The resistance in an electrical connector (standard wire) is typically less than 0.1 ohm. Therefore, the wire's resistance is not mentioned in most textbook problems, especially if the resistors involved in the problem are of large values.

A **short circuit** occurs when there is almost zero resistance between the voltage source's high and low potentials. Connecting a wire to the positive and negative ends of a battery is an example of a short circuit: with almost zero resistance in the electrical pathway, the result would be a dangerously large current. A short circuit can occur unintentionally in the wiring of circuits, so it is definitely something to be aware of in the physics lab.

In the following diagram, the path ABCDEF represents a short circuit. This alternative path around the bulb would cause the light to go out, which is a sure sign of a short circuit.

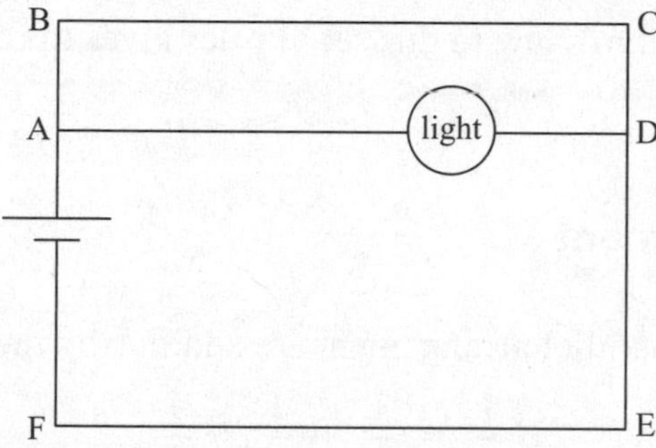

CIRCUIT ANALYSIS

A circuit often contains some combination of light bulb, resistors, and voltage sources (eventually, capacitors as well). The resistors can be combined in interesting ways to get the various current and energy outcomes necessary for various circuit devices. Typically, AP Physics B focuses on the series, parallel, and combination circuits.

Here are some of the basic rules of circuits:

Series Arrangement

- Resistors in a series circuit are additive:

$$R_E = R_1 + R_2 + R_3 + ...R_N,$$

where R_E stands for **equivalent resistance**.

- Voltage measurements in a series circuit are also additive:

$$V_T = V_1 + V_2 + V_3 + ...V_N$$

- Current in a series circuit is the same value at all points. This is represented mathematically as

$$I_{total} = I_1 + I_2 + I_3 = I_N,$$

where I_{total} represents the current in the battery or voltage source. This is typically called the total current or operating current. The other current measurements, I_1, I_2, and so on, are simply currents measured at specific resistors.

- Bringing in Ohm's law to this set of rules gives the following analysis:

$$V_{total} = I_{total}R_{equivalent}$$

Parallel Arrangement

- Resistors in parallel arrangement are additive by their inverses:

$$\frac{1}{R_E} = \frac{1}{R_1} + \frac{1}{R_2} + \frac{1}{R_3}$$

- Voltage in parallel arrangement is the same measurement for all resistors:

$$V_T = V_1 = V_2 = V_3$$

- The current in a parallel circuit is additive:

$$I_T = I_1 + I_2 + I_3$$

- Essentially, there are alternative pathways for circuit flow. Each pathway has a measurable current, so the total current will have the total sum of all of the alternative pathways' currents—like the flow of traffic onto a highway. The total flow of traffic onto a highway is the sum of all of the entrance ramp flows onto that highway.
- In a parallel circuit, the important factor is not that resistors are aligned in parallel lines but that the voltages across the resistors have the same potential difference between them, because they are attached to the same two points (A and B), like this:

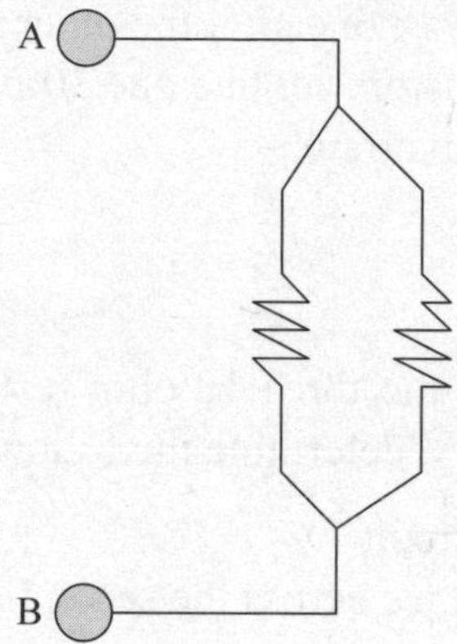

The steps in solving any circuit problem are: (1) to reduce the entire circuit's resistance to an equivalent resistance, a process called **reducing a circuit**; (2) determine the operating current; and (3) determine all other currents and voltages based on the rules just outlined.

Here is an example of three 10-ohm resistors in series:

10 Ω

10 Ω

10 Ω

This circuit reduces to the following:

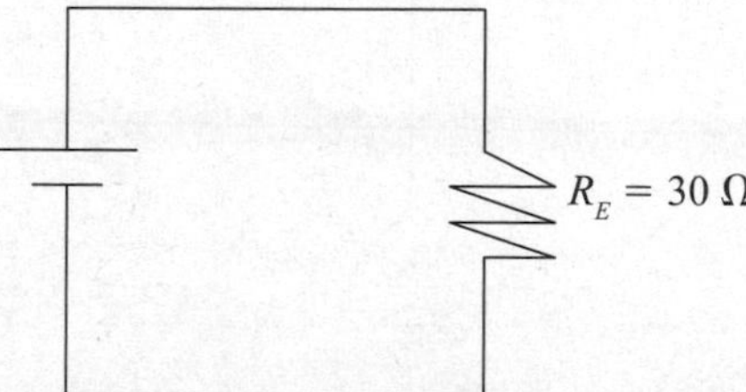

Circuit diagrams are typically drawn as rectangular boxes or squared out loops, mainly to make them easier to interpret. You won't always encounter this in your physics lab, but textbooks will stick to this formalized drawing format. In the example shown here, the three resistors could have been arranged in any way—all three clumped together, one on each of the square's lengths—as long as they are arranged in a pathway, one after the other after the other. The net effect is that the three 10-ohm resistors act like one 30-ohm resistor to the battery, as shown in the final reduced diagram.

Sample Problem 1

Using the diagram of the three 10-ohm resistors shown in the previous section and a voltage of 10 V, determine the following:

- The current in the circuit
- The potential difference across the second resistor

Solution

As shown in the diagram, the equivalent resistance is 30 ohms. We can determine the current using Ohm's law:

$$I = \frac{V}{R} = \frac{10\ \text{V}}{30\ \Omega} = 0.33\ \text{A}$$

Using this current value, we can determine the voltage at any point:

$$V = IR = (0.33\ \text{A})(10\ \Omega) = 3.33\ \text{V},$$

which is one-third of the total voltage. This is what you would expect for three equal resistors in series. Each resistor would consume one-third of the total potential difference.

Sample Problem 2

All resistors have a value of 10 ohms in the following diagram:

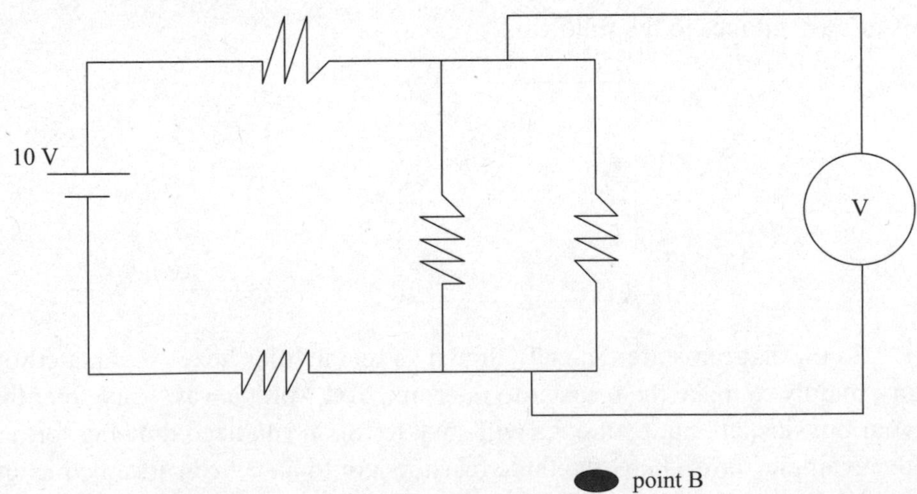

Using this diagram, determine the following:

- The current in the circuit
- The voltage measurement in the voltmeter
- What would happen to the circuit's operating current if the circuit were broken at point B

Solution

First, we must reduce the circuit. This is the most important step in solving circuit problems. There are two resistors attached to the same two points. These two 10-ohm resistors are in a parallel arrangement. We can calculate the effective resistance with these two resistors as follows:

$$\frac{1}{R_E} = \frac{1}{10} + \frac{1}{10} = \frac{2}{10} = \frac{1}{5} \Rightarrow R_E = 5 \text{ ohms}$$

Now we redraw the circuit to show this new effective resistance:

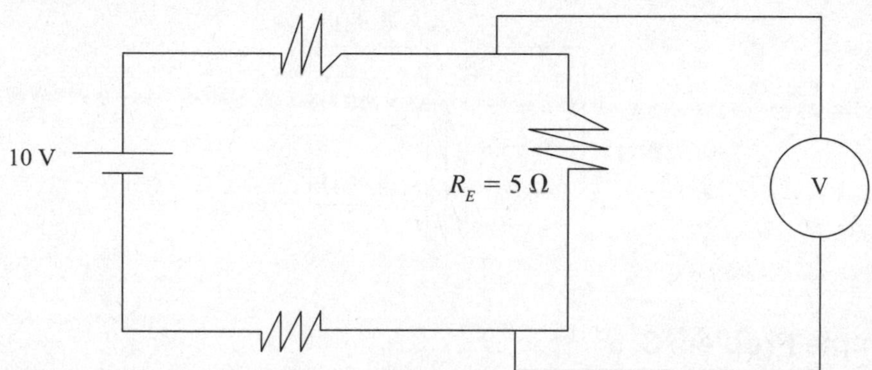

This gives a "new" circuit of three resistors in series, and we know what to do with that—just add up the total resistance:

$$R_E = R_1 + R_2 + R_3 = 10\ \Omega + 5\ \Omega + 10\ \Omega = 25\ \Omega$$

This gives a total current in the circuit of $I_t = \dfrac{10\text{ V}}{25\ \Omega} = 0.4\text{ A}$.

To determine the voltage measurement by the voltmeter, we simply take the net current through that 5-ohm equivalent resistance and apply Ohm's law:

$$V = IR = (0.4\text{ A})\,(5\ \Omega) = 2\text{ V}$$

The two parallel resistor combinations have a voltage of 2 volts across their end points.

To answer the third question, we simply redraw the circuit with the cut at point B, thereby eliminating that branch from the circuit path. The new circuit path looks like this:

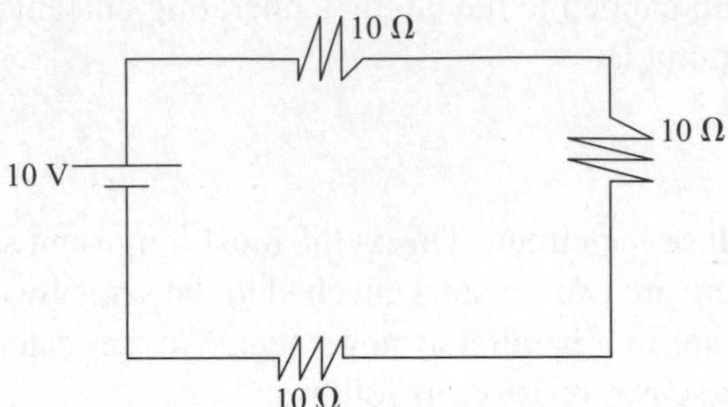

The new circuit has an increased resistance of 30 ohms. This will drop the operating current lower to a value of 0.33 amperes. Thus, cutting out a resistor actually increases resistance and lowers the current.

$R_1 = 5\ \Omega$

$I_t = 2$ A

$R_2 = 10\ \Omega$

$R_2 = 20\ \Omega$

Sample Problem 3

In the previous figure, a current of 2 amperes enters the branch point of the three-resistor arrangement. Determine the current in each branch.

Solution

The parallel arrangement has an equivalent resistance of:

$$\frac{1}{R_E} = \frac{1}{5} + \frac{1}{10} + \frac{1}{20} \Rightarrow \frac{1}{R_E} = \frac{4}{20} + \frac{2}{20} + \frac{1}{20} = \frac{7}{20}$$

$$\Rightarrow R_E = \frac{20}{7}\ \Omega$$

Applying Ohm's law to the entire parallel arrangement gives us

$$V_{parallel} = I_{parallel} R_E = (2\text{ A})\left(\frac{20}{7}\right) = \frac{40}{7}\text{ V.}$$

Voltage is the same value across each of the three resistors. This follows the rules for parallel circuits. Now we apply Ohm's law to each branch to determine the current in each branch:

$$I_{5\Omega} = \frac{\left(\frac{40}{7}\text{V}\right)}{5\ \Omega} = \frac{8}{7}\text{ A},\ I_{10\Omega} = \frac{\left(\frac{40}{7}\text{V}\right)}{10\ \Omega} = \frac{4}{7}\text{ A},\ I_{20\Omega} = \frac{\left(\frac{40}{7}\text{V}\right)}{20\ \Omega} = \frac{2}{7}\text{ A}$$

Notice that the total current adds up to the sum of the three individual branch currents, a condition of parallel circuits:

$$2\text{ A} = \frac{8}{7}\text{ A} + \frac{4}{7}\text{ A} + \frac{2}{7}\text{ A} = \frac{14}{7}\text{ A}$$

One way to approach this problem is to use a little math trickery. The resistors' values are inversely proportional to their currents; in other words, the largest resistance gets the smallest currents. We can use this inverse approach to solve the problem. First, we write out the ratio of resistances:

$$5\ \Omega : 10\ \Omega : 20\ \Omega$$

Then we take the inverse of each resistance:

$$\frac{1}{5} : \frac{1}{10} : \frac{1}{20} \Rightarrow \text{Clear the fraction … giving: } 4 : 2 : 1$$

Thus, the currents will be in the ratio of 4 : 2 : 1, with the 4 corresponding to the 5-ohm resistor. The total current of 2 amperes can be broken into seven units: $4 + 2 + 1 = 7$. This means that $\frac{4}{7}I_t = \frac{4}{7} \cdot 2\text{A} = \frac{8}{7}\text{A}$. The other two currents can be determined in the same way. This trick is especially quick when the parallel circuit only has two resistors.

ELECTRICAL POWER AND ENERGY

You can think of a circuit pathway as a closed-loop system that conserves energy. The energy source (battery or power supply) pumps energy into the system. The resistors, light bulbs, connectors, and capacitors all consume energy. The energy output of the battery should add up to the energy drawn from the circuit. Electrical power is a way to measure this principle. The definition of electrical power is $P = VI$. This relationship can be rearranged in two other ways:

$P = I^2R = \frac{V^2}{R}$. The relationship that is used in any particular problem will depend on the circuit characteristics that are known or given at that point.

Going a little further with this idea, we can see that if it is electrical energy that we are interested in, we will have to take that rate of energy use (power) and multiply it by time. This gives a relationship of $Energy = P \cdot \Delta t = VI\Delta t$.

We can inspect the units of this expression and see that it is indeed an expression of energy:

$$VI\Delta t \Rightarrow \frac{\text{Joule}}{\text{coulomb}} \cdot \frac{\text{coulomb}}{\text{second}} \cdot \text{second} = \text{Joule}$$

CAPACITORS IN CIRCUITS

Capacitors can also show up in the AP Physics B exam in a circuit problem. You should know how capacitors behave in a steady-state circuit. Additionally, you should know how arrangements of capacitors can be reduced to an equivalent capacitance in a circuit.

Typically, a capacitor placed at some point in a circuit will simply gain a potential difference across the plates. Charge will be induced on its plates, and the capacitor will retain that charge until it is needed. Usually, a switch attached to the capacitor will enable the charge to be used elsewhere in another circuit.

A capacitor will usually be attached in parallel across some part of a circuit. Thus, the voltage across the capacitor will be the same as that particular circuit element. Here is a picture of what this would look like:

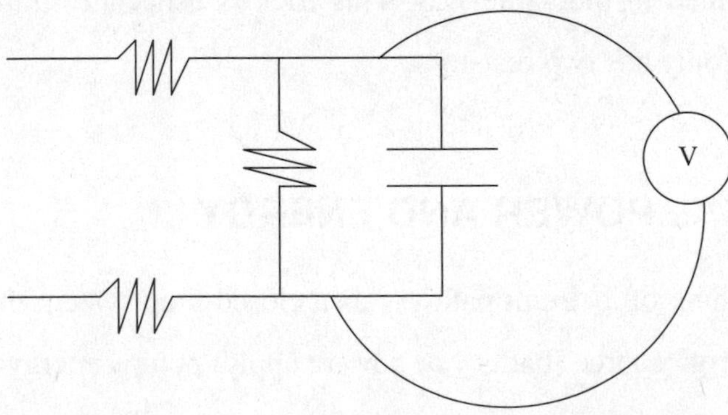

The voltage measured by the voltmeter is the same for the resistor and capacitor that are attached in parallel.

Capacitors also have equivalent capacitance relationships when they are arranged in series or parallel. The rules for capacitors are the inverse of the rules for resistors. Be careful when solving questions quickly. Try not to mix these two concepts. Here are the rules for capacitors:

- In series, capacitors add reciprocally:

$$\frac{1}{C_E} = \frac{1}{C_1} + \frac{1}{C_2} + \frac{1}{C_3}$$

- In parallel, capacitors add linearly:

$$C_E = C_1 + C_2 + C_3$$

Knowing the basis for these rules helps in understanding the nature of capacitors.

When capacitors are arranged in series, only one plate gets charged. The other capacitors in the series get charged by induction. Therefore, the total charge on each capacitor is the same as the total charge that left the battery. You will need to think about that for a moment. Because each capacitor is essentially sharing the same total charge, the equivalent capacitance will be smaller than any one of the capacitors.

Another property of the capacitors in series is that the voltage across each capacitor must add up to the total voltage across the network of capacitors. Here is a picture of that property:

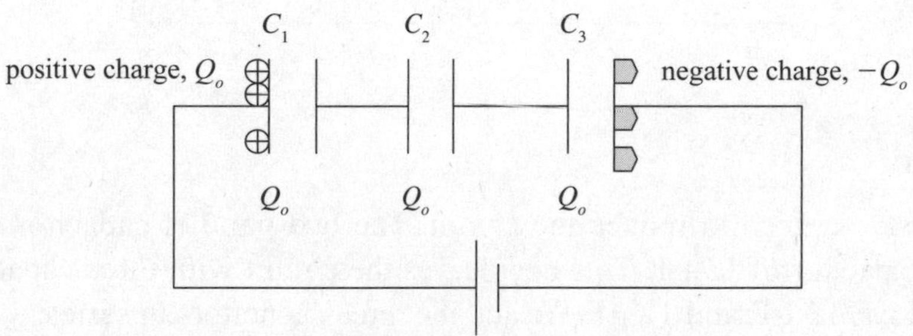

The diagram shows each capacitor with an equal amount of charge on each capacitor. The picture also shows only the two outer plates getting charged by the conductive wires attached directly to the battery. The other four plates get charged equally and oppositely by induction. This leaves each capacitor with a charge of Q_0. Because the voltage (energy) around a circuit pathway must add up to the batteries voltage, the following is true:

$V_b = V_1 + V_2 + V_3 \Rightarrow$

Replace with capacitor relationship, $C = \dfrac{Q}{V} \rightarrow V = \dfrac{Q}{C}$

$$\frac{Q_t}{C_E} = \frac{Q_1}{C_1} + \frac{Q_2}{C_2} + \frac{Q_3}{C_3} \Rightarrow \text{All } Q\text{'s are } Q_o \Rightarrow$$

$$\frac{Q_o}{C_E} = \frac{Q_o}{C_1} + \frac{Q_o}{C_2} + \frac{Q_o}{C_3} \Rightarrow \frac{1}{C_E} = \frac{1}{C_1} + \frac{1}{C_2} + \frac{1}{C_3}$$

Sample Problem 4

In the following diagram, determine the amount of charge stored on the 2-μF capacitor.

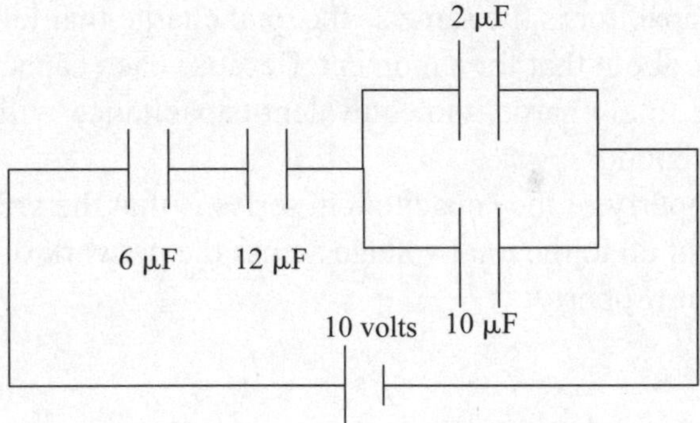

Solution

First, we need to reduce the circuit. The two parallel capacitors behave as one capacitor of 12 μF. This now leaves the circuit with three capacitors in series: 6 μF, 12 μF, and 12 μF. We add the three capacitors in series:

$$\frac{1}{C_E} = \frac{1}{C_1} + \frac{1}{C_2} + \frac{1}{C_3} = \frac{1}{6} + \frac{1}{12} + \frac{1}{12} \Rightarrow C_E = 3\ \mu\text{F}$$

Now we apply the definition of capacitance to the network:

$$C = \frac{Q}{V} \Rightarrow Q_{system} = C_E V_{system} = (3\ \mu\text{F})\,(10\ \text{V}) = 30\ \mu\text{C}$$

Thus, there is 30 μC on the 6-μF capacitor, 30 μC on each 12-μF capacitor, and 30 μC on the parallel network. The charge on each capacitor in the network adds up to 30 μC:

$$C_{parallel} = 12\ \mu F = C_1 + C_2 \Rightarrow \text{ Replace } C \text{ with } \frac{Q}{V} \Rightarrow$$

$$C_E = \frac{Q_{total}}{V} = \frac{Q_1}{V_1} + \frac{Q_2}{V_2} \Rightarrow \text{ In parallel all voltages are the same value:}$$

$$\text{so, } Q_{total} = Q_1 + Q_2$$

The 2-μF capacitor is 2/12 or 1/6 of the total capacitance, so it will take 1/6 of the 30 μC charge. Therefore, the 2-μF capacitor has 5 μC of charge, and the 10-μF capacitor has 25 μC of charge.

Practice Session Problems

Multiple Choice

1. The combination of *farad* · *ohm* is equivalent to which of the following units?
   - (A) Volt
   - (B) Ampere
   - (C) Second
   - (D) Watt
   - (E) Tesla

In the following circuit, all the bulbs have a resistance of 6 Ω. Initially, the switch is open. Use this diagram to answer questions 2 and 3.

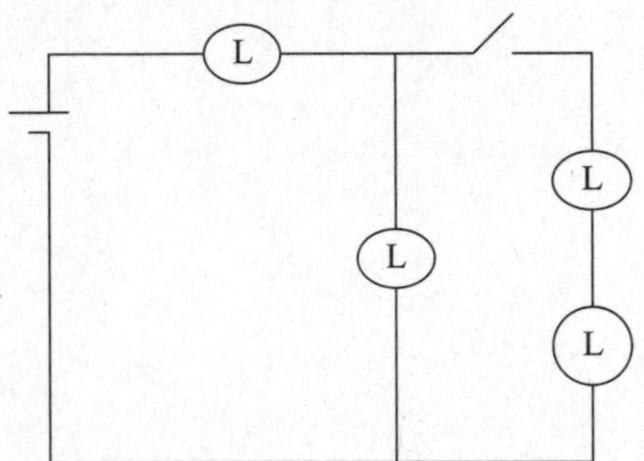

2. What is the equivalent resistance in the circuit when the switch is in the open position?
   - (A) 3 Ω
   - (B) 6 Ω
   - (C) 12 Ω
   - (D) 24 Ω
   - (E) 36 Ω

3. What is the equivalent resistance in the circuit when the switch is in the closed position?
   - (A) 24 Ω
   - (B) 10 Ω
   - (C) 8 Ω
   - (D) 6 Ω
   - (E) 4 Ω

4. What is the equivalent resistance of the following circuit? All the resistances are 6 ohms.

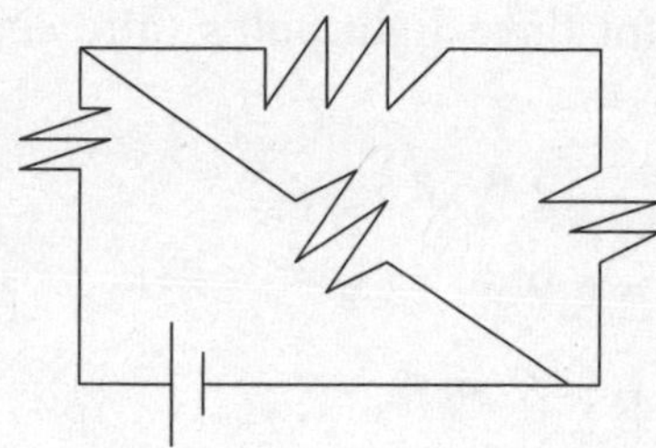

(A) 3 ohms
(B) 6 ohms
(C) 8 ohms
(D) 10 ohms
(E) 24 ohms

The following circuit diagram shows a capacitor in a circuit. All the resistances are 6 ohms. The battery is 12 V. The capacitor has a value of 5 μF. Use the diagram to answer questions 5 and 6.

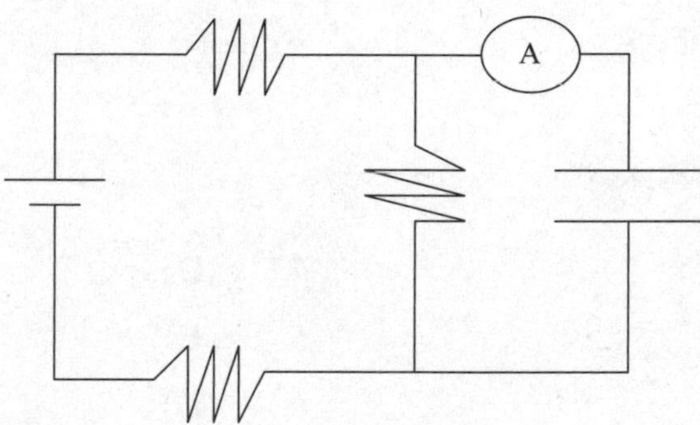

5. What is the charge on the capacitor?

(A) 60 μC
(B) 30 μC
(C) 20 μC
(D) 15 μC
(E) 5 μC

6. What is the current value in the Ammeter?

(A) 0.67 A
(B) 2.0 A
(C) 1.5 A
(D) 0 A
(E) Short circuit

Free Response

1. The specifications for three light bulbs (all behave according to Ohm's law) are as follows:

   Light 1: Power = 12 W at 12 V

   Light 2: Power = 6 W at 12 V

   Light 3: Power = 3 W at 12 V

   a. Draw a circuit diagram that shows the three bulbs in series with a 12-volt battery. Put an ammeter in your diagram to measure the total current.
   b. Determine the total power and operating current for this circuit.
   c. Draw a new circuit diagram that shows the three bulbs arranged in parallel with a 12-volt battery. Put an ammeter in your diagram to measure the total current.
   d. Determine the total power and operating current for this circuit.

Solutions

Multiple Choice

1. (C)
2. (C)
3. (B)
4. (D)
5. (C)
6. (D)

Free Response

1. a.

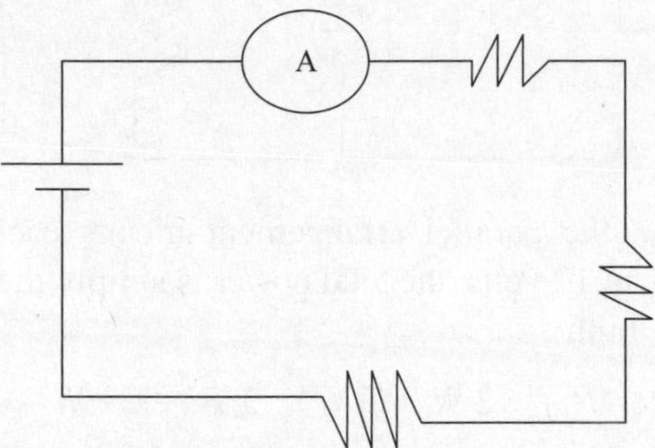

b. Determining the power and current for this setup requires determining the resistance of each bulb as follows:

$$P = \frac{V^2}{R} \Rightarrow R = \frac{V^2}{P}$$

$$R_{12\text{W}} = \frac{V^2}{P} = \frac{12^2\text{ V}}{12\text{ W}} = 12\ \Omega$$

$$R_{6\text{W}} = \frac{12^2\text{ V}}{6\text{ W}} = 24\ \Omega$$

$$R_{3\text{W}} = \frac{12^2\text{ V}}{3\text{ W}} = 48\ \Omega$$

$$\therefore R_E = 12\ \Omega + 24\ \Omega + 48\ \Omega = 84\ \Omega$$

So, the circuit has 84 ohms of resistance and is attached to a 12-volt battery, resulting in an operating current of $I_T = \frac{12\text{ V}}{84\ \Omega} = \frac{1}{7}\text{ A} \approx 0.14\text{ A}$. This gives a total power output of

$$P_{total} = VI\,(12\text{ V})(0.14\text{ A}) = 1.7\text{ W.}$$

Thus, the total power of three bulbs arranged in series is less than any of the individual power ratings at 12 volts. This results in very diminished light for each bulb, because in series, each bulb is receiving less than 12 volts.

c.

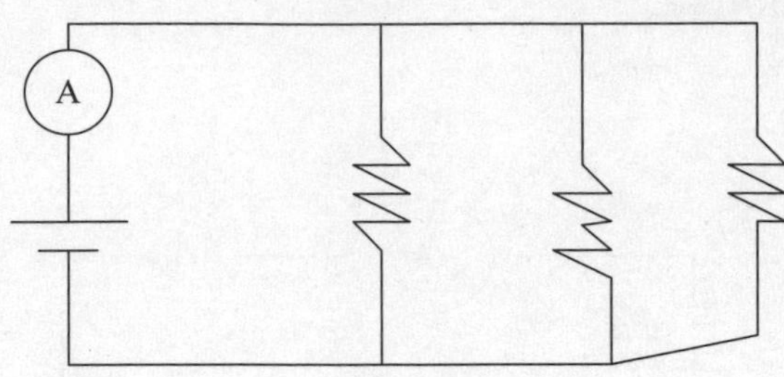

d. Because the parallel arrangement means each bulb is attached directly to 12 volts, the total power is simply the sum of the powers of each bulb:

$$P_t = 12\text{ W} + 6\text{ W} + 3\text{ W} = 21\text{ W}$$

The total current in the circuit can also be determined from the power relationship. The total current is

$$\Rightarrow P = VI \Rightarrow I = \frac{P}{V} = \frac{21\text{ W}}{12\text{ V}} = 1.75\text{ A}.$$

Chapter 13

Magnetism

EXAM OVERVIEW

The topic of magnetism brings together all the principles of electricity. Therefore, you must have a good understanding of electrostatics, charge behavior, current, and circuits before attempting to master magnetism. This chapter reviews the major topics in magnetism:

- **Force on moving charges**
- **Force on current carrying wires**
- **Moving charge in uniform circular motion in a magnetic field**
- **Sources of fields: wires and solenoids**
- **Induced currents, fields, and forces**
- **Faraday's law**

SOURCE OF ALL MAGNETISM

The source of all magnetic fields is the moving charge. A charge at rest produces an electrostatic field, and a charge in motion produces a magnetic field. Only like fields will interact with each other. Therefore, a static electric field interacts only with other static electric fields, and a static magnetic field interacts only with other static magnetic fields. A moving charge can interact with another external magnetic field or another moving charge.

The three most common fields you will be working with on the AP Physics exam are the field of a current carrying wire, the field of a solenoid (the classic electromagnet), and the fields of permanent magnets. In all cases, the magnetic field is a field line that completes a loop.

Many physics textbooks do not include the complete loop of a magnetic field in their illustrations. Rather, they highlight the areas of large field strength and line density. These areas are the poles. The magnetic field is always determined by the "north seeking south" convention. Thus, the direction of the magnetic field vector at any point will correspond to this convention.

The following diagram is the classic permanent magnetic field showing the poles marked. The field is a complete loop (that continues inside the magnet). The arrows indicate the direction of the field.

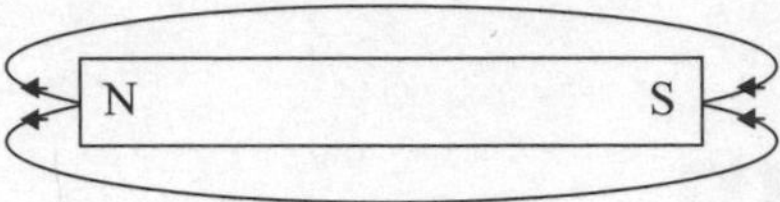

To produce a fairly constant strong field, two magnets' opposite poles can be placed near each other, as show here:

This is still a closed-loop field; it continues through each magnet and around the magnets with a very small line density. Because this part of the field is irrelevant and too large in area, it is rarely drawn in textbooks or in problems using this setup. The only area with a large line density (field strength) is the area shown between the north and south poles. This is how a fairly strong and constant magnetic field could be obtained for use in a typical physics problem requiring a constant field.

UNITS OF MAGNETIC FIELD

The symbol for a magnetic field is $\vec{B}$, and the unit of measure of a magnetic field is the tesla (T). This is a vector measurement. Magnetic field lines describe the field that exists in some point in space. The magnetic field strength vector is tangent to the field line at that point. Sometimes the magnetic field strength is called magnetic induction, although no modern textbook uses that term. A smaller unit measurement is the gauss; 1 gauss = 10^{-4} tesla. Although the tesla is the unit for magnetic field, a field equivalent to 1.0 T is rare in the typical high school laboratory situation; rather, most fields are in the milligauss range.

The dimensional equivalency of the magnetic field unit brings together a few areas of physics, as shown here:

$$Tesla = \frac{N}{A \cdot m}$$

Why the magnetic field unit, the tesla, is based on a force unit, the newton, is discussed in the next section.

MAGNETIC FORCE ON A MOVING CHARGE

If a moving charge exists in an external magnetic field, the field of the moving charge will interact with the external field, and the two fields will interact. The force will be large enough to bend the trajectory of the moving charge. This occurs with charged particles entering the Earth's atmosphere at the poles of the Earth's magnetic field. The charged particles end up spiraling in circular motion around the Earth's magnetic field lines. This effect also occurs in standard TV and computer monitors (before LCD screens). Moving charges emitted from a vacuum tube are bent by magnetic fields onto the proper spot on the screen.

By experimentation and observation, we can see that a charged particle moving through a magnetic field experiences a magnetic force perpendicular to the magnetic field lines and the velocity vector. This force depends on three factors:

$$F_B = qvB\sin\theta,$$

where q is the magnitude of charge, v is the velocity of the charge, and B is the magnitude of the magnetic field. The angle θ is defined as the angle between the velocity vector and the magnetic field vector. When the two vectors are 90 degrees apart, the force is a maximum. When the two vectors are parallel, the force is 0.

The direction of the magnetic force must be determined separately by what is called the "Right-Hand Rule for Force on a Moving Charge." To demonstrate, hold up your right hand (the right hand is used by convention for a positive charge moving) with your palm facing toward you, your thumb pointing up, and your first and second fingers pointing out, as shown here:

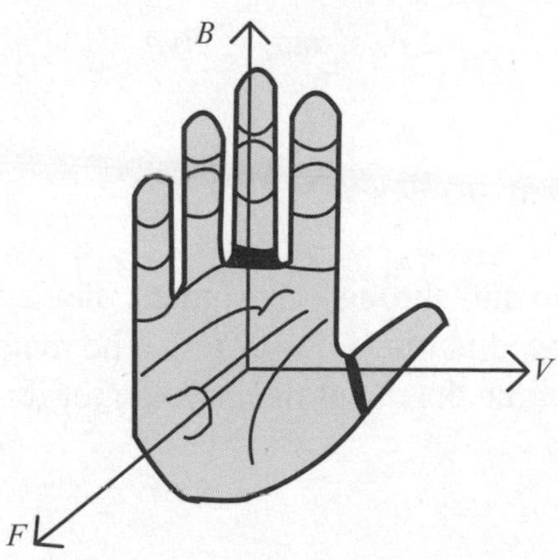

Your fingers represent the magnetic field vector, the palm represents the force on the moving charge, and the thumb represents the velocity of the charge. This is basically a memory device for remembering that the three vector quantities create a right-handed system.

The right-hand rule is exemplified by the following diagram, which shows a positive charge entering a region of magnetic field that is directed into the paper. Based on the right-hand rule (thumb to the right, fingers into the paper, and palm pointing upwards), this gives a force that is directed upwards initially as the charge enters.

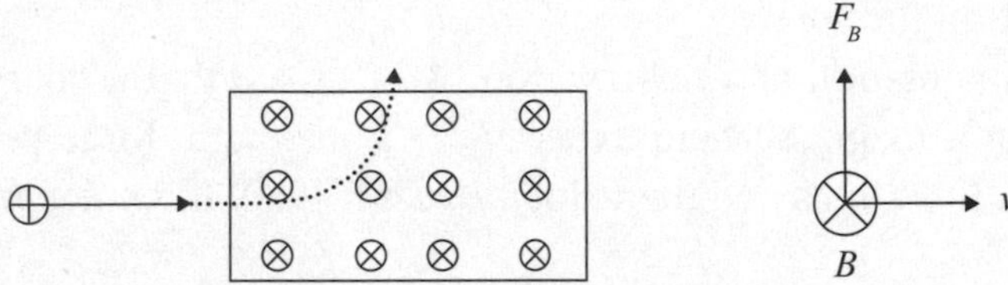

Notice how it forms a mutual right-handed system of three perpendicular vectors: *B*, *v*, and *F*.

The moving charge as it enters the field is initially pushed upward, resulting in a circular trajectory while it is in the field. This occurs because, as the magnetic force pushes the velocity of the charge upward, the new magnetic force must be perpendicular to the new velocity. Therefore, the magnetic force is always perpendicular to the velocity vector. We know of this situation from mechanics. This is also the behavior of a centripetal force on a particle moving in circular motion. Thus, any particle moving in a magnetic field and experiencing a magnetic force will experience the following:

$$\Sigma F_c = ma_c = Bvq$$

Sample Problem 1

An electron is moving through a magnetic field, as shown in the diagram. The electron's speed is $v = 1 \times 10^6$ m/s. The magnetic field strength is $B = 2 \times 10^{-4}$ T. Determine the radius of curvature for this electron's trajectory, and draw the trajectory.

Solution

The trajectory is shown in the diagram.

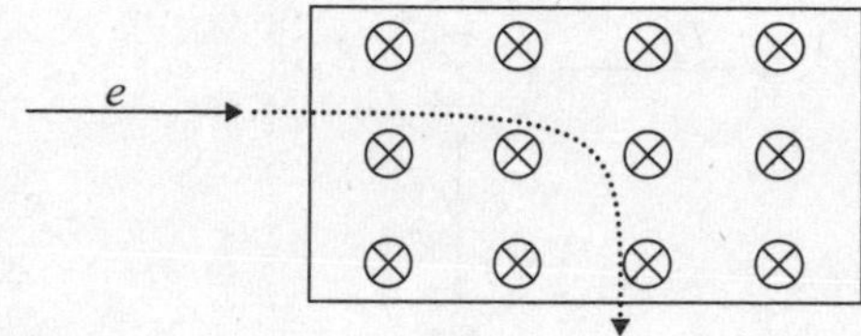

This is determined by the left-hand rule, which is the same as the right-hand rule, but we switch hands for a negative charge:

$$\Sigma F = ma_c = Bvq \sin 90 \Rightarrow m\frac{v^2}{R} = Bvq$$

$$R = \frac{mv}{Bq} = \frac{9.1 \times 10^{-31}\text{ kg} \cdot 1 \times 10^{6}\text{ m/s}}{2 \times 10^{-4}\text{ T} \cdot 1.6 \times 10^{-19}\text{ C}} = 0.028\text{ m}$$

FORCE ON A CURRENT-CARRYING WIRE

The same principle that causes a moving charge to experience a magnetic force will also cause a wire with current to experience a force. The rule to determine the direction of the force is the same as the moving charge, except the current direction replaces the moving charge's velocity vector. The force relationship is also very similar:

$$F_B = BIl \sin\theta,$$

where I is the current and θ is the angle between the current and the field. Again, if θ is a 90-degree angle, the magnetic force is a maximum; if the two vectors are parallel, there is no magnetic force.

Sample Problem 2

A wire carrying current is supported by cables and suspended in midair at an angle of 30 degrees with respect to the vertical. It is placed in a magnetic field as shown in the following diagram:

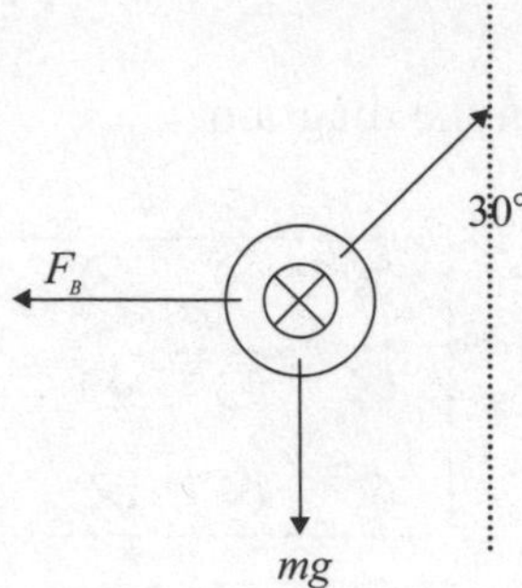

In the diagram the wire's current is directed into the page, which is indicated by the cross vector symbol. The current in the wire is 2 amperes, the magnetic field is 1.5 tesla, and the wire's length is 0.5 meters. Determine the mass of the wire and the direction of the magnetic field.

Solution

The magnetic field must be directed down to get the wire to be forced to the left:

$$\Sigma F_x = 0 = F_b - T_x$$

$$\Sigma F_y = 0 = T_y - mg \Rightarrow T \sin 30 = mg$$

$$\Rightarrow F_B = mg \cot 30$$

$$BIl \sin 90 = mg \cot 30$$

$$m = \frac{BIl}{g \cot 30} = \frac{1.5\ \text{T} \cdot 2\text{A} \cdot 0.5\ \text{m}}{10\ \text{m/s}^2 \cdot 1.73} = 0.087\ \text{kg}$$

FIELD OF A WIRE

The magnetic field of a wire is a complete circular path around the wire's current. This path's sense of north to south is determined by another right-hand rule. Position your right thumb (for a positive conventional current) in the direction of the current, and let your fingers naturally curl to correspond to the directional sense of the wires' magnetic field. The following diagram shows the field of a wire carrying current. The current is coming out of the page (indicated by the vector dot), and the field lines are shown with the correct sense indicated by arrows.

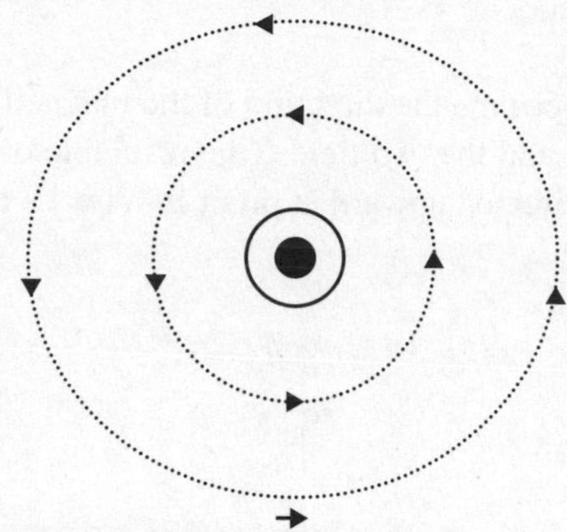

EX: Field of a wire carrying current. The wire's current is coming out of the page (indicated by the vector dot). The field lines are shown with the correct sense indicated by arrows.

At the top of the wire, we would say that the magnetic field is directed to the left (tangent to the circular field line at that point).

The strength of the field of a wire is determined by two factors: distance from wire and the magnitude of the current in the wire:

$$B_{wire} = \frac{\mu_o I}{2\pi r} = \frac{2kI'}{r},$$

where

$$k' = \text{magnetic constant} = 1 \times 10^{-7} \frac{\text{T} \cdot \text{m}}{\text{A}}$$

and

$$\mu_o = \text{permeability of free space} = 4\pi \times 10^{-7} \frac{\text{T} \cdot \text{m}}{\text{A}}$$

Sample Problem 3

Find the magnetic field at point *P* in the following diagram. The current in each wire is 2.0 amperes. The two wires are oriented in the page, and the currents are perpendicular to the plane of the page.

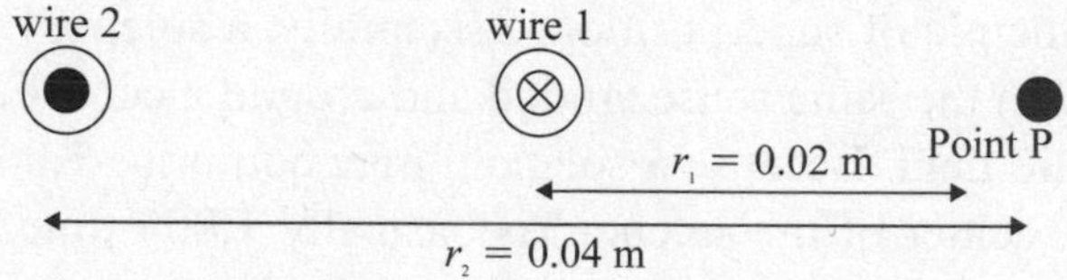

Solution

First, we must determine the direction of the magnetic field caused by each current. Then we must add the two fields (the principle of superposition).

Wire 2's field is directed upward at point P. Wire 1's field is directed downward at point P.

Thus, the net field will be downward and will equal the vector sum of these two fields:

$$B_{net} = \vec{B}_1 - \vec{B}_2 = \frac{\mu_o I_1}{2\pi r_1} - \frac{\mu_o I_2}{2\pi r_2} = \frac{\mu_o I}{2\pi}\left(\frac{1}{r_1} - \frac{1}{r_2}\right)$$
$$= \frac{(4\pi \times 10^{-7})\,(2\text{ A})}{2\pi}\left(\frac{1}{0.02} - \frac{1}{0.04}\right)$$
$$= 1 \times 10^{-5}\text{ T}$$

This field strength is about one-half of the Earth's horizontal component near the Earth's surface. Therefore, these wires with fairly large currents would just be able to move a compass around a bit if placed this close to it.

TWO OTHER IMPORTANT SOURCES OF MAGNETIC FIELDS

The solenoid is important in physics. It has a fairly strong and constant field through its core and at its ends. The solenoid's field becomes intense through the principle of superposition. Essentially, a solenoid is a coil of wire that is wrapped in the same sense around and around a core. Each loop creates a small magnetic field. Because a solenoid may comprise 1,000 loops, the net field inside the center of the solenoid is basically 1,000 times the strength of one loop.

Another way to increase the strength of the solenoid is by placing an iron core inside it. Iron is ferromagnetic, which means in the presence of an external field, it will create its own field, and the two fields will combine to create a larger field. Iron can hold a magnetic field up to about 2 T. This is quite large and quite useful in creating large fields; just think about the magnets in your speakers.

The direction of the magnetic field of one loop or a continuation of loops (solenoid) is also determined by the right-hand rule. The current is indicated by the curl of the fingers of the right hand, and the thumb naturally points to the north pole.

The following diagram shows the field of a loop. The field is still "circular" and would create a large complete loop; however, it is not drawn in the figure because it would be too large. Thus, only the north and south ends are drawn.

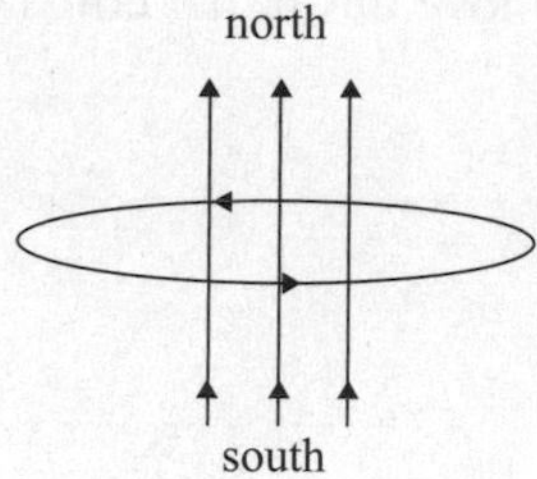

The field at the center of the loop is

$$B_{loop} = \frac{\mu_o I}{2R}.$$

The field of a solenoid throughout the center of the core is

$$B_{solenoid} = \mu_o nI$$

where n is turns per length.

INDUCED CURRENT

Whenever a changing magnetic field exists within a loop or whenever a loop moves through a magnetic field, induced current is created in the conductor. Faraday's law explains why a generator produces current. Induced-current production requires a flux of magnetic field that passes through a conductive loop and changes over time.

The formal representation of Faraday's law is

$$\varepsilon_i = -\frac{d\phi_b}{dt}, \text{ where } \phi_b = BA.$$

The negative sign refers to the direction of the induced current. This is essentially a way to conserve energy in the system. If energy created the changing flux, then the energy that appears in the system in the form of current cannot act to increase the total energy of the system. In other words, the energy put into this system will simply change from mechanical to electrical or vice versa.

The flux part is important. Without a field going through a conductive loop, flux cannot occur. The unit of flux is the weber:

$$Weber = T \cdot m^2 \text{, and } \frac{Weber}{s} = Volt$$

Typically, there are a few ways to create flux changes in conductors. One of the simplest is to have a rod move through a constant field, as shown here:

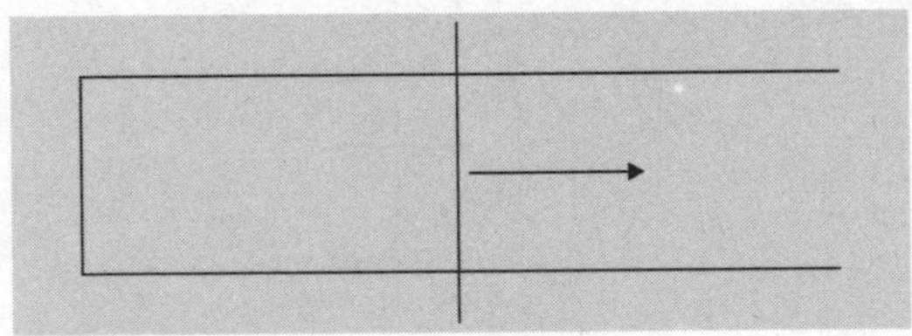

The gray region represents a constant field directed perpendicular into the plane of the paper, and the rod moves to the right. The flux would be increasing in this diagram as the area enclosed by the movable rod/loop gets larger over time.

Using Faraday's law, this example simplifies to

$$\varepsilon_i = Bvl,$$

where v is the velocity of the movable rod, and l is the length of the rod that creates one side of the rectangle of the enclosed loop.

We can figure out the direction of the induced current by using the right-hand rule for a moving charge: The rod is moving to the right (like a moving charge), and the field is directed inward, which leaves the palm upward. So the induced current is directed upward at that part of the rod. That means an induced magnetic force will be on the movable rod because it is now a current-carrying conductor in an external field. This new induced force is directed to the left on the rod. It directly opposes the motion of the rod. This is what the negative sign is about in the law. The energy does not come for free; rather, you will work against this induced force.

Another way to induce current is to have a set conductive loop linked to a magnetic field that changes over time through the loop. A simple version of this is to take small permanent magnets and move them in or out of a solenoid that has its ends connected to form a complete loop. The solenoid will have an induced current within its wire as long as the permanent magnet is moving. Here is an illustration:

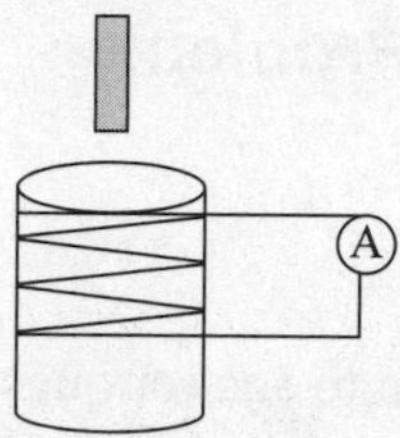

If the north end of the magnet is pushed into the solenoid, the solenoid will create a north at its top end to "oppose" the changing field. When the magnet is inside the solenoid and begins to move out of the solenoid, the solenoid will try to "oppose" the changing field and create a south at the top end. This is an attempt to keep the magnet from leaving. Loops or induced currents always behave this way, trying to "save a dying field" or "kill an increasing field." Just think that whatever field is created will do so with an opposing force on the changing object.

Practice Session Problems

Multiple Choice

Use the following diagram to answer questions 1 and 2.

1. A wire is shown with current moving as indicated. What is the direction of the magnetic field caused by the wire at point P?

   (A) Toward the top of the page

   (B) Toward the bottom of the page

   (C) Into the page

   (D) Out of the page

   (E) No field exists at that point.

2. An electron moves to the right at point P in the diagram. What is the direction of the magnetic force on the electron at point P?

   (A) Toward the top of the page

   (B) Toward the bottom of the page

   (C) Into the page

   (D) Out of the page

   (E) No force exists at that point.

3. An electron of charge e and mass m moves in complete circular orbit in a magnetic field of strength B. The radius of the orbit is R. The speed is constant at v_o. What is the period of circular orbit?

   (A) $T = 2\pi\frac{m}{Be}$

   (B) $T = 2\pi\frac{e}{Bm}$

   (C) $T = \frac{2\pi m v_o}{R}$

   (D) $T = \frac{2\pi m v_o}{B}$

   (E) $T = \frac{2\pi v_o}{Be}$

4. If the speed of the electron described in question 3 is doubled, what is the new period (T') of circular motion compared with the period determined in question 3?

(A) $T' = T_o$

(B) $T' = 2T_o$

(C) $T' = 4T_o$

(D) $T' = \frac{T_o}{2}$

(E) $T' = \sqrt{2}T_o$

5. An electron moves through a magnetic field with a speed of 2/3 c. An observer measures a magnetic force of zero on the electron. Which of the following statements could explain the observation?

I. The electron speed is too fast for a magnetic field to interact with it.
II. The electron will not interact with the magnetic field because it is a negative charge.
III. The electron is traveling parallel to the magnetic field lines.

(A) I

(B) II

(C) III

(D) I and III

(E) I and II

Free Response

1. Two wires with currents in opposite directions are shown in the following diagram. Determine the force on wire 1 caused by wire 2 in terms of I, r, l, and any other constants. Each wire has a current of I, and each wire has a length of l.

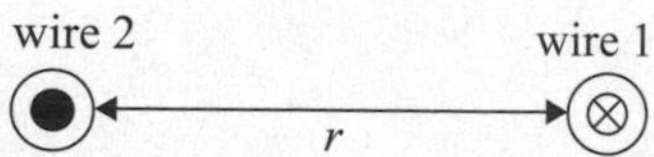

2. An electron is shot into a magnetic field as shown. The electron is projected into the field using an electron gun composed of two plates at a difference of potential V that accelerates the charge into the field. Determine the radius of orbit of the electron in terms of e, V, m, and B. Draw the trajectory of the charge.

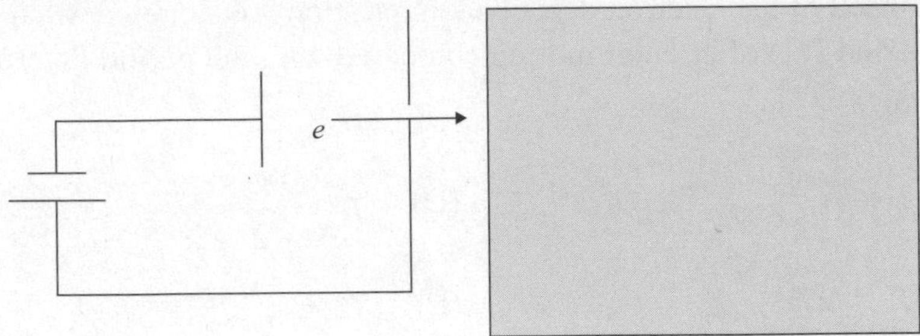

region of magnetic field directed into the plane of the paper

3. A conductive loop of resistance R travels through a region of magnetic field B_o with a speed of v_o. It maintains this speed the whole time. The loop's dimensions are a by a. The region of field B is $4a$ wide, as shown here:

region of B directed out of the page

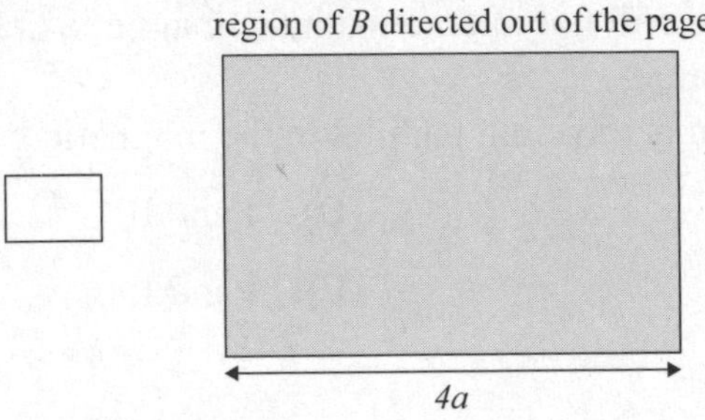

a. Sketch a graph of the flux through the loop as a function of the position of the leading edge of the loop, starting at the point where the leading edge of the loop just hits the field region.

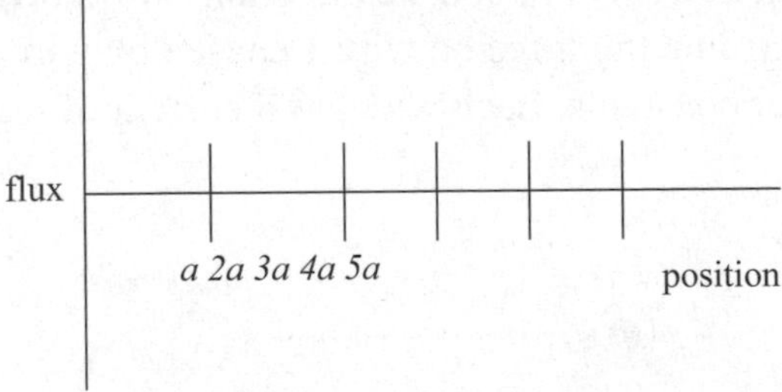

b. What is the current in the loop at the instant the loop breaks into the field?

c. What is the current in the loop when the loop is completely in the field?

d. What is the magnetic force on the loop the instant it breaks into the field?

Solutions

Multiple Choice

1. (D)
2. (A)
3. (A)
4. (A)
5. (C)

Free Response

1. $F_{wire2} = \dfrac{\mu_o I^2 l}{2\pi r}$. This force is directed to the right.

2. $R = \sqrt{\dfrac{2mV}{B^2 e}}$. The trajectory would be a circular path directed downward initially.

3. a.

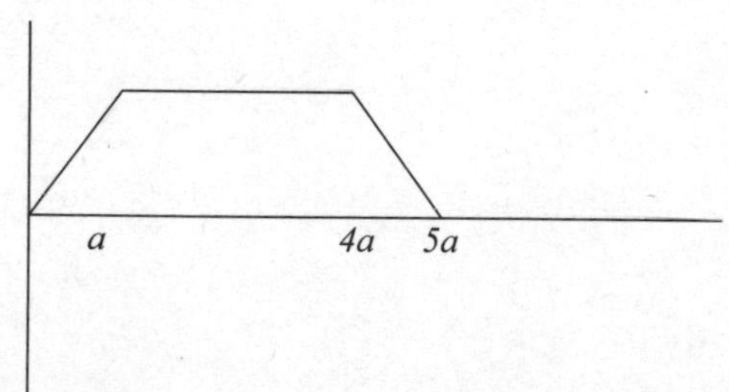

b. $i = \dfrac{B_o v_o a}{R}$

c. 0

d. $F_B = \dfrac{B_o\,(B_o v_o a)\,a}{R} = \dfrac{B_o^2 a^2 v_o}{R}$. This force is directed to the left.

Chapter 14

Geometrical Optics

For Physics B Test Takers

EXAM OVERVIEW

Two principles are at the heart of geometrical optics:

1. Light travels in straight lines.
2. Light will bend in accordance with Snell's law at the interface of two media.

These two principles and a little geometry will give you the tools you need to solve most optics problems.

THE NORMAL

As it relates to reflection and refraction, the **normal** is defined as the perpendicular line to the boundary of the interface between two mediums. The normal is important in optics because all the angles in geometrical optics are measured with respect to the normal.

The following diagram shows light reflecting off a mirror, with the incident angle measured with respect to the normal:

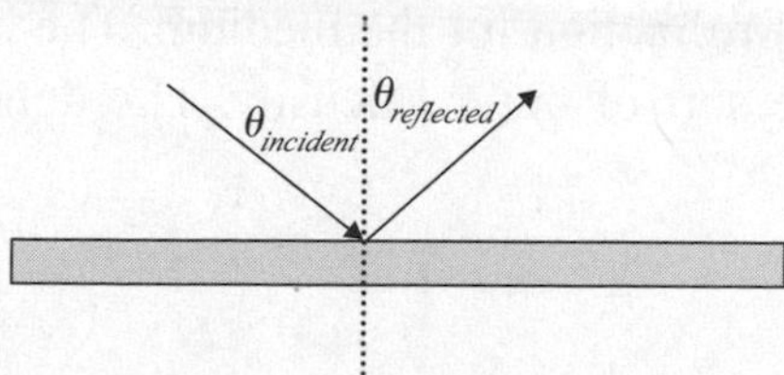

This also shows the law of reflection, which states that

$$\theta_{incidence} = \theta_{reflection}.$$

Sample Problem 1

A ray of light strikes a completely mirrored surface as shown in the diagram. Determine the unknown angle θ.

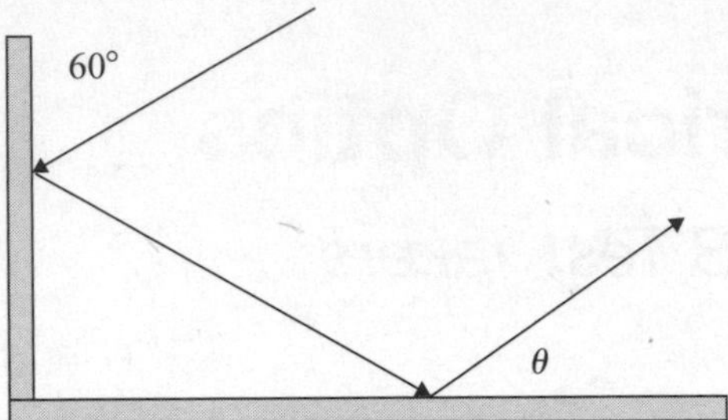

Solution

Solving this problem requires us to draw the normal for the incident light and work through the geometry from that point. The unknown angle is 30 degrees.

The problem would be more interesting if the second mirror were at an angle other than 90 degrees to the first mirror.

SNELL'S LAW AND REFRACTION

Refraction occurs when light traveling in one medium is incident in a second medium. The speed of light will change in the second medium. This causes the light to bend at the interface of the two media. The exception to the bending is when the angle of incidence is 0 degrees. The law that explains this behavior is called Snell's law:

$$n_1 \sin \theta_{inc} = n_2 \sin \theta_{refraction},$$

where n is the index of refraction for the medium. The index of refraction can be thought of as some sort of optical density. The definition of the index of refraction is

$$n = \frac{c}{v_{medium}},$$

where c is the speed of light and v_{medium} is the speed of light in the medium. The index of refraction for glass is about 1.5. Thus, the speed of light in glass is about $\frac{2}{3}c$. It is impossible to have an index of refraction greater than the speed of light, so if you ever get a value for n that is greater than c, you will know that you need to recheck your algebra.

You need to understand refraction from a visual perspective. The light ray undergoing refraction will bend *away* from the normal when going from one medium to another that is less dense. The ray will bend *toward* the normal when going from one medium to another that is more dense. Here is an example from air to glass ($n_{air} = 1$):

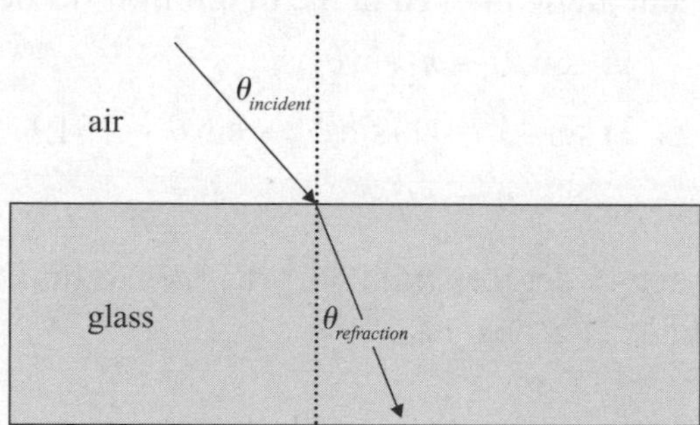

Notice that the light bends toward the normal in the diagram.

Sample Problem 2

Draw the light refracting through the following prism, which is a 45-45-90 prism. Determine the angle above or below the horizontal that the beam emerges with. The index of refraction for the glass block is 1.3.

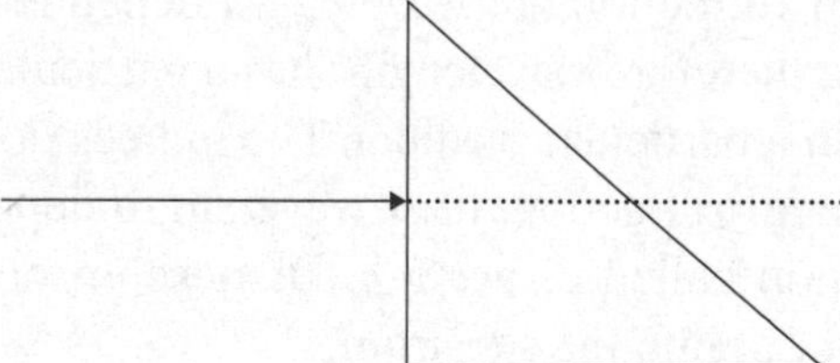

Solution

First, we sketch what will happen. The light *will not bend* at the first interface. Any light that is incident perpendicular to a surface ($\theta_{inc} = 0$) will not bend at the interface. Next, we draw a normal on the other interface to determine the angle of incidence, and then draw the second point of refraction bending away from the normal. Our diagram will look like this:

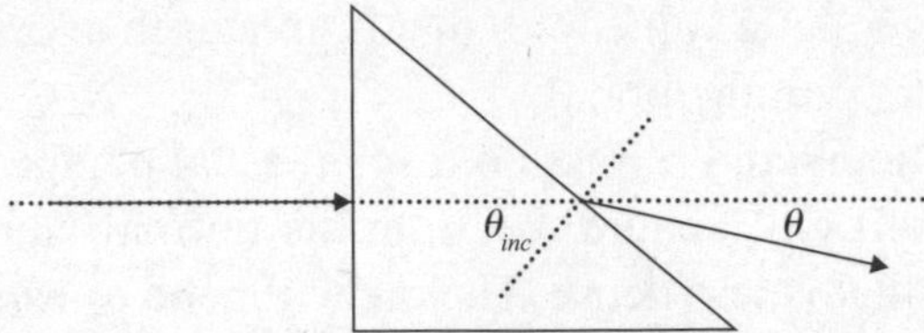

We use Snell's law to determine the unknown angle. Our equation must reflect that the incident angle marked in the diagram is 45 degrees:

$$n_1 \sin\theta_1 = n_2 \sin\theta_2$$

$$(1.3)\sin 45 = (1)\sin\theta \Rightarrow \sin\theta = .919$$

$$\theta = 66.8^\circ$$

Then we subtract 45 degrees from 66.8 degrees to find that the angle indicated in the diagram is 21.8 degrees.

EXPERIMENTAL FACTS ABOUT REFRACTION

Here are some interesting facts that can be seen with some laboratory investigations with refraction:

- When light strikes the boundary between two media, there will always be some reflected light and some refracted light. The amount of each depends on the media.
- The indices of refraction are wavelength dependent. Each color in the spectrum (and therefore wavelength) has a particular value for the index of refraction in a particular medium. The indices do not vary greatly, but at large angles of refraction, their wavelength dependence shows up in the phenomenon called dispersion. **Dispersion** occurs when refracted light is spread out into the spectrum.

THE CRITICAL ANGLE

The critical angle is the angle at which all the incident light is reflected back by an interface boundary. This can only occur when going from one medium to another medium that is less dense. This reflection has a name as well: **total internal reflection**. Here is a diagram of this phenomenon:

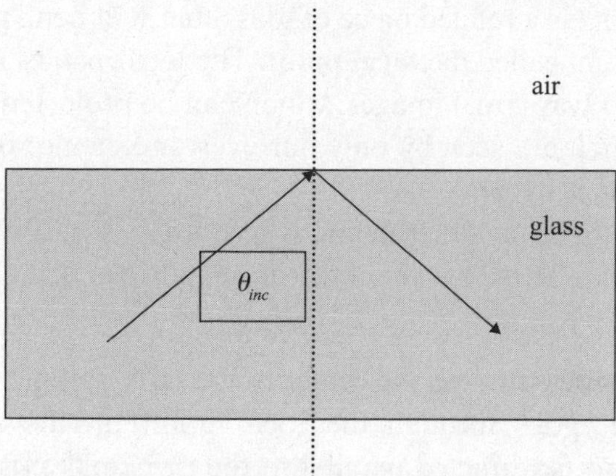

The light ray begins in the glass block, hits the interface between the glass and the air, and reflects back into the block. The light never gets out. If the light is incident at an angle greater than one particularly critical angle, all the light will be reflected and none will be refracted.

That critical angle is easy to determine. The boundary condition is simply that the refracted angle must be 90 degrees. That means we would not see the light exit the glass.

$$n_1 \sin \theta_{critical} = n_2 \sin 90^\circ$$

$$\sin \theta_c = \frac{n_2}{n_1} \cdot 1$$

$$\theta_c = \sin^{-1}\left(\frac{n_2}{n_1}\right)$$

If the second medium is air, the expression becomes

$$\theta_c = \sin^{-1}\left(\frac{1}{n_1}\right).$$

The critical angle is an interesting phenomenon and is the reason fiber optic cable works. The light pulses in fiber optic cable never exit the cable because the light bounces off of the boundary at angles always greater than the critical angle. This ensures that the light pulse travels down the cable at the speed of light in that medium and none of the pulse is lost as a result of refraction out of the cable.

LENSES AND MIRRORS

Lenses and mirrors both work with the same mathematics and geometry. So if you learn to apply the lens equation in one situation, it also has an analog situation with mirrors.

Basically, a lens is a refined piece of glass that will bend parallel light rays through an exact point called the **focal point**. The lens enables images of objects to be formed in two ways: real images, which can be projected on a screen, and virtual images, which are seen by only our eyes and cannot be projected (like the image in a plane mirror).

The lens has three rays that define where images will be with respect to the object placement. These are the three principal rays that can be drawn in a **ray diagram**:

1. A ray that goes through the center of the lens without bending.
2. A ray that goes through the focal point on the incident side of the lens and is refracted parallel to the principal axis on the real side of the lens.
3. A ray that is parallel to the principal axis on the incident side of the lens and refracts through the focal point on the real side of the lens.

Here is an example of a ray diagram of a lens with focal point f and showing all three principal rays:

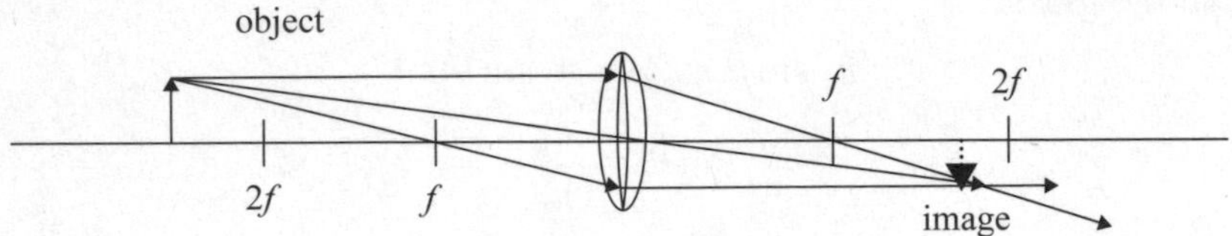

This geometry is represented by the lens equation:

$$\frac{1}{f} = \frac{1}{d_o} + \frac{1}{d_i}$$

This works for all lenses of all types, including diverging lenses, which have negative focal lengths.

CONVERGING LENSES AND SIGN CONVENTIONS

The following table organizes the possible image locations for converging lenses:

- All focal lengths are positive for converging lenses.
- All object distances are positive.

Focal length	Object position	Image position
$+f$	$d_o < f$	Negative and virtual, $d_i < 0$
	$f < d_o < 2f$	Real and > than $2f$
	$d_o > 2f$	Real and $f < d_i < 2f$

MAGNIFICATION IN LENSES

Magnification is the ratio of the image size to the object's size:

$$M = -\frac{d_i}{d_o}$$

The negative sign reminds us of the real image being inverted. The magnification of a virtual image will come out positive because of the virtual image's negative object distance. There is one object location that gives a magnification of 1.0. That location is twice the focal length. Try the math out for yourself.

Sample Problem 3

An object is placed at two different places in front of a lens. The lens has a focal length of *f*. In one position, the image produced is twice the magnification and is negative. In the other position, the magnification is twice also, but it is a positive magnification. Find both locations of the object.

Solution

The problem tells us that one location has to be greater than *f* and one location has to be less than *f*. We also know that the virtual image distance will be a negative value. The image distance in the first position is $d_i = 2d_o$.

$$\frac{1}{f} = \frac{1}{d_o} + \frac{1}{2d_o} \Rightarrow \frac{1}{f} = \frac{2}{2d_o} + \frac{1}{2d_o} \Rightarrow \frac{1}{f} = \frac{3}{2d_o}$$

$$\therefore d_o = \frac{3}{2}f$$

The second position follows similarly, except the image distance is negative:

$$\frac{1}{f} = \frac{1}{d_o} + -\frac{1}{2d_o} \Rightarrow \frac{1}{f} = \frac{2}{2d_o} - \frac{1}{2d_o} = \frac{1}{2d_o}$$

$$\therefore d_o = \frac{f}{2}$$

Thus, $3f/2$ and $f/2$ are the two possible object locations.

Practice Session Problems

Multiple Choice

1. Which of the following statements about virtual images is (are) true?

    I. Virtual images are inverted.

    II. Virtual images are always smaller than the object.

    III. Virtual images can only be formed by diverging lenses.

    IV. Virtual images can be formed by both lenses and mirrors.

    (A) I and II only
    (B) II only
    (C) III only
    (D) I and III only
    (E) IV only

2. An image of an object is formed by a lens. The focal length of the lens is +20 cm. The object is placed 40 cm from the lens. Where is the image located?

    (A) 20 cm on the same side of the lens as the object
    (B) 40 cm on the same side of the lens as the object
    (C) 60 cm on the opposite side of the lens as the object
    (D) 40 cm on the opposite side of the lens as the object
    (E) The image cannot be located because it is virtual.

Free Response

1. A prism has an index of refraction of $n_{blue} = 1.46$ and $n_{red} = 1.42$. White light is incident in the glass-to-air interface at an angle of 40 degrees.
    a. Using the information below, draw a diagram showing the refraction from prism to air:

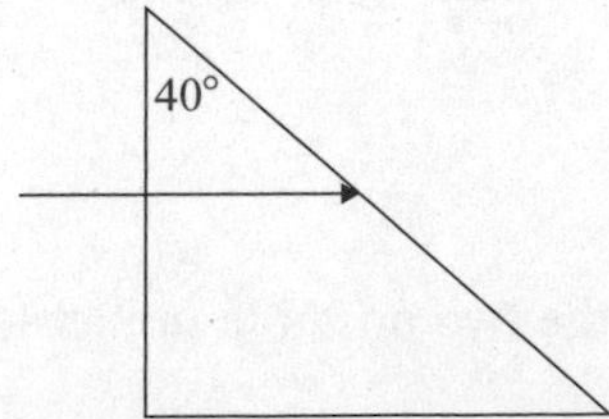

b. Determine the angle between the red and blue light rays as they emerge from the prism.
c. Determine the angle of the prism for which absolutely no light will refract out of the prism.

2. Draw a ray diagram of a convex mirror of focal length f and an object located at $3f$.

Solutions

Multiple Choice

1. (E)
2. (D)

Free Response

1. a.

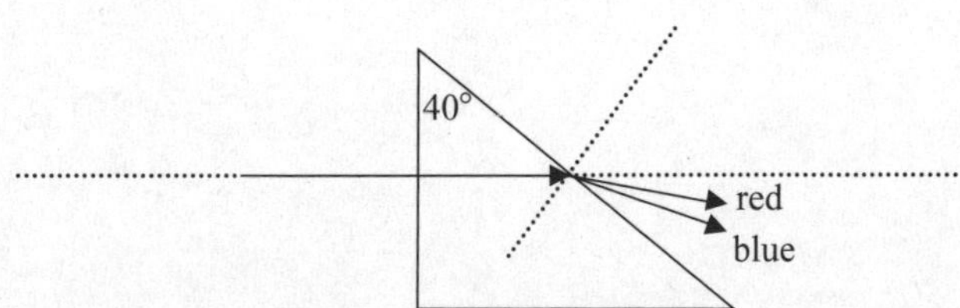

b. The angle between the red and blue is 5.8 degrees.
c. The angle of the prism at which no light will emerge is the 43.2-degree angle where the 40-degree angle is currently located. This is because all the light will be totally internally reflected at 43.2 degrees.

2.

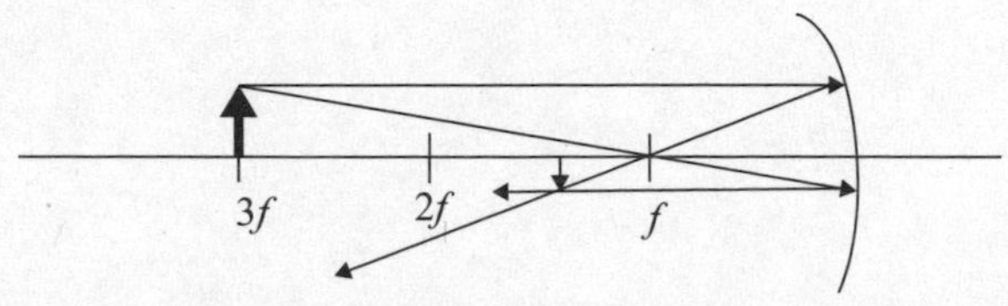

Chapter 15

Modern Physics

For Physics B Test Takers

EXAM OVERVIEW

The term *modern physics* refers to the principles of physics developed since 1900. These principles include Planck's law of black-body radiation, atomic theory, quantum mechanics, and particle and nuclear physics. AP Physics B lightly touches on a few of the major ideas in some of these areas. This chapter focuses on the three major areas of modern physics covered by the AP Physics B curriculum:

- The complementary nature of light and the quantization of light
- The photoelectric effect
- The absorption and emission of light

COMPLEMENTARY NATURE OF LIGHT AND THE QUANTIZATION OF LIGHT

Planck's work with black-body radiation was essential in setting the stage for modern physics, revealing that light carried energy in quantized bundles now called photons. This idea undermined physicists' previous model of the energy of light moving in a wave. Planck's model predicted that light could have all possible energies in a continuous spectrum. During that time of transition in the world of physics, scientists dubbed the model the ultraviolet catastrophe. It was a "catastrophe" because it predicted that infinite power would be needed to radiate energy at frequencies approaching infinity.

Einstein added to this body of knowledge with his groundbreaking 1905 paper that used Planck's black-body radiation work as the foundation for his theories about the photoelectric effect. Two major ideas emerged from Einstein's work:

- Light radiates energy according to the following relationship:

$$E = hf,$$

where E is the energy of the light, h is Planck's constant, and f is the frequency of the light defined as follows.

$$h = 6.626 \times 10^{-34}\ \text{J} \cdot \text{s},$$

$$h = 4.14 \times 10^{-15}\ \text{eV} \cdot \text{s}$$

Planck's constant in eV · s can be very useful in solving problems involving light energies, which are typically given in eV units.

- Light behaves as both a wave and a particle. This is called the **complementary nature of light**. Which model of light is applicable depends on the experiment being conducted. If light is incident on two small slits (Young's double-slit experiment), the wave model of light applies, and interference of light is the idea behind the dark fringes. If light is incident on a metal surface and electrons start spraying off the metal, the particle model of light applies.

Sample Problem 1

A photon of light of 5 eV is used in an experiment. Determine the wavelength of this light.

Solution

$$E = hf \text{ and } c = f\lambda \Rightarrow E = h\frac{c}{\lambda}$$

$$\lambda = \frac{hc}{E} = \frac{(4.14 \times 10^{-15}\ \text{eV} \cdot \text{s})(3 \times 10^{8}\ \text{m/s})}{5.0\ \text{eV}}$$

$$= \frac{1.242 \times 10^{-6}\ \text{eV} \cdot \text{m}}{5.0\ \text{eV}} = 2.48 \times 10^{-7}\ \text{m}$$

The product of hc is used frequently in computations with light. So the value 1.242×10^{-6} eV m could be kept around when performing multiple computations with energy and wavelength of light.

Another important idea revealed by this sample problem is that 5 eV of light is ultraviolet light. The visible wavelength of the highest energy that we can see is about 380 nanometers. Thus, the edge of our visible spectrum is at about a light energy of 3.28 eV and a lower energy bound of 1.77 eV.

THE PHOTOELECTRIC EFFECT

Usually, the photoelectric effect is presented in a laboratory format. But the equipment cost is too high for most high school physics classes to conduct the photoelectric effect experiment in the classroom. Nonetheless, as a physics student, you must be aware of the typical photoelectric experiment and what each piece of equipment contributes to it, because the experiment is the topic of some problems on the AP Physics B exam.

The general idea of the photoelectric effect is pretty simple. It is also a significant physical effect used in many devices around us today. Any device that uses a phototube or photomultiplier (e.g., a light sensor or motion detector) relies on the photoelectric effect.

Essentially, if light of a specific energy is incident on a metal surface, the light will interact one to one with electrons in the metal. The interaction will be such that the light and the electron will conserve energy (like particles colliding). The light must have sufficient energy to at least "knock" an electron out of the atom. This energy is called the **work function**, usually denoted by the symbol φ. This energy is a property of the metal and varies from metal to metal.

If the light incident on the metal has energy greater than the work function, then the electron is released and will have extra kinetic energy. This kinetic energy will show up in the circuit created to analyze this process.

Because the electrons are ejected by a one-to-one interaction with the photons, the number of electrons (i.e., current) is proportional to the intensity of light (i.e., the number of photons). The following diagram shows a theoretical schematic of the apparatus for the photoelectric effect experiment:

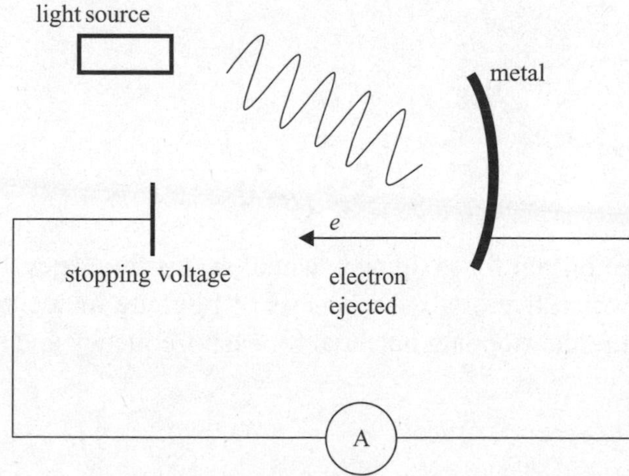

The apparatus is termed *theoretical* because most of it is enclosed in a black box and cannot be seen.

The **stopping voltage** is a measure of the kinetic energy of the electron. If we can just "stop" the electron from entering the circuit (and thus creating current in the ammeter), we can measure the maximum kinetic energy of the ejected electron.

By measuring the current and intensity, we can determine the relationship between intensity of light and current. This photoelectric relationship is simply a restatement of conservation of energy between the photon of light and the ejected electron.

The photoelectric system has two forms of energy: the light's energy and the energy necessary for the electron to overcome the metal's work function and be ejected. When the electron is ejected, any excess energy becomes kinetic energy. This kinetic energy is measured by the stopping potential. The work function is measured by investigating the frequency of light, which does not produce a current. A current will be present only if electrons are moving to the negative plate, and that will happen only at the point where the light has at least a minimum energy of the work function of the metal.

This relationship between the energies involved in the photoelectric effect is represented by the following equation:

$$E_{light} = \varphi + KE_{\max}.$$

The kinetic energy of the electron is found using the stopping potential measurement of the voltage across that negative plate. Each electron can be stopped by the value of the stopping voltage. Therefore, $KE_{\max} = eV$. An electron volt is one electron charge (e) times the stopping voltage (V). Putting this value into the relationship results in another relationship for the frequency of light:

$$E = \varphi + KE_{\max}$$

$$hf = \varphi + eV \Rightarrow V = \frac{h}{e}f - \frac{\varphi}{e}$$

This gives a relationship for stopping potential versus frequency. In a laboratory experiment in which five or six frequencies of light are incident on the metal, we could measure the stopping potential for each frequency and then graph the result. Let's try it.

Sample Problem 2

From the following data and graph of an experiment of the photoelectric effect, determine the work function and Planck's constant.

Frequency (Hz)	Stopping potential (V)
5.1×10^{14}	0.12
6.0×10^{14}	0.45
7.0×10^{14}	0.98
8.0×10^{14}	1.28
9.5×10^{14}	1.55

Stopping potential vs. frequency

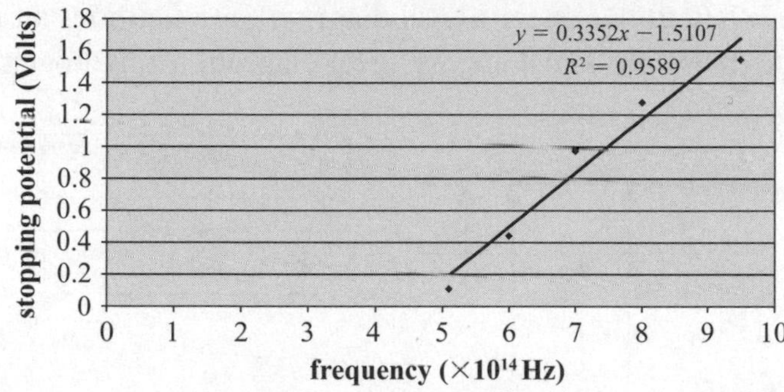

Solution

The graph gives us the answers. The work function is simply the x-intercept. You could eyeball this or draw an extension of the line. The answer should be around 4.5×10^{14} Hz. The value for Planck's constant comes from the slope. The slope of the graph is $\frac{h}{e}$. Therefore,

$$\frac{h}{e} = 3.35 \times 10^{-15}\ \text{eV} \cdot \text{s} \Rightarrow h$$
$$= \left(3.35 \times 10^{-15}\ \text{eV} \cdot \text{s}\right)\left(1.6 \times 10^{-19}\ \text{C}\right)$$
$$= 4.51 \times 10^{-34}\ \text{J} \cdot \text{s}$$

Well, this value for Planck's constant is about 20 percent less than the actual value, but remember this was an experimental question.

ABSORPTION AND EMISSION OF LIGHT

The typical light absorption or emission problem on the AP Physics exam centers on a "hypothetical" atom depicted in an "energy diagram." Using a hypothetical atom avoids the complexity of real atoms and their accompanying energy diagrams.

Underlying the idea of an atom absorbing or emitting light is another quantized property of light. Light incident on an atom can cause an electron in a ground state to move up to another excited state. If the light is energetic enough, it could even cause the electron to completely leave the atom, or **ionize**. This process of exciting up to another energy level can occur only if the light has the exact energy needed to bump an electron up from one level to another. This is the idea of **quantized energy**. If the light has too much energy, no excitation occurs. Similarly, if the light has too little energy, no excitation occurs.

An energy-level diagram shows the excited states the electrons are allowed to be in. Here is a fictitious energy-level diagram for a fictitious atom. (Look in your physics textbook for a real energy-level diagram for hydrogen.)

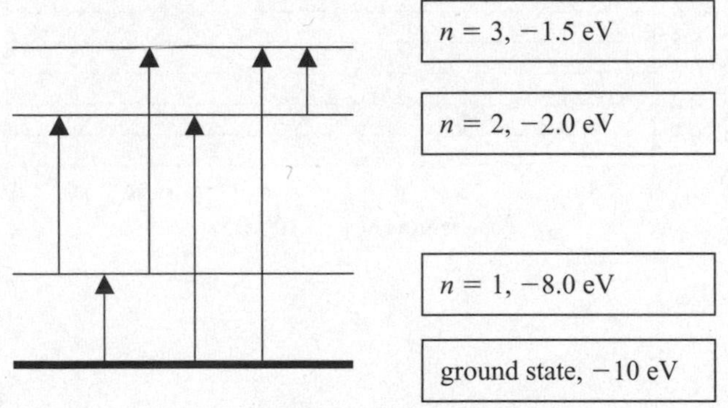

The arrows in the diagram show all the allowed transitions. For instance, an electron could gain 2.0 eV from a light source and jump from $n = 0$ to $n = 1$, gain 8 eV and jump from $n = 0$ to $n = 2$, or gain 8.5 eV and jump from $n = 0$ to $n = 3$. An electron could also gain 10.0 eV or greater and completely ionize. Another possible transition consists of electrons sitting in $n = 1$ and exciting to $n = 2$ or $n = 3$. Thus, energies of 6.0 eV, 6.5 eV, and 0.5 eV could also cause an electron to excite to another level.

The evidence of this occurring is in the **absorption spectrums** of atoms. Examples of these spectrums and pictures of the absorption that undoubtedly appear in your physics textbook would show that light of many wavelengths incident on a particular atom (hydrogen gas or sodium gas sources) actually has certain wavelengths of light not passing through the gas but rather absorbed by the gas. The wavelengths of the absorbed light correspond to the excited energy levels gained by the electrons in the atom.

The reverse of this phenomenon is also true. When electrons are in excited states, they can spontaneously jump down to a lower energy level, thereby releasing light of a wavelength and energy equal to the loss of energy in the jump to a lower energy level. In other words,

$$E_{light} = hf = E_n = E_{n-1}.$$

An electron drops 3.0 eV in an energy-level diagram, and then the atom will emit a light of

$$3.0\,\text{eV} = hf = \frac{hc}{\lambda} \Rightarrow \lambda = \frac{hc}{3.0\text{ eV}} = \frac{1.242 \times 10^{-6}\text{ eV}\cdot\text{m}}{3.0\text{ eV}} = 4.14 \times 10^{-7}\text{ m}.$$

Sample Problem 3

Here is an energy-level diagram for a hypothetical atom:

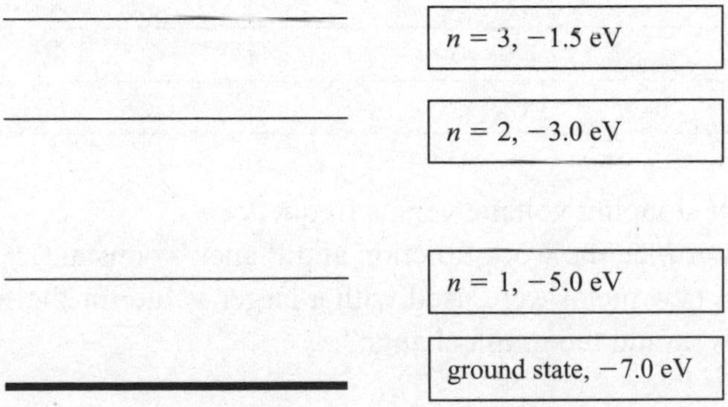

$n = 3$, -1.5 eV

$n = 2$, -3.0 eV

$n = 1$, -5.0 eV

ground state, -7.0 eV

What is the longest wavelength of light that could be emitted by this atom? Excited electrons exist at all energy levels.

Solution

The light of the longest wavelength is the light of the lowest energy. The lowest possible energy difference is between $n = 3$ and $n = 2$, a drop of 1.5 eV. We compute this wavelength of light as follows:

$$E = hf = \frac{hc}{\lambda} \Rightarrow \lambda = \frac{hc}{E} = \frac{1.242 \times 10^{-6}\text{ eV}\cdot\text{m}}{1.5\text{ eV}} = 8.28 \times 10^{-7}\text{ m}$$

This wavelength is too long to be visible light, but it would be considered infrared light.

Practice Session Problems

Free Response

1. A hypothetical atom has a ground state energy value of $E_o = -5.5$ eV. Determine the wavelength of the photon that will ionize this atom.

2. Here is a table of measurements made by a physics student performing the photoelectric effect experiment:

Frequency of light ($\times 10^{15}$ Hz)	Stopping voltage (volts)
1.25	0
1.75	2.0
2.0	3.0
2.25	4.0
2.75	5.8
3.0	6.6

a. Plot stopping voltage versus frequency.
b. Determine the work function and Planck's constant.
c. If a new metal were used with a larger value for the work function, how would the graph change?

Solutions

1. $\lambda = 2.26 \times 10^{-7}$ m

2. a.

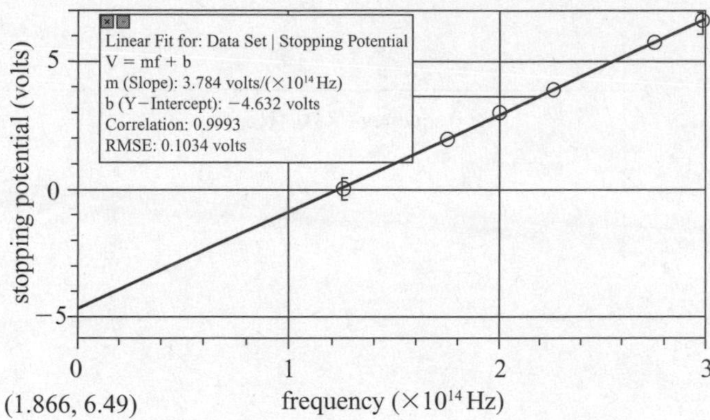

b. The work function is determined graphically; it is the y-intercept of the graph, $\varphi = 4.6$ eV. Because

$$E = KE + \varphi \Rightarrow KE = E - \varphi$$

$$KE = hf - \varphi$$

and KE is stopping voltage multiplied by charge

$$Ve = hf - \varphi \Rightarrow V = \frac{h}{e}f - \frac{\varphi}{e}$$

The slope of this graph is

$$\frac{h}{e} = 3.78 \times 10^{-14} \Rightarrow h = \left(3.78 \times 10^{-14}\right) e = 6.05 \times 10^{-33}\ \text{J} \cdot \text{s}$$

This value is a factor of 10 higher than the actual Planck's constant. Remember, this was an experiment.

c. If a new metal is used with a larger work function, this would shift the graph to the right. The slope would theoretically remain the same.

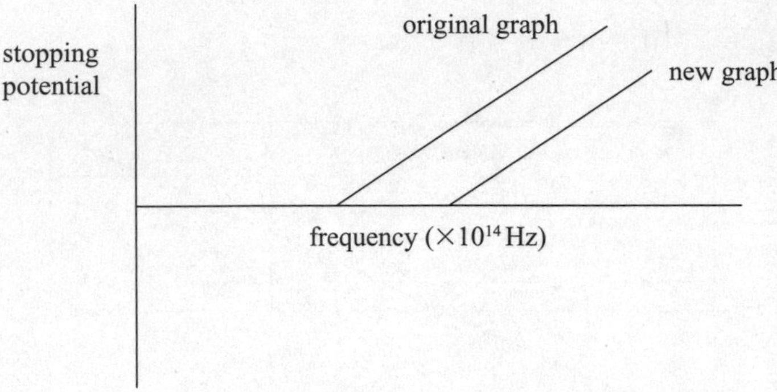

Chapter 16

Calculus Topics

For Physics C Test Takers

EXAM OVERVIEW

Calculus is a major part of the AP Physics C exam. Having gone through changes over the last few years, Physics C now places an increased emphasis on calculus applications. Therefore, all students enrolled in Physics C and preparing for the AP Physics exam should master calculus concepts in physics.

CALCULUS CONCEPTS TO MASTER

Most of the calculus that will appear on the AP Physics C exam will not be difficult. The actual derivatives and integrals will be familiar ones if you have practiced all year in your physics and calculus classes. Here is a list of the most common and useful derivatives and integrals that you should know and be prepared to encounter in the exam:

- Derivatives:

$$\frac{d}{dt}[At^n] = nAt^{n-1},\ \frac{d}{dt}\left[e^{kt}\right] = ke^{kt},\ \frac{d}{dt}[\sin \omega t] = \omega \cos \omega t,\ \frac{d}{dt}\left[\cos \omega t\right] = -\omega \sin \omega t,\ \frac{d}{dt}[\ln kt] = \frac{1}{t}$$

Note: The derivatives are in common physics symbols and language.

- Integrals:

$$\int At^n = \frac{A}{n+1}t^{n+1},\ \int \frac{dt}{t} = \ln|t|,\ \int e^{kt}dt = \frac{1}{k}e^{kt},\ \int \sin \omega t dt = -\frac{1}{\omega}\cos \omega t$$

You can probably find a few other useful concepts listed in the back of your physics textbook. Integrals that include the term $\frac{1}{\sqrt{x^2 + a^2}}$ are particularly useful in working with electric fields or magnetic fields, where the term occurs frequently in calculations of the distance between point charges and points in space. You will have access to the basic calculus concepts on your AP Physics equations sheet.

The following are other advanced mathematical ideas that come up during AP Physics C and thus should be mastered before the exam:

- The dot and cross product
- The idea of flux and the surface integral
- The idea of the line integral
- The binomial expansion approximation:
  $(1 + x)^n \approx 1 + nx$, when $x << 1$

CALCULUS IN KINEMATICS

AP Physics C includes calculus in the study of kinematics almost immediately. Therefore, proficiency in calculus early on in the course is very helpful.

We can derive the set of uniformly accelerated motion equations starting with a constant acceleration:

$$a = \frac{dv}{dt}, v = \frac{dx}{dt} \Rightarrow a = constant \Rightarrow dv = adt \Rightarrow$$

$$\int dv = \int adt \Rightarrow v = at + C, \text{ where } C = v_o$$

$$\Rightarrow v = v_o + at \Rightarrow \frac{dx}{dt} = v_o + at \Rightarrow dx = (v_o + at)dt$$

$$\Rightarrow \int dx = \int (v_o + at)dt \Rightarrow x = v_o t + \frac{1}{2}at^2 + C, \text{ where } C = x_o$$

These three equations can be derived from the calculus definitions in kinematics. Let's try some sample problems.

Sample Problem 1

An object travels with the velocity function of $v(t) = 2t + \frac{3}{2}t^2$. The object begins its motion at $x = 0$ m. Determine the following:

- The position of the object at $t = 4$ seconds
- The velocity of the object at $t = 2$ seconds
- The average velocity during the time interval from $t = 0$ to $t = 2$ seconds

Solution

Integrating the velocity expression will yield an expression for displacement. Once the displacement expression is determined we can determine the exact position of the object by evaluating the displacement at $t = 4$ seconds.

$$\int dx = \int \left(2t + \frac{3}{2}t^2\right) dt \Rightarrow x = t^2 + \frac{t^3}{2} + C \Rightarrow C = 0 \text{ m} \therefore x(t) = t^2 + \frac{t^3}{2}$$

$$x(4) = (4)^2 + \frac{4^3}{2} = 48 \text{ m}$$

The velocity of the object at $t = 2$ seconds is

$$v(2) = 2(2) + \frac{3}{2}(2)^2 = 10 \text{ m/s}.$$

What is the average velocity over the interval from $t = 0$ to $t = 2$ seconds?

Don't be fooled by this classic question. The definition of average velocity is still $v_{avg} = \frac{\Delta x}{\Delta t}$. Thus, Δx must be determined for the time interval:

$$x(2) = (2)^2 + \frac{1}{2}(2)^3 = 4 + 4 = 8 \text{ m}$$

The average velocity is $v = \frac{\Delta x}{\Delta t} = \frac{8 \text{ m} - 0 \text{ m}}{2 \text{ s} - 0 \text{ s}} = 4 \text{ m/s}$.

Sample Problem 2

An object moves with a velocity function of $v(t) = 10 \text{ m/s } (1 - e^{-0.2t})$ and begins its motion at $x = 0$ m. Determine the following:

- Acceleration of this object at time $t = 10$ seconds
- Velocity of the object at time $t = 10$ seconds
- Position of the object at time $t = 10$ seconds

Finally, sketch a graph of acceleration versus time.

Solution

The acceleration function appears often in physics, so make sure you are comfortable with its behavior:

We calculate the object's acceleration when $t = 10$ seconds as follows:

$$a = \frac{dv}{dt} = \frac{d}{dt}\left[10\left(1 - e^{-.2t}\right)\right] = -0.2 \cdot -10 \cdot e^{-0.2t} = \left(2 \text{ m/s}^2\right) e^{-0.2t}$$

$$a(10) = \left(2 \text{ m/s}^2\right) e^{-0.2(10 \text{ sec})} = 2 \cdot e^{-2} = \frac{2}{e^2} = 0.27 \text{ m/s}^2$$

The object's velocity is

$$v(10s) = 10(1 - e^{-0.2(10)}) = 10(1 - 0.135) = 8.65 \text{ m/s}.$$

We calculate position (x) like this:

$$x = \int vdt = \int 10\left(1 - e^{-0.2t}\right)$$

$$= 10t - 10 \cdot (-5) \int e^{-0.2t}(-.2)dt = 10t + 50e^{-0.2t} \Rightarrow$$

However, we must integrate with limits of $t = 0$ to $t = t$:

$$x = 10t + \left[50e^{-0.2t}\right]_0^t = 10t + 50e^{-0.2t} + 50 = 50 + 10t + 50e^{-0.2t}$$

$$\therefore x(10 \text{ sec}) = 50 + 10(10) + 50e^{-(0.2 \cdot 10)} = 150 + 6.76 = 156.76 \text{ m}$$

Here is our graph:

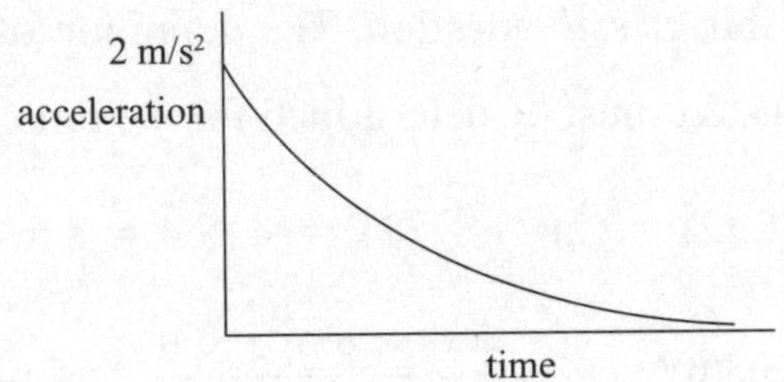

THE RESISTIVE FORCE PROBLEM

The resistive force problem is used frequently by physics teachers and on the AP Physics C exams. Students often call the resistive force problem the "air resistance" problem. Because air resistance is a force that depends on velocity, the mathematics of this problem becomes quite interesting.

Typically, the air resistance force is defined by $\vec{F}_r = -b\vec{v}$. Notice that the resistive force is always opposite the velocity vector.

Let's use the definition of resistive force in a ball falling freely from a very tall building. The free-falling ball is dropped from rest, gains speed because of the gravitational force, and experiences an increasing resistive force the entire time it is falling.

A free-body diagram for this event at some time $t > 0$ is shown here:

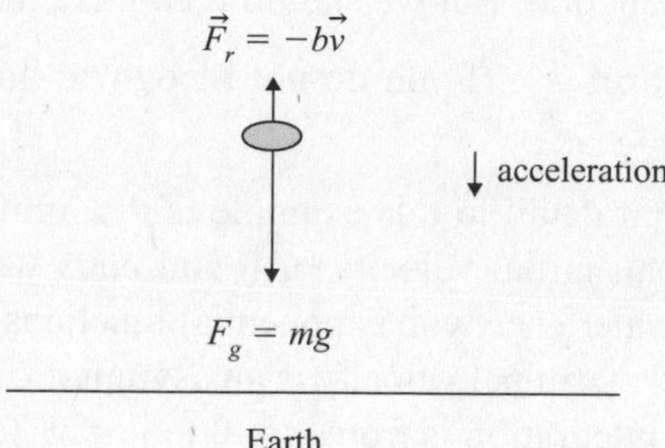

Now we should write Newton's second law for the falling mass:

$$\sum F = m\frac{dv}{dt} = mg - bv$$

This is called a **differential equation** because it contains differentials. We can solve for one of the variables in the equation in terms of another. We want to know what the velocity of the object is at any given time, so we want to solve for velocity in terms of time.

Our first step in reaching a solution is to recognize another physical property of this falling ball situation: **terminal velocity**. If the ball falls for a long enough period, then the ball's resistive force will eventually equal the ball's weight. When this happens, the net force on the ball will become 0. The ball will still continue to fall, but at a terminal velocity. This value is determined completely by the mass of the ball and the constant b. In our example, we can determine the terminal velocity as follows:

$$\sum F = 0 = mg - bv_t \Rightarrow v_t = \frac{mg}{b}$$

This term will appear in our differential equation when we manipulate the equation a bit:

$$\sum F = m\frac{dv}{dt} = mg - bv$$

(divide all terms by b) $\quad \Rightarrow \frac{m}{b}\frac{dv}{dt} = \frac{mg}{b} - v$

(recognize terminal velocity) $\quad \Rightarrow \frac{m}{b}\frac{dv}{dt} = v_t - v$

(rearrange equation to be able to integrate) $\quad \Rightarrow \frac{dv}{v_t - v} = \frac{b}{m}dt$

$$\int \frac{dv}{v_t - v} = \int \frac{b}{m}dt$$

The result of this manipulation is a bit more difficult to deal with than just integrating a simple function. But we should recognize that the left side of the expression is in the form $\frac{du}{u}$. If you do not recognize this fact, you probably need to review your calculus.

Another important detail in this example is the limits of integration. The problem begins with an initial velocity of 0 and ends with terminal velocity. However, after some experience with exponential functions and natural log functions, we should realize terminal velocity is an asymptotic value in our solution. So the actual limit of integration is from $v = 0$ to $v = v$. Terminal velocity cannot be used as a limit of integration.

Back to our differential equation, with the correct limits of integration:

$$\int_{v=0}^{v=v} \frac{dv}{v_t - v} = \int_{t=0}^{t=t} \frac{b}{m}$$

$$(-\ln|(v_t - v)|]_0^v = \left(\frac{b}{m}t\right]_0^t$$

$$\ln(v_t - v) - \ln(v_t) = -\frac{b}{m}t$$

$$\ln\frac{(v_t - v)}{v_t} = -\frac{b}{m}t$$

$$\frac{(v - v_t)}{v_t} = e^{-\frac{b}{m}t} \Rightarrow v = v_t\left(1 - e^{-\frac{b}{m}t}\right)$$

This resistive force problem has plenty of details in its lines of mathematics. You need to master these details and work as many calculus problems as you can so that you can master some of the trickier aspects of problems involving resistive forces.

The graph of the solution to this problem is a very familiar graph in the world of physics:

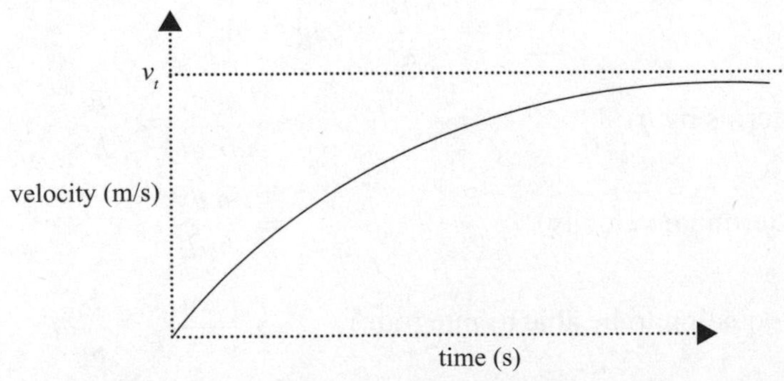

Sample Problem 3

From the resistive force problem just discussed, determine the acceleration function and sketch its graph.

Solution

The acceleration function is

$$a(t) = ge^{-\frac{b}{m}t}.$$

The graph looks like this:

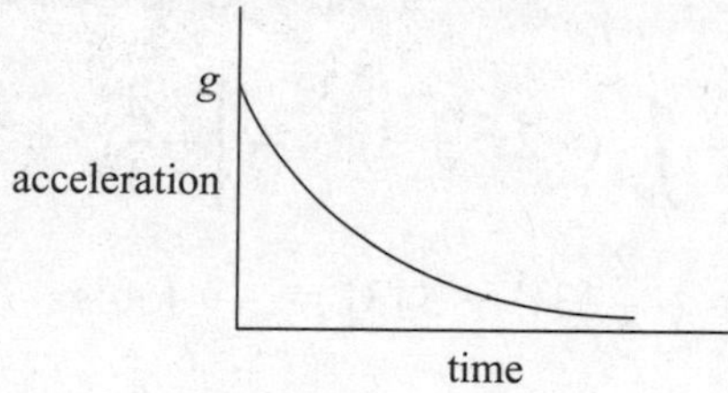

CALCULUS IN WORK AND ENERGY

There are two major calculus definitions in the area of work and energy. The definition of work is

$$W = \int \overrightarrow{F} \cdot \overrightarrow{dx}.$$

The connection of work, potential energy, and conservative force gives rise to the following definition:

$$F_{conservative} = -\frac{dU}{dx}$$

Using these definitions, we can define potential energy functions for springs or gravitation:

$$\Delta U_{spring} = -W_s = \int_0^x \overrightarrow{F_s} \cdot \overrightarrow{dx} = -\int (F_s dx) = -\int (-kx)\,dx = \frac{kx^2}{2}$$

We can do the same for the potential energy of the gravitational force, F_g. You can do this proof as an exercise for yourself.

$$U_g = -\frac{Gmm}{r}$$

Sample Problem 4

A nonlinear spring is defined by the relationship $F_s = -2x^2 + 3$. Determine the work done by the spring in stretching from $x = 0$ meters to $x = 3$ m.

Solution

$$W_s = \int_0^3 (-2x^2 + 3)dx = \left[-\frac{2}{3}x^3 + 3x\right]_0^3$$

$$= -\frac{2}{3}[3]^3 + 3[3] = -9 \text{ Joules}$$

The spring force did –9 J of work, and the spring gained 9 J of potential energy.

Practice Session Problems

Multiple Choice

1. A mass is falling through a viscous fluid. The resistive force relationship is given the expression $F_r = -kmv^2$. What is the terminal velocity of the mass?

(A) $v_t = \sqrt{\frac{mg}{k}}$

(B) $v_t = \sqrt{\frac{k}{mg}}$

(C) $v_t = \sqrt{\frac{g}{k}}$

(D) $v_t = \sqrt{\frac{k}{g}}$

(E) $v_t = \sqrt{kg}$

2. The potential energy of a particular conservative force is expressed as $U(x) = -2x^2 + 3x$. At what position on the x-axis is the conservative force 0?

(A) $x = -\frac{9}{4}$ m

(B) $x = -\frac{3}{4}$ m

(C) $x = \frac{9}{4}$ m

(D) $x = \frac{3}{4}$ m

(E) $x = 0$ m

3. The acceleration of an object is expressed by this function: $a(t) = ge^{-\frac{b^2}{2m}t}$. What is the terminal speed of the object?

(A) $v_t = \frac{mg}{2b^2}$

(B) $v_t = \frac{2mg}{b^2}$

(C) $v_t = \frac{b^2}{2\text{ m}}$

(D) $v_t = \frac{2b^2}{m}$

(E) $v_t = \frac{g}{2b^2}$

4. A car has a kinetic energy described as $KE = -\frac{2}{3}t^3 + 6t^2$. At what time does this car have a maximum power output?

(A) $t = 0$ sec

(B) $t = 3$ sec

(C) $t = 6$ sec

(D) $t = 12$ sec

(E) $t = 0.333$ sec

Free Response

1. A car has a constant force of F_o applied by engine. The car starts from rest and is driving into a headwind, producing a resistive force of $\vec{F}_r = -mb\vec{v}$. The mass of the car is m, and b is a constant with units $\frac{1}{s}$.

   a. Draw a free-body diagram at $t = 0$ and at $t > 0$.
   b. Determine an expression for the velocity of the car at any time.
   c. Sketch a graph of velocity versus time.

Solutions

Multiple Choice

1. (C)
2. (D)
3. (B)
4. (B)

Free Response

1. a. At time $t = 0$ sec:

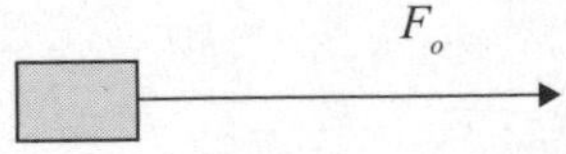

At time $t > 0$:

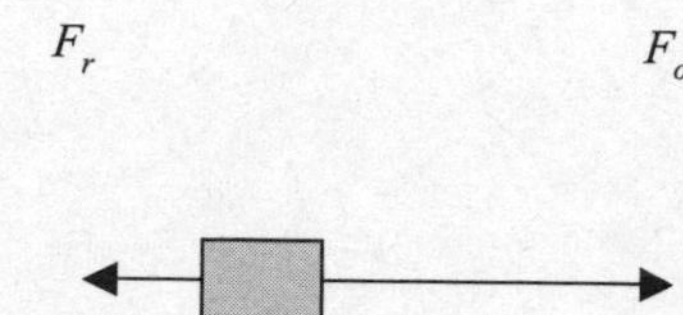

b. $\sum F = m\frac{dv}{dt} = F_o - mbv$

$$\Rightarrow m\frac{dv}{dt} \cdot \frac{1}{mb} = F_o \cdot \frac{1}{mb} - mbv \cdot \frac{1}{mb}$$

$$\frac{1}{b}\frac{dv}{dt} = \frac{F_o}{mb} - v, \text{ where } \frac{F_0}{mb} = v_{terminal}$$

$$\frac{1}{b}\frac{dv}{dt} = v_t - v \Rightarrow \frac{dv}{(v_t - v)} = bdt$$

$$\int_0^v \frac{dv}{(v_t - v)} = \int_0^t bdt \Rightarrow [-\ln|v_t - v|]_0^v = [bt]_0^t$$

$$\ln\left[\frac{(v_t - v)}{v_t}\right] = -bt \Rightarrow \frac{v_t - v}{v_t} = e^{-bt} \Rightarrow v = v_t\left(1 - e^{-bt}\right)$$

$$\therefore v(t) = \frac{F_0}{mg}\left(1 - e^{-bt}\right)$$

c.

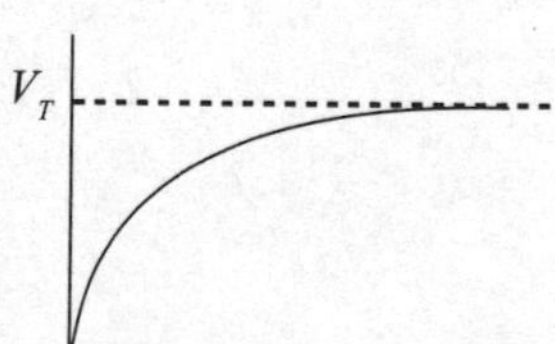

Chapter 17

Angular Mechanics

For Physics C Test Takers

EXAM OVERVIEW

Angular mechanics is roughly 15 to 20 percent of the AP Physics C exam. Therefore, mastering the concepts discussed in this chapter can mean the difference between a 4 and a 5 on the exam.

ANGULAR KINEMATICS

Angular kinematics is simply kinematics in the angular mode of motion. All the linear kinematic relationships apply in angular motion. Simply changing the symbols in the linear kinematic relationships will give you the angular kinematic relationships. The symbols to use are as follows:

- Angular displacement: θ, measured in radians
- Angular velocity: ω, measured in radians per second
- Angular acceleration: α, measured in radians per second squared

And these are the primary angular kinematic relationships:

- Average angular velocity: $\omega_{avg} = \dfrac{\Delta\theta}{\Delta t}$
- Average angular acceleration: $\alpha_{avg} = \dfrac{\Delta\omega}{\Delta t}$
- Constant acceleration:

$$\theta = \omega_o t + \frac{1}{2}\alpha t^2,\ \omega_f = \omega_o + \alpha t,\ \omega_f^2 = \omega_o^2 + 2\alpha\Delta\theta$$

You use the conversion of 2π radians (rad) = 1 revolution (rev) to go back and forth between revolutions and radians.

Sample Problem 1

A turntable is initially rotating at 45 revolutions per minute (rpm). It is turned off and is brought to rest uniformly in 10 seconds. Determine the angular acceleration and the number of rotations the turntable made during the stopping process.

Solution

Our first step is to change revolutions per minute into radians per second. Once we have converted to the proper units, we can proceed to apply the kinematic relationships:

$$45 \text{ rpm} = 45\frac{\text{rev}}{\text{min}} \cdot \frac{\text{min}}{60 \text{ s}} \cdot \frac{2\pi \text{ rad}}{\text{rev}} = \frac{3\pi}{2}\frac{\text{rad}}{\text{s}} \approx 4.71\frac{\text{rad}}{\text{s}}$$

We then use the relationships to find angular acceleration:

$$\omega_f = \omega_o + \alpha t \Rightarrow \alpha = \frac{\omega_f - \omega_o}{t} = \frac{0 - \frac{3\pi}{2}}{10} = -\frac{3\pi}{20}\frac{\text{rad}}{\text{s}^2}$$

$$\theta = \omega_o t + \frac{1}{2}\alpha t^2 \Rightarrow \theta = \frac{3\pi}{2}(10) - \frac{1}{2}\left(\frac{3\pi}{20}\right)(10)^2$$

$$= 15\pi - \frac{15\pi}{4} = \frac{45\pi}{4} \text{ rad}$$

$$\frac{45\pi}{4} \text{ rad} \cdot \frac{\text{rev}}{2\pi \text{ rad}} = \frac{45}{8} \text{ rev} = 5.625 \text{ rev}$$

RELATING LINEAR VELOCITY TO ANGULAR VELOCITY AND ROLLING MOTION

We can also determine the linear velocity of a point on an object moving in an angular mode. For example, in Sample Problem 1, a piece of tape on the edge of the turntable would have a linear velocity at that point. The velocity vector would be tangent to the circular path, as shown in the following diagram:

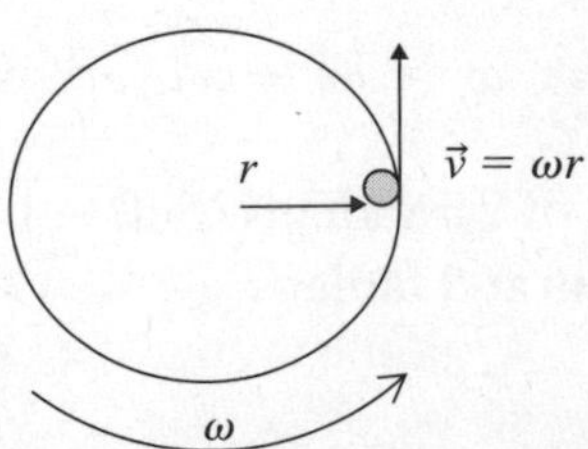

The linear velocity relates to the angular velocity with the following relationship:

$$\| \vec{v} \| = \omega r,$$

where r is the distance from the center of rotation to the point in question. Thus, if the angular velocity is 10 rad/s and the piece of tape on the edge of the turntable is located 0.2 m from the center, the linear velocity of that piece of tape is 2 m/s.

If we have an object rolling without slipping, the same relationship applies. The velocity of the center of mass of any rolling object is equivalent to the angular velocity times the radius of the object rotating. Here are the relationships for objects that are rotating:

$$\text{rolling: } v_{cm} = \omega R_{object} \text{ and } a = \alpha R \text{ and } x = R\theta$$

The relationship between angular velocity and the velocity of the center of mass is shown in the following diagram, in which a sphere with a radius $R = 0.5$ m is rolling down an incline onto a horizontal surface:

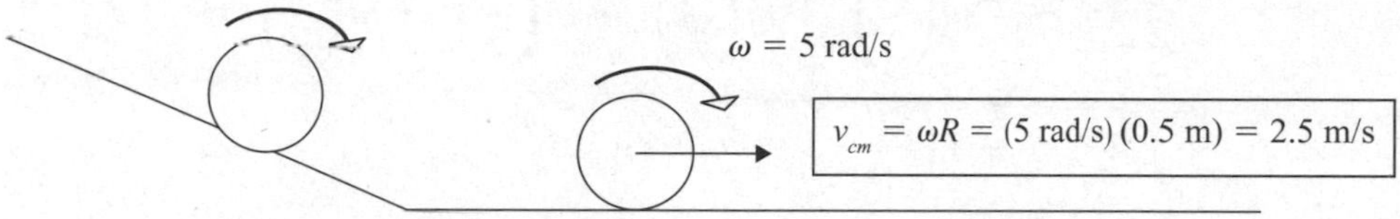

$\omega = 5$ rad/s

$v_{cm} = \omega R = (5 \text{ rad/s})(0.5 \text{ m}) = 2.5 \text{ m/s}$

MOMENT OF INERTIA

The property of inertia in a rotating system is called the **moment of inertia**. This is defined conceptually as a system's resistance to a change in the state of rotational motion. The physics definition looks like this:

For discrete masses:

$$I = \sum_i m_i r_i^2$$

For continuous mass distribution:

$$I = \int dm r^2$$

Let's focus on the discrete or **point mass** definition. The calculus in that definition is part of AP Physics C, but the integrals that usually occur in applying the definition may be quite a bit of work. Essentially, a rotating object's inertia depends on its shape and geometry. The location of the mass (r) has more of an effect than the actual mass. The moment of inertia definition is actually fairly simple to apply. Let's take a look at a typical moment of inertia calculation.

Sample Problem 2

Determine the moment of inertia of the rotating object shown in the following diagram, in which all masses equal m and the separation of all masses is L.

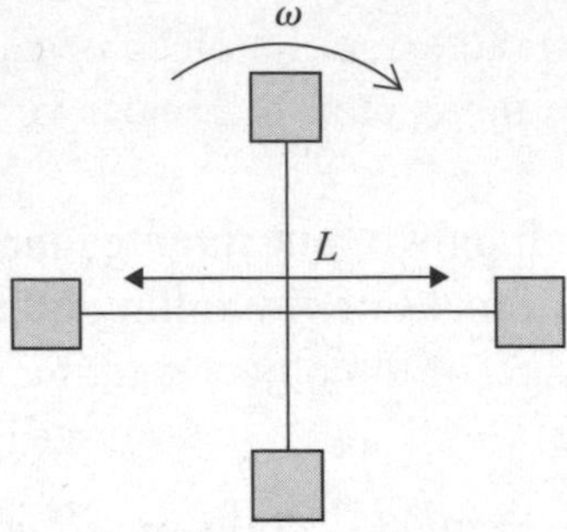

Solution

Applying the definition gives the following statement:

$$\sum m_i r_i^2 = m\left(\frac{L}{2}\right)^2 + m\left(\frac{L}{2}\right)^2 + m\left(\frac{L}{2}\right)^2 + m\left(\frac{L}{2}\right)^2$$

$$= 4\left(\frac{mL^2}{4}\right) = mL^2 \text{ kg} \cdot \text{m}^2$$

The units for moment of inertia are kg · m^2. In this solution, each mass is a distance of $L/2$ away from the center of the rotating system.

Determining the moment of inertia of some common solid objects—like solid spheres, disks, rings, and rods—are typically done with the calculus definition of moment of inertia. The details of some of those calculations are beyond the scope of this review book. However, these objects are typically used in physics problems and should be familiar to you. Here are the common moments:

$$I_{sphere} = \frac{2}{5}MR^2 \quad I_{soliddisk} = \frac{1}{2}MR^2 \quad I_{thin\ ring} = MR^2 \quad I_{rod} = \frac{1}{12}ML^2$$

R is the radius of the object. All these moments are given about the center of mass (CM) of the rotating object.

THE PARALLEL AXIS THEOREM

If an object with a known moment of inertia about its CM is forced to rotate about another point other than the CM, we can calculate the new moment of inertia about the new point using the following theorem, which is called the **parallel axis theorem**:

$$I_{new\ axis} = I_{CM} + Md^2,$$

where d is the distance that the axis has been moved from the CM.

Sample Problem 3

Determine the moment of inertia of a rod with mass M and length L when rotated about the end of the rod, as shown in the following diagram:

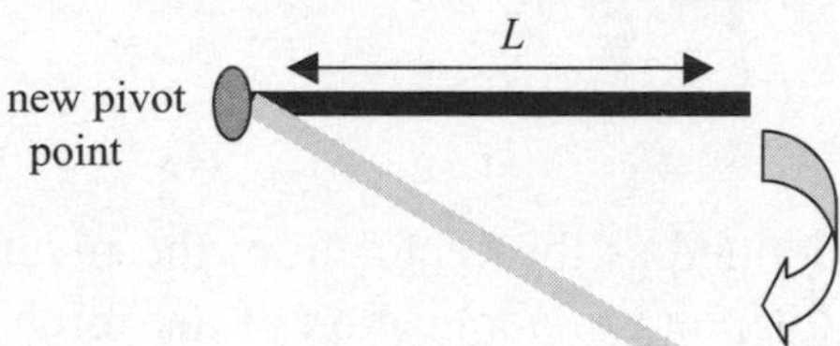

Solution

Because the new pivot point has been moved from the CM to the end, it has moved a distance $d = L/2$. We can apply the parallel axis theorem to compute the new moment of inertia:

$$I_{end} = \frac{1}{12}ML^2 + M\left(\frac{L}{2}\right)^2 = \frac{ML^2}{12} + \frac{ML^2}{4} = \frac{ML^2}{3}$$

Thus, it is four times harder to rotate the rod from the end than from the center of mass.

TORQUE AND NEWTON'S SECOND LAW

Torque is a force that is applied at a point located some distance (called the **moment arm**) from the pivot point of an object and causes an object to rotate. Whereas force causes a mass to accelerate linearly, torque causes an extended body to angularly accelerate. The definition of torque is

$$\vec{\Gamma} = \vec{r} \times \vec{F} = \|\vec{r}\| \cdot \left\|\vec{F}\right\| \cdot \sin\theta.$$

Torque has direction. The direction of the torque is perpendicular to the plane that contains the vectors $\vec{r}$ and $\vec{F}$. The direction is predicted using the right-hand screw rule from the definition of the cross product.

Using the moment arm, we can compute the torque without having to go through the entire cross product definition. The moment arm is the perpendicular distance between the line of action of the force vector and the pivot point.

In the following diagram, an extended body (the cube) will be rotated about its center by the force applied at one corner:

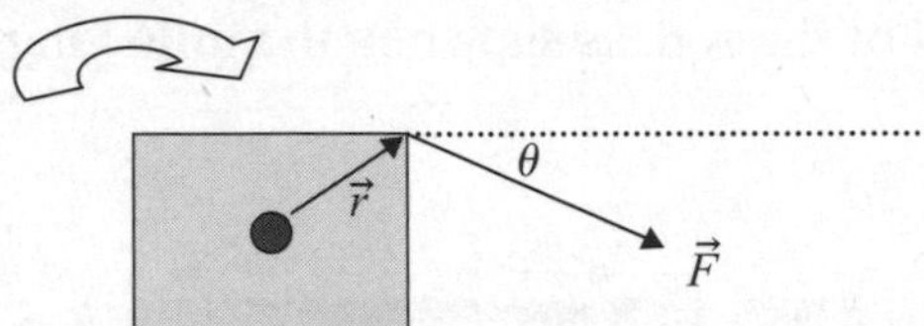

The vector $\vec{r}$ is defined as the vector from the pivot point (the center of mass, in this case) to the point of application of the force vector. Note that the angle θ is *not* the angle indicated in the definition of torque. That angle is the angle between the two vectors when both vectors are drawn from a common origin ($\theta + 45$, in this case). Thus, the torque on the cube caused by the applied force in the diagram is calculated as follows:

$$\Gamma = \|\vec{r}\| \cdot \|\vec{F}\| \cdot \sin(\theta + 45^\circ)$$

The following diagram shows the moment arm as a dashed line. It is the perpendicular distance between the line of action of the force and the pivot point. In some instances, that distance is an easy computation. Here it is simply drawn for identification purposes.

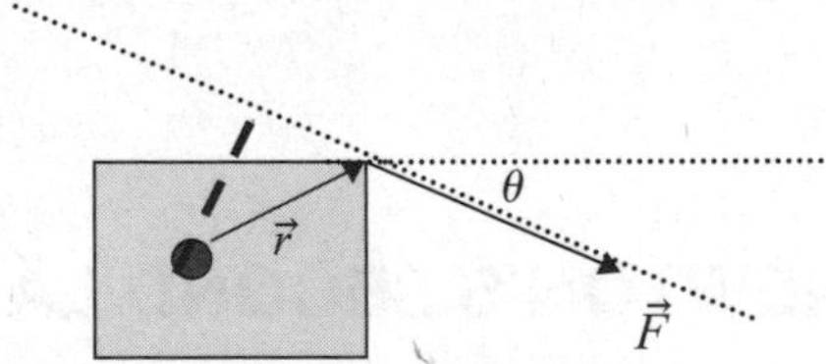

Sample Problem 4

Three forces are applied to a solid object of length a and width b, as shown in the following diagram:

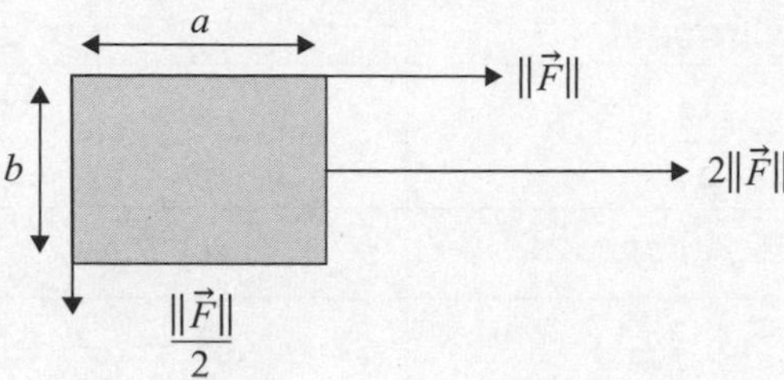

Determine the torques applied in all three cases.

Solution

- $\left\|\vec{F}\right\|$: The torque in this case is

$$\Gamma = \left\|\vec{F}\right\| \cdot \left\|\frac{b}{2}\right\| \cdot \sin(90°) = \frac{\left\|\vec{F}\right\| b}{2}.$$

- $2\left\|\vec{F}\right\|$: The torque is 0 in this case. The force vector goes through the pivot point (the center) and therefore has no moment arm.

- $\frac{\left\|\vec{F}\right\|}{2}$: This force has a moment arm of $a/2$. Therefore, the torque is

$$\Gamma = \frac{\left\|\vec{F}\right\|}{2} \cdot \frac{a}{2} \cdot \sin 90° = \frac{\left\|\vec{F}\right\| a}{4}.$$

Newton's second law has its appropriate form in the world of rotational physics. The sum of net torques on a system can produce either rotational equilibrium or angular acceleration.

- Second condition of equilibrium: $\Sigma\Gamma = 0$
- Newton's second law (rotation): $\Sigma\Gamma = I\alpha$

Using these two conditions of Newton's laws and understanding rotational kinematics and moment of inertia, many new and interesting physics can be analyzed.

Realizing that there is a connection between the rotational and linear versions of these relationships is useful. Here are all of the relationships in translational mechanics and their rotational equivalents.

Translational	Angular
$v = \dfrac{\Delta x}{\Delta t}$	$\omega = \dfrac{\Delta \theta}{\Delta t}$
$v_f = v_o + at$	$\omega_f = \omega_o + \alpha t$
$v_f^2 = v_o^2 + 2a\Delta x$	$\omega_f^2 = \omega_o^2 + 2\alpha\Delta\theta$
$\Delta x = v_o t + \frac{1}{2}at^2$	$\Delta\theta = \omega_o t + \frac{1}{2}\alpha t^2$
Linear motion connected to rolling motion, $x = r\,\theta$, $v = \omega r$, $a = r\alpha$ (if there is no slipping)	
Mass, M Force, F $\sum F = 0$ $\sum F = ma$ $KE = \frac{1}{2}mv^2$ $\vec{p} = m\vec{v}$ $W = \int F dx$ $\vec{F}\,\Delta t = \Delta\vec{p}$	Moment of inertia, $I = \sum m_i r_i^2$ $\Gamma = \vec{r} \times \vec{F}$ $\sum \Gamma = 0$ $\sum \Gamma = I\alpha$ $KE_{rot} = \frac{1}{2}I\omega^2$ $L = I\omega$ and $\vec{L} = \vec{r} \times \vec{p}$ $W = \int \Gamma d\theta$ $\Gamma dt = \Delta L$

It is useful to look at all the connections in these relationships. Notice that in each case, the new (rotational) relationship is merely connecting an old concept in a new mode of motion.

Sample Problem 5

As shown in the following diagram, a sphere rolls (without slipping) down a ramp of height h, starting from rest:

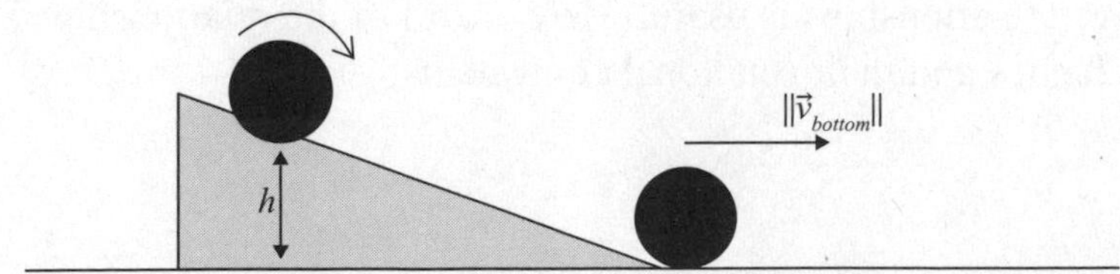

The moment of inertia of the sphere is $I = \frac{2}{5}MR^2$. The frictional force does net work of zero on the sphere, thus conserving total mechanical energy. Determine the following:

- The speed of the sphere at the bottom of the ramp.
- How much of the the sphere's kinetic energy is rotational KE and how much is translational KE?

Solution

Because the sphere will conserve total mechanical energy, the total gravitational potential energy will transfer completely into total kinetic energy. Because the sphere is rolling, the kinetic energy has two parts: the rotational KE and the translational KE. And because the sphere is rolling without slipping, the linear speed of the sphere's CM is related to the angular velocity by $v_{cm} = \omega R$. Therefore, we compute the speed of the sphere at the bottom of the ramp as follows:

$$U_g = Mgh$$

$$KE_{total} = \frac{1}{2}Mv_{cm}^2 + \frac{1}{2}I\omega^2 = \frac{1}{2}Mv_{cm}^2 + \frac{1}{2}\left(\frac{2}{5}MR^2\right)\left(\frac{v_{cm}}{R}\right)^2$$

$$U_g = KE_{total} \Rightarrow Mgh = \frac{7}{10}Mv_{cm}^2 \Rightarrow v_{cm} = \sqrt{\frac{10}{7}gh}$$

The percentage of the energy that is translational KE is

$$\frac{KE_{translational}}{KE_{total}} = \frac{\frac{1}{2}Mv^2}{\frac{7}{10}Mv^2} = \frac{5}{7} \approx 71\%.$$

Thus, the percentage of rotational KE would be 29 percent.

Sample Problem 6

A uniform rod of mass M and inertia $I_{cm} = \frac{1}{12}ML^2$ (about its center) is pivoted about its end. A large ball of putty of mass 3 M is added to the end of the rod. The rod is initially in a horizontal position, as shown in the following diagram. It is then released from rest and allowed to begin rotating clockwise.

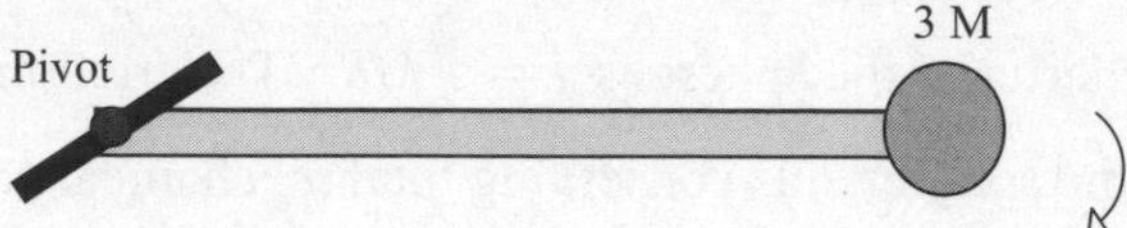

Determine the initial angular acceleration.

Solution

This problem shows the importance of using the center of mass. Our first step is to find the center of mass of this two-mass system. The net torque on the system will occur from the gravitational force acting on the system's center of mass:

$$x_{cm} = \frac{\sum m_i x_i}{M_{total}} = \frac{M\left(\frac{L}{2}\right) + 3M(L)}{4M} = \frac{7ML}{8M} = \frac{7}{8}L$$

This puts the system's CM at $\frac{7}{8}L$ from the pivot end.

A rigid-body diagram of the system looks like this:

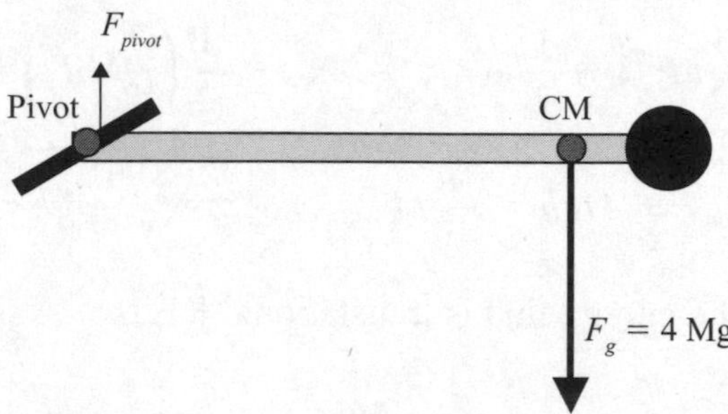

Now we need to find the moment of inertia about the end of the rod. The rod's moment of inertia about one end is $\frac{1}{3}ML^2$. We must add that to the mass's effect on the moment of inertia. The mass acts as a point mass and has a moment of inertia of $3ML^2$. We combine the two moments to determine the system's moment of inertia:

$$I_{pivot} = \frac{1}{3}ML^2 + 3ML^2 = \frac{10}{3}ML^2$$

Applying Newton's second law, we can determine the net torque on the system and the initial acceleration:

$$\sum \Gamma_{pivot} = I\alpha = (4Mg)\left(\frac{7}{8}L\right)$$

This is the statement for the initial horizontal state of the rod. Remember that once the rod begins to move, the torque changes because of the cross product between the gravitational force and the *r* vector. Also, note that the force on the pivot from the axle does not contribute to the net torque. Any force through the pivot contributes zero torque to the system.

We solve for the initial angular acceleration as follows:

$$\sum \Gamma_{pivot} = I\alpha = (4Mg)\left(\frac{7}{8}L\right) \Rightarrow \frac{10}{3}ML^2\alpha_o = \frac{28}{8}MgL$$

$$\alpha_o = \frac{21g}{20L}$$

ANGULAR MOMENTUM

The concept of angular momentum is very similar to that of linear momentum. Angular momentum in a rotating object is defined as the product of the object's inertia times the object's angular velocity: $\vec{L} = I\omega$. This mirrors the linear momentum definition: $\vec{p} = m\vec{v}$.

The direction of the angular momentum vector is determined by the right-hand rule. The fingers of the right hand wrap in the direction of the angular velocity, and the thumb on the right hand points in the direction of the angular momentum vector.

Angular momentum is conserved in a rotating system if no outside torques are acting on the system. This can occur in many interesting physics problems—most notably, any central force problem. The orbits of satellites or the swinging of a mass on a string all have central forces or radially directed forces. These forces never produce a torque on the system because they go through the pivot point.

One of the more interesting examples of the conservation of angular momentum is a figure skater rotating with arms and hands outward. As the skater brings in the arms, the angular velocity of the skater increases. Angular momentum is conserved in the system (there are no outside torques on the skater, and friction is negligible) and the skater actually changes the moment of inertia of the body by bringing in the arms. This decreased moment of inertia results in an increased angular velocity of the system. The orbit of the Earth in its ellipse around the sun works in much the same way. At the Earth's farthest approach from the sun, the moment of inertia of the Earth with respect to the sun is larger than its moment of inertia when the Earth is at its closest approach to the sun. Thus, the Earth's angular velocity is actually a little bit greater at the point of closest approach.

Sample Problem 7

The rotating system shown in the following diagram has an internal mechanism that can slowly bring in the system's arms. The initial speed of the system, when the arms are in the outward position, is 2 rad/s.

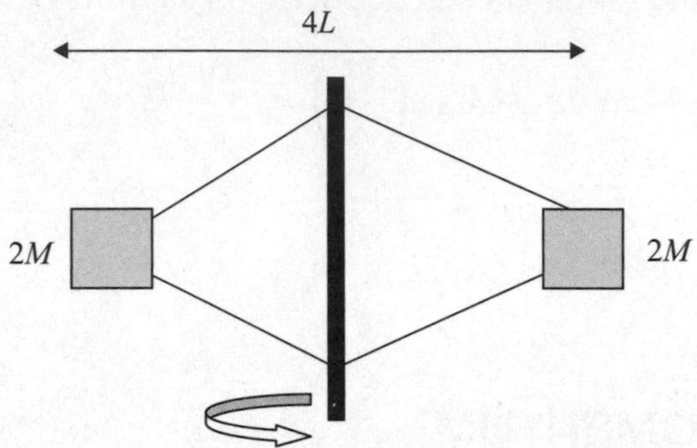

initial position of system

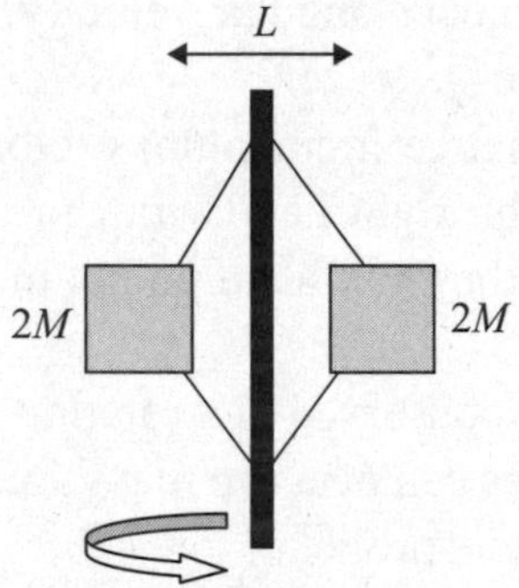

final position of system

Determine the speed of the system when the arms are brought in to the final position. Also, determine the change in energy of the system.

Solution

First, we need to compute initial angular momentum of the system:

$$L_o = I_o\,\omega_o \Rightarrow I_o = (2M)\,(2L)^2 + (2M)(2L)^2 = 16ML^2$$

The moment of inertia in the final position is

$$I_f = (2\text{ M})\left(\frac{L}{2}\right)^2 + (2\text{ M})\left(\frac{L}{2}\right)^2 = ML^2.$$

Now we equate the initial angular momentum to the final angular momentum and solve for the unknown final angular velocity:

$$L_o = L_f \Rightarrow \left(16ML^2\right)(2\text{ rad/s}) = \left(ML^2\right)\omega_f$$
$$\omega_f = 32\text{ rad/s}$$

Another interesting aspect of this problem is that the momentum stays constant, but the kinetic energy of the system increases, as shown here:

$$KE_o = \frac{1}{2}I_o\omega_o^2 = \frac{1}{2}\left(16ML^2\right)(2)^2 = 32ML^2$$
$$KE_f = \frac{1}{2}I_f\omega_f = \frac{1}{2}\left(ML^2\right)(32)^2 = 512ML^2$$
$$\Delta KE = 512ML^2 - 32ML^2 = 480ML^2 \Rightarrow \frac{\Delta KE}{KE_o} = \frac{480ML^2}{32ML^2} = 15$$

Thus, the system increased its energy by a factor of 15. This energy increases from the internal mechanism doing work in moving the masses inward. When applying conservation of angular momentum, be aware that sometimes one conservation law can be applied but not the other.

ANGULAR MOMENTUM OF AN OBJECT MOVING LINEARLY

Sometimes it is necessary to define the angular momentum of a linearly moving object, like a bullet moving through the air. This is necessary when a linearly moving object interacts with an angular system and causes a rotational motion in the angular system. An example of this would be a baseball moving linearly and striking a door, which then begins to rotate about its hinges. This seems like a case of the linear momentum of the baseball changing into the angular momentum of the door. However, to compensate for this inconsistency, we simply define the linearly moving baseball as having an angular momentum about the same axis that the door has as its pivot point.

The definition of the angular momentum of a linearly moving object is

$$L = \vec{r} \times \vec{p}.$$

The following diagram illustrates the relationship:

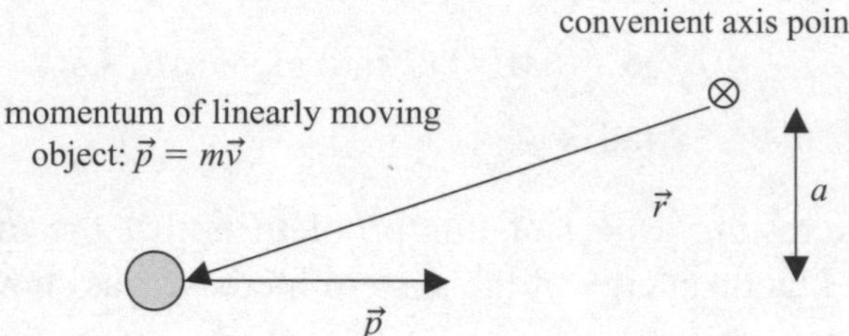

In this case, $L = mva$. The direction of the angular momentum, which in the diagram is out of the page, is determined by applying the cross product correctly. Remember, to apply the cross product correctly, you must draw the two vectors from a common origin and then rotate vector r into vector p, using the right-hand rule, as shown in the following diagram. The thumb of the right hand will then be pointing in the direction of the angular momentum vector.

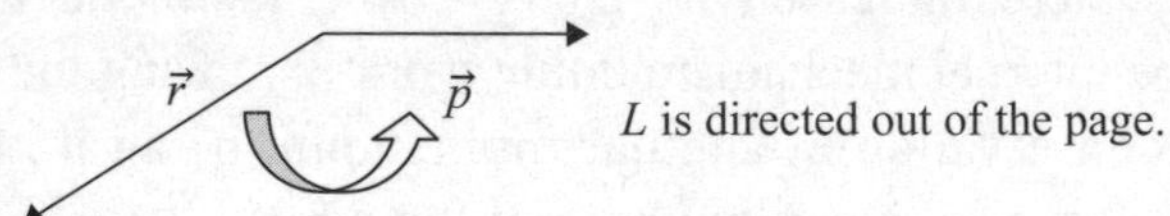

Practice Session Problems

Multiple Choice

1. A thin, massless rod has three point masses attached to it, as shown in the following diagram:

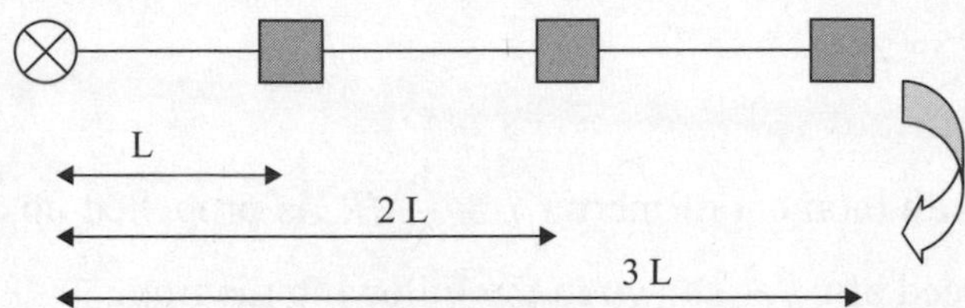

Each point mass has a mass of M. The rod is pivoted about one end and rotated with an angular velocity of 2 rad/s. What is the angular momentum of the system?

(A) $L = 6\ ML^2$

(B) $L = 12\ ML^2$

(C) $L = 28\ ML^2$

(D) $L = 56\ ML^2$

(E) $L = 112\ ML^2$

2. A sphere, a solid disk, and a hoop all of equal mass and equal radius, are set down an inclined ramp at the same time, as shown in the following diagram:

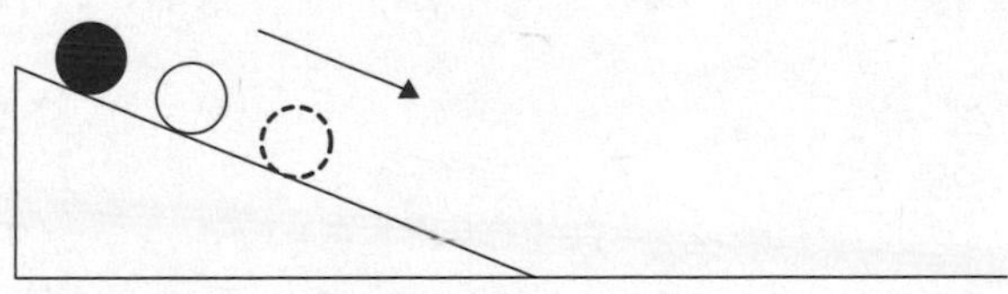

Which object will reach the end of the ramp first, second, and third?

(A) First, sphere; second, disk; third, hoop

(B) First, disk; second, sphere; third, hoop

(C) First, hoop; second, disk; third, sphere

(D) First, sphere; second, hoop; third, disk

(E) All objects arrive at the same time.

3. A merry-go-round is rotating with an angular velocity of 5 rad/s. The moment of inertia of the merry-go-round is $I = 100 \text{ kg} \cdot \text{m}^2$. A bag of sand is dropped on the merry-go-round at a distance of 3 meters from the center of the merry-go-round. The bag of sand has a mass of 2 kg. What is the new angular velocity of the merry-go-round after the bag of sand hits it?

(A) 4.58 rad/s
(B) 4.71 rad/s
(C) 4.23 rad/s
(D) 4.0 rad/s
(E) Cannot be determined

4. A disk with moment of inertia $I = \frac{1}{2}MR^2$ is propelled up a ramp with a linear speed of v_o, as shown in the following diagram:

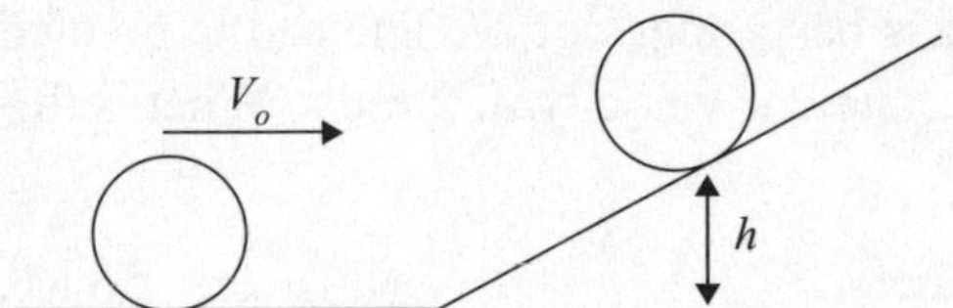

The disk rolls without slipping. What is the height h of the disk's rise above the ground?

(A) $h = \frac{v_o^2}{2g}$
(B) $h = \frac{2v_o^2}{3g}$
(C) $h = \frac{2v_o^2}{5g}$
(D) $h = \frac{3v_o^2}{4g}$
(E) $h = \frac{v_o^2}{g}$

Free Response

1. A disk with moment of inertia $I = \frac{1}{2}MR^2$ rolls from rest (without slipping) down an incline at an angle of θ.

   a. Draw a rigid-body diagram for the disk.

b. Determine the acceleration the disk acquires while rolling down the incline.
c. Determine the minimum coefficient of static friction, such that the disk will not slip on the incline.

2. A pulley with a moment of inertia of $I = \frac{1}{5}MR^2$ and two masses is set up on a frictionless table, as shown here:

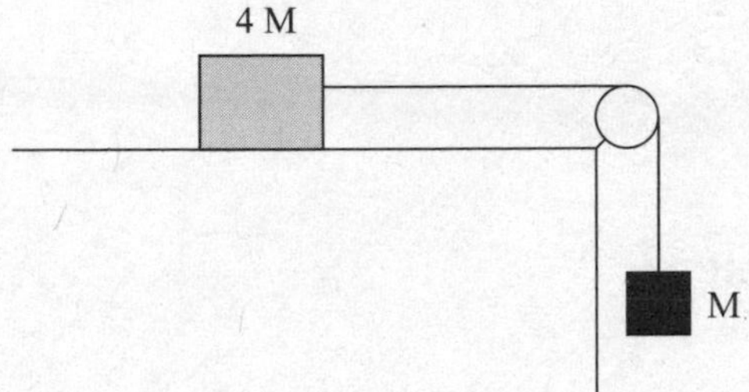

Determine the following for this problem:

a. The tension in the vertical cord
b. The acceleration of the system in terms of M, g, and R
c. The hanging mass is dropped a distance of 5 R from its starting position and how much energy (%) the pulley has at the instant the hanging mass has dropped 5 R

3. A ball of putty of mass m is projected at a rod of mass 4 M and hits the rod in two different ways, as shown in the following diagrams:

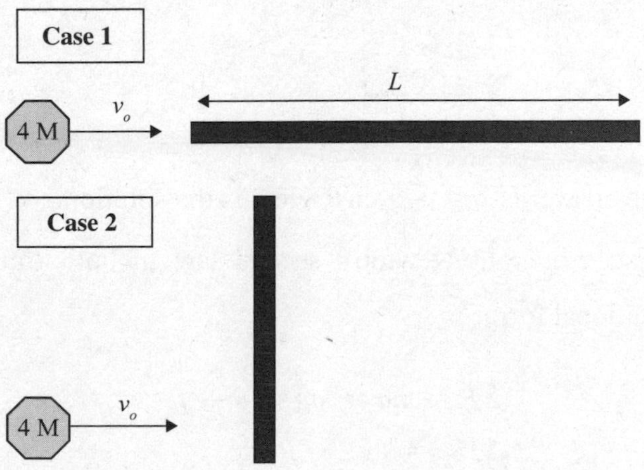

In each case, the putty sticks to the rod, and the putty and rod move together in accordance to the laws of physics. The putty–rod system is far away from any other masses or interactions.

Determine the following for case 1 and case 2:

a. The linear and angular velocity of the rod/putty system after the hit
b. The loss of energy that occurs from the inelastic collision

Answers

Multiple Choice

1. (C)
2. (A)
3. (C)
4. (D)

Free Response

1. a. The rigid-body diagram is as follows:

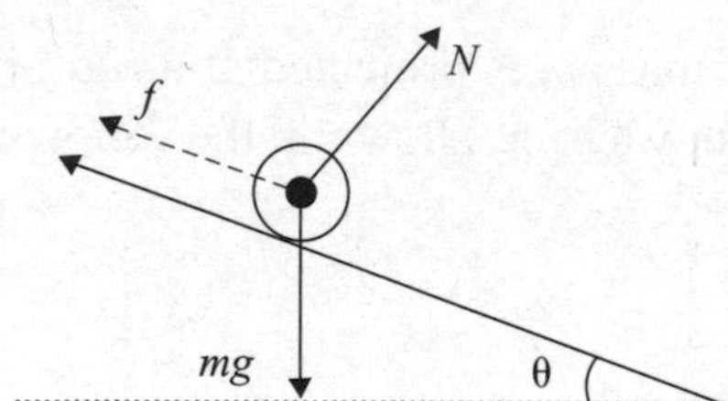

b. The answer is $a = \frac{2}{3} g \sin\theta$. Here is the solution:

First, write out Newton's second law in both translational and rotational form:

$$\Sigma F = ma = mg\sin\theta - f_s$$

$$\Sigma \Gamma_{cm} = I\alpha = f_s R$$

Recognize that in the condition of no slipping, $a = \alpha R$. Solve for the unknown acceleration:

$$I\alpha = f_s R \Rightarrow \frac{1}{2}MR^2\alpha = f_s R, \alpha = \frac{a}{R} \Rightarrow f_s = \frac{1}{2}ma$$

$$\sum F = ma = mg\sin\theta - f_s \Rightarrow ma = mg\sin\theta - \frac{1}{2}ma$$

$$\frac{3}{2}ma = mg\sin\theta \Rightarrow a = \frac{2}{3}g\sin\theta$$

c. To determine the minimum coefficient of friction, equate the expression for the frictional force to the definition of static friction:

$$f_s = \frac{1}{2}ma \leq \mu_s N \Rightarrow \mu_s \geq \frac{\frac{1}{2}ma}{N} = \frac{\frac{1}{2}m\left(\frac{2}{3}g\sin\theta\right)}{mg\cos\theta} = \frac{1}{3}\tan\theta$$

2. a. $T_{lowercord} = \frac{21}{26}mg$

b. $a = \frac{5}{26}g$

c. $KE_{pulley} = \frac{1}{26}KE_{total} \approx 3.8\%$ of total energy

3. **Case I:** The ball of putty hits the rod on a line that contains the center of the rod, producing no torque on the system; therefore, the rod will not rotate. The rod–putty system will move linearly (on the same line as v_o) without any rotational velocity.

$$\vec{p}_{putty} = \vec{p}_{putty/rod}$$

$$mv_o = (m + 4m)v' \Rightarrow v' = \frac{v_o}{5}$$

The system will have zero angular velocity and a linear speed of $\frac{v_o}{5}$, in the same direction as v_o.

The energy loss is computed by the difference in kinetic energy before and after:

$$KE_o = \frac{1}{2}mv_o^2 \quad KE_f = \frac{1}{2}(m + 4m)\left(\frac{v_o}{5}\right)^2 = \frac{1}{10}mv_o^2$$

$$\Delta KE = KE_f - KE_o = -\left[\frac{1}{10}mv_o^2 - \frac{1}{2}mv_o^2\right]$$

$$= -\frac{1}{2}mv_o^2\left(1 - \frac{1}{5}\right) = -\frac{4}{5}KE_o$$

The collision produces a loss of 80% of its original kinetic energy.

Case II: Because the ball of putty hits the end of the rod (about the CM of the rod), the rod will rotate about its CM, as shown here:

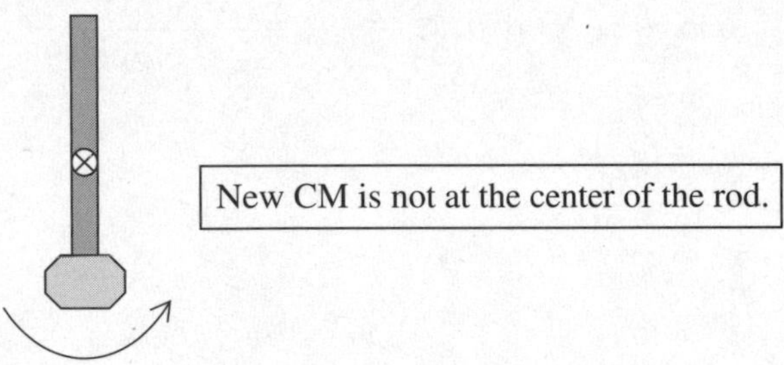

The system will conserve both angular momentum and linear momentum. The first thing to compute is the new CM:

$$y_{cm} = \frac{\sum m_i r_i}{M} = \frac{4\text{ M} \cdot \frac{L}{2} + M \cdot L}{5\text{ M}} = \frac{3}{5}L$$

This puts the CM at 3/5 L from the top of the rod or 2/5 L from the putty end of the rod. The CM was basically shifted 1/10 L by the putty being on the end.

The moment of inertia of the rod about the CM is calculated as follows:

$$I_{rod} = \frac{1}{12}(4\text{ M})L^2 + (4\text{ M})\left(\frac{L}{10}\right)^2 = \frac{28}{75}ML^2$$

The conservation of linear momentum of this case is the same as in case I. In other words, the rod–putty system still moves with a linear speed of $\frac{v_o}{5}$ in the same direction as v_o. The difference is that in this case, the rod is now rotating.

To compute the angular velocity of the rod, conservation of angular momentum must be applied as follows:

$$L_{before} = L_{after}$$

$$Mv_o\left(\frac{2}{5}L\right) = I\omega \Rightarrow \omega = \frac{Mv_o\frac{2}{5}L}{\frac{28}{75}ML^2} = \frac{15v_o}{14L}$$

Computing the total energy of the rod–putty system goes like this:

$$KE_{total} = KE_{translational} + KE_{rotational}$$

$$KE_{rotational} = \frac{1}{2}I\omega^2 = \frac{1}{2}\left(\frac{28}{75}ML^2\right)\left(\frac{15v_o}{14L}\right)^2 = \frac{3}{14}Mv_o^2$$

$$KE_{total} = \frac{Mv_o^2}{10} + \frac{3}{14}Mv_o^2 = \frac{11}{35}Mv_o^2$$

$$\therefore \Delta KE = \frac{11}{35}Mv_o^2 - \frac{1}{2}Mv_o^2 = -\frac{13}{70}Mv_o^2 = -\frac{26}{70}KE_o \approx -37\%KE_o$$

Thus, in the rotating case, the collision lost only 37 percent of its original energy compared with 80 percent in the nonrotating case. The rotation enabled the system to keep more energy.

Chapter 18

Electricity and Magnetism

For Physics C Test Takers

EXAM OVERVIEW

AP Physics C is filled with calculus-based ideas in the areas of electricity and magnetism. This review cannot address all the details of the physics and math involved in this area of the course; you will have to rely on your textbook for many of these details. Chapters 10 through 13 in this book provide a review of the basics of electricity and magnetism.

This chapter focuses on some of the main calculus-based ideas in electricity and magnetism, including Gauss's law, Faraday's law, and Ampere's law. The sample problems presented here should give you a good idea of the skills you should master for the AP Physics exam.

CHARGE DENSITY

Charge density, λ, in its various forms, plays a very important role in electricity and magnetism. Many of the concepts of electricity and magnetism are based on the principle of **superposition**, which states that the net field at any point in space is equal to the sum of all of the individual fields that contribute a field at that point. When a wire or ring is charged, every part of the charged wire or ring contributes a field into space. This idea is managed mathematically with the concept of charge density. If a conductive wire is continuously charged, the charge spreads out uniformly across the length of the wire. In the following diagram, the conductive wire has charge spread out on its surface:

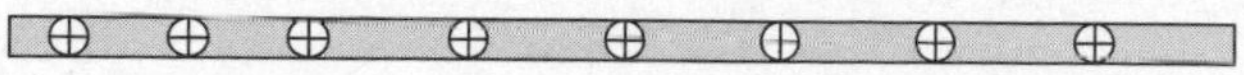

The entire amount of charge is $+Q$, and the length of the conductor is L. The linear charge density is $\lambda = \frac{+Q}{L}$. Using the concept of charge density, we can effectively work with an infinitesimal amount of charge (dq) as follows:

$$Q = \lambda L \Rightarrow dq = \lambda dl$$

In many cases, dl will become dx or dy, depending on the geometry of the problem.

Similarly, we can calculate surface charge density (σ) and volume charge density (ρ). Sample problems later in this chapter will give you some practice using each term.

PRINCIPLE OF SUPERPOSITION

Superposition is one of the most important principles in physics. It states that the net electric field (or force) at any point is the vector sum of all of the fields acting at that point. Mathematically, it looks like this:

$$\vec{E}_{net} = \vec{E}_1 + \vec{E}_2 + \vec{E}_3 = \sum \vec{E}_i$$

For a point charge, the equation turns into this:

$$\vec{E}_{net} = \sum \frac{kq_1}{r_i^2}\hat{r}$$

For a continuous charge distribution, it is

$$E_{net} = \int \frac{kdq}{r^2}\hat{r}.$$

Sample Problem 1

Using the following diagram of a uniformly charged rod ($+\lambda$), determine the electric field's magnitude and direction at point P.

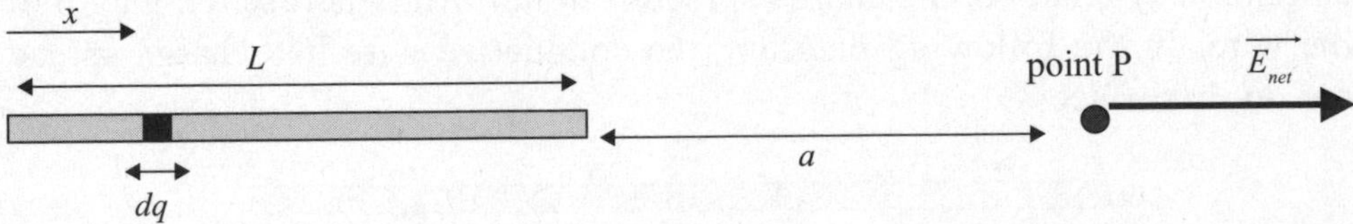

Solution

The net electric field is composed of many infinitesimal fields created by *dq*'s on the wire. One *dq* is shown on the diagram. Each positive *dq* creates a field that points in the $+x$ direction, as shown in the diagram. The sum of the fields that the *dq*'s contribute is the net electric field at point P. This is also shown in the diagram. Once we realize what makes up the net field, we can add up (integrate) the actual field elements created by each *dq*. Here is how this looks:

$$dq = \lambda dx$$

The distance from each *dq* to point P is

$$\vec{r} = L + a - x$$

The next step is to write out the definition of the electric field with all these defined values:

$$\vec{E}_{net} = \int \frac{kdq}{r^2} = k \int \frac{\lambda dx}{(L + a - x)^2}$$

Now we can add the limits of integration from the limits of the wire, from $x = 0$ to $x = L$:

$$\int_0^L \frac{k\lambda dx}{(L + a - x)^2} = k\lambda \int_0^L \frac{dx}{(L + a - x)^2}$$

$$= -k\lambda \int_0^L \frac{-dx}{(L + a - x)^2} = -k\lambda \left[\frac{-1}{(L + a - x)}\right]_0^L$$

$$= k\lambda \cdot \left[\frac{1}{a} - \frac{1}{L + a}\right] = k\lambda \left[\frac{(L + a) - a}{a(L + a)}\right] = k\lambda \left(\frac{L}{a(L + a)}\right)$$

If we replace linear charge density with charge per length, the expression reduces down further, as shown here:

$$E_p = k\lambda \cdot \left(\frac{L}{a(L + a)}\right) = k \cdot \frac{Q}{L} \cdot \left(\frac{L}{a(L + a)}\right) = \frac{kQ}{a(L + a)}$$

DETERMINING POTENTIAL CAUSED BY A CONTINUOUS CHARGE DISTRIBUTION

In much the same way that we determined the electric field caused by a charged wire, we can determine the potential resulting from charged rings, wires, spheres, and other types of continuous charge distributions.

Recall the following from Chapter 10 on electrostatics:

$$V_{point\ charge} = \frac{kq}{r} \quad V_{sphere} = \frac{kQ}{R} \quad V_{point} = \sum \frac{kq_i}{r_i}$$

As we did to determine the net electric field at one point, we can use the principle of superposition to determine the potential resulting from many charges. There is one important distinction, however: potential is a *scalar*. That means we do not need to add the x and y components; they do not exist in the scalar world. In differential form, the equation $V_{point} = \sum \frac{kq_i}{r_i}$ becomes the following:

$$V_p = \int \frac{kdq}{r}.$$

Sample Problem 2

A conductive ring filled with a continuous charge distribution λ has a radius R. Determine the potential at a point P shown on the x-axis in the following diagram:

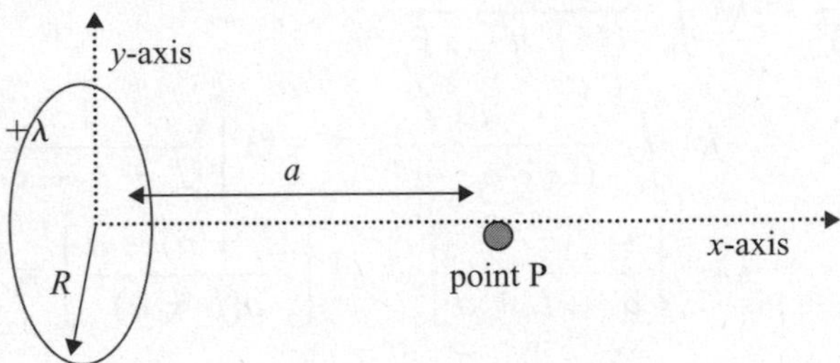

Solution

Each elemental dq is a distance $\sqrt{(a^2 + R^2)}$ from point P. (Think about this statement and prove it to yourself before we move on.) We set up the potential relationship like this:

$$V_p = \int \frac{kdq}{\sqrt{a^2 + R^2}} = \frac{k}{\sqrt{a^2 + R^2}} \int dq$$

We could integrate dq the difficult way, or we could realize that the integration of dq around the ring is simply Q, the total charge on the ring. If we need to put the answer in terms of the linear charge density, the total charge on the ring is equivalent to $Q_t = \lambda \cdot 2\pi R$, giving the following for the potential at point P: $V_p = k\lambda \cdot \frac{2\pi R}{\sqrt{a^2 + R^2}}$. We could also state this as $V_p = \frac{kQ}{\sqrt{a^2 + R^2}}$.

GAUSS'S LAW

Gauss's law is one of the most powerful and elegant laws in electricity and magnetism. The point of Gauss's law is to be able to determine the electric field of simple, or not so simple, charge arrangements. In many instances, Gauss's law makes this determination easier than the method of $E = \int \frac{kdq}{r^2}$. The geometry and charge arrangement of a problem will determine whether applying Gauss's law will lead to the solution.

Gauss's law is based on the idea that if a charged region creates an electric field around its surrounding space, the flux through some shape that contains these charges will be a constant. This is a powerful and simple concept. Flux depends on the vector field and the area through which that field is cutting. Because an electric field is dependent on $\frac{1}{r^2}$ and the surface area (for the flux calculation) is dependent on r^2, the two contributions cancel each other out, leaving the flux calculation as a constant value. The formal statement of Gauss's law is

$$\phi = \oint \vec{E} \cdot d\vec{A} = \frac{q_{enclosed}}{\varepsilon_o}.$$

The surface area integral is simple. An actual integral is rarely involved. Because the electric field is usually constant at some radial distance away from the source charges, the value of the electric field is a constant value at the boundary of the surface in question. Employing Gauss's law requires using the idea of a **Gaussian surface**. This is the imaginary surface enclosing the charges. The Gaussian surface usually fits the geometry of a problem; that is, if the problem is about a sphere of charges, the Gaussian surface should be an imaginary sphere that is larger than the actual sphere and bounds the actual sphere.

Let's apply Gauss's law to the simplest example as a starting point for our discussion.

Two concentric conducting spheres—an inner sphere of radius a and an outer sphere of radius b—both have charges on their surfaces. The inner sphere has a total net charge of $+3Q$ on its surface, and the outer sphere has a total charge of $-2Q$ on its surface, as shown in the following diagram:

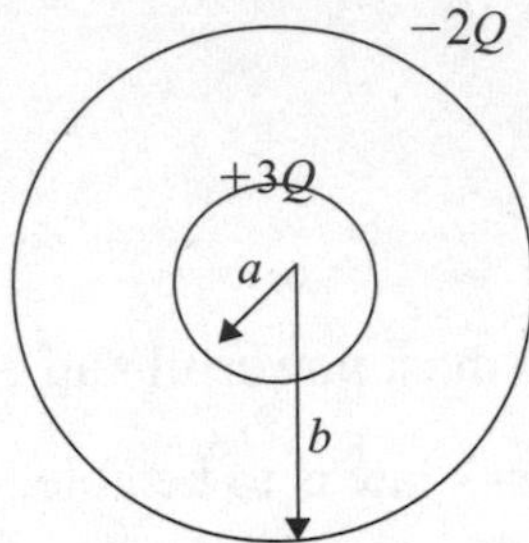

Gauss's law can answer two interesting questions for us: what is the value of the electric field for r when $a < r < b$ and when $r > b$?

Let's start with the first problem: determining the field for $a < r < b$. Because the region of space identified is the region of space between the two spheres, we can draw (or imagine) a Gaussian sphere of radius r that fits in that space as follows:

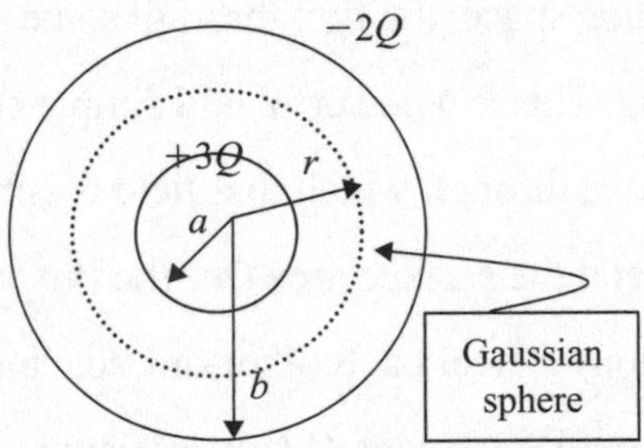

The next step is to determine how much charge the Gaussian sphere encloses. In this case, the Gaussian sphere encloses the entire $+3Q$ charge on the inner sphere, which is located inside the Gaussian surface. The $-2Q$ charge is outside the Gaussian surface and therefore is not a consideration. When we put this information into the equation for Gauss's law, we get this:

$$\oint \vec{E} \cdot \vec{dA} = \frac{+3Q}{\varepsilon_o}$$

Now, considering the left side of the relationship, we know that the area vector of a sphere is perpendicular to the sphere and parallel to the electric field vector that emanates from the sphere. This is significant because it gives a dot product of $\|\vec{E}\| \cdot \|\vec{dA}\| \cos 0° = EdA$. The other significant detail of applying

Gauss's law is that the magnitude of the electric field's value is constant at all radial distances r from the inner sphere. Noting this fact and realizing that the imaginary spherical Gaussian surface is a radial distance r at all points from the center, we realize that the value of the electric field at the surface of the Gaussian sphere is a constant.

$$\oint EdA = \frac{+3Q}{\varepsilon_o} \Rightarrow E\oint dA = \frac{+3Q}{\varepsilon_o}$$

Our final step is to realize that the total surface area of the Gaussian sphere is the result of the surface integral of dA. We are basically "adding up" all the little area elements, the dA's, that make up the Gaussian sphere.

The final solution looks like this:

$$E\oint dA = \frac{+3Q}{\varepsilon_o} \Rightarrow E(\text{Area of Gaussian sphere}) = \frac{+3Q}{\varepsilon_o}$$

$$E\left(4\pi r^2\right) = \frac{+3Q}{\varepsilon_o} \Rightarrow E = \frac{+3Q}{4\pi\varepsilon_o r^2}$$

Now that we have the value of the electric field for values of $a < r < b$, determining the electric field in the other regions is simple. We can skip over all the redundant details and focus on the significant steps. The Gaussian surface this time is a sphere that surrounds both conductive shells, as shown in the following diagram:

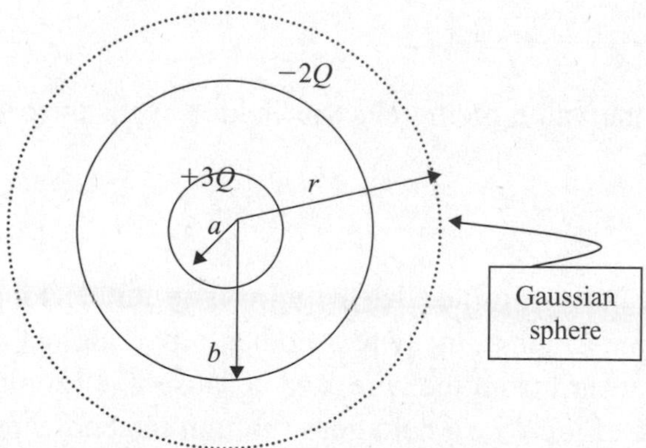

When we apply Gauss's law, the left side of the equation is identical to the first example. What changes is the right side of the equation. Because the Gaussian sphere encloses both conductive shells with their charges, the total charge enclosed by the Gaussian sphere is $+3Q + -2Q = +Q$. The result is

$$\oint E \cdot dA = \frac{Q_{enclosed}}{\varepsilon_o} \Rightarrow E(4\pi r^2) = \frac{+Q}{\varepsilon_o} \Rightarrow E = \frac{+Q}{4\pi\varepsilon_o r^2}.$$

Thus, the linear charge line density of the field lines between the two spheres is three times the line density of the field lines outside the outer sphere.

This was a relatively simple problem. However, Gauss's law is very useful for some interesting arrangements of charge. Cylinders, wires, plates, and spheres are all very typical surfaces used in Gauss's law problems. Here is a sample problem.

Sample Problem 3

A charged wire with a uniform charge density λ is shown in the diagram. Although it is impossible to show in the diagram, the wire is infinitely long.

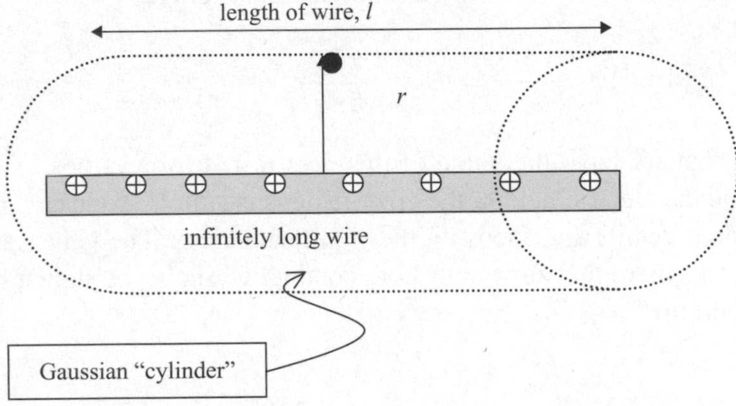

Determine the value of the electric field at a distance r from the wire. Essentially $l_{wire} >> r$.

Solution

We need to keep in mind that the wire is infinitely long. The Gaussian cylinder is the same length as the wire. Another important fact is that the electric field emanates outward from the wire, and because it is infinitely long, we can assume that none of the wire's field goes through the end caps of the cylinder. The electric field lines penetrate only the lateral surface area of the cylinder. Here is the formal mathematics behind these ideas:

$$\oint \vec{E} \cdot \vec{dA} = \frac{Q_{enclosed}}{\varepsilon_o} \Rightarrow E(2\pi rl) = \frac{Q_e}{\varepsilon_o}$$

So the trick is to put the enclosed charge in terms of the surface charge density

$$Q_E = \lambda l,$$

giving us

$$E(2\pi rl) = \frac{Q_e}{\varepsilon_o} \Rightarrow E\left(2\pi rl\right) = \frac{\lambda l}{\varepsilon_o} \Rightarrow E = \frac{\lambda}{2\pi\varepsilon_o r}.$$

We just determined the electric field of a very long wire and it was relatively easy. Using the other method (adding up *dq*'s) would have been much more complicated. This sample problem shows the simplicity and power of Gauss's law.

DIFFERENCE IN POTENTIAL

One of the definitions of difference in potential involves integration. It is the simplest and most powerful definition of the difference in potential:

$$\Delta V = V_b - V_a = -\int_a^b \vec{E} \cdot \vec{dl}$$

This is also a fairly straightforward definition. Notice the negative sign. It implies that the decreasing potential differences are in the direction of the electric field vector. In general, if we integrate a $1/r^2$ electric field function, we will get a potential difference that depends on $1/r$. If a $1/r$ function (as in Sample Problem 3) is integrated, the natural log of r will be the potential dependency.

This definition of difference in potential is the best definition to use when a general relationship is necessary. It is also the best to use when a question asks about the potential difference between two points situated in an electric field. (If you have point charges creating the field, simply use the point charge definition.)

Sample Problem 4

An electric field directed along the x-axis has the following definition:

$$\vec{E} = \left(10 + 4x + x^2\right)\frac{\text{volt}}{\text{meter}}\hat{\imath}$$

Determine the difference in potential between the origin ($x = 0$) and the value $x = 3$.

Solution

$$\Delta V = V_{3m} - V_0 = -\int_0^3 (10 + 4x + x^2) = -\left(10x + 2x^2 + \frac{x^3}{3}\right)_0^3$$

$$= -(30 + 18 + 9) = -57 \text{ Volts}$$

Thus, the origin is 57 V higher in potential than the 3-m mark.

Sample Problem 5

Determine the difference of potential between a long, uniformly charged wire and some point P a radial distance *r* away from the wire.

Solution

The solution to Sample Problem 4 can help us in solving the first part of Problem 5. In the previous problem, the electric field of a long wire of uniform charge density was $E = \dfrac{\lambda}{2\pi\varepsilon_o r}$. This expression will be integrated between the inner radius of the wire ($r = a$) and some other point *r* away from the wire.

To make the problem realistic and mathematically doable, we will need to make the long thin wire a little thicker by giving it a cylindrical shape with a radius of $r = a$. This will not change the value of the electric field at all. The field would be the same whether the wire had an infinitesimal thickness or a large thickness.

$$\Delta V = V_{wire} - V_r = -\int_r^a \frac{\lambda}{2\pi\varepsilon_o r} dr = \frac{-\lambda}{2\pi\varepsilon_o} \int_r^a \frac{dr}{r} = \frac{-\lambda}{2\pi\varepsilon_o} [\ln r]_r^a$$

$$= \frac{-\lambda}{2\pi\varepsilon_o} [\ln a - \ln r] = \frac{\lambda}{2\pi\varepsilon_o} \ln\left(\frac{r}{a}\right)$$

CALCULUS AND THE RC CIRCUIT

The RC circuit is full of interesting mathematics. The derivation for RC circuit equations comes from applying Kirchhoff's loop rule around the circuit and then carefully solving a differential equation for *dq* and *dt*. You should review this proof in your textbook. Once this is proven, the equations work out to the following for any RC series circuit:

In the charging of a capacitor: $q(t) = Q_f(1 - e^{-\frac{t}{RC}})$ and $i(t) = I_o e^{-\frac{t}{RC}}$.

In the discharging process of a capacitor: $q(t) = Q_o e^{-\frac{t}{RC}}$ and $i(t) = I_o e^{-\frac{t}{RC}}$,

where $q(t)$ creates the charge on the capacitor at any given time and creates the current in the circuit at any given time.

An important characteristic of the RC circuit equations is the product of R and C. This product RC is called the **time constant**. When time is equal to RC, the exponent in the equation equals –1. This gives some easy markers to remember.

At one time constant: $q(RC) = Q_f(1 - e^{-\frac{RC}{RC}}) = Q_f\left(1 - e^{-1}\right) \approx 63\%Q_f$

At five time constants ($5RC$):

$$q(5RC) = Q_f(1 - e^{-\frac{5RC}{RC}}) = Q_f(1 - e^{-5}) = 99.5\%Q_f$$

These markers are important because they give our increasing exponential function the characteristic shape of approaching the Q_f asymptote, as shown in the following diagram:

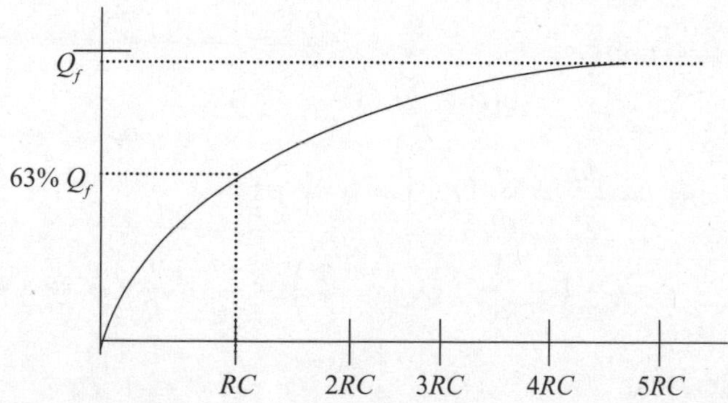

If the time constant for a circuit is 5 seconds, it will take approximately 25 seconds (five times the constant) to fully charge the capacitor.

Current may be found by taking the derivative with respect to time of the charge relationship. The current equation is simply exponential decay. The idea of the time constant is still the same, except this time the time constant gives 37 percent of the value. The current in the circuit while charging a capacitor is

$$i(t) = I_o e^{-\frac{t}{RC}}$$

$$i(RC) = I_o e^{-\frac{RC}{RC}} = I_o e^{-1} \approx 37\%I_o$$

$$i(5RC) = I_o e^{-\frac{5RC}{RC}} = I_o e^{-5} \approx 0.5\%I_o$$

Thus, the current in the circuit dips to basically zero in five time constants. The graph looks like this:

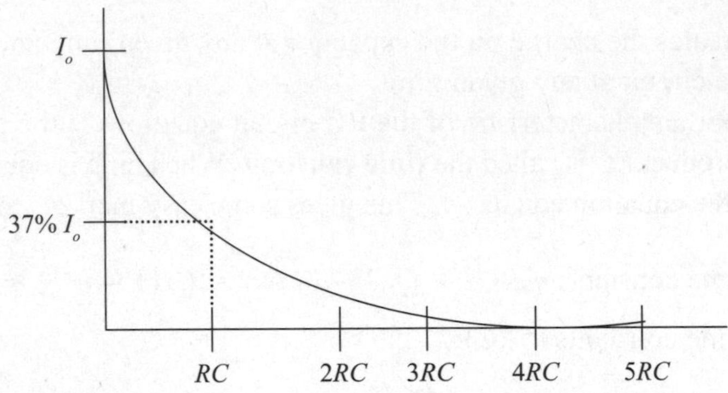

Sample Problem 6

Starting from the charge relationship of a capacitor filling up over time, prove that the current relationship is $i(t) = I_o e^{-\frac{t}{RC}}$.

Solution

$$q(t) = Q_f(1 - e^{-\frac{t}{RC}})$$

$$i(t) = \frac{dq}{dt} = \frac{d}{dt}\left(Q_f(1 - e^{-\frac{t}{RC}})\right)$$

$$= -\left(-\frac{1}{RC} \cdot Q_f \cdot e^{-\frac{t}{RC}}\right) = \frac{Q_f}{C} \cdot \frac{1}{R} \cdot e^{-\frac{t}{RC}}$$

Remember, that

$$\frac{Q_f}{C} = Voltage \Rightarrow \frac{V}{R}e^{-\frac{t}{RC}} = I_o e^{-\frac{t}{RC}}$$

MAGNETIC FLUX

Magnetic flux is very similar to electric flux. It has the same mathematical definition of any vector field flux:

$$\phi_b = \int \vec{B} \cdot \vec{dA}$$

If the magnetic field is constant over the area through which it is passing, the flux definition simplifies to just the product $\phi_b = \vec{B} \cdot \vec{A}$.

However, if the magnetic field is changing over the area, the magnetic flux calculation is more interesting. Here is a common example of this happening in a typical AP Physics C exam problem.

Sample Problem 7

A wire with current I_o creates a magnetic field around the wire that has the magnitude of $B_{wire} = \dfrac{\mu_o I}{2\pi r}$. As shown in the following diagram, a rectangular loop with the dimensions w and l is placed next to the wire at a distance a from the wire:

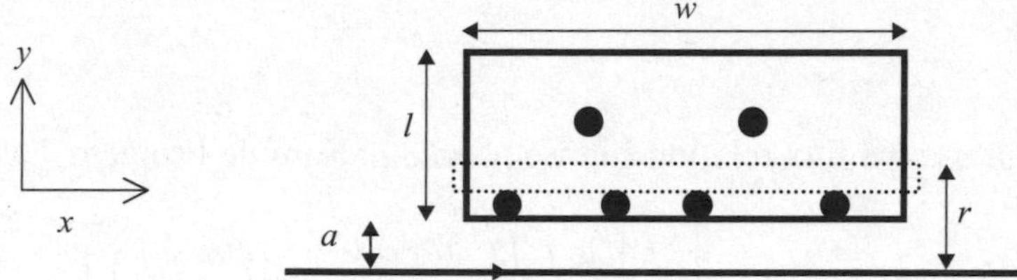

In the diagram, the dots represent the changing magnetic field strength coming out of the page. The field strength decreases moving away from the wire.

Determine the flux through the loop.

Solution

First, we must imagine an infinitesimal area (shown in diagram as the dashed rectangular area). This area is represented by $dA = wdr$.

$$\phi_b = \int \vec{B} \cdot \vec{dA} = \int_a^{a+l} \left(\frac{\mu_o I_o}{2\pi r}\right)(wdr)$$

$$= \frac{\mu_o I_o w}{2\pi} \int_a^{a+l} \frac{dr}{r} = \frac{\mu_o I_o w}{2\pi} \ln r]_a^{a+l}$$

$$= \frac{\mu_o I_o w}{2\pi} \cdot \ln\left(\frac{a+l}{a}\right)$$

FARADAY'S LAW

Faraday's law is one of the most physically interesting laws in all of electricity and magnetism. Conceptually, Faraday's law implies that when there is a changing flux through some conductive loop, the conductive loop will contain an induced current while the flux change exists. This is represented mathematically as follows:

$$\varepsilon_{induced} = -\frac{d\phi_b}{dt}$$

The negative sign is a reference to the fact that the induced current and voltage create a new induced magnetic field that opposes the original changing flux.

Sample Problem 8

Continuing from Sample Problem 7, let's consider the wire to have a changing current of $I = I_o(1 - \alpha t)$. Determine the induced current created in the wire and indicate the direction of the current on the diagram.

Solution

We can use the flux relationship we proved in Sample Problem 7 as follows:

$$\varepsilon_i = -\frac{d\phi_b}{dt} = -\left[\frac{d}{dt}\left[\frac{\mu_o I_o (1 - \alpha t) w}{2\pi} \cdot \ln\left(\frac{a+l}{a}\right)\right]\right]$$

All the terms in the equation (except αt) are constants, so the derivative is

$$\varepsilon_i = -\left[\frac{-\mu_o I_o \alpha w}{2\pi} \cdot \ln\left(\frac{a+l}{a}\right)\right].$$

Because the current is diminishing, so is the flux through the loop. The loop will have its new induced magnetic field in the same direction as the diminishing field. An easy way to remember this is by thinking of the adage "save a dying field."

The current in the loop would be the induced magnetic field divided by the resistance of the loop. The direction of the current would be counterclockwise around the loop to produce an induced outward flux.

AMPERE'S LAW

Ampere's law is a convenient way to find magnetic fields of current carrying conductors in particular situations. It is similar to Gauss's law for electric fields. Just as Gauss's law uses geometry and flux to determine unknown electric fields, Ampere's law uses geometry and a **line integral** to determine unknown magnetic fields of current-carrying conductors.

The law states the following:

$$\oint \vec{B} \cdot \vec{dl} = \mu_o I_{enclosed}$$

If we take a closed path (the line integral part) and the dot product of the magnetic field contribution at that point with the *dl* and add them all together, we get the total current enclosed by this closed path (times a constant). Like the Gaussian surface, the **Amperian loop** is an imaginary closed path that we draw for convenience when using Ampere's law.

Sample Problem 9

Using Ampere's law, determine the magnetic field around a wire with a current I_o.

Solution

First, we draw the wire with the field around it, as shown here:

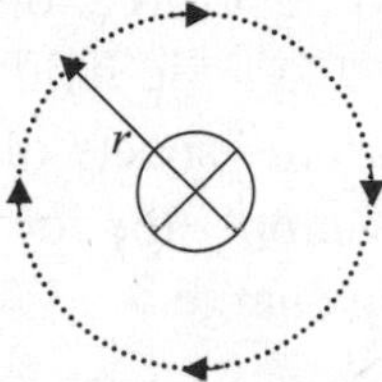

This is the end view of the wire, with the current directed into the page. The field is indicated by the dashed circle.

The magnetic field of the wire encircles the wire and the sense indicated by the arrows in the diagram. This "sense" is determined by the right-hand rule. The thumb points with the current direction (into the page), and the right fingers naturally curl in the circular direction of the field. The sense tells you that at a point tangent to the field line, the B field is seeking south.

The obvious Amperian loop would be a circle coinciding with the circular field. That would mean the dot product between the B field and *dl* at every point would yield $\vec{B} \cdot \vec{dl} = \|B\| \, \|dl\| \cos 0 = Bdl$. In other words, the B field and the Amperian loop are always tangent to each other at every point. Because magnetic fields vary with $1/r$, the B field is constant at any distance r from the center of the wire, which means Ampere's law shortens to

$$\oint \vec{B} \cdot \vec{dl} = \mu_o I \Rightarrow B \oint dl = \mu_o I \Rightarrow B(l) = \mu_o I,$$

and the integration of dl gives the total circumference of the Amperian loop, which is simply $2\pi r$.

$$B(2\pi r) = \mu_o I_o \Rightarrow B = \frac{\mu_o I_o}{2\pi r}$$

Ampere's law is typically only used for determining magnetic fields of cylinders (wires) or coaxial cables. It is a powerful idea, but it is difficult to apply to many different situations.

For difficult or more generic magnetic fields, the **Biot-Savart law** must be used. This law states the following:

$$\overrightarrow{dB} = \frac{\mu_o}{4\pi} \cdot \frac{q\left(\vec{v} \times \hat{r}\right)}{r^2} \text{ or } \overrightarrow{dB} = \frac{\mu_o}{4\pi} \cdot \frac{I\left(\overrightarrow{dl} \times \hat{r}\right)}{r^2}$$

Applying the Biot-Savart law is more difficult than applying Ampere's law and is beyond the scope of a review book. The general relationship may be tested in AP Physics C, but the actual computation of a B field using the Biot-Savart law most likely will not appear in the AP Physics C exam. The general idea that the magnetic field has a cross product directional relationship with velocity of the charge and the idea that the magnetic field has an inverse square law with distance are the two most important aspects of the Biot-Savart law. The cross product in the Biot-Savart law is simply the formal representation of why the B field always encircles the moving charge.

Practice Session Problems

Note: These problems are more difficult than those in previous chapters because they include the calculus discussed in this chapter. The answer section does not contain complete solutions to all problems for the sake of brevity.

1. A line of charge is shown in the following diagram (with the dots representing spaces filled with a positive charge):

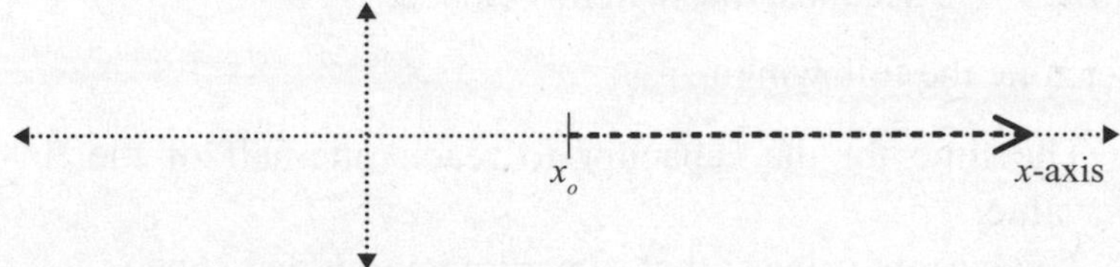

The line of charge starts at x_o and goes to infinity. It is represented by the linear charge density relationship $\lambda(x) = \dfrac{\lambda_o x_o}{x}$.

a. Draw a vector at the origin of the x-y-axis to show the direction of the electric field at this point.
b. Determine the magnitude of the electric field at the same point.

2. At a point x on the x-axis, determine the electric field caused by the uniformly charged ring (total charge Q) shown in the diagram. The ring has a radius R and is centered at the origin in the y-z plane.

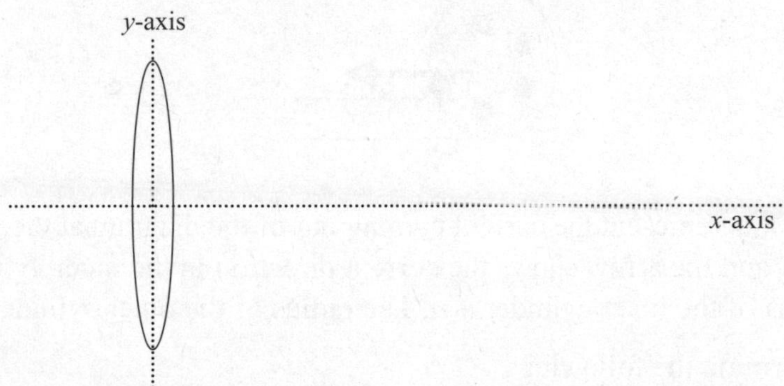

3. The RC circuit shown in the following diagram begins with a switch open (not operating):

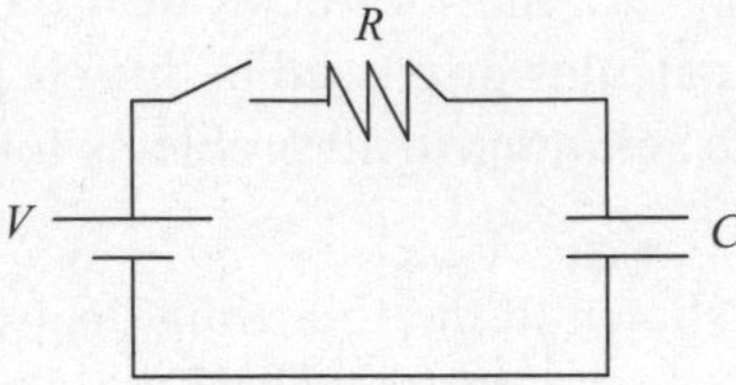

At time $t = 0$ seconds, the switch is closed.

Determine the following:

a. The time for the capacitor to reach one-half of the final charge value.
b. The current value at that same time computed above.
c. The rate at which the power developed by the battery is changing at the instant the switch is closed.

4. An electric field in some region of space follows the following relationship:

$$E = 2x + x^2$$

Determine the difference in potential between the origin and $x = 3$.

5. A coaxial cable has an inner cylinder current of I_o and an outer cylinder current of I_o, as shown in the following diagram:

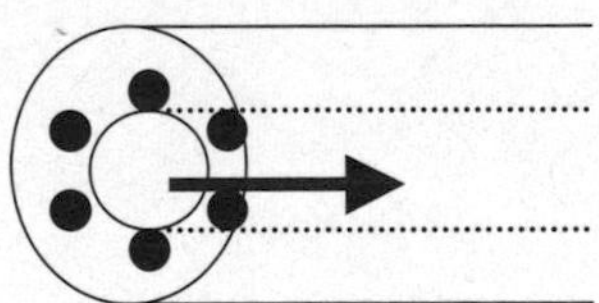

The dots represent the current coming out of the diagram at the end of the wire, and the arrow shows the current direction in the inner cylinder. The radius of the inner cylinder is a. The radius of the outer cylinder is b.

Determine the following:

a. An expression for the magnetic field in the outer cylinder ($a < r < b$)
b. An expression for the magnetic field for distances completely outside the wire ($r > b$)

Solutions

1. a. The vector is directed in the $-x$ direction.

   b. $E = \dfrac{k\lambda_o}{x_o}$

   Here are the steps to the solution:

$$dq = \lambda dx = \frac{\lambda_o x_o}{x} dx$$

   and $r = x$, as measured from dq to the origin.

$$E = \int_{x_o}^{\infty} \frac{kdq}{r^2} = \int_{x_o}^{\infty} \frac{k\frac{\lambda_o x_o}{x}dx}{x^2} = k\lambda_o x_o \int_{x_o}^{\infty} \frac{dx}{x^3} = k\lambda_o x_o \left[-\frac{1}{2x^2}\right]_{x_o}^{\infty}$$

$$= k\lambda_o x_o \left[\frac{-1}{\infty} - \frac{-1}{x_o^2}\right] = k\lambda_o x_o \left[\frac{1}{2x_o^2}\right]$$

$$= \frac{k\lambda_o}{x_o}$$

2. $E = \dfrac{1}{4\pi\varepsilon_o} \cdot \dfrac{Qx}{(x^2 + R^2)^{\frac{3}{2}}}$

3. a. $t = RC\text{In}2$

   b. $\dfrac{I_o}{2}$

   c. $-\dfrac{2V^2}{R^2C}$

4. $\Delta V = 18$ volts, with the origin at the higher potential.

5. a. $B = \dfrac{\mu_o I_o}{2\pi r} \cdot \dfrac{b^2 - r^2}{b^2 - a^2}$

   b. $B = 0$

TEXTBOOKS AND WEBSITES FOR FURTHER STUDY

General Physics:

Cutnell, John D., and Kenneth W. Johnson, *Physics*, New York: Wiley, 2006

Halliday, David, Robert Resnick, and Jearl Walker, *Fundamentals of Physics*, New York: Wiley, 2004

Knight, Randall, *Physics for Scientists and Engineers –A Strategic Approach*, New York: Pearson Education, Inc., 2004

AP Physics B

Young, Hugh D., and Robert Geller, College Physics, New York: Addison Wesley, 2006

Giancoli, Douglas, C., *Physics: Principles and Applications*, Englewood Cliffs, N.J.: Prentice-Hall Inc., 2004

Walker, James S., *Physics*, Englewood Cliffs, N.J.: Prentice-Hall Inc., 2001

AP Physics C

Young, Hugh D., and Roger Freedman, *Sears and Zemansky's University Physics,* New York: Addison Wesley Longman, 2007

Tipler, Paul A., and Gene Mosca, *Physics for Scientists and Engineers*, New York: W.H. Freeman, 2007

WEBSITES

http://apcentral.collegeboard.com—Website maintained by the College Board for all AP course information, including course and exam descriptions and released AP exams.

http://apphysicsb.homestead.com/—One of the longest running and most useful websites for AP physics students, created and maintained by AP Physics teacher Dolores Gende.

http://phet.colorado.edu/index.php—A very engaging and interesting interactive simulation site for physics teachers and students. Created by the University of Colorado Physics Education Research Group.

http://www.physicsclassroom.com—A very useful page by AP Physics teacher Tom Henderson that provides online physics tutorials.

http://www.fearofphysics.com—This site contains simulations, a homework tutorial section, and an "ask an expert" section.

http://www.aapt.org/Contests/olympiad.cfm—The official U.S. Physics Team website. Contains links to previous years tests and solutions. A great site for difficult and challenging physics questions.

http://www.aapt.org/Contests/physicsbowls.cfm—The official Physics Bowl site sponsored by The American Association of Physics Teachers. This site offers access to previous Physics Bowl exams, which are less difficult than the Olympiad Tests, and more in line with AP types of questions.

http://www.physlink.com—A general physics website that contains fun and educational links for the physics enthusiast.

PRACTICE EXAMS

AP Physics B

PRACTICE EXAM 1

This exam is also on CD-ROM in our special interactive AP Physics B TestWare®

AP Physics B

Section I

Time: 90 Minutes
70 Multiple-Choice Questions

DIRECTIONS: Each of the questions or incomplete statements below is followed by five answer choices. Select the one that is best in each case and fill in the oval on the corresponding answer sheet.

NOTE: Units associated with numerical quantities are abbreviated, using the abbreviations listed in the Table of Information and Equations found at the back of this book. To simplify calculations, you may use $g = 10\ \text{m/s}^2$ for all problems.

1. Which of the following graphs depicts a car moving with a changing acceleration? All the graphs are velocity (v) versus time (t).

(A)

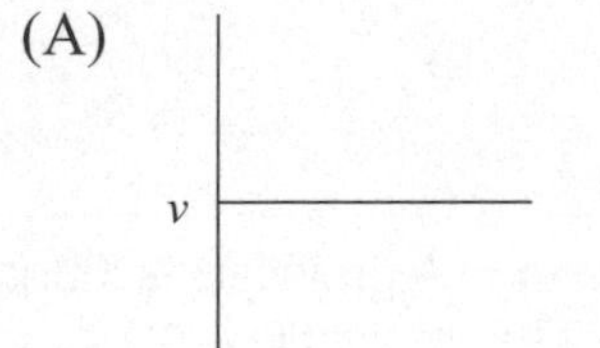

(D)

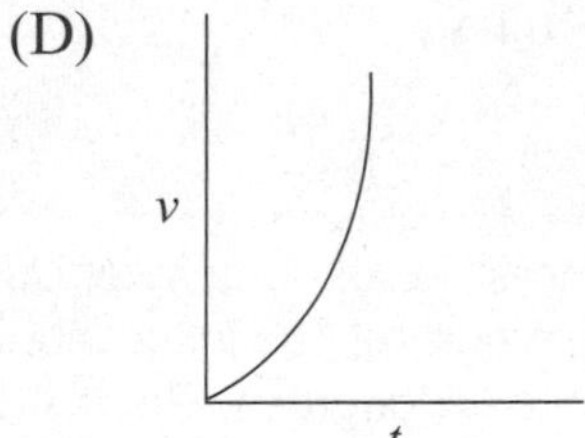

(B)

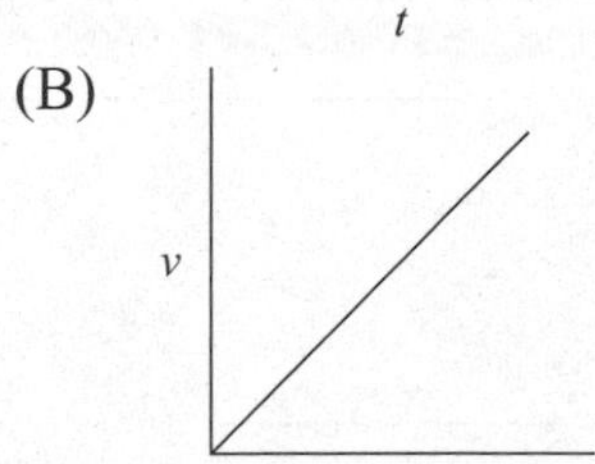

(E)

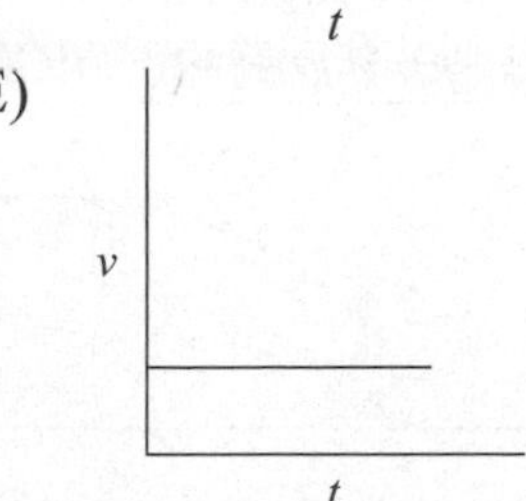

(C)

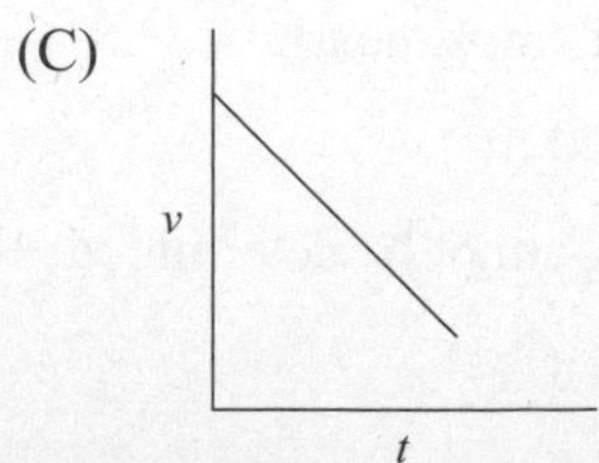

Use the following situation to answer questions 2 and 3. As shown in the diagram, a uniform mass m is sitting stationary on a uniform wood incline set to 37 degrees. The force of static friction between the mass and the incline has a magnitude of f. (Note: $\sin 37 = 0.6$ and $\cos 37 = 0.8$.)

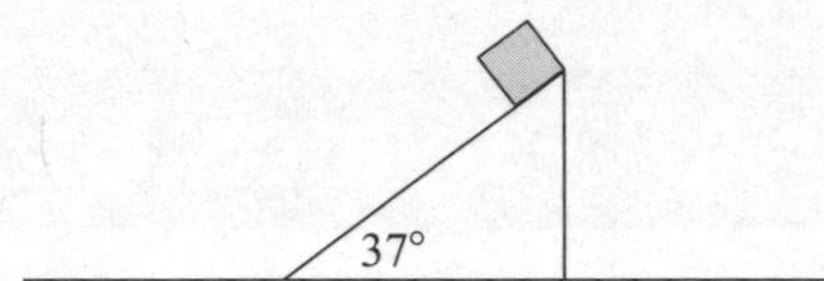

2. A mass made of the same material replaces the stationary mass. This mass has a mass of $2m$. What is the new force of *static friction* between this new mass and the incline?

(A) $(2mg)(\cos 37)$
(B) $2f$
(C) $(2mg)(\sin 37)$
(D) Both B and C
(E) 0

3. If the 37-degree angle turned out to be the exact angle at which mass m began to slip on the incline, determine the coefficient of static friction for the mass and the incline.

(A) $\mu = 0.333$
(B) $\mu = 0.5$
(C) $\mu = 0.666$
(D) $\mu = 0.707$
(E) $\mu = 0.75$

Use the following situation to answer questions 4 and 5. A projectile is launched as shown in the diagram. The initial launch speed of the projectile is 10 m/s. The angle of launch is 45 degrees. Point A is the launch point, point C is the point of impact, and point B is at the maximum height.

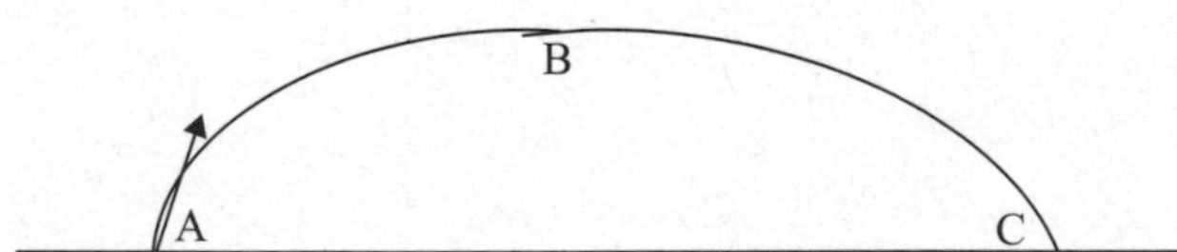

4. The distance between point A and point C is most nearly

(A) 2.5 m
(B) 7.5 m
(C) 10 m
(D) 20 m
(E) Cannot be determined

5. Which set of vectors correctly describes the velocity and acceleration direction at point B? (Each answer choice shows velocity first and acceleration second.)

(A) $v = 0, a = 0$

(B) $v = 0, \downarrow$

(C) $\rightarrow \quad \downarrow$

(D) $\rightarrow, a = 0$

(E) $\downarrow \; \downarrow$

6. The following graph shows the data that a physics student collected from an experiment. In the experiment, the student stretched a spring by a certain displacement and then measured the force that the spring exerted at that displacement.

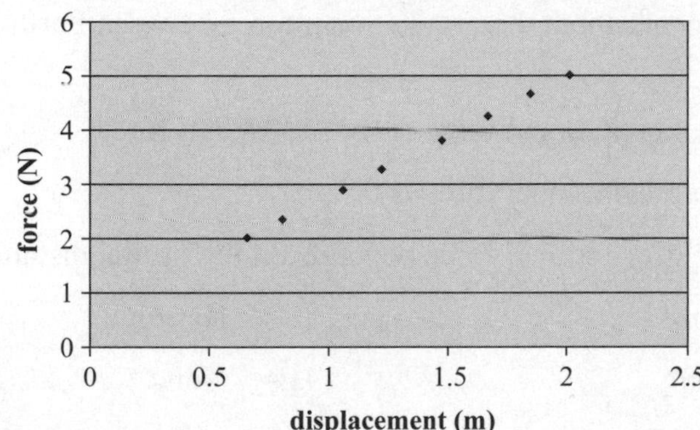

The spring constant of the spring used in the experiment is most nearly

(A) 3 N/m

(B) 2.5 N/m

(C) 2 N/m

(D) 5 N/m

(E) 2.7 N/m

7. A car travels one-half of a 1-km trip at a constant speed of 10 km/hr. It then travels the other half of the trip at twice the speed (20 km/hr). What is the average speed for the whole 1-km trip?

(A) 10 km/hr

(B) 13.33 km/hr

(C) 15 km/hr

(D) 16.66 km/hr

(E) 18 km/hr

8. A ball swings in a conical pendulum, as shown in the following diagram. The ball moves around the path with a constant speed. Which of the following vectors best describes the direction of the ball's net acceleration at the instant shown in the diagram?

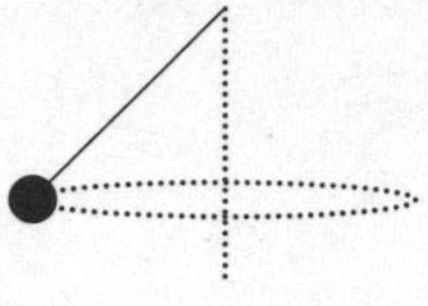

(A) ↗
(B) →
(C) ↓
(D) ←
(E) None

9. A space shuttle is orbiting Earth in its standard orbit. Which of the following statements about the gravitational force between Earth and the shuttle is true?

I. The gravitational force is the centripetal force.
II. The gravitational force is 0.
III. The gravitational force depends on the orbital distance.

(A) I only
(B) II only
(C) I and III only
(D) III only
(E) None

10. The combination of units $\text{kg} \cdot \frac{\text{m}^2}{\text{s}^3}$ is equivalent to which of the following units?

(A) Newton
(B) N/m
(C) Joule
(D) Watt
(E) Nm

Use the following situation to answer questions 11 and 12. A dense metal ball of mass m is projected horizontally off a ledge, as shown in the diagram.

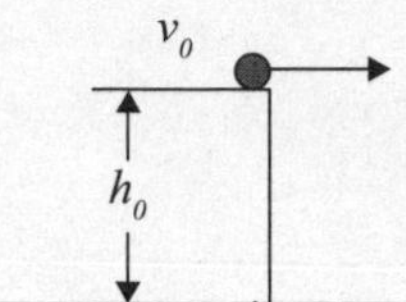

11. Which expression correctly determines the time of flight?

(A) $t = \dfrac{v_o + \sqrt{v_o^2 - 2gh_o}}{g}$

(B) $t = \sqrt{\dfrac{h_o}{g}}$

(C) $t = \sqrt{\dfrac{2h_o}{g}}$

(D) $t = \sqrt{2gh}$

(E) $t = \sqrt{\dfrac{g}{h_o}}$

12. What is the total energy of the ball at the point of impact?

(A) $TE = mgh_o$

(B) $TE = mgh_o + \dfrac{1}{2}mv_o^2$

(C) $TE = mv_o^2$

(D) $TE = 2mgh_o$

(E) $TE = \dfrac{1}{4}mv_o^2$

Use the following situation to answer questions 13 and 14. A block with a mass of 1 kg slides down a 37-degree incline with friction. The coefficient of kinetic friction between the block and the incline is $\mu = 0.5$. (Note: $\sin 37 = 0.6$.)

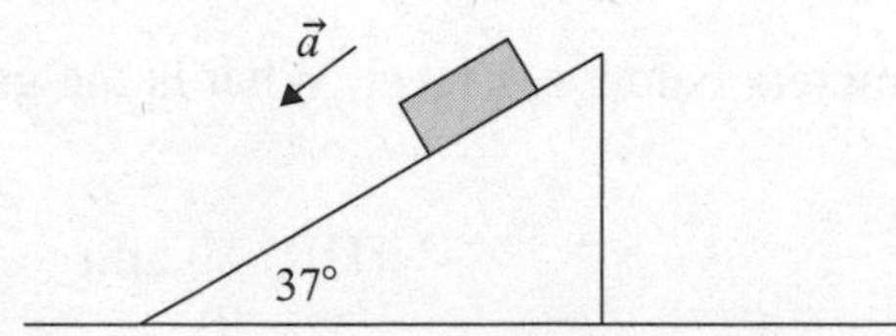

13. The frictional force between the incline and the block is most nearly

(A) 6 N

(B) 5 N

(C) 4 N

(D) 2 N

(E) 1 N

14. The acceleration of the block down the incline is most nearly

(A) 0 m/s^2
(B) 1 m/s^2
(C) 2 m/s^2
(D) 3 m/s^2
(E) 4 m/s^2

Use the following situation to answer questions 15 and 16. A block of mass $m = 2$ kg is lifted by a motor at a constant speed of $||\vec{v}|| = 2$ m/s. The block is lifted a height of 0.5 m.

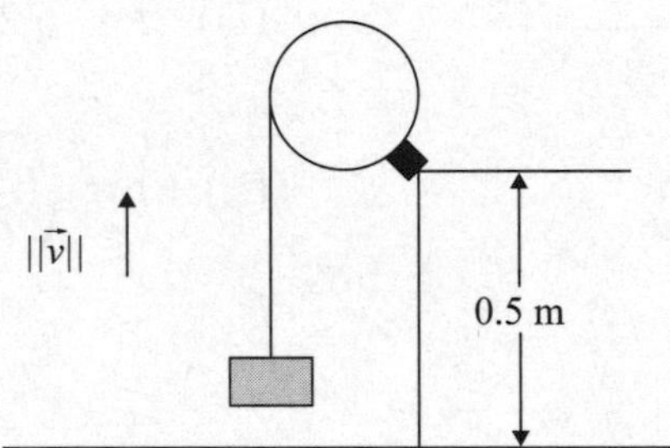

15. The power developed by the motor is most nearly

(A) 0.4 W
(B) 4 W
(C) 40 W
(D) 1 W
(E) 10 W

16. The gain in potential energy for the block is most nearly

(A) 0.4 J
(B) 4 J
(C) 40 J
(D) 1 J
(E) 10 J

17. A diver is 100 meters below sea level. What is the gauge pressure at that location?

(A) 0.1 atm
(B) 1.0 atm
(C) 1.1 atm
(D) 10 atm
(E) 11 atm

18. A piece of metal with a density of 1,500 kg/m^3 is suspended in a liquid of unknown density, as shown in the following diagram. The tension in the cord is measured to be 60% of the metal's actual weight.

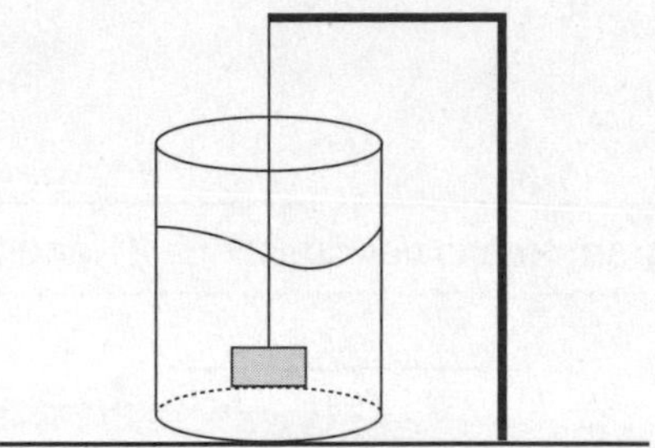

What is the density of the liquid?

(A) 2,400 kg/m^3

(B) 900 kg/m^3

(C) 800 kg/m^3

(D) 600 kg/m^3

(E) 400 kg/m^3

Use the following diagram to answer questions 19 and 20. It depicts a pendulum bob released from rest at point A.

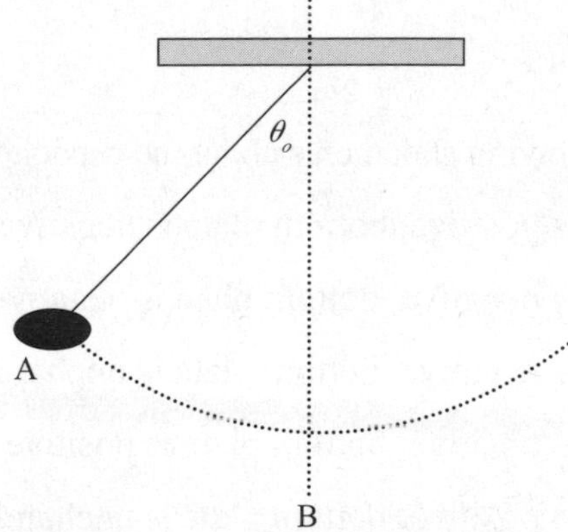

19. Which vector best describes the acceleration vector at point A?

(A) ↘

(B) →

(C) ↑

(D) ←

(E) None

20. Which vector best describes the velocity vector at point B?

(A) ↘

(B) →

(C) ↑

(D) ←

(E) None

Use the following diagram to answer questions 21 and 22.

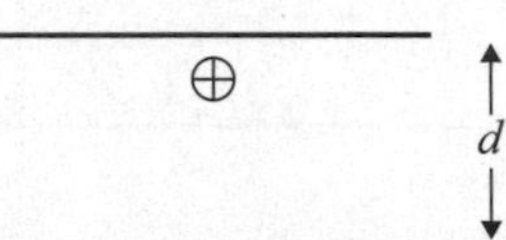

21. A charged particle of mass m and charge $+q$ is suspended by an electric field. The voltage difference between the two plates is ΔV. The distance between the plates is d. Determine the mass of the charged particle in terms of these other quantities.

(A) $m = \dfrac{q\Delta Vd}{g}$

(B) $m = \dfrac{q\Delta V}{dg}$

(C) $m = \dfrac{q}{g\Delta Vd}$

(D) $m = \dfrac{gd}{q\Delta V}$

(E) $m = \dfrac{\Delta V}{d}$

22. Which of the following statements about the capacitor plates could be true?

(A) Top plate is positive, bottom plate is negative

(B) Top plate is negative, bottom plate is negative

(C) Top plate is negative, bottom plate is uncharged

(D) Top plate is positive, bottom plate is positive

(E) Top plate is positive, bottom plate is uncharged

Use the following diagram to answer questions 23 and 24. The graph shows the characteristics of a mechanical wave. It is a graph of vertical displacement versus time.

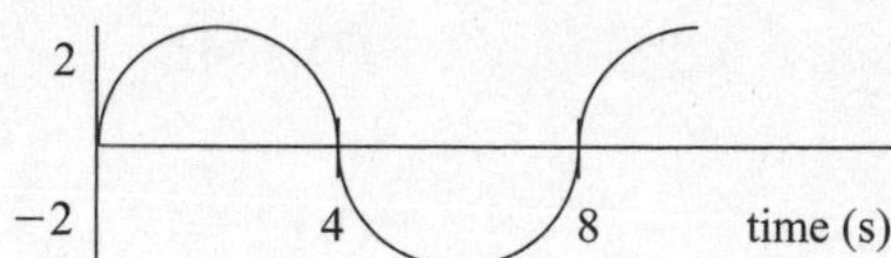

23. What is the amplitude of the wave?

(A) 2 units
(B) −2 units
(C) 4 units
(D) 8 units
(E) 16 units

24. What is the frequency of the wave?

(A) 2 Hz
(B) 4 Hz
(C) 8 Hz
(D) 0.25 Hz
(E) 0.125 Hz

25. The wave pulse shown in the following diagram is traveling on a taut string and traveling toward a rigid boundary (a wall). Which of the following statements best describes what happens to the pulse after hitting the rigid boundary?

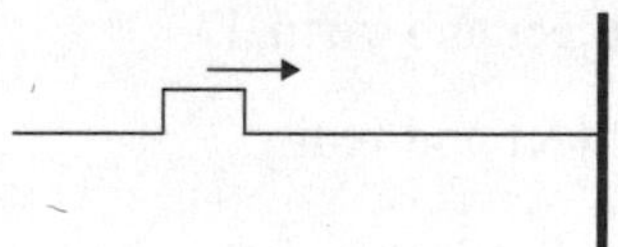

(A) Thc pulse is inverted and the same size.
(B) The pulse is not affected in any way.
(C) The pulse is inverted and smaller in amplitude.
(D) The pulse is traveling in the same orientation, with the same amplitude.
(E) The pulse gets smaller in width.

26. A guitar string of length L_o is plucked in its second harmonic mode. The string's first harmonic has a frequency of f_o. What is the wavelength of the standing wave formed by the second harmonic?

(A) $\frac{L_o}{2}$

(B) L_o

(C) $2L_o$

(D) $4L_o$

(E) $\frac{L_o}{4}$

27. A lens with a focal length of 0.1 m is forming a real image of an object. For the image to be twice the size of the object, the image must be located how far from the lens?

(A) 0.05 m

(B) 0.1 m

(C) 0.15 m

(D) 0.067 m

(E) 0.30 m

28. A diverging lens is forming an image of an object. Which of the following best describes the image produced from a diverging lens?

(A) Larger than object and virtual

(B) Larger than object and real

(C) Same size as object and real

(D) Smaller than object and virtual

(E) Smaller than object and real

29. A piece of glass has an index of refraction of $n = 1.5$. Determine the speed of light in the piece of glass.

(A) 3.0×10^8 m/s

(B) 1.5×10^8 m/s

(C) 2.0×10^8 m/s

(D) 1.0×10^8 m/s

(E) 4.5×10^8 m/s

30. A beam of electrons has energy ranging from 0.6 to 0.7 MeV. What is the order of magnitude of the wavelength of these electrons?

(A) 10^{-6} m
(B) 10^{-9} m
(C) 10^{-12} m
(D) 10^{-13} m
(E) 10^{-15} m

31. A toaster oven draws a current of 10 A at full power of 1,200 W. If the toaster is running at one-half of the current, what is the new power consumption of the toaster? (Assume a constant resistance for the toaster.)

(A) 200 W
(B) 300 W
(C) 600 W
(D) 900 W
(E) 1,000 W

Use the following circuit diagram to answer questions 32 and 33.

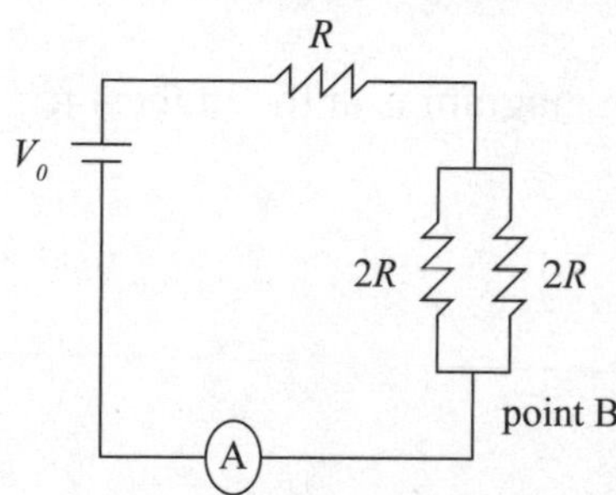

32. What is the current in ammeter A?

(A) $\frac{V_o}{R}$
(B) $\frac{V_o}{2R}$
(C) $\frac{V_o}{3R}$
(D) $\frac{V_o}{5R}$
(E) $\frac{5V_o}{6R}$

33. If the wire at point B is cut, what is the current in the ammeter?

(A) 0

(B) $\frac{V_o}{R}$

(C) $\frac{V_o}{2R}$

(D) $\frac{V_o}{3R}$

(E) $\frac{2V_o}{3R}$

Use the following diagram to answer questions 34 through 36. It is a PV diagram for a thermodynamic engine cycle (ABCDA). A mole of gas starts at point A and goes through the four processes and returns to point A.

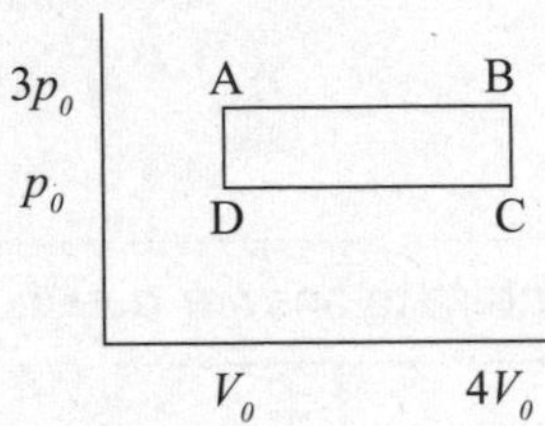

34. Which point on the diagram is at the highest temperature?

(A) A

(B) B

(C) C

(D) D

(E) All points are at equal temperatures.

35. Which processes added heat to the system?

I. Process AB

II. Process DA

III. Process BC

(A) I only

(B) I and II only

(C) I and III only

(D) II and III only

(E) III only

36. What is the net work done by the complete cycle (ABCDA)?

(A) $6p_oV_o$
(B) $8p_oV_o$
(C) $12p_oV_o$
(D) $3p_oV_o$
(E) $2p_oV_o$

37. A Carnot engine operates between the temperatures of 100°C and 300°C. Determine the efficiency of the engine.

(A) 25%
(B) 75%
(C) 35%
(D) 45%
(E) 67%

Use the following diagram to answer questions 38 and 39. The wire shown is carrying conventional current. An electron is placed at point P.

point P

38. What is the direction of the magnetic field at point P?

(A) Up
(B) Down
(C) Into the page
(D) Out of the page
(E) No field

39. What is the direction of the magnetic force on the electron placed at P?

(A) Up
(B) Down
(C) Into the page
(D) Out of the page
(E) No magnetic force

Use the following situation to answer questions 40 and 41. Three positive point charges, each equivalent to q, are placed at the vertices of an equilateral triangle, as shown in the diagram. The triangle has sides of length d. Point P is the midpoint of the base of the triangle.

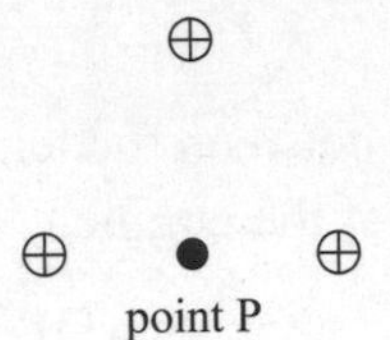

40. What is the direction of the electric field at point P.

(A) 0

(B) →

(C) ←

(D) ↓

(E) →

41. What is the electric potential at point P?

(A) $V_p = \frac{2kq}{d}\left(\frac{2\sqrt{3}+1}{\sqrt{3}}\right)$

(B) $V_p = \frac{kq}{\sqrt{3}d}$

(C) $V_p = \frac{2kq}{\sqrt{3}d}$

(D) $V_p = \frac{2kq}{d}$

(E) 0

42. A photoelectron has a kinetic energy of 2.5 eV. The work function of the metal that released the photoelectron has a work function of 0.5 eV. Determine the wavelength of the incident light in nanometers (nm).

(A) 621 nm

(B) 414 nm

(C) 497 nm

(D) 249 nm

(E) 100 nm

43. The uniform magnetic field B is directed into the page, as shown in the diagram. A wire with a current is placed in the field, as shown. Determine the direction of the force on the wire.

B field, into page

(A) Top of the page
(B) Bottom of the page
(C) No force
(D) Into the page
(E) Out of the page

Use the following situation to answer questions 44 through 46. Two lab carts are resting on a frictionless lab track. The two carts have a spring-loaded plunger between them. The plunger is exploded, and the two carts fly apart in opposite directions. Cart I has a mass of M. Cart II has a mass of $3M$. Cart I moved off with a speed of 2 m/s.

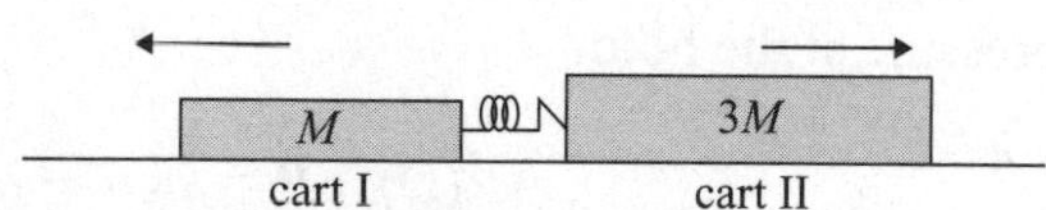

44. What is the speed of cart II?

(A) 3/2 m/s
(B) 2/3 m/s
(C) 2 m/s
(D) 3 m/s
(E) 5/3 m/s

45. What is the ratio of the kinetic energy of cart I to that of cart II?

(A) $\frac{KE_I}{KE_{II}} = \frac{1}{3}$

(B) $\frac{KE_I}{KE_{II}} = \frac{2}{3}$

(C) $\frac{KE_I}{KE_{II}} = \frac{3}{2}$

(D) $\frac{KE_I}{KE_{II}} = \frac{3}{1}$

(E) $\frac{KE_I}{KE_{II}} = \frac{1}{9}$

46. Which of the following statements about the energy change in the system is correct?

(A) Energy was not conserved because of friction in the track.

(B) There was a loss of energy in the system.

(C) There was a gain of energy because of the spring's potential energy.

(D) There was a gain of energy because cart II's mass is larger.

(E) There was a gain of energy because of gravitational potential energy.

Use the following situation to answer questions 47 and 48. A tall beaker (height *h*), is open to the air, and completely filled with water (density of ρ). A small hole is located at the side of the beaker at a distance *h*/2 above the table.

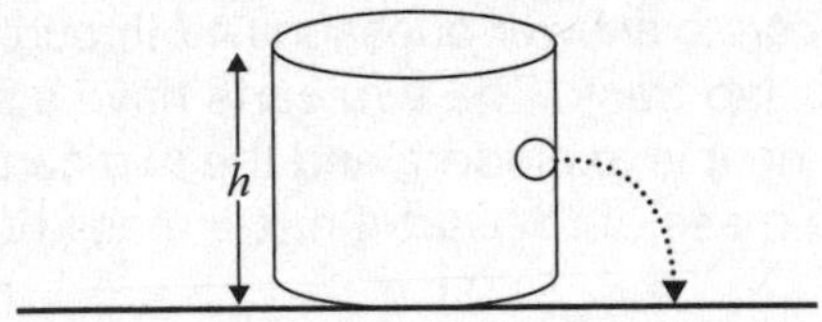

47. What is the pressure at the hole?

(A) $P = \rho g \frac{h}{2}$

(B) $P = \rho gh$

(C) $P = 2\rho gh$

(D) $P = \rho gh + atm$

(E) $P = \rho g \frac{h}{2} + atm$

48. What is the speed of the water coming out of the hole?

(A) $v = \sqrt{2gh}$

(B) $v = \sqrt{gh}$

(C) $v = \frac{\sqrt{2gh}}{2}$

(D) $v = 2\sqrt{2gh}$

(E) $v = \sqrt{\frac{gh}{2}}$

Use the following situation to answer questions 49 and 50. Three capacitors are arranged as shown in the diagram. A potential of V_o is applied to points A and B. The total charge on the $4C_o$ capacitor is Q_o.

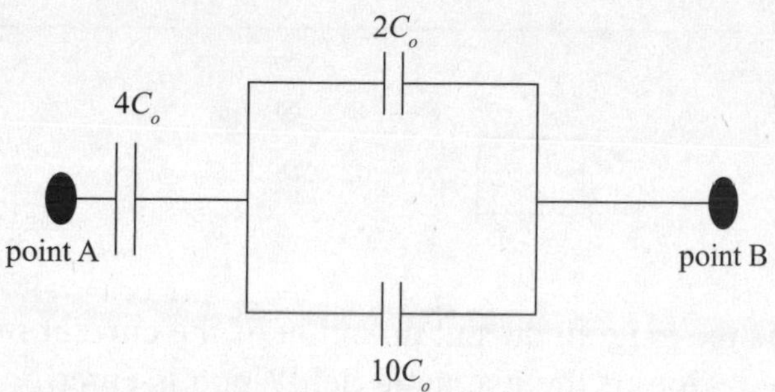

49. What is the magnitude of charge on the $10C_o$ capacitor?

(A) $10Q_o$

(B) $\frac{2}{3}Q_o$

(C) $\frac{1}{3}Q_o$

(D) $\frac{5}{6}Q_o$

(E) $\frac{1}{6}Q_o$

50. What is potential difference across the $2C_o$ capacitor?

(A) V_o

(B) $\frac{V_o}{4}$

(C) $\frac{3V_o}{4}$

(D) $\frac{V_o}{2}$

(E) $\frac{V_o}{3}$

Use the following situation to answer questions 51 and 52. A square conductive loop is dragged through a uniform magnetic field B, as shown in the diagram. The resistance of the wire is 5 ohms. The loop is dragged with a constant speed of 2 m/s. The uniform B field has a magnitude of 0.2 tesla. The side of the square loop is 0.5 m.

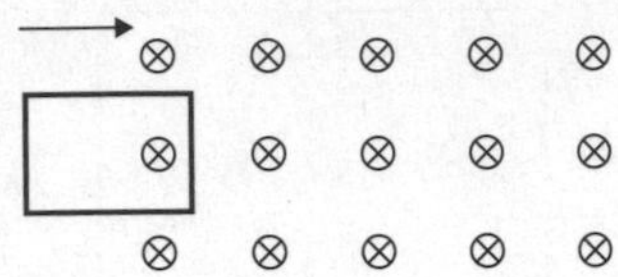

51. Determine the magnitude and direction of the current in the loop as it enters the region of the magnetic field (loop is entering and not completely in the field).

(A) 0.04 A, counterclockwise

(B) 0.04 A, clockwise

(C) 0.4 A, counterclockwise

(D) 0.4 A, clockwise

(E) 0.2 A, counterclockwise

52. Determine the magnitude and direction of the magnetic force on the loop as it moves into the field.

(A) 0.016 N, left

(B) 0.016 N, right

(C) 0.004 N, left

(D) 0.004 N, right

(E) 0.4 N, left

Use the following diagram to answer questions 53 and 54. Three identical bulbs (L_1, L_2, and L_3) are arranged in a circuit with two switches.

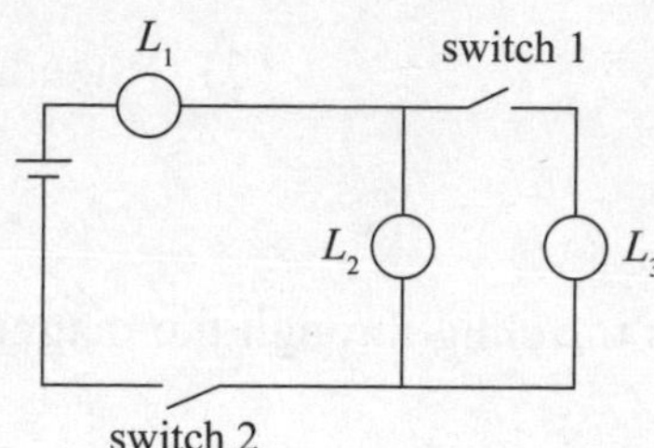

53. Both switches are put in the closed position, and the bulbs light up. Rank the three bulbs in order of increasing brightness.

(A) $L_1 < L_2 = L_3$

(B) $L_2 = L_3 < L_1$

(C) $L_1 = L_2 = L_3$

(D) $L_3 < L_2 < L_1$

(E) $L_2 = L_1 < L_2$

54. Switch 1 is now in the open position, and switch 2 is in the closed position. Rank the brightness of the bulbs.

(A) $L_1 > L_2$, L_3 goes out

(B) $L_1 = L_2$, L_3 goes out

(C) $L_2 > L_1$, L_3 goes out

(D) $L_1 = L_2 = L_3$

(E) All three bulbs go out.

55. An incoming ray of light enters a glass block as shown in the following diagram:

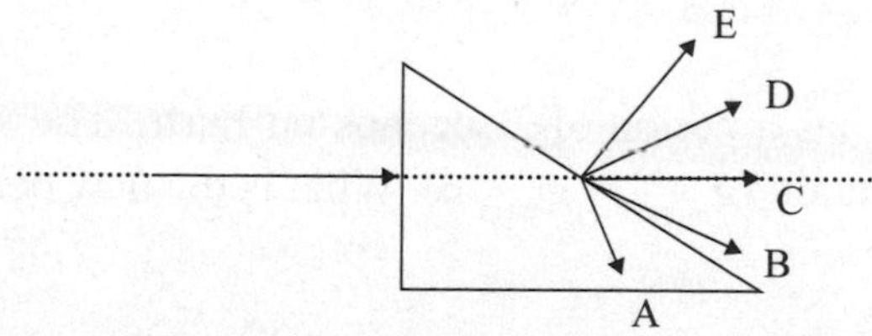

The light ray is traveling in air before it encounters the glass block. Which of the following best represents the refracted ray of light as it leaves the glass block?

(A) Ray A

(B) Ray B

(C) Ray C

(D) Ray D

(E) Ray E

56. The Michelson interferometer is an instrument used to measure the wavelength of light. On what wave principle is the interferometer based?

(A) Diffraction
(B) Polarization
(C) Interference
(D) Malus's law
(E) Standing waves

57. An alpha particle is traveling through the magnetic B field shown in the following diagram:

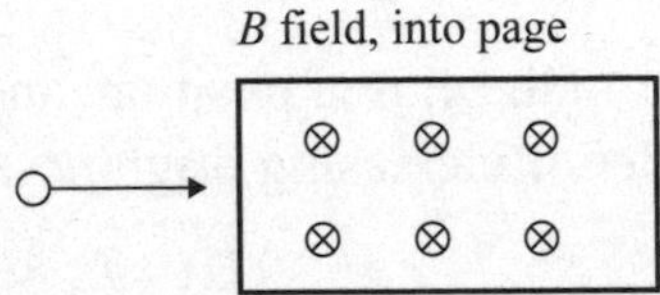

Which of the following descriptions best describes what will happen to the alpha particle as it goes into the B field?

(A) Goes through undeflected
(B) Deflects upward
(C) Deflects downward
(D) A circular path upward
(E) A circular path downward

58. A beam of gamma photons has an energy of 0.65 MeV. Determine the momentum of the gamma photons.

(A) 1.04×10^{-13} kgm/s
(B) 1.04×10^{-7} kgm/s
(C) 3.47×10^{-22} kgm/s
(D) 3.47×10^{-16} kgm/s
(E) 3×10^{-8} kgm/s

59. A pendulum has a period of 2 seconds on Earth. The same pendulum is taken to the moon ($g_{moon} = g_{earth}/6$). What is the new period of the pendulum on the moon?

(A) 0.33 s
(B) $\frac{\sqrt{6}}{3}$ s
(C) 12.0 s
(D) $2\sqrt{6}$ s
(E) 2 s

Use the following situation to answer questions 60 through 62. Two charges are aligned on a line, as shown in the following diagram. Both charges are fixed in space and cannot move. Point P on the line is a distance d away from the $-Q$ charge. Point M is at the midpoint of the two charges.

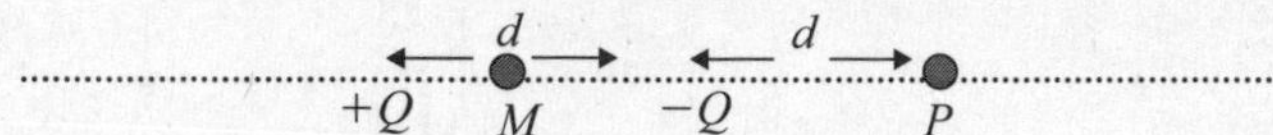

60. What is the magnitude and direction of the electric field at the midpoint between the two charges?

(A) 0

(B) $\frac{8kQ}{d^2}$, right

(C) $\frac{8kQ}{d^2}$, left

(D) $\frac{2kQ}{d^2}$, right

(E) $\frac{2kQ}{d^2}$, left

61. An electron (magnitude of charge E) is placed at point P. What is the magnitude of the force on the electron?

(A) 0

(B) $\frac{2kQe}{d^2}$

(C) $\frac{kQe}{4d^2}$

(D) $\frac{3kQe}{4d^2}$

(E) $\frac{5kQe}{4d^2}$

62. What is the electric potential at point P?

(A) 0

(B) $\frac{kQ}{2d}$

(C) $-\frac{kQ}{2d}$

(D) $\frac{2kQ}{d}$

(E) $-\frac{2kQ}{d}$

Use the following diagram to answer questions 63 and 64. The table is frictionless.

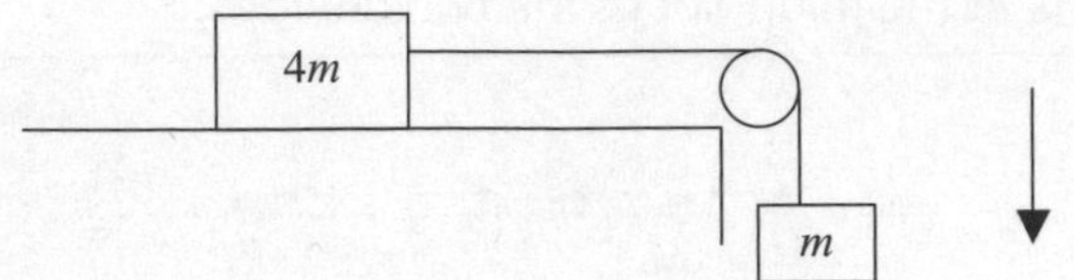

63. What is the acceleration of mass m?

(A) g
(B) $g/2$
(C) $g/3$
(D) $g/4$
(E) $g/5$

64. What is the tension in the cord attached to the $4m$ mass?

(A) $T = \frac{4mg}{5}$
(B) $T = \frac{3mg}{5}$
(C) $T = \frac{mg}{3}$
(D) $T = \frac{2mg}{3}$
(E) $T = \frac{4mg}{3}$

Use the following situation to answer questions 65 and 66. A box with a mass of 5 kg is pulled by a force of 25 N, as shown in the diagram. The coefficient of kinetic friction between the box and the surface is $\mu_k = 0.5$. The box is being pulled by the force over a distance of 2.0 m. (Note: $\sin 37 = 0.6$ and $\cos 37 = 0.8$.)

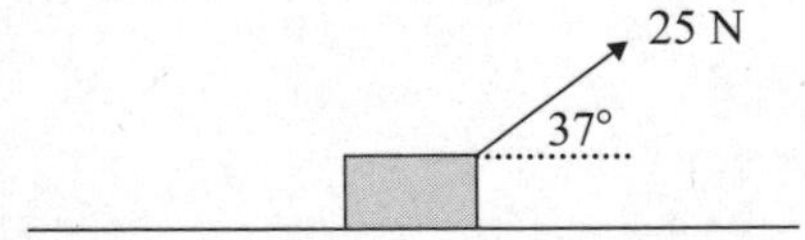

65. What is the work done by the applied force?

(A) 50 J
(B) 40 J
(C) 35 J
(D) 30 J
(E) 25 J

66. What is the increase in the kinetic energy of the box after this event?

(A) 40 J
(B) 13.5 J
(C) 6 J
(D) 24 J
(E) 16 J

67. An atom absorbs a light of wavelength 400 nm. The excited state that an electron jumps to from the ground state must be ______ above the ground state.

(A) 1.1 eV
(B) 2.1 eV
(C) 3.1 eV
(D) 4.1 eV
(E) 5.1 eV

68. Light of 700 nm is incident on a diffraction grating with slit spacing ($d = 1 \times 10^{-4}$ m). An interference pattern is made on the wall 2.0 m away from the slit. What is the distance between the bright central fringe and the first-order bright fringe?

(A) .014 cm
(B) 1.4 cm
(C) 14 cm
(D) 1.4×10^{-4} cm
(E) 1.4×10^{-7} cm

Use the following velocity-versus-time graph to answer questions 69 and 70. The graph describes an object in motion for the times $0 < t < 5$ seconds.

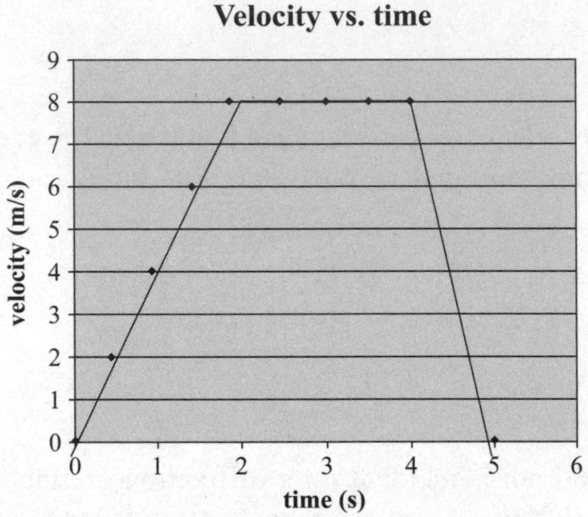

Velocity vs. time

69. What is the distance traveled by this object during the 5 seconds of motion?

(A) 40 m
(B) 48 m
(C) 16 m
(D) 24 m
(E) 28 m

70. What it is the average velocity of the object during the 5-second interval?

(A) 4 m/s
(B) 5.6 m/s
(C) 8 m/s
(D) 2 m/s
(E) 1.6 m/s

STOP

This is the end of Section I.
If time still remains, you may check your work only in this section.
Do not begin Section II until instructed to do so.

Section II

Time: 90 Minutes
6 Free-Response Questions

<u>DIRECTIONS</u>: Carefully read each question and be sure to answer *each part* of the question. Show your work. Crossed-out work will not be graded. You may use your calculator and the equation tables for Physics B found at the back of this book for this section of the exam.

1. A mass m of 10 kg is on an incline plane attached to an unknown mass M arranged in the pulley system, as shown in the following diagram. The incline has friction with coefficients noted in the diagram. The pulley is frictionless.

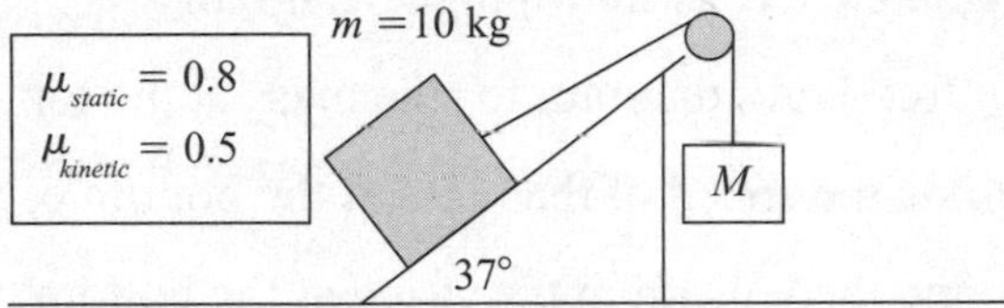

(a) Determine the smallest m (to the nearest whole number) that will cause the system to accelerate up the incline.

(b) Using the value for m determined in part (a), determine the acceleration of the system.

(c) Determine the tension in the cord attached the two masses.

2.

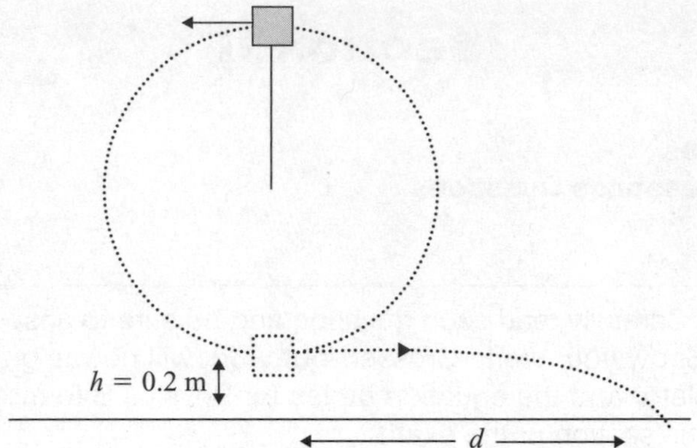

A mass of 2 kg is rotating on a string in vertical circular motion. The radius of the circle is 0.5 m. The speed at the top of circle is $v_{top} = 5$ m/s. After rotating through a complete cycle, the string is cut at the bottom of the circle. The mass goes flying off and lands a distance d away from the point of being launched, as shown in the diagram.

(a) Draw a free-body diagram for the mass at the top of the circle.

(b) Determine the speed of the mass at the bottom of the circle.

(c) Determine the tension in the string at the bottom of the circle.

(d) Determine the distance d.

3. A physics student is performing an experiment on buoyancy. The student takes a rectangular slab of metal (area A and length h) and hangs it from a force sensor, as shown in the following diagram. The force sensor measures the tension in the cord. The student then slowly drops the metal into a large container of water. The new tension is measured each time the metal goes deeper into the water. The student makes a data table as shown under the diagram and plots a graph of $\left[\frac{T}{mg}\right]$ *vs* depth. From this graph, the density of the metal (ρ_{metal}) can be determined. The height of the metal slab is h = 15 cm. The density of water is $\rho_{water} = 1000\ \text{kg/m}^3$. The weight of the slab is 20 N. The variable for depth is y, as shown in the diagram.

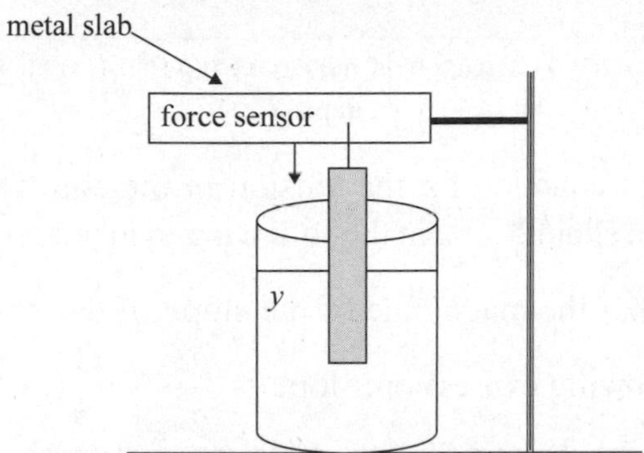

This is the data taken by the student:

Tension	Weight	$\left[\frac{T}{mg}\right]$	Depth
20.0 N	20 N	1.0	0.0 m
19.1 N	20 N	0.96	0.01 m
18.2 N	20 N	0.91	0.02 m
16.5 N	20 N	0.82	0.04 m
13.8 N	20 N	0.69	0.07 m
10.2 N	20 N	0.51	0.11 m
6.7 N	20 N	0.33	0.15 m

(a) Plot $\left[\frac{T}{mg}\right]$ vs depth in the following grid:

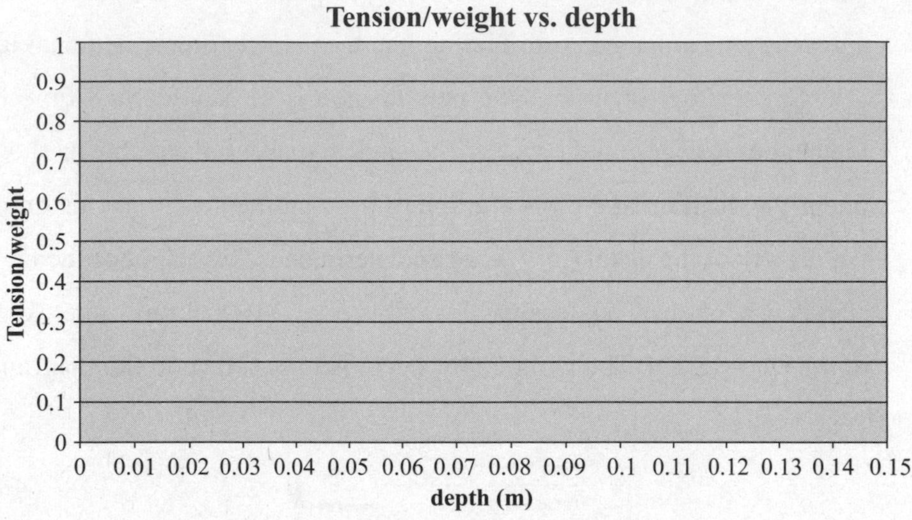

(b) Write an equation for the tension in the cord for any depth y. The equation should contain the following symbols: ρ_{metal}, h, y, ρ_{water}, A_{slab}

(c) Show that the magnitude of the slope of the graph is equivalent to the following expression: slope $= \frac{\rho_{water}}{\rho_{metal}} \cdot \frac{1}{h} \cdot y$.

(d) Determine the metal's density from your graph.

(e) How would the graph change if a thicker piece of metal (of the same length) were used?

4. A physics student is making various circuits in the physics laboratory. The student has access to three lightbulbs with the following power ratings:

   (1) 3 W power at 30 V

   (2) 5 W power at 30 V

   (3) 15 W power at 30 V

   For the first part of the experiment, the student arranges the three bulbs in parallel attached to a 30-V battery source.

   (a) Draw a circuit diagram of this arrangement. Include in the diagram an ammeter to measure the *total current* in the circuit.

   (b) Determine the total power rating of the three bulbs in parallel.

   (c) Determine the total number of electrons that pass through the battery in 1 minute of operation.

   For part two of the experiment, the student arranges all three lightbulbs in series and attaches them to the 30-V battery.

   (d) Determine the total power rating of the three bulbs arranged in series.

5. (a) An object (use an arrow) is placed at a distance of 20 cm from a concave mirror ($f = 15$ cm). Draw a ray diagram showing the object and the image. Make the diagram to scale. Draw at least two rays (use a straight edge with centimeter marks).

   (b) An object (use an arrow) is placed 20 cm from a convex lens ($f = 15$ cm). Draw a ray diagram locating the image. Draw at least two rays.

   (c) If the object moves from 20 cm to 30 cm away from the lens, what happens to the size of the image?

6. A mole of gas enclosed in a chamber with a moveable piston undergoes the following three processes in a complete thermodynamic cycle. The gas starts the cycle with the following initial conditions:

$$T_1 = 300 \text{ Kelvin}, p_1 = 1.0 \times 10^5 \text{ pascals}, V_1 = 0.02 \text{ m}^3$$

Process I The gas is heated under constant volume. The final temperature of the gas is $T_2 = 600$ kelvin.

Process II The gas is now allowed to expand the volume of the chamber and expands to a new greater volume, V_2, and it reaches the atmospheric pressure of $p_1 = 1.0 \times 10^5$ pascals. During this process the gas cools to a temperature of 485 kelvin.

Process III The gas is now cooled at a constant pressure (atmospheric pressure -1.0×10^5 pascals). The gas is cooled until it reaches the initial temperature of 300 kelvin.

(a) What is the pressure of the gas at the end of process I?

(b) What is the new volume of the gas at the end of process II?

(c) How much heat was expelled during the cooling phase (process III)?

(d) Make a sketch of pressure versus volume for the complete cycle.

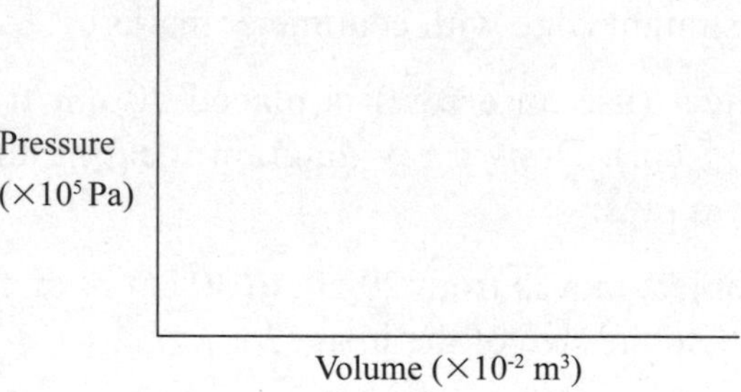

END OF EXAM

PRACTICE EXAM 1

AP Physics B

Answer Key

1. (D)	15. (C)	29. (C)	43. (A)	57. (D)
2. (D)	16. (E)	30. (C)	44. (B)	58. (C)
3. (E)	17. (D)	31. (B)	45. (D)	59. (D)
4. (C)	18. (D)	32. (B)	46. (C)	60. (B)
5. (C)	19. (A)	33. (D)	47. (A)	61. (D)
6. (B)	20. (B)	34. (B)	48. (B)	62. (C)
7. (B)	21. (B)	35. (B)	49. (D)	63. (E)
8. (B)	22. (C)	36. (A)	50. (B)	64. (A)
9. (C)	23. (A)	37. (C)	51. (A)	65. (B)
10. (D)	24. (E)	38. (C)	52. (C)	66. (C)
11. (C)	25. (C)	39. (E)	53. (B)	67. (C)
12. (B)	26. (B)	40. (D)	54. (B)	68. (B)
13. (C)	27. (C)	41. (A)	55. (B)	69. (E)
14. (C)	28. (D)	42. (B)	56. (C)	70. (B)

PRACTICE EXAM 1

AP Physics B

Detailed Explanations of Answers

Section I

1. **(D)**

The slope of a velocity-versus-time graph is the acceleration. Only the graph in answer choice (D) has a changing slope representing a changing acceleration.

2. **(D)**

In equilibrium, the frictional force up the incline equals the downward component of the weight $(mg)(\sin 37)$. If the mass is doubled, then both forces change proportionally. Therefore, $(2mg)(\sin 37)$ is a correct value for the frictional force as well as $2f$. The new block cannot go into sliding mode. The slipping angle is the same for all values of mass and only dependent on the material (μ) and the angle. Because both those factors did not change, the system will remain in equilibrium, thus eliminating choice (E) from consideration.

3. **(E)**

At the slipping point, $\mu s = \tan \phi$. $\text{Tan}\,37 = 0.75$.

4. **(C)**

$$R = \frac{v_o^2 \sin(2\theta)}{g} = \frac{(10)^2 \sin(2 \cdot 45)}{10} = 10 \text{ m}$$

5. **(C)**

At point B, the projectile has a completely horizontal velocity. And as a funny physics teacher once said, "Gravity never takes a holiday," so the projectile has a downward vertical acceleration.

6. **(B)**

The slope of the force-versus-displacement graph is the spring constant. Therefore, the spring constant is 2.5 N/m.

7. **(B)**

This question can trick many physics students. Don't fall for it! Calculating *average velocity* requires the total displacement and the total time. The car spends different amounts of time at each velocity. The average velocity is not simply the average of the two speeds (15 km/hr). Find the total time of the trip as follows:

$$t_{firsthalf} = \frac{\Delta x}{v} = \frac{1\text{ km}}{10\text{ km/hr}} = \frac{1}{10}\text{ hr}$$

$$t_{secondhalf} = \frac{\Delta x}{v} = \frac{1\text{ km}}{20\text{ km/hr}} = \frac{1}{20}\text{ hr}$$

$$v_{avg} = \frac{\Delta x}{\Delta t} = \frac{2\text{ km}}{\left[\frac{1}{10}\text{ hr} + \frac{1}{20}\text{ hr}\right]} = \frac{2\text{ km}}{\frac{3}{20}\text{ hr}} = \frac{40}{3}\text{ km/hr} = 13.33\text{ km/hr}$$

8. **(B)**

The acceleration is center directed along the radial direction of the circle that is circumscribed by the pendulum bob.

9. **(C)**

Two of the three statements are true. The gravitational force is not 0.

10. **(D)**

$$\frac{\text{kg}\cdot\text{m}^2}{\text{s}^3} = \frac{\text{kg}\cdot\text{m}}{\text{s}^2}\cdot\frac{1}{\text{s}}\cdot\text{m} = \text{N}\cdot\text{m}\cdot\frac{1}{\text{s}} = \frac{\text{Joule}}{\text{s}} = \text{Watt}$$

11. **(C)**

Because the initial velocity is completely horizontal, the vertical component of the initial velocity is 0. Therefore, solve for time as follows:

$$\Delta y = v_{oy}t + \frac{1}{2}gt^2 \Rightarrow h = 0 + \frac{1}{2}gt^2 \Rightarrow t = \sqrt{\frac{2h_o}{g}}$$

12. **(B)**

The total energy at impact is equivalent to the total energy at the initial point of the projectile's motion because of conservation of total mechanical energy (gravity is the only force doing work in the example). The total energy at the initial point of the projectile's motion is a kinetic energy and a potential energy equivalent to *mgh*.

13. **(C)**

Because the block is sliding and accelerating, this problem requires the use of the definition for kinetic frictional force. First, draw a free-body diagram of the accelerating mass:

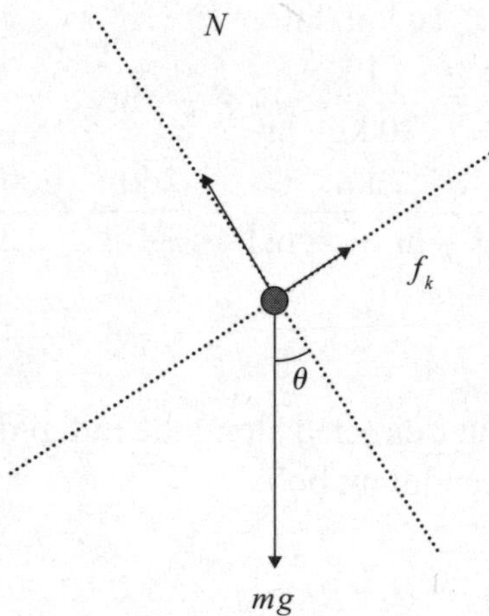

$$\sum F_x = ma = mg\sin 37 - f_k$$

$$\sum F_y = 0 = \mathrm{N} - mg\cos 37$$

$$f_k = \mu_k \mathrm{N} = (0.5)(mg\cos 37) = (0.5)\left((1\text{ kg})(10\text{ m/s}^2)(.8)\right) = 4\text{ N}$$

$$\sum F_x = ma = mg\sin 37 - f_k \Rightarrow a = g\sin 37 - \frac{f_k}{m} = (10\text{ m/s}^2)(0.6) - \frac{4\text{ N}}{1\text{ kg}}$$

$$a = 6 - 4 = 2\text{ m/s}^2$$

14. **(C)**

See the explanation for question 13.

15. **(C)**

Because the block is being lifted at a constant speed, the lifting force has the same magnitude as the weight. A relationship between power and velocity is $P = Fv$. Thus,

$$\text{Power} = (\text{mg})(2\text{ m/s}) = (2\text{ kg})(10\text{ m/s}^2)(2\text{ m/s}) = 40\text{ W.}$$

16. **(E)**

The gain in potential energy is simply

$$\Delta U_g = mg\Delta h = (2\,\text{kg})(10\,\text{m/s}^2)(0.5) = 10\text{ Joules.}$$

17. **(D)**

The change in pressure at a certain depth below sea level is calculated as follows:

$$p = \rho gh = (1000\text{ kg/m}^3)(10\text{ m/s}^2(100\text{ m})) = 1 \times 10^6\text{ Pa}$$

$$1 \times 10^6\text{ Pa} = 10\text{ atm}(1\text{ atm} = 1 \times 10^5\text{ Pa})$$

Gauge pressure is simply the pressure that a gauge would read at that location. Gauge pressure can only measure pressure differences above or below atmospheric pressure (1 atm).

18. **(D)**

The free-body drawing of the metal object is shown here:

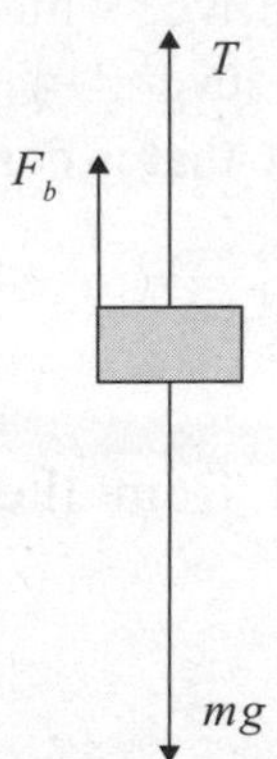

$$\sum F = 0 = T + F_b - mg \Rightarrow F_b = 40\% \cdot mg$$

$$F_b = \text{weight of liquid displaced}$$

$$\text{So, } F_b = \rho_{liquid} V g = 0.4mg_{object}$$

$$\rho_{liq} V_{obj} g = 0.4(\rho_{object}) V_{obj} g$$

$$\rho_{liq} = 0.4\rho_{obj} = 0.4 \cdot 1500 = 600\text{ kg/m}^3$$

19. **(A)**

Because the pendulum is at an amplitude, it has an instantaneous velocity of 0. That means the centripetal acceleration is 0. The only acceleration is the tangential acceleration (perpendicular to the pendulum cord).

20. **(B)**

The velocity vector is always tangent to the trajectory.

21. **(B)**

The weight of the charged particle must equal the electric force for the particle to be suspended between the plates.

$$F_e = mg$$

$$qE = mg$$

The E field magnitude is unknown, but the potential difference between the plates is known. The relationship between the electric field between parallel plates and the potential difference between the plates is $\Delta V = Ed$.

Solve for mass as follows:

$$m = \frac{qE}{g} = \frac{q\Delta V}{dg}$$

22. **(C)**

The suspended charge is positive, which means the electric field must be directed upward. There are several ways to make that possible with conductive plates, but the only one that is correct to have the top plate negative and the bottom plate uncharged.

23. **(A)**

The amplitude is measured from the maximum location from the equilibrium, which is 2 units.

24. **(E)**

The period of the wave is 8 seconds. The frequency is the reciprocal of the period: $f = 1/8$ Hz $= 0.125$ Hz.

25. **(C)**

After hitting a rigid barrier, a wave will invert and lose energy. The loss of energy is shown in a reduction of the original amplitude.

26. **(B)**

The second harmonic has one full wavelength between endpoints. Thus, the length of the guitar, L_o, is the wavelength of the second harmonic.

27. **(C)**

If an image is twice the size of the object, the image distance is twice the object distance:

$$M = -\frac{h_i}{h_o} = \frac{d_i}{d_o} = 2$$

$$\Rightarrow d_i = 2d_o$$

Ignore the negative sign because it only refers to the image being inverted or upright.

Apply the lens equation and solve for the object distance:

$$\frac{1}{f} = \frac{1}{d_o} + \frac{1}{d_i} \Rightarrow \frac{1}{0.1} = \frac{1}{d_o} + \frac{1}{2d_o} = \frac{3}{2d_o}$$

$$0.1 = \frac{2d_o}{3} \Rightarrow d_o = 0.15$$

28. **(D)**

All diverging lenses produce images that are virtual and smaller than the object.

29. **(C)**

The index of refraction is defined as

$$n = \frac{c}{c_n} \Rightarrow c_n = \frac{c}{n} = \frac{3 \times 10^8}{1.5} = 2 \times 10^8 \text{ m/s}.$$

Remember, the speed of light in any medium will be less than the speed of light. So any answer choice greater than the speed of light can be eliminated.

30. **(C)**

According to the DeBroglie wavelength, a beam of electrons also has the ability to interfere with itself and produce interference patterns. The energy of the electron beam is between 0.6 and 0.7 MeV. The energy of a photon is $E = hf$:

$$E = hf = \frac{hc}{\lambda} \Rightarrow \lambda = \frac{hc}{E} = \frac{(4.14 \times 10^{-15} \text{ eV} \cdot \text{s})(3 \times 10^8 \text{ m/s})}{0.6 \times 10^6 \text{ eV}}$$

$$= \frac{1.24 \times 10^{-6}\ \text{eV} \cdot \text{m}}{0.6 \times 10^{6}\ \text{eV}}$$

$$\Rightarrow \lambda = 2.2 \times 10^{-12}\ \text{m}$$

Therefore, the correct answer is 10^{-12} m. This is a factor of 10^5 smaller than the wavelength of light. That is a way to keep these values in perspective.

31. **(B)**

At constant resistance, the toaster consumes energy at the rate of $P = I^2R$. Thus, if the current is halved, the power decreases by a factor of one-fourth. That means the new power consumption is 300 W.

32. **(B)**

The current in the marked ammeter is equivalent to the total operating current in the circuit. First, reduce the circuit and find the equivalent resistance.

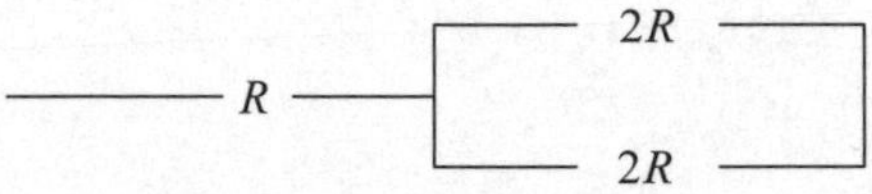

R 2R 2R

The two resistors in parallel make an equivalent of R:

$$\frac{1}{R_{eq}} = \frac{1}{2R} + \frac{1}{2R} = \frac{2}{2R} \Rightarrow R_{eq} = R$$

Add this resistance to the original resistance of R, giving a total resistance of $2R$. This gives a total operating current of $I = V_o/2R$.

33. **(D)**

If the wire is cut at point B, the circuit becomes a one-loop circuit with resistances of R and $2R$ in series. This gives a new operating current of $I = V_o/3R$.

34. **(B)**

The point on the diagram with greatest temperature is point B. It is the point with the greatest product of pressure times volume ($pV = nRT$).

35. **(B)**

Heat is added to the system in AB and DA. A quick way to determine this is to use the molar heat capacity relationship:

$$\Delta Q = nC_V \Delta T$$

$$\Delta Q = nC_p \Delta T$$

One expression is used under constant pressure, and one is used under constant volume. These two processes show temperature increases at their endpoints, which indicates positive heat input. The other two processes have a lower final temperature; therefore, heat is lost during those processes.

36. **(A)**

The net work is the net area enclosed by the cycle:

$6p_oV_o$.

37. **(C)**

This is a classic "trick question." When working in thermodynamics, remember that all absolute temperatures must be measured in kelvin. The change in kelvin has the same magnitude as the change in Celsius, so this is never an issue with computations involving ΔT. However, for the gas law and other computations involving an absolute temperature, the value must be measured in kelvin. The efficiency of a Carnot engine can be represented by "hot" and "cold" reservoir temperatures alone. Here is the computation for this efficiency:

$$e = 1 - \frac{T_c}{T_h} = 1 - \frac{([100\text{ C}^\circ + 273\text{ C}^\circ]\text{ K})}{([300\text{ C}^\circ + 273\text{ C}^\circ]\text{ K})} = 1 - \frac{373\text{ K}}{573\text{ K}} = 0.35$$

Watch out for the "trick" incorrect answer. Forgetting to change the temperatures to kelvin results in the following calculation:

$$1 - \frac{100}{300} = 0.67$$

38. **(C)**

The field of a current-carrying wire encircles the wire in a sense predicted by the right-hand rule. With the right-hand thumb in the direction of the current, the fingers wrap in the sense of the field. At point P, the field is directed into the page.

39. **(E)**

There is no magnetic force on the electron. The stationary electron has no magnetic field associated with it. Therefore, there is no second magnetic field to interact with the current's field.

40. **(D)**

The two charges at the base of the triangle produce equal and oppositely directed electric fields. These two cancel, leaving only the vertically downward-directed field of the top charge.

41. **(A)**

The potential resulting from the three charges is calculated using the relationship of potential resulting from point charges. Remember to use geometry to find the distance of the top charge to point P. That distance is $\frac{\sqrt{3}}{2}d$.

$$V_p = \sum \frac{kq_i}{r_i} = \frac{kq}{\left(\frac{d}{2}\right)} + \frac{kq}{\left(\frac{d}{2}\right)} + \frac{kq}{\left(\frac{\sqrt{3}}{2}d\right)} = \frac{4kq}{d} + \frac{2kq}{\sqrt{3}d}$$

$$= \frac{2kq}{d}\left(2 + \frac{1}{\sqrt{3}}\right) = \frac{2kq}{d}\left(\frac{2\sqrt{3}+1}{\sqrt{3}}\right)$$

42. **(B)**

The photoelectric effect relationship equates the incoming energy of a photon of light to the maximum kinetic energy of an ejected electron. This is the relationship $E = \vartheta_{workfunct.} + KE_{max}$

In this problem, the work function is 0.5 eV and the maximum kinetic energy is 2.5 eV. Thus, the incoming light must be 3.0 eV. Compute the wavelength of light from the energy of a photon relationship:

$$E = hf = h\frac{c}{\lambda} = \frac{hc}{\lambda} \Rightarrow \lambda = \frac{hc}{E} = \frac{(4.14 \times 10^{-15} \text{ eV} \cdot \text{s})(3 \times 10^{8} \text{ m/s})}{3.0 \text{ eV}}$$

$$\lambda = 4.14 \times 10^{-7} \text{ m} = 414 \text{ nm}$$

43. **(A)**

Using the right-hand rule for magnetic force: thumb of the right hand matches the current's direction, fingers of the right hand point into the page (with B), leaving the palm (magnetic force) facing upward toward the top of the page.

44. **(B)**

$$p_1 - p_2 = 0 \Rightarrow p_1 = p_2 \Rightarrow (M)(2 \text{ m/s}) = (3M)v$$

$$v = \frac{2}{3} \text{ m/s}$$

45. **(D)**

$$KE_{\text{I}} = \frac{1}{2}M(2)^2 = 2M$$

$$KE_{\text{II}} = \frac{1}{2}(3M)\left(\frac{2}{3}\right)^2 = \frac{2}{3}M$$

$$\frac{KE_{\text{I}}}{KE_{\text{II}}} = \frac{2M}{\left(\frac{2}{3}M\right)} = \frac{3}{1}$$

46. **(C)**

The gain in energy in the system came from the energy that was present in the spring before the carts were released.

47. **(A)**

Pressure caused by a liquid at a certain depth is defined by the following relationship: $P = \rho gh$. At a depth of $h/2$, this gives a pressure of $\rho g\frac{h}{2}$.

48. **(B)**

Using the Bernoulli equation, solve for the velocity of the water at the hole:

$$p_1 + \rho g y_1 + \frac{1}{2}\rho v_1^2 = p_2 + \rho g y_2 + \frac{1}{2}\rho v_2^2$$

$p_1 = p_2 = p_{atm}$ (both the top of the container and the hole are exposed to the air)

$y_1 = \frac{h}{2}$ and $v_1 \approx 0$ m/s

(the water at the top of the container moves at an imperceptable velocity)

$y_2 = 0$, $v_2 = \textit{unknown}$

So, $\Rightarrow \rho g\frac{h}{2} = \frac{1}{2}\rho v_2^2 \Rightarrow v_2 = \sqrt{gh}$

49. **(D)**

First, find the equivalent capacitance of the network. The $2C_o$ and $10C_o$ capacitors in parallel make a $12C$ capacitor. That $12C$ is in series with the $4C_o$. The $4C_o$ and $12C$ in series add reciprocally:

$$\frac{1}{C_e} = \frac{1}{4C} + \frac{1}{12C} = \frac{4}{12C} = \frac{1}{3C} \Rightarrow C_e = 3C$$

Therefore, the net charge in the system is the product of this capacitance times the voltage: $Q_o = 3C_oV_o$. The $4C_o$ and the parallel branch both have equal amounts of charges on the capacitor due to induction. But the $10C_o$ and the $2C_o$ in parallel must add up to the total charge on the system. So $10C_o$ is five-sixths of the total $12C$ capacitance, which means it will have five-sixths of the total charge on it. Remember, the voltage is equal across the parallel branch, so the charge on each capacitor is simply proportional to the capacitance value. Thus, the charge on the $10C_o$ capacitor is $\frac{5}{6}Q_o$.

50. **(B)**

The voltage across the $2C_o$ capacitor is the same as the voltage across the entire parallel branch. The voltage is equal to the net charge on the system divided by the equivalent capacitance of the two parallel capacitors:

$$V = \frac{Q_{net}}{C_e} = \frac{3C_oV_o}{12C_o} = \frac{V_o}{4}$$

51. **(A)**

The EMF produced by a conductive wire moving through a field is equivalent to $\varepsilon = Bvl$. Thus, the induced voltage is

$$\varepsilon = (0.2T)(2\text{ m/s})(0.5\text{ m}) = 0.2\text{ Volts}$$

$$I = \frac{V}{R} = \frac{0.2\text{ V}}{5\text{ ohms}} = 0.04\text{ A}$$

Determining the direction of the current requires applying Lenz's law to the situation. The field that is causing the flux change in the loop is directed into the page (because the flux change is positive, or increasing). Therefore, the induced current will create an opposition to this positive flux change. The current will be counterclockwise around the loop to produce an outward-induced magnetic field.

52. **(C)**

The force on the wire that is in the field is equivalent to $F = BIL$. Computing the force gives $F = (0.2\text{ T})(0.04\text{ A})(0.5\text{ m}) = 0.004\text{ N}$. This force is directed to the left because the changing flux will oppose the flux change. The system will try to resist the incoming loop and try to force it out of the field (to the left).

53. **(B)**

In this case, L_2 and L_3 will "split" the current in half in each bulb. Thus, the total current is in L_1, and L_2 and L_3 each have half of the total current.

54. **(B)**

In this new configuration, L_3 goes out and L_1 and L_2 are in series. In series, the current is the same at all points, so the two bulbs have the same current.

55. **(B)**

Take the time to draw a diagram. The ray is unrefracted at the first interface (left side), hits the other interface (right side), and then bends away from the normal as it heads back into the air. This leaves ray B as the only possible option.

56. **(C)**

It is based on the interference of light.

57. **(D)**

The alpha particle has a net positive charge. Therefore, it will move in a circular path in the B field. Applying the right-hand rule yields a circular upward path in this case. The right thumb is in the velocity direction and the fingers follow the field into the page, leaving the right hand palm upward, indicating the direction of the deflected charge.

58. **(C)**

The momentum of a photon is

$$p = \frac{h}{\lambda} = \frac{6.626 \times 10^{-34}\ \text{J/s}}{\lambda} \Rightarrow \lambda = \frac{hc}{E} = \frac{(4.14 \times 10^{-15}\ \text{eVs})(3 \times 10^{8}\ \text{m/s})}{0.65 \times 10^{6}\ \text{eV}}$$

$$= \frac{1.242 \times 10^{-6}}{0.65 \times 10^{6}} = 1.9 \times 10^{-12}\ \text{m}$$

$$\therefore p = \frac{h}{\lambda} = \frac{6.626 \times 10^{-34}\ \text{J/s}}{1.91 \times 10^{-12}\ \text{m}} = 3.47 \times 10^{-22}\ \text{kgm/s}$$

59. **(D)**

Because the same pendulum (of the same length) is taken to the moon, the only thing that is changed is the gravitational acceleration. The period of a pendulum is

$$T = 2\pi\sqrt{\frac{l}{g}} \Rightarrow T^2 = 4\pi^2\frac{l}{g}$$

$$T_e^2 = 4\pi^2\frac{l}{g} \text{ and } T_m^2 = 4\pi^2\frac{l}{\frac{g}{6}}$$

$$\frac{T_m^2}{T_e^2} = \frac{4\pi^2\frac{l}{\frac{g}{6}}}{4\pi^2\frac{l}{g}} = 6 \Rightarrow T_m^2 = T_e^2 \cdot 6 \Rightarrow T_m = T_e\sqrt{6} = 2\sqrt{6} \approx 4.9\,\text{s}$$

60. **(B)**

At the midpoint, both the $+Q$ and $-Q$ charges exert a field to the right. The two fields are of the same magnitude and are additive to the right:

$$E_{mid} = 2\left\|E_Q\right\| = 2\left[\frac{kQ}{\left(\frac{d}{2}\right)^2}\right] = \frac{8kQ}{d^2}$$

61. **(D)**

The force on an electron placed at point P is dependent on the electric field at point P. This field must be determined. The distance from the $+Q$ charge is $2d$ and the distance from the $-Q$ charge is d:

$$\vec{E}_p = \vec{E}_{+Q} + \vec{E}_{-Q}$$

the field from the negative charge is larger than the field from the + charge.

$$\Rightarrow \vec{E}_p = \|E_{-Q}\| - \|E_{+Q}\| = \frac{kQ}{d^2} - \frac{kQ}{(2d)^2} = \frac{3kQ}{4d^2}$$

$\therefore F = qE = e\left[\frac{3kQ}{4d^2}\right]$, directed opposite of the field (to the right)

62. **(C)**

$$V = \sum \frac{kQ}{r} = \frac{k(+Q)}{2d} + \frac{k(-Q)}{d} = -\frac{kQ}{2d}$$

63. **(E)**

$$\sum F_{system} = mg = (totalmass)a \Rightarrow a = \frac{mg}{total\ mass}$$

$$a = \frac{mg}{m + 4m} = \frac{g}{5}$$

64. **(A)**

There is only one horizontal force on the $4M$ mass: the tension. The net force on the mass is $4Ma$, which must equal the tension. The acceleration is $g/5$, as computed in question 63. So the tension force is $T = (4/5)mg$.

65. **(B)**

Simply convert the work done by the definition of work:

$$W = Fx\cos\theta = (25\,\text{N})(2\,\text{m})(\cos 37) = 40\,\text{J}$$

66. **(C)**

To find the increase in kinetic energy, determine the amount of work done by friction (which is negative). The frictional work is

$$W_f = f_k \cdot \Delta x \cdot \cos 180 = -(\mu_k)(\text{Normal}).$$

Now you must compute the normal. But be careful not to just write down that the normal is equivalent to the weight, because it is not in this case. The tension's vertical component is $25 \sin 37 = 15$ N, so the normal is added to this force to get the weight of the block: $T_y + \text{N} = \text{mg}$:

$$N = mg - T_y = (5\,\text{kg})(9.8) - 15 = 34\,\text{N}$$

Therefore, the frictional force is $0.5 \times 34\,\text{N} = 17\,\text{N}$. The work done by friction is then $-(17\,\text{N})(2\,\text{m}) = -34\,\text{J}$. So the increase in kinetic energy is $+6\,\text{J}$.

67. **(C)**

Simply find the energy of the photon, which is equivalent to the increase in energy of the electron:

$$E = hf = h\frac{c}{\lambda} = \frac{hc}{\lambda} = \frac{1.242 \times 10^{-6}\,\text{eV} \cdot \text{m}}{400 \times 10^{-9}\,\text{m}} = 3.1\,\text{eV}$$

68. **(B)**

The interference pattern relationship is

$$m \sin\theta = \frac{\lambda}{d} \Rightarrow \tan\theta = \frac{x}{L}$$

for small angles ... $\tan\theta = \sin\theta$,

$$\frac{x}{L} = \frac{\lambda}{d} \Rightarrow x = \frac{\lambda}{d}L = \frac{700 \times 10^{-7}}{1 \times 10^{-4}}(2\,\text{m}) = 0.014\,\text{m}$$

which is 1.4 cm.

69. **(E)**

The distance traveled by this object is equivalent to the area under the velocity-versus-time curve. Compute this area by breaking it up into three shapes: two triangles and a rectangle. The total area is

$$Area_{total} = \frac{1}{2}(8\,\text{m/s})(2\,\text{s}) + (8\,\text{m/s})(2\,\text{s}) + \frac{1}{2}(8\,\text{m/s})(1\,\text{s}) = 28\,\text{m}$$

70. **(B)**

The average velocity is simply

$$v = \frac{\Delta x}{\Delta t} = \frac{28\,\text{m}}{5\,\text{s}} = 5.6\,\text{m/s}.$$

Section II

1. (a) The first step is to draw a free-body diagram of each mass, as shown here:

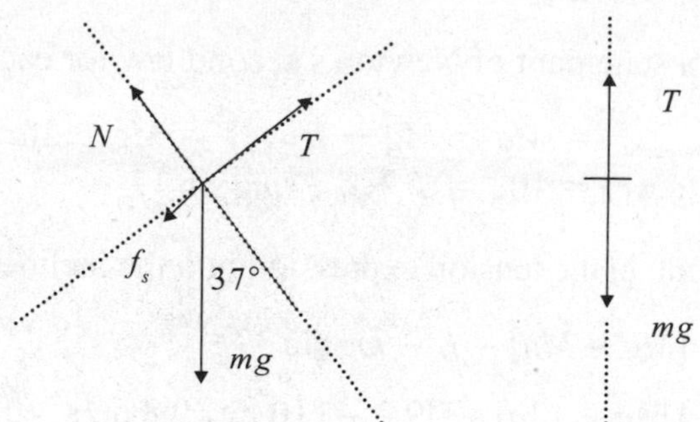

Set up statements of equilibrium for each mass:

For the 10-kg mass (m): $\sum F_x = 0 = T - f_s - mg \sin 37$
$\sum F_y = 0 = N - mg \cos 37$

For the unknown mass (M): $\sum F_y = 0 = T - Mg$

For the maximum static frictional force (which would give the minimum weight necessary to begin to accelerate the system), use the maximum static frictional relationship: $f_{static} \leq \mu_s N$.

Solving for this value:

$$f_{static\,\max} = \mu_s N = (0.8)(mg \cos 37) = (0.8)(10 \text{ kg})(9.8 \text{ m/s}^2)(0.8) = 62.7 \text{ N}$$

Put this value back in the equilibrium statement:

$$\sum F_x = 0 = T - f_s - mg \sin 37 \Rightarrow T = mg \sin 37 + f_{static\,\max}$$

$$T = (10 \text{ kg})(9.8 \text{ m/s}^2)(0.6) + 62.7 = 121.5 \text{ N}$$

From the equilibrium statement on the unknown mass, the tension in the cord is equivalent to the unknown mass's weight:

$$T = Mg \Rightarrow M = \frac{T}{g} = \frac{121.5 \text{ N}}{9.8 \text{ m/s}^2} = 12.4 \text{ kg}$$

Therefore, to the nearest whole number, a mass of 13 kg will cause the system to accelerate.

(b) Computing the acceleration of the system requires remembering two important ideas. First, once the system is sliding, the kinetic coefficient must be used. Second, the accelerations of each mass are the same value because they are attached.

First, find the new frictional force:

$$f_k = \mu_k N = (0.5)(mg\cos 37) = (0.5)(10\text{ kg})(9.8\text{ m/s}^2)(0.8) = 39.2\text{ N}$$

Set up a statement of Newton's second law for each mass:

$$\sum F_{hangingmass} = Ma = Mg - T \Rightarrow T = Mg - Ma$$
$$\sum F_{inclinedmass} = 10a = T - f_k - mg\sin 37$$

Substitute in the tension expression into the inclined mass statement:

$$10a = [Mg - Ma] - f_k - mg\sin 37$$

$$10a = [13g - 13a] - 39.2 - (10\text{ kg})(9.8\text{ m/s}^2)(0.6)$$

$$10a = 127.4 - 39.2 - 58.8 - 13a$$

$$23a = 29.4$$

$$a = 1.3\text{ m/s}^2$$

(c) Based on the answers of the previous parts of this problem, the tension expression is $T = Mg - Ma$.

$$T = (13\text{ kg})(9.8\text{ m/s}^2) - (13\text{ kg})(1.3\text{ m/s}^2) = 110.5\text{ N} \approx 111\text{ N}$$

2. (a) The free-body diagram for the mass at the top of the circle looks like this:

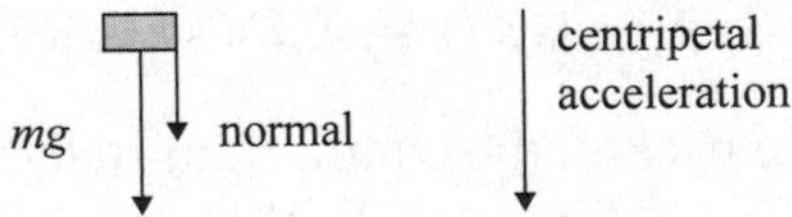

(b) The only force doing work on the system is the weight. Remember, the tension does no work because it is directed radially and contributes zero work. Therefore, mechanical energy in the system can be conserved. The energy at the top of the circle is equal to the energy at the bottom of the circle.

$$TE_{top} = KE_{top} + U_g = \frac{1}{2}mv_t^2 + mg(2R)$$

$$TE_{bottom} = KE_{bottom} + U_g = \frac{1}{2}mv_b^2 + 0$$

$$TE_{top} = TE_{bottom}$$

$$\frac{1}{2}mv_t^2 + mg(2R) = \frac{1}{2}mv_b^2$$

$$v_b^2 = v_t^2 + 4\,gR = (5\text{ m/s})^2 + 4(10\text{ m/s}^2)(0.5\text{ m}) = 45$$

$$v_b = \sqrt{45} = 6.7\text{ m/s}$$

(c) To solve for the tension at the bottom, draw a free-body diagram for that point:

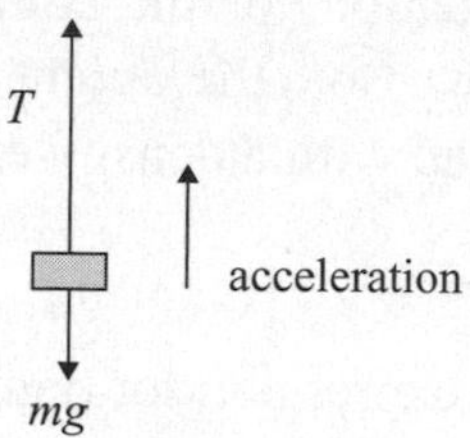

$$\sum F_{cent} = ma_c = T - mg \Rightarrow T = ma_c + mg$$

$$T = ma_c + mg = (2\text{ kg})\left(\frac{v_b^2}{0.5}\right) + (2\text{ kg})(9.8\text{ m/s}^2)$$

$$T = (2\text{ kg})\left(\frac{6.7^2}{0.5}\right) + (2\text{ kg})(9.8\text{ m/s}^2) = 198\text{ N}$$

(d) This is a projectile motion problem. The mass leaves the circular path with a completely horizontal velocity. Therefore, the time to travel vertically a distance of 0.2 m is

$$t = \sqrt{\frac{2h}{g}} = \sqrt{\frac{0.4}{9.8}} = 0.2\text{ s.}$$

Because the mass has a constant horizontal velocity of 6.7 m/s, the distance d traveled by the mass is

$$d = v_{ox}t = (6.7\text{ m/s})(0.2\text{ s}) = 1.35\text{ m.}$$

3. (a) A plot of the data looks like this:

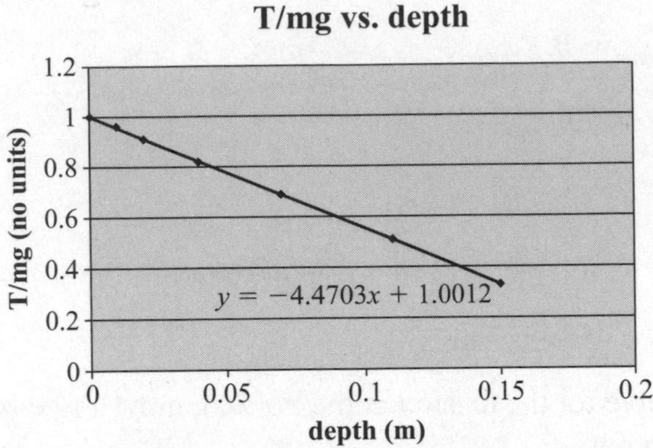

(b) and (c) Writing an equation for the equilibrium statement involves using Archimedes' law. Both the weight of the object and the buoyant force can be expressed with a density expressions:

$$\sum F_{metal} = 0 = T + F_{bouy} - mg \Rightarrow T = mg - F_b$$

Now, write an expression for bouyant force:

$$F_b = \text{weight of water displaced} = \rho_{water} V_{water} g$$

$$V_{waterdisp} = A_{metal} y$$

$$\therefore F_b = \rho_w A y g$$

$$\therefore T = mg - F_b = mg - \rho_w A y g$$

Now, going further to get a better expression ...

An expression for the weight of the metal in terms of its density is:

$$weight = \rho_{metal} V_{metal} g$$

$$V_{metal} = Ah$$

$$\therefore weight = \rho_{metal} A h g$$

Dividing the entire force statement by the weight of the metal provides a better statement:

$$\frac{T}{mg} = \frac{mg}{mg} - \frac{F_b}{mg} \Rightarrow \frac{T}{mg} = 1 - \frac{F_b}{mg}$$

$$\frac{T}{mg} = 1 - \frac{[\rho_w A y g]}{[\rho_{metal} A h g]} = 1 - \frac{\rho_w}{\rho_m} \cdot \frac{1}{h} \cdot y$$

Notice that this expression is in the form of $y = mx + b$ for the graph in part (a). The slope is the coefficient of the variable for depth (y).

(d) The slope of the graph is approximately 4.44 (the negative is not necessary). Solve for the metal's density as follows:

$$\text{slope} = 4.44\ \text{m}^{-1} = \frac{\rho_w}{\rho_m} \cdot \frac{1}{h} \Rightarrow \rho_m = \frac{\rho_w}{4.44} \cdot \frac{1}{h}$$

$$\rho_m = \frac{1000\ \text{kg/m}^3}{4.44\ \text{m}^{-1}} \cdot \frac{1}{0.15\ \text{m}} = 1500\ \text{kg/m}^3$$

(e) If the area of the slab is increased, the graph is exactly the same. In this analysis, the relationship is independent of the metal's area.

4. (a) The circuit diagram looks like this:

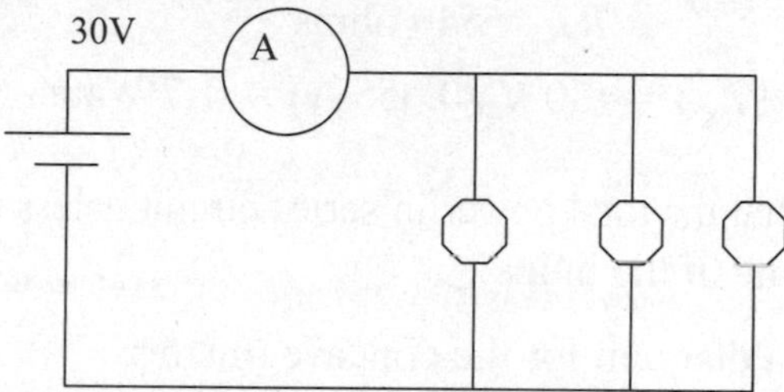

(b) Because each of the three light bulbs is directly attached to the 30-V source, each bulb is consuming the rated power. So the total power consumption is equal to the sum of the individual powers:

$$P_{total} = 3W + 5W + 15W = 23W$$

(c) To determine the total charge moving through the battery, calculate the total operating current of the circuit:

$$P = VI \Rightarrow I = \frac{P}{V} = \frac{23\ W}{30\ V} = 0.77\ A$$

$$I = \frac{\Delta Q}{\Delta t} \Rightarrow \Delta Q = I \cdot \Delta t = (0.77\ A)(60\ \text{s}) = 46\ \text{Coulombs}$$

$$\#\text{electrons} = 46\ C \cdot \frac{6.25 \times 10^{18}\ \text{electrons}}{C} = 2.07 \times 10^{20}\ \text{electrons}$$

(d) When the bulbs are arranged in series, the power consumption is drastically different. To compute the power, compute the resistance of each bulb (assume that the resistance of each bulb is constant, although this is not necessarily true for most standard incandescent bulbs).

$$P = \frac{V^2}{R} \Rightarrow R = \frac{V^2}{P}$$

$$R_{3W} = \frac{30^2}{3} = 300\ \Omega$$

$$R_{5W} = \frac{30^2}{5} = 180\ \Omega$$

$$R_{15W} = \frac{30^2}{15} = 60\ \Omega$$

Now apply the laws of series circuits to get the total current:

$R_e = 300 + 180 + 60 = 540$ ohms

$$I_{tot} = \frac{V}{R_e} = \frac{30 \text{ volt}}{540 \text{ ohms}} = 0.055 \text{ Amperes}$$

$$P_{total} = VI_{total} = (30\text{ V})(0.055\text{ A}) = 1.7 \text{ Watts}$$

Notice that the total power in series circuit is less than the least power of any one of the bulbs.

5. (a) Here is a diagram for the concave mirror:

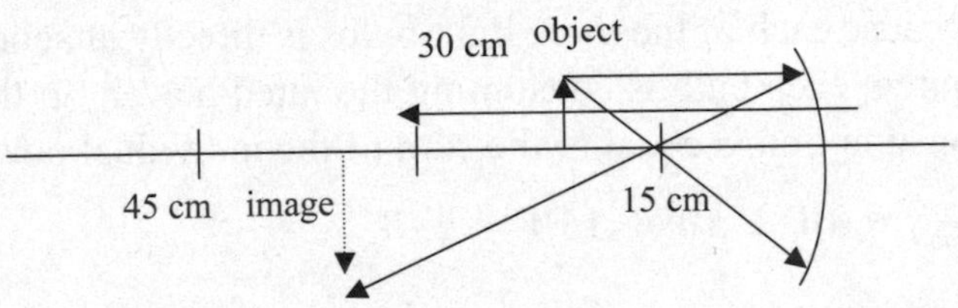

(b) Here is a diagram for the convex mirror:

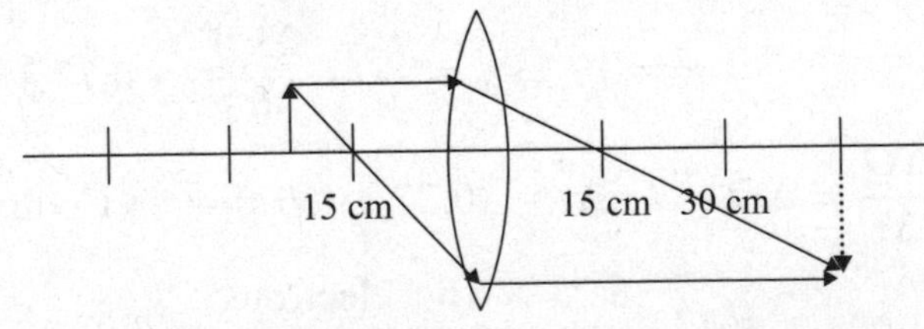

(c) If the object moves from 20 cm to 30 cm, the object's distance goes from $4/3f$ to $2f$. The image size, $M = \frac{d_i}{d_o}$, goes from $4x$ to $2x$. So the image size decreases.

6. (a) Using the gas law:

$$\frac{p_1 V_1}{T_1} = \frac{p_2 V_2}{T_2} \Rightarrow p_2 = \frac{T_2}{T_1} \cdot \frac{V_1}{V_2} \cdot p_1 = \frac{600 \text{ K}}{240 \text{ K}} \cdot \frac{0.02}{0.02} \cdot 1 \times 10^5 \text{ Pa}$$

$$p_2 = 2.5 \times 10^5 \text{ Pa}$$

(b) Apply the gas law again:

$$pV = nRT \Rightarrow V = \frac{nRT}{p} = \frac{(1)(8.31 \text{ J/Kmole})(485 \text{ K})}{1 \times 10^5 \text{ Pa}} = 0.04 \text{ m}^3$$

(c) Computing the total amount of heat expelled requires the temperatures of the initial and final states:

$$\Delta Q = nC_p \Delta T \text{ and } C_p = \frac{5}{2}R$$

$$\Rightarrow \Delta Q = (1 \text{ mole}) \left(\frac{5}{2}\right) (8.31 \text{ J/mole} \cdot \text{K})(240 \text{ K} - 485 \text{ K}) = -5090 \text{ Joules}$$

(d)

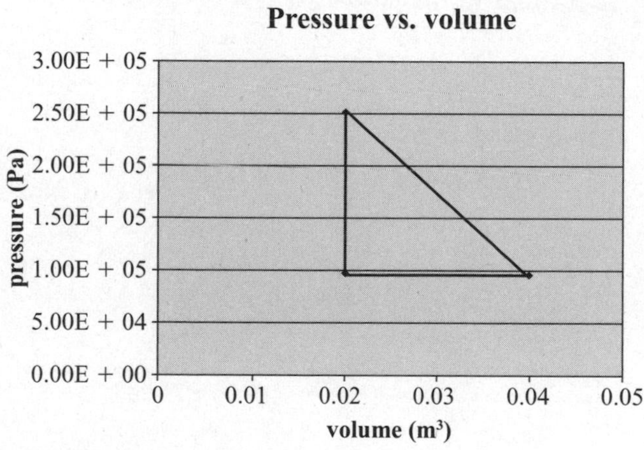

PRACTICE EXAM 2

This exam is also on CD-ROM in our special interactive AP Physics B TestWare®

AP Physics B

Section I

Time: 90 Minutes
70 Multiple-Choice Questions

DIRECTIONS: Each of the questions or incomplete statements below is followed by five answer choices. Select the one that is best in each case and fill in the oval on the corresponding answer sheet.

NOTE: Units associated with numerical quantities are abbreviated, using the abbreviations listed in the Table of Information and Equations found at the back of this book. To simplify calculations, you may use g = 10 m/s^2 for all problems.

1. A dense metal ball is projected horizontally from a table, as shown in the following diagram. The ball hits the wall at a height of y above the floor. Determine the height y.

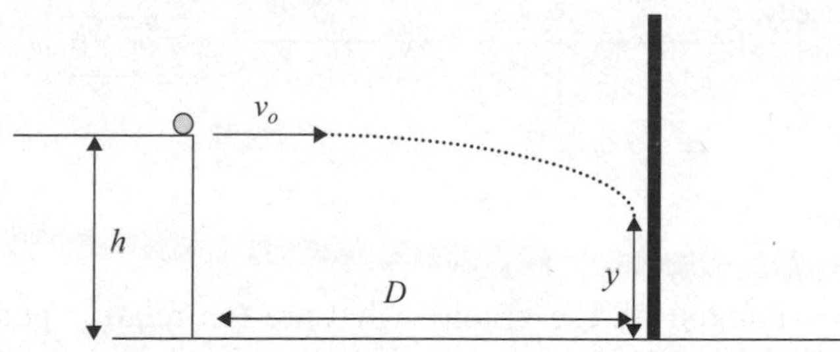

(A) $y = \frac{gD^2}{2v_o^2}$

(B) $y = \frac{gh^2}{2v_o^2}$

(C) $y = \frac{gD^2}{2v_o}$

(D) $y = h - \frac{gD^2}{2v_o^2}$

(E) $y = h - \frac{gh^2}{2v_o^2}$

Use the following situation to answer questions 2 and 3. A 50-kg man is standing on a scale inside an elevator. The scale measures forces in newtons.

2. While the elevator is moving at a constant speed of $v = 2$ m/s, what is the reading on the scale?

   (A) 400 N
   (B) 500 N
   (C) 600 N
   (D) 450 N
   (E) 100 N

3. While the elevator is accelerating downward at a rate of $a = 2$ m/s^2, what is the reading on the scale?

   (A) 400 N
   (B) 500 N
   (C) 600 N
   (D) 450 N
   (E) 100 N

Use the following velocity-versus-time graph to answer questions 4 and 5. Both car A and car B begin their motion at the position $x = 0$ m.

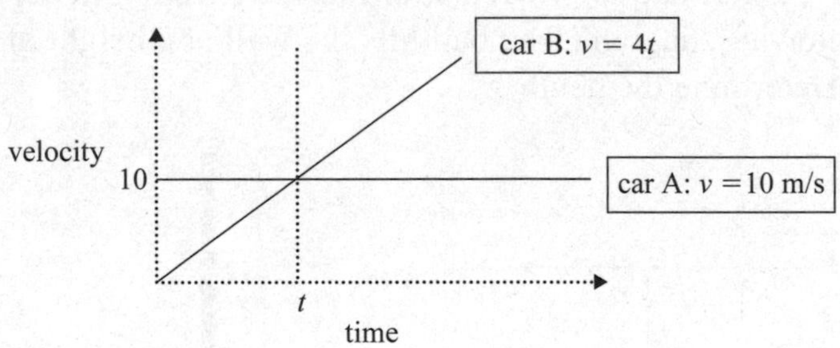

4. At time t (marked on the graph), what are the relative positions of the two cars?

   (A) Car A is behind car B.
   (B) Car A is passing car B.
   (C) Car A is ahead of car B.
   (D) Cars A and B are at the same position at time t.
   (E) Not enough information is given.

5. Determine the time t at which cars A and B have the same position.

(A) 2.5 seconds
(B) 4 seconds
(C) 5 seconds
(D) 10 seconds
(E) Not enough information

6. A spring with a natural length of 20 cm is suspended vertically. A 2-kg mass is attached to the spring. The spring's length stretches to 25 cm when the mass is attached. Determine the spring constant of the spring.

(A) 100 N/m
(B) 200 N/m
(C) 267 N/m
(D) 400 N/m
(E) 800 N/m

Use the following graph to answer questions 7 and 8. The graph shows the period of a pendulum squared (T^2) versus the length of the pendulum (l).

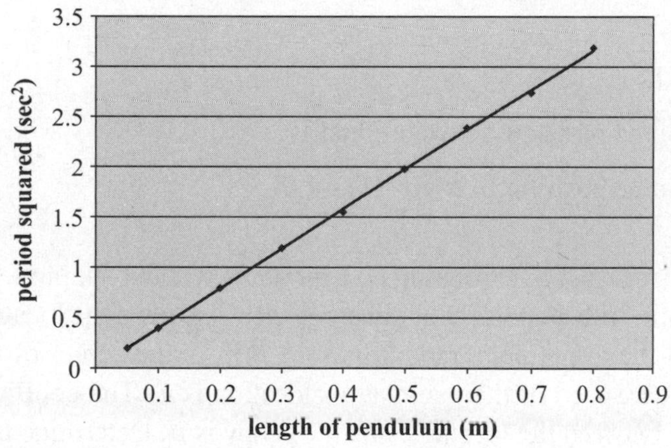

7. Based on the graph, which of the following expressions best determines the relationship of T to l of the pendulum.

(A) $T^2 = 2l$
(B) $T = 2\sqrt{l}$
(C) $T^2 = \frac{l}{4}$
(D) $T = \frac{\sqrt{l}}{2}$
(E) $T = \frac{\sqrt{l}}{4}$

8. What is the value of the pendulum's period when the pendulum's length is 0.5 m?

(A) 2 seconds
(B) 4 seconds
(C) 1.4 seconds
(D) 2.8 seconds
(E) 0.707 second

9. A pendulum is released from rest at position I, as shown in the following diagram. The tension in the cord will be the greatest at which position?

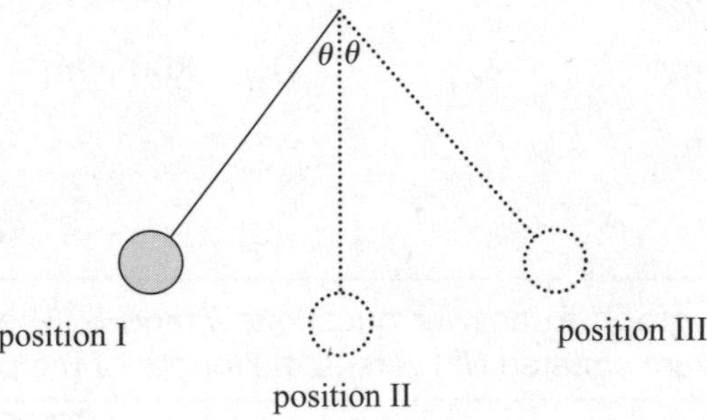

(A) I
(B) II
(C) III
(D) Some position between I and II
(E) Some position between II and III

10. A penny of mass m is rotating on a turntable without slipping. The turntable is rotating with a constant angular velocity. The penny is located at the very edge of the turntable, a radial distance R from the center of the turntable. The linear speed of the penny at its location is v_o. The coefficient of static friction between the turntable and the penny is μ. Determine the magnitude of the static frictional force between the penny and the turntable.

(A) $f = \frac{mv_o^2}{R}$
(B) $f = \mu mg$
(C) $f = \frac{\mu mv_o^2}{R}$
(D) $f = mg$
(E) $f = \mu g$

11. A spring-loaded projectile launcher has a spring constant of k. The launcher is placed on the ground, and a ball of mass m is placed in the launcher, as shown in the following diagram. The launcher's spring is compressed a distance of x and then released. How high does the ball rise above the launcher?

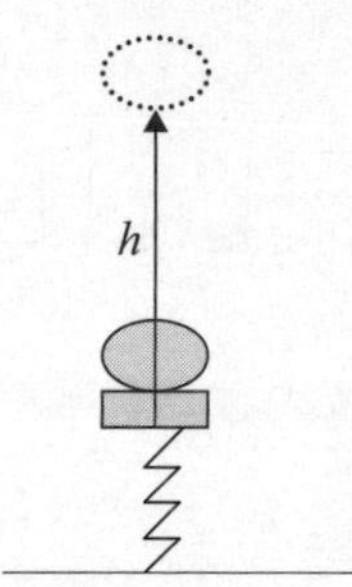

(A) $h = \frac{gx^2}{2}$

(B) $h = kx^2$

(C) $h = \frac{kx^2}{2mg}$

(D) $h = \frac{kx^2}{2g}$

(E) $h = \frac{mg}{2k}x^2$

12. A two-block system is pulled by a constant force F, as shown in the following diagram. There is no friction between the $3M$ block and the horizontal surface. There is friction between the M block and the $3M$ block. The coefficient of static friction between the two blocks is μ. If a constant force F pulls the two blocks without the two blocks slipping, what is the value of the static frictional force f_s between the two blocks?

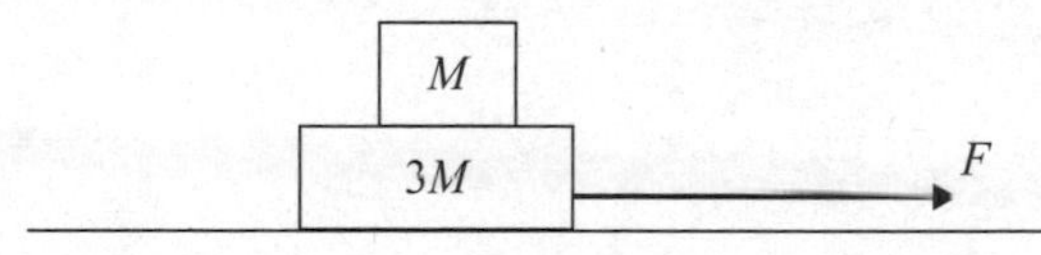

(A) $f_s = \mu Mg$

(B) $f_s = \mu 3Mg$

(C) $f_s = \mu 2Mg$

(D) $f_s = \frac{F}{4}$

(E) $f_s = F$

13. A wood block of density $\rho_{wood} = 600\frac{\text{kg}}{\text{m}^3}$ is a cube of length L. The block is placed in a container of water and is observed to float. How much of the wood block appears above the water line? (The density of the water is $\rho_{water} = 1000\frac{\text{kg}}{\text{m}^3}$.)

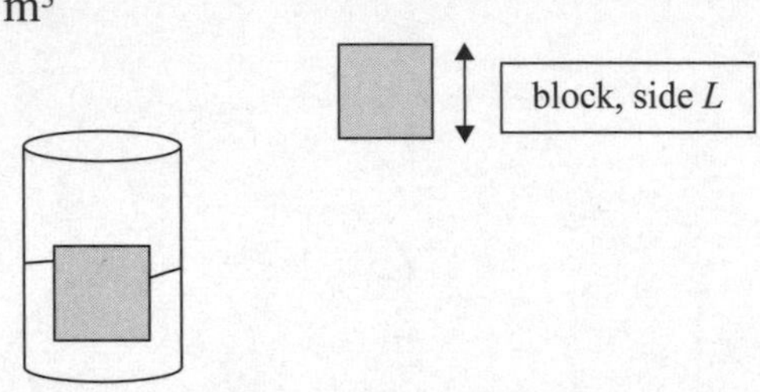

(A) $0.6L$

(B) $0.4L$

(C) $0.8L$

(D) $0.2L$

(E) The block's edge is even with the water line.

Use the following situation to answer questions 14 and 15. A bullet of mass m_o is shot into a large suspended block of mass $M - m_o$. The bullet's initial velocity is v_o. The bullet becomes embedded in the large block, and the two objects move off as a simple pendulum that rises to a maximum height of h.

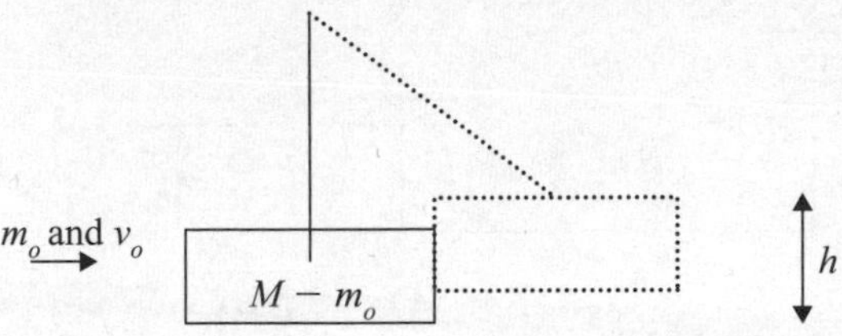

14. Determine the maximum height that the block rises.

(A) $h = \frac{v_o^2}{2g}$

(B) $h = \frac{m_o}{M} \cdot \frac{v_o^2}{2g}$

(C) $h = \frac{M}{m_o} \cdot \frac{v_o^2}{2g}$

(D) $h = \frac{M^2}{m_o^2} \cdot \frac{v_o^2}{2g}$

(E) $h = \frac{m_o^2}{M^2} \cdot \frac{v_o^2}{2g}$

15. Determine the loss of energy in the collision.

(A) $\Delta E_{system} = KE_o\left(\frac{M - m_o}{M}\right)$

(B) $\Delta E_{system} = KE_o\left(\frac{M - m_o}{m_o}\right)$

(C) $\Delta E_{system} = KE_o\left(\frac{m_o}{M}\right)$

(D) $\Delta E_{system} = KE_o\left(\frac{M^2 - m_o^2}{M^2}\right)$

(E) $\Delta E_{system} = KE_o\left(\frac{M + m_o}{M}\right)$

16. A 12-V battery is attached to three capacitors, as shown in the following diagram. What is the total amount of charge that flows from the battery after completely charging the capacitors?

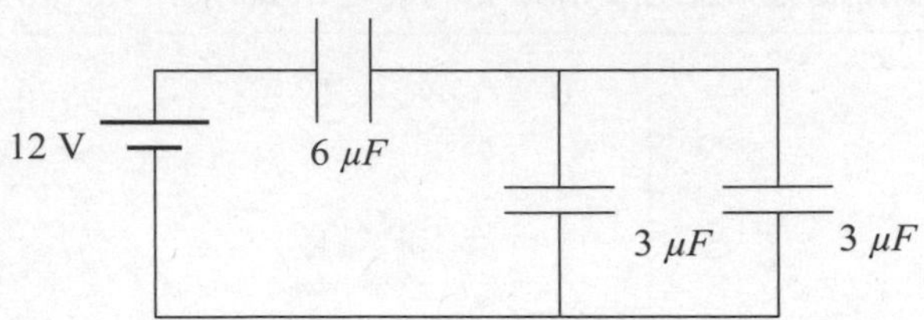

(A) 90 μC

(B) 144 μC

(C) 36 μC

(D) 12 μC

(E) 288 μC

Use the following diagram to answer questions 17 through 19. A conductive metal sphere of radius *R* has a total charge of Q placed on it. Point P is a distance 4*R* from the center of the sphere.

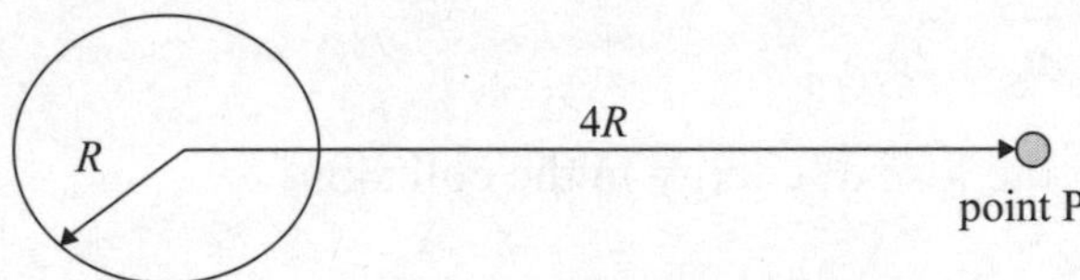

17. What is the magnitude of the electric field at the center of the sphere?

(A) 0

(B) $\frac{kQ}{R^2}$

(C) $\frac{kQ}{R}$

(D) $\frac{kQ}{R^3}$

(E) $\frac{kQ}{R^{\frac{3}{2}}}$

18. What is the magnitude of the electric field at point P?

(A) 0

(B) $\frac{kQ}{R^2}$

(C) $\frac{kQ}{4R^2}$

(D) $\frac{kQ}{16R^2}$

(E) $\frac{kQ}{4R}$

19. What is the electric potential at the center of the sphere?

(A) 0

(B) $\frac{kQ}{R}$

(C) $\frac{kQ}{R^2}$

(D) $\frac{2kQ}{R}$

(E) Infinite

Use the following situation to answer questions 20 and 21. The planet M_p has a radius of R_p. The satellite M_s is orbiting the planet at an orbital distance of $4R_p$.

20. What is the centripetal acceleration of the satellite?

(A) $\frac{GM_s}{R_p^2}$

(B) $\frac{GM_p}{4R_p^2}$

(C) $\frac{GM_p}{16R_p^2}$

(D) $\frac{GM_s}{16R_p^2}$

(E) 0

21. What is the gravitational acceleration at the surface of the planet?

(A) $\frac{GM_p}{R_p^2}$

(B) $\frac{GM_p}{4R_p^2}$

(C) $\frac{GM_p}{R_p}$

(D) $\frac{GM_p}{2R_p^2}$

(E) 0

22. An ideal spring with a spring constant of k has mass M attached to it, as shown in the diagram. The system is displaced vertically a small distance and then set into simple harmonic motion (SHM). The period of this SHM is T_o. The mass is removed and replaced with a new mass of $2M$. The system is once again put into vertical oscillations. What is the period of the new system?

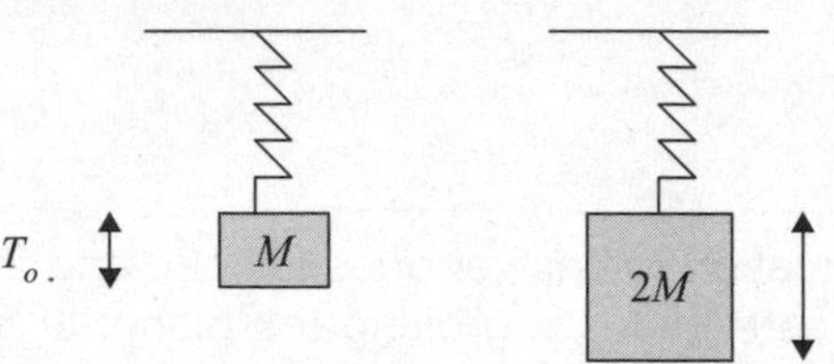

(A) T_o

(B) $2T_o$

(C) $\sqrt{2}T_o$

(D) $\frac{T_o}{\sqrt{2}}$

(E) $\frac{T_o}{2}$

23. A pipe open at one end and closed at the other end has a length of 80 cm. A student hears a resonance at the lowest possible frequency from this tube. This frequency is measured at 110 Hz. The speed of sound in this experiment is closest to which value?

(A) 330 m/s

(B) 345 m/s

(C) 350 m/s

(D) 352 m/s

(E) 362 m/s

24. A photon has an energy of 3.0 eV. What is the wavelength of this photon in nanometers (nm)?

(A) 414 nm

(B) 828 nm

(C) 207 nm

(D) 104 nm

(E) 621 nm

25. An interference pattern is created on a screen using a laser and a diffraction grating. A physics student performing this experiment measures the locations of the maximums in the interference pattern. The student then wants to see what would happen if the entire experiment were done in water. The laser, grating, and screen are placed underwater (in the same positions as the first experiment), and the student again measures the locations of the maximums. Which of the following statements best describes what the student saw in the second experiment?

(A) The distance between the maximums increased.

(B) The distance between the maximums decreased.

(C) There is no change in the pattern.

(D) The refraction from the water completely distorts the image of the pattern.

(E) There is no evidence of the pattern.

26. An electron is in an excited state ($n = 2$) in a fictitious atom, as shown in the diagram. When this electron returns to ground state, what are the possible energies of photons that will be released by the atom?

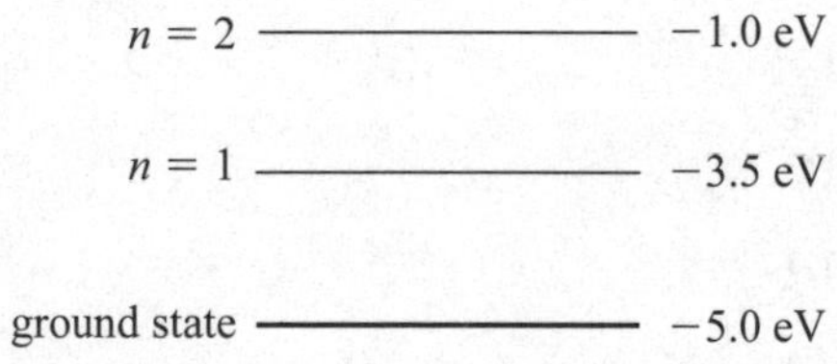

$n = 2$ ———————— -1.0 eV

$n = 1$ ———————— -3.5 eV

ground state ———————— -5.0 eV

(A) Only 4 eV

(B) Only 5 eV

(C) 4 eV and 1.5 eV

(D) 1.5 eV and 2.5 eV

(E) 4 eV, 2.5 eV, and 1.5 eV

27. An electron of charge e is moving to the right above a wire with current, as shown in the following diagram. At point P, the direction of the magnetic force will be in which direction?

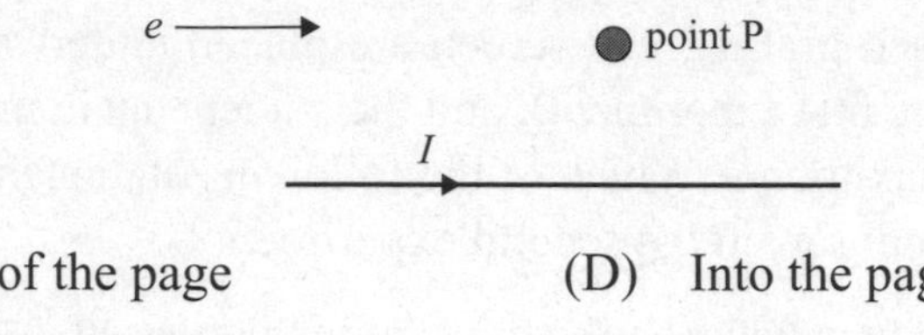

(A) Top of the page
(B) Bottom of the page
(C) Out of the page
(D) Into the page
(E) No force

28. Two wires are oriented as shown in the following diagram. The two wires are fixed at these locations. One wire has a current of $4I$, and the other wire has a current of I. At what location would the magnetic field equal zero?

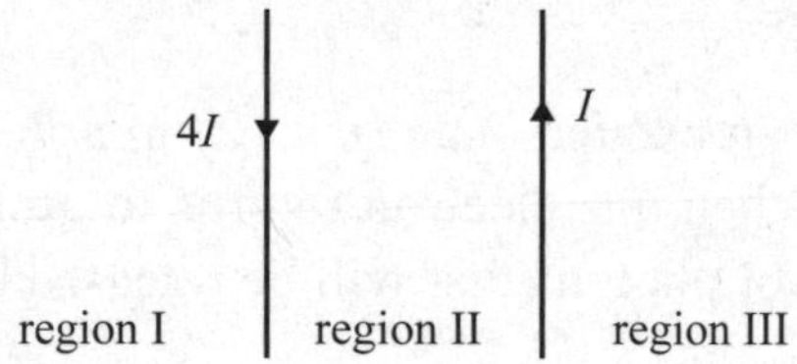

(A) In region I
(B) In region II
(C) In region III
(D) Exactly midway between the two wires
(E) No location would have a net field of 0.

29. The switch in the circuit is initially open, and the current in ammeter A reads I_o. When the switch is closed, what will happen to the ammeter measurement?

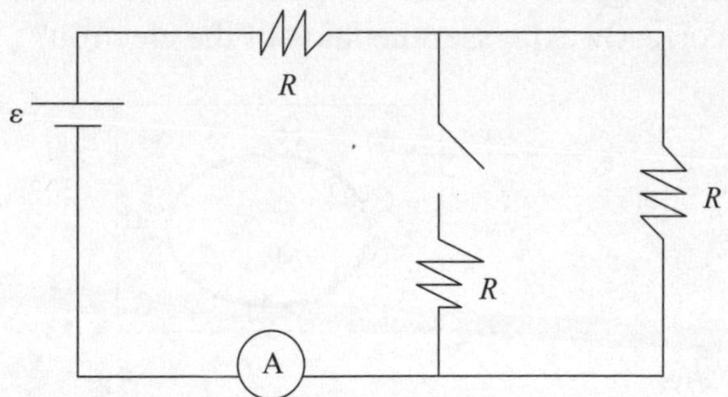

(A) Increase by 33%

(B) Decrease by 33%

(C) Increase by 50%

(D) Decrease by 50%

(E) No change in measurement

30. A circuit is operating as shown in the following diagram. What is the reading in voltmeter *V*?

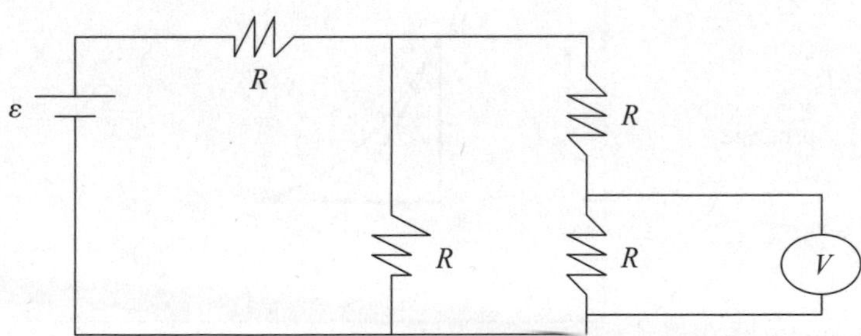

(A) $\frac{\varepsilon}{4}$

(B) $\frac{2\varepsilon}{5}$

(C) $\frac{\varepsilon}{5}$

(D) $\frac{\varepsilon}{2}$

(E) ε

31. An electron of charge e enters a region of uniform magnetic field strength. The electron is initially moving with speed v_o as it enters the field. The electron begins moving in a circular motion in the uniform B field, as shown in the diagram. The circular path has a radius of r. Which of the following correctly expresses the mass of the electron?

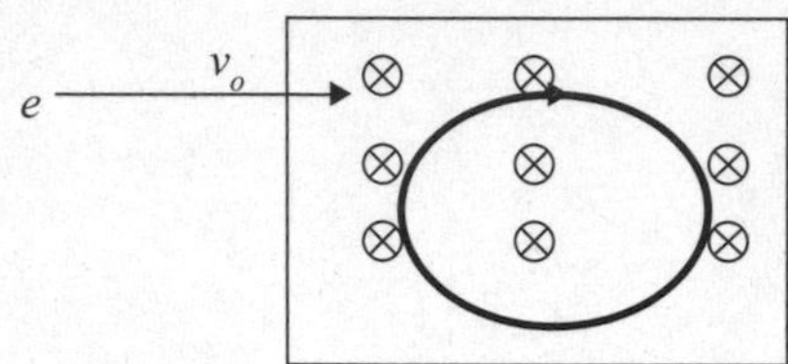

(A) $m = \frac{Bve}{r}$

(B) $m = \frac{Ber}{v_o}$

(C) $m = \frac{v_o}{Br}$

(D) $m = \frac{Bv_o}{er}$

(E) $m = \frac{B}{e}$

Use the following diagram to answer questions 32 and 33. The letters A, B, C, and D indicate thermodynamic processes.

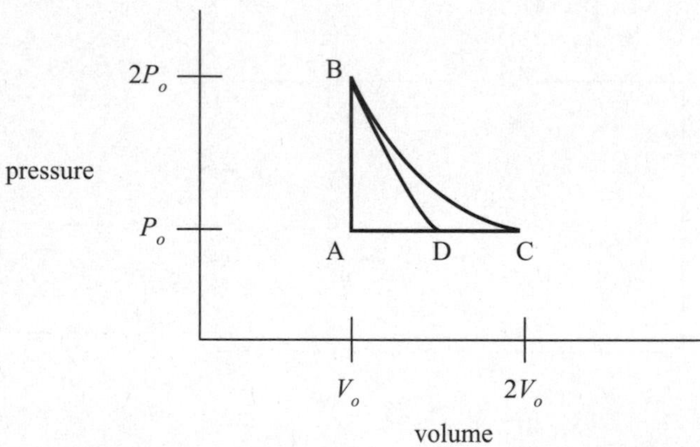

32. Which of the processes represents an isothermal process?

(A) $A \rightarrow B$

(B) $B \rightarrow C$

(C) $B \rightarrow D$

(D) $C \rightarrow A$

(E) No isothermal process is shown in the diagram.

33. Which of the processes best represents an adiabatic process?

(A) $A \to B$

(B) $B \to C$

(C) $B \to D$

(D) $C \to A$

(E) No adiabatic process is shown in the diagram.

34. A mass of weight w is suspended by two cords, as shown in the diagram.

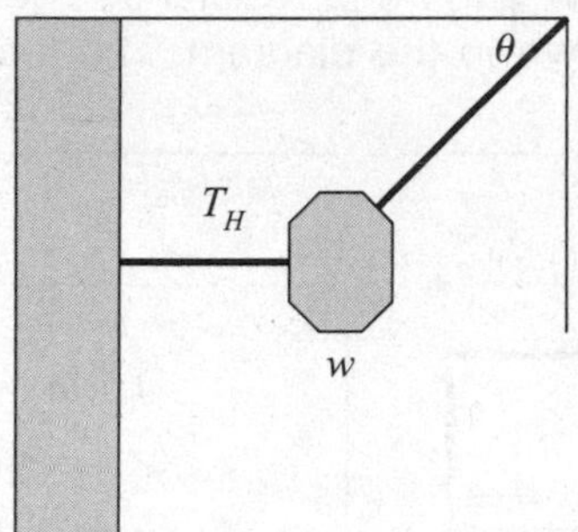

Which of the following expresses the magnitude of tension in the horizontal cord T_H?

(A) $T_H = w\tan\theta$

(B) $T_H = w\cos\theta$

(C) $T_H = w\cot\theta$

(D) $T_H = w\sin\theta$

(E) $T_H = w/\cos\theta$

35. A book of mass m is propelled along a rough horizontal floor with an initial speed of v_o. The book travels a distance d from the starting point to stopping. Which of the following expressions represents the coefficient of kinetic friction between the book and the floor?

(A) $\mu = \frac{gd}{v_o^2}$

(B) $\mu = \frac{mv_o}{d}$

(C) $\mu = \frac{mv_o^2}{2d}$

(D) $\mu = \frac{mv_o^2}{2gd}$

(E) $\mu = \frac{v_o^2}{2gd}$

36. A physics student looks into a large convex mirror and notices that his physics book is exactly one-quarter of its actual size. The book is located exactly 60 cm from the mirror. What is the focal length of the mirror?

(A) −20 cm
(B) 20 cm
(C) −15 cm
(D) 15 cm
(E) 12 cm

Use the following situation to answer questions 37 through 39. A conductive wire loop of dimensions *w* and *l* and resistance *R* enters a region of uniform magnetic *B* field, as shown in the diagram. The loop enters the field with a speed of v_o.

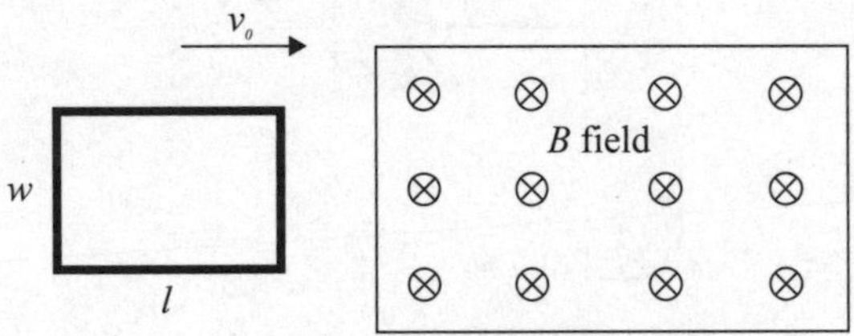

37. What are the directions of the current in the conductive loop as it enters the field region and as it exits the field region?

(A) Enters counterclockwise, exits clockwise
(B) Enters clockwise, exits clockwise
(C) Enters counterclockwise, exits counterclockwise
(D) Enters clockwise, exits counterclockwise
(E) Enters zero current, exits zero current

38. Which of the following expressions gives the magnitude of current as it enters the field?

(A) $i = \frac{Blv_o}{R}$

(B) $i = \frac{Bwlv_o}{R}$

(C) $i = \frac{4Bwlv_o}{R}$

(D) $i = \frac{Bwv_o}{R}$

(E) $i = 0$

39. What is the magnitude of the magnetic force on the loop when the loop is completely in the magnetic field region?

(A) $F_B = \frac{B^2w^2v_o}{R}$

(B) $F_B = \frac{B^2l^2v_o}{R}$

(C) $F_B = \frac{B^2l^2v_o^2}{R}$

(D) $F_B = \frac{B^2w^2v_o^2}{R}$

(E) 0

40. A parallel-plate capacitor has a capacitance of C_o and a charge of Q_o. An electron of charge e and mass m_e is placed at the negative plate of the capacitor and then accelerated through the capacitor's electric field. Which of the following expressions represents the electron's speed when it strikes the positive plate?

(A) $v = \sqrt{\frac{2e}{m_e}}$

(B) $v = \sqrt{\frac{2e}{m_eC_o}}$

(C) $v = \sqrt{\frac{2Q_oe}{m_eC_o}}$

(D) $v = \sqrt{\frac{2Q_o}{m_eC_o}}$

(E) $v = \sqrt{\frac{2e}{C_o}}$

41. In the following diagram, the circuit is in a steady-state condition. The capacitor is completely charged. What is the amount of charge on the capacitor?

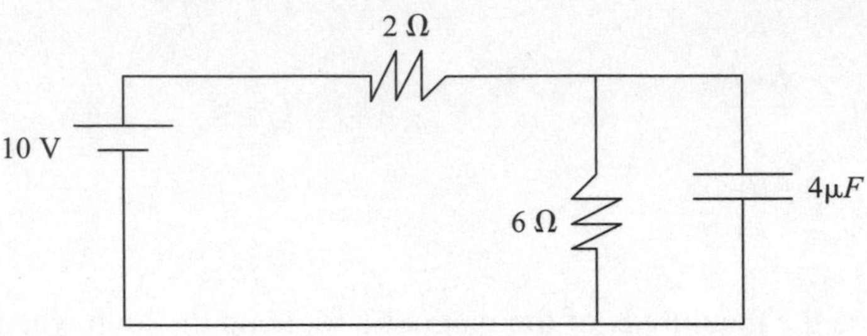

(A) 40μC
(B) 24μC
(C) 8μC
(D) 30μC
(E) 0

42. A heat engine undergoes a complete thermodynamic cycle. In this cycle, the engine takes in 500 J of heat and ejects 300 J of heat. What is the efficiency of the engine?

(A) 33%
(B) 40%
(C) 60%
(D) 75%
(E) 80%

43. A UV photon of wavelength 300 nanometers hits a photoelectric metal. The metals work function is 3 eV. The maximum kinetic energy of the photoelectron ejected from the metal is most nearly

(A) 0
(B) 1.0 eV
(C) 1.5 eV
(D) 2.0 eV
(E) 2.5 eV

44. A collection of gas at temperature T_o in a closed container is heated. The speeds of the gas molecules triple because of this heating process. How much does the temperature of the gas increase?

(A) $\sqrt{3}T_o$

(B) $3T_o$

(C) $\frac{\sqrt{3}}{3}T_o$

(D) $9T_o$

(E) $18T_o$

Use the following velocity-versus-time graphs of an object in motion to answer questions 45 through 47.

(I)
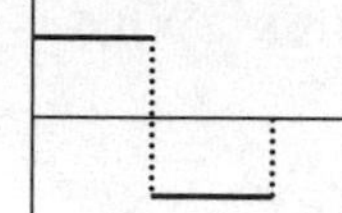

(III)
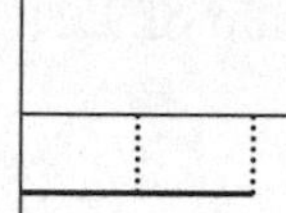

(V)
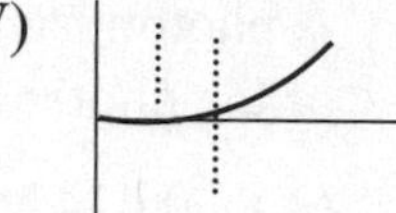

(II)
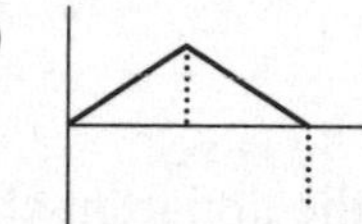

(IV)
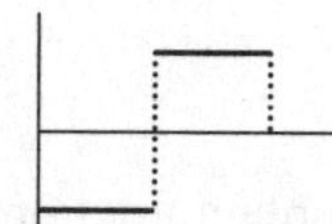

45. Which graph indicates an object that is the furthest distance from the starting point?

(A) I

(B) II

(C) III

(D) IV

(E) V

46. Which graph indicates an object with a continuously changing acceleration?

(A) I

(B) II

(C) III

(D) IV

(E) V

47. Which graph indicates that the object returned to its starting point?

(A) I only
(B) II only
(C) I and IV only
(D) IV only
(E) None of the graphs

48. A mass of 0.5 kg has a momentum of 10 kg · m/s. What is the kinetic energy of the mass?

(A) 25 J
(B) 50 J
(C) 100 J
(D) 200 J
(E) 400 J

49. A photon has a momentum of 2.21×10^{-21} kg · m/s^2. What is the energy of the photon?

(A) 0.414 MeV
(B) 4.14 MeV
(C) 414 MeV
(D) 4.14 KeV
(E) 414 KeV

50. The Doppler effect is a phenomenon that affects the apparent change in

(A) wavelength
(B) amplitude
(C) frequency
(D) energy
(E) speed of wave

51. A diffraction grating with 1,200 lines per millimeter is used to create a diffraction pattern on a wall. The grating is replaced with a second grating with 1,600 lines per millimeter, and the same experiment is performed. How does the pattern change from the first to the second experiment?

(A) There is no change.
(B) The distance between the maximums decreases.
(C) The distance between the maximums increases.
(D) The maximums are more intense.
(E) The maximums are less intense.

52. A ray diagram shows how light bends when it hits a mirror or a lens. Which of the following is not correct for a ray diagram of a convex lens?

    (A) A ray parallel to the principal axis will pass through the focal point after refraction.

    (B) A ray that passes through the focal point will be parallel to the principal axis after refraction.

    (C) A ray that passes through the exact center of the lens will go through unrefracted.

    (D) A ray that passes through the point $2f$ will refract parallel to the principal axis.

    (E) A ray that starts at an infinite distance away from the lens will refract through the focal point of the lens.

53. A concave mirror of focal length f produces a virtual image that is twice the size of the object. In terms of f how far away is the object from the mirror?

    (A) $2f$
    (B) f
    (C) $f/2$
    (D) $f/4$
    (E) $2f/3$

54. Tungsten (W^{166}_{74}) decays with an alpha particle. The subsequent daughter particle decays again with another alpha particle decay. What is the final product after these two decays?

    (A) Hf^{162}_{72}
    (B) Hf^{162}_{70}
    (C) Yb^{156}_{70}
    (D) Yb^{158}_{71}
    (E) Yb^{158}_{70}

55. An object of density ρ_o, mass m, and volume V_o is placed in water. The density of water is ρ_w, and $\rho_o > \rho_w$. Which of the following expressions represents the buoyant force?

    (A) $\rho_o V_o g$
    (B) $\rho_w V_o g$
    (C) $\rho_o g$
    (D) mg
    (E) $\frac{\rho_o}{\rho_w} mg$

56. A light bulb has a power rating of 60 W and is attached to a voltage of 120 V. How many electrons move through the filament in 1 minute?

(A) 10^{16} electrons
(B) 10^{17} electrons
(C) 10^{18} electrons
(D) 10^{19} electrons
(E) 10^{20} electrons

57. A guitar string is vibrating with frequency f_o in the standing wave pattern shown in the following diagram:

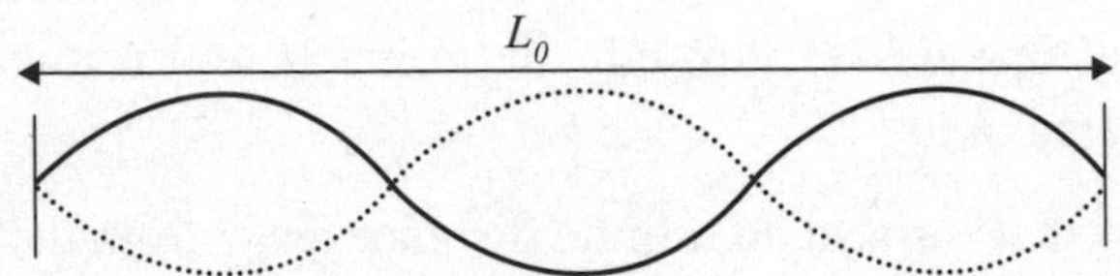

Which of the following expressions indicates the speed of the wave on the string?

(A) $v = f_o L_o$
(B) $v = \frac{f_o L_o}{2}$
(C) $v = \frac{2}{3} f_o L_o$
(D) $v = \frac{3}{2} f_o L_o$
(E) $v = \frac{f_o L_o}{3}$

58. Rutherford scattering was the first experiment to show which property of the atom?

(A) The electron has a negative charge.
(B) The atom is electrically neutral.
(C) The nucleus of the atom contains the positive charge in a very small volume.
(D) A photon will scatter from a free electron in a metal.
(E) A photon will release an electron from a metal if it has some minimum energy.

59. Which statement best explains the dispersion of white light through a prism into its constituent colors (red, orange, yellow, blue, etc.)?

    (A) The index of refraction changes with wavelength of light.

    (B) The prism polarizes each color in a different orientation.

    (C) The light hits the critical angle inside the prism.

    (D) Diffraction occurs at the boundary of the prism and air.

    (E) Dispersion is a consequence of only the refraction caused by the glass.

60. A wire with current directed into the page is in a static magnetic field, as shown in the following diagram:

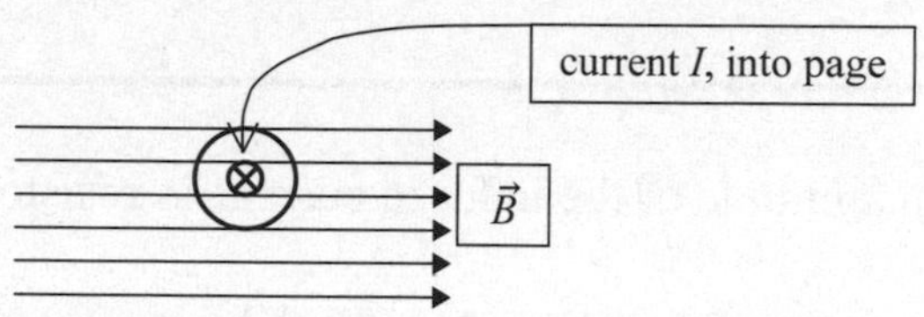

What is the direction of the magnetic force on the wire?

(A) Left

(B) Right

(C) Top of page

(D) Bottom of page

(E) No force

Use the following situation to answer questions 61 through 63. A wire of length b moves across conductive rails initially with speed v_o, as shown in the diagram. A magnetic field directed into the page is contained everywhere in the large rectangular box.

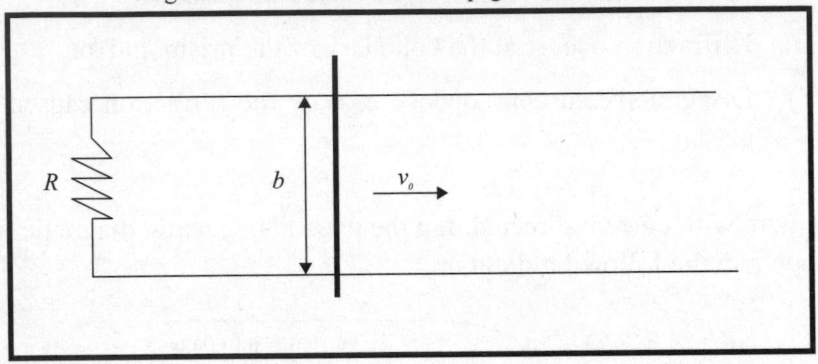

61. What is the magnitude of the induced current in resistor R?

(A) $\frac{Bv_o}{R}$

(B) $\frac{Bv_o b}{R}$

(C) $\frac{B^2 v_o^2 b}{R}$

(D) $\frac{B}{R}$

(E) 0

62. What is the direction of the magnetic force on the moving rod?

(A) Left

(B) Right

(C) Up

(D) Down

(E) No magnetic force

63. What is the direction of the induced magnetic field created by this moving rod?

(A) Into the page

(B) Out of the page

(C) Left

(D) Right

(E) No induced field exists.

Use the following diagram to answer questions 64 through 66. The conical pendulum is moving in a circular motion of radius *R*. The mass of the pendulum is *M* and the length of the pendulum is *L*. This picture shows the pendulum at one moment in time during its circular motion.

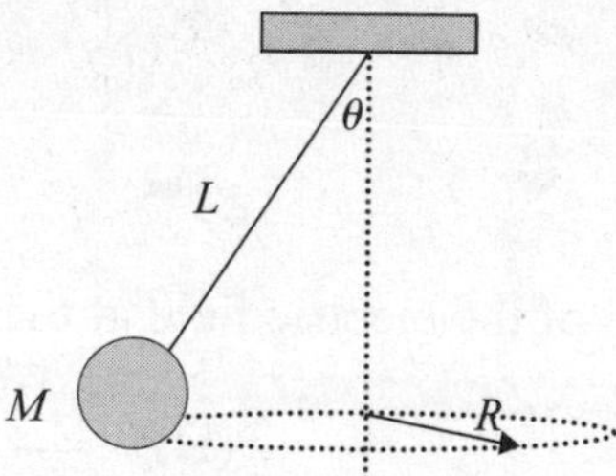

64. What is the direction of the acceleration of the mass at this instant?

(A) ↘

(B) ↓

(C) →

(D) ↗

(E) Zero acceleration

65. Which of the following is an expression for the magnitude of the tension in the cord?

(A) $T = \dfrac{mg}{\cos\theta}$

(B) $T = mg\cos\theta$

(C) $T = \dfrac{mg}{\sin\theta}$

(D) $T = mg\sin\theta$

(E) $T = mg$

66. Which expression represents the period of circular motion?

(A) $2\pi\sqrt{\dfrac{R}{g}}$

(B) $2\pi\sqrt{\dfrac{R\cos\theta}{g}}$

(C) $2\pi\sqrt{\dfrac{L\cos\theta}{g}}$

(D) $2\pi\sqrt{\dfrac{L}{g}}$

(E) $2\pi\sqrt{\dfrac{L}{g\tan\theta}}$

Use the following diagram to answer questions 67 through 69. Four point charges, all of magnitude Q, are arranged in a square.

67. What is the direction of the electric field at the center of the square?

(A) ←

(B) ↑

(C) ↓

(D) →

(E) The field is zero at the center.

68. What is the magnitude of the potential at the center of the square?

(A) $\frac{kQ}{a}$

(B) $\frac{4kQ}{a}$

(C) $\frac{2\sqrt{2}kQ}{a}$

(D) $\frac{\sqrt{2}kQ}{2a}$

(E) 0

69. What is the magnitude of force between two charges diagonally opposite from each other?

(A) $F = \frac{kQ^2}{a^2}$

(B) $F = \frac{kQ^2}{2a^2}$

(C) $F = \frac{kQ^2}{\sqrt{2}a^2}$

(D) $F = \frac{2kQ^2}{a^2}$

(E) $F = \frac{\sqrt{2}kQ^2}{a^2}$

70. A very dense object is dropped from a tall building of height h. The time it takes to hit the ground is t_o. The same object is taken up to a height of $2h$ and dropped again. What is the time to hit the ground from the new height?

(A) $2t_o$

(B) $4t_o$

(C) $\frac{t_o}{\sqrt{2}}$

(D) $\sqrt{2}t_o$

(E) $2\sqrt{2}t_o$

STOP

This is the end of Section I.
If time still remains, you may check your work only in this section.
Do not begin Section II until instructed to do so.

Section II

Time: 90 Minutes
6 Free-Response Questions

DIRECTIONS: Carefully read each question and be sure to answer *each part* of the question. Show your work. Crossed-out work will not be graded. You may use your calculator and the equation tables for Physics B found at the back of this book for this section of the exam.

1. A car is moving in one dimension on the x-axis. When $t = 0$, the position and velocity are both 0. The car's subsequent motion is displayed in the following velocity-versus-time graph:

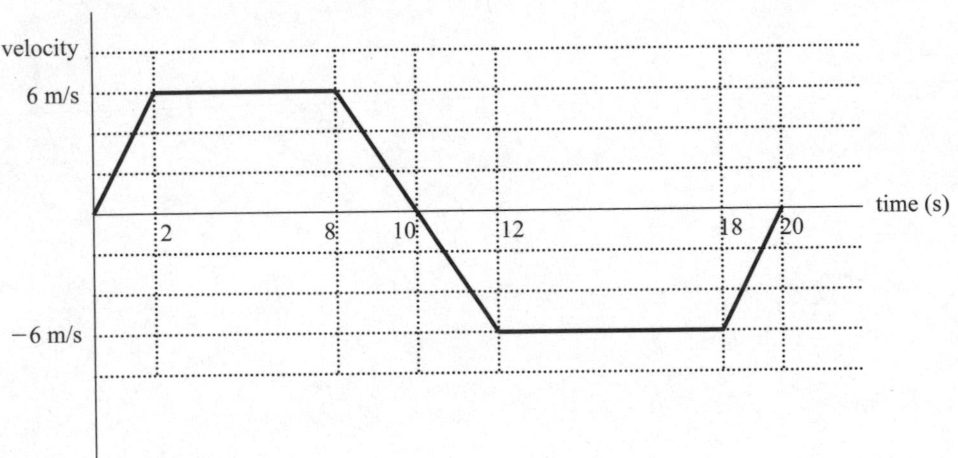

(a) Determine the acceleration of the car at the time $t = 10$ seconds.

(b) Determine the distance traveled by the car during the time interval $8 \leq t \leq 12$ seconds.

(c) What is the position of the object at the time $t = 20$ seconds?

(d) Sketch a position-versus-time graph of the object's motion.

2. A system of masses attached with cords is shown in the following diagram. The coefficients of friction between the blocks and the surfaces are given in the box of values. The pulleys have negligible friction and inertia, and the cords have negligible mass. The unknown mass is just able to move the system.

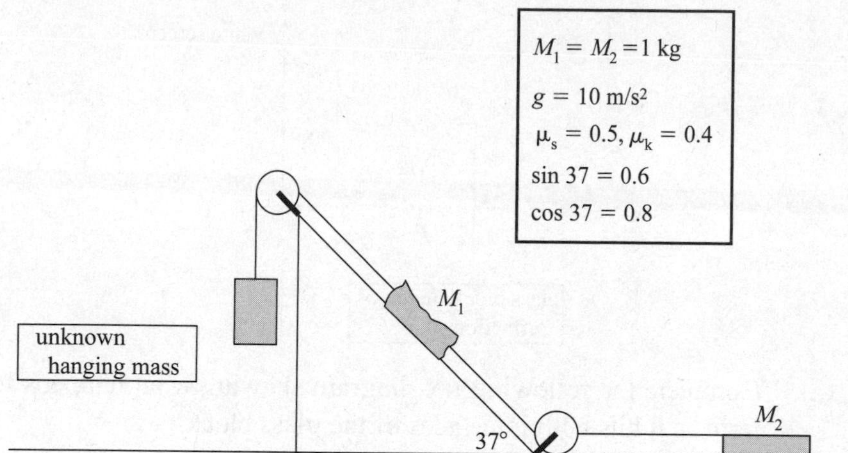

(a) Draw a free-body diagram of mass M_1 at the point of slipping.

(b) Determine the maximum static frictional force on M_1 in this case.

(c) Determine the unknown mass that causes the system to slip and move.

(d) Describe what happens if a mass larger than the mass determined in part (c) is placed in the unknown mass's position.

3. A physics class is performing an experiment with the refraction of light. The students have the following setup on the lab table. The students use a white light source as the light ray. The incident light ray is shown in the diagram.

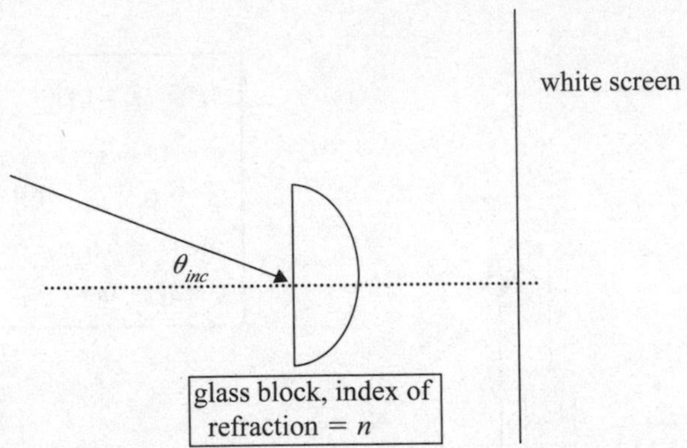

(a) Complete the following ray diagram showing what happens to the light as it hits both interfaces of the glass block.

(b) For a particular measurement, the students measure an incident angle of 45 degrees and a refracted angle of 30 degrees. Determine the index of refraction for the glass block using these data.

(c) White light is sent in at a very large incident angle of 75 degrees. The physics students notice something different on the white screen that they did not observe at the smaller angles. Describe what the students might have noticed on the screen.

(d) The students then reverse the light source to the other side of the block. They put the light ray through and observed what is illustrated in the following diagram. Describe what is happening to the light in this picture.

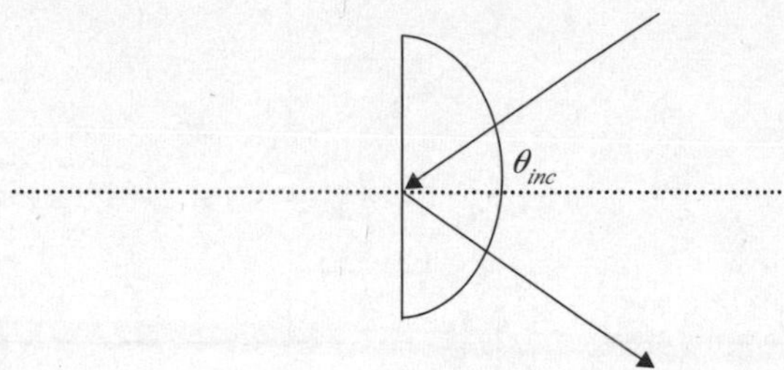

4. A large parallel-plate capacitor is charged by a voltage source to a voltage of V. A singly charged ion (charge e and mass m) is suspended vertically in the electric field of the capacitor plates, as shown in the diagram.

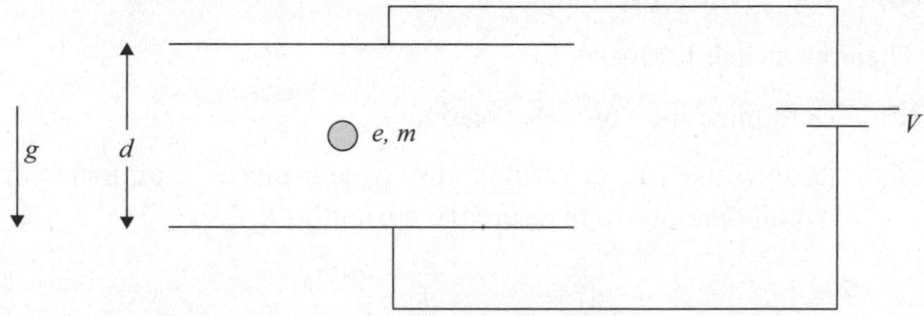

(a) Draw the electric field lines for the capacitor.

(b) Determine the sign on the charge that makes this happen.

(c) In terms of e, V, d, and g, determine the mass of the ion.

(d) A doubly charged ion of $+2q$ is placed on the positive capacitor plate. The ion is of the same mass as determined in part (c). Determine the speed with which it hits the negative plate when it is released from rest at the positive plate. (You may ignore gravitational potential energy in your answer.)

5. The circuit shown in the following diagram starts out with the switch in the open position.

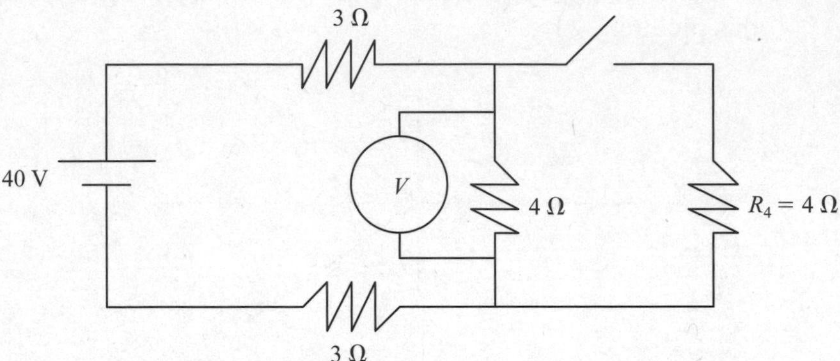

With the switch in the open position as shown, determine the following:

(a) The current in the battery

(b) The voltmeter reading

Then the switch is closed.

(c) Determine the voltmeter reading.

(d) Redraw the circuit (switch closed) and place an ammeter in your circuit diagram to measure the current in R_4.

6. The following diagram depicts a mass spectrometer. A singly charged ion with a negative charge ($-e$) and mass m is shown projected with a speed of v_o into a region of uniform magnetic field. It goes into circular motion with a radius of R and comes out of the mass spectrometer at the point indicated.

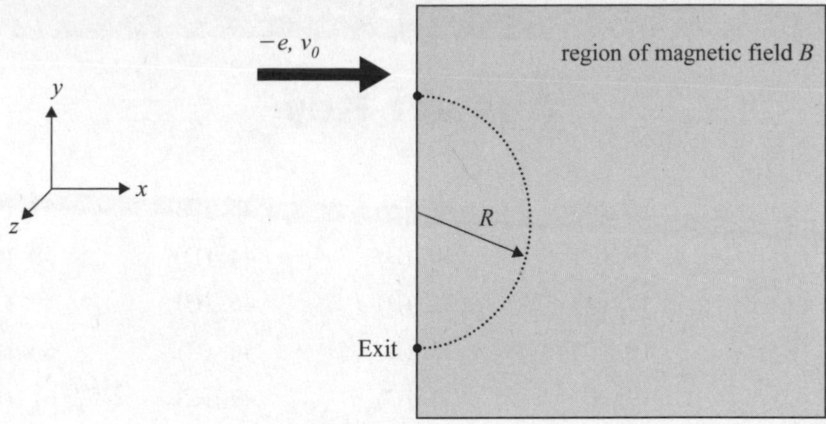

(a) Using the given coordinate system, state the direction of the magnetic field.

(b) Determine the magnetic force at point P in the diagram.

(c) Determine R in terms of m, v_o, e, and B.

(d) Another ion with the same mass as the first ion but with twice the charge is sent into the mass spectrometer. Determine R', the radius of circular motion of this new charge. Give your answer in terms of R.

END OF EXAM

PRACTICE EXAM 2

AP Physics B

Answer Key

1. (D)	15. (A)	29. (A)	43. (B)	57. (C)
2. (B)	16. (C)	30. (B)	44. (D)	58. (C)
3. (A)	17. (A)	31. (B)	45. (C)	59. (A)
4. (C)	18. (D)	32. (B)	46. (E)	60. (D)
5. (C)	19. (B)	33. (C)	47. (C)	61. (B)
6. (D)	20. (C)	34. (C)	48. (C)	62. (A)
7. (B)	21. (A)	35. (E)	49. (B)	63. (B)
8. (C)	22. (C)	36. (A)	50. (C)	64. (C)
9. (B)	23. (D)	37. (A)	51. (C)	65. (A)
10. (A)	24. (A)	38. (D)	52. (D)	66. (C)
11. (C)	25. (B)	39. (E)	53. (C)	67. (C)
12. (D)	26. (E)	40. (C)	54. (E)	68. (E)
13. (B)	27. (A)	41. (D)	55. (B)	69. (B)
14. (E)	28. (C)	42. (B)	56. (E)	70. (D)

PRACTICE EXAM 2

AP Physics B

Detailed Explanations of Answers

Section I

1. **(D)**

The time for the ball to drop to the indicated point is the same time that it takes the ball to travel the horizontal distance D at a constant velocity of v_o: $t_{hit} = \frac{D}{v_o}$. The vertical displacement for this amount of time can then be computed:

$$\Delta y_{drop} = \frac{1}{2}g\left(\frac{D}{v_o}\right)^2$$

The position y on the wall is then determined by subtracting Δy_{drop} from h:

$$y = h - \frac{gD^2}{2v_o^2}$$

2. **(B)**

The elevator is moving at a constant speed. Because it is in equilibrium, so is everything inside of it (the scale and the person). Thus, the upward normal force on the person is equal in magnitude to the weight of the person. The weight of the person is $mg = (50 \text{ kg})(10 \text{ m/s}^2) = 500 \text{ N}$, and the scale will read the normal force.

3. **(A)**

When the elevator is accelerating downward at 2 m/s², the free-body diagram on the person looks like this:

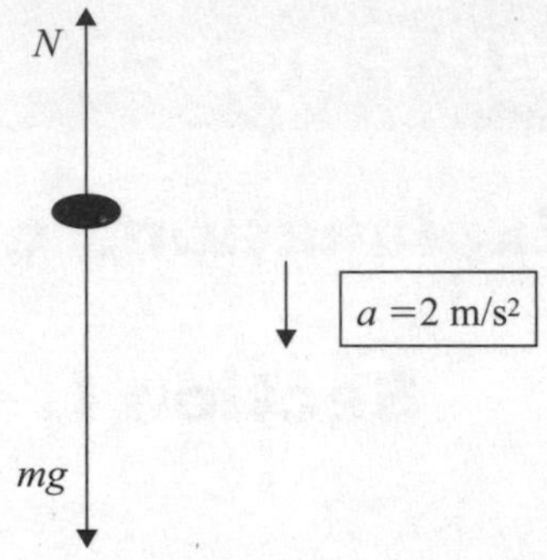

Applying Newton's second law:

$$\sum F_{person} = ma = mg - \text{N} \Rightarrow (50\text{ kg})(2\text{ m/s}^2) = 500\text{ N} - \text{N}$$

$$\therefore \text{N} = 400\text{ N}$$

4. **(C)**

At the time marked t on the graph, the cars' velocities are equal. However, their positions are a different story. Car A has traveled twice the displacement of car B at time t.

5. **(C)**

The two cars have the same position at only one time. That time can be computed by equating the position relationships of the cars. The position of each car is computed by finding the area under the velocity-versus-time curve for each car:

$$CarB - x = \frac{1}{2}(4t)(t) = 2t^2 \text{ (Area of triangle)}$$

$$CarA - x = 10t \text{ (Area of rectangle)}$$

$$10t = 2t^2$$

$$t = 5\text{ s}$$

6. **(D)**

The spring stretches a distance $\Delta x = 25 \text{ cm} - 20 \text{ cm} = 5 \text{ cm}$. The force that stretches this spring is the weight of the mass on the spring, which is 20 N:

$$F_s = k\Delta x \Rightarrow k = \frac{F}{\Delta x} = \frac{20 \text{ N}}{0.05 \text{ m}} = 400 \text{ N/m}$$

7. **(B)**

By inspection, the slope of the T^2-versus-l graph is approximately 4. That would make the relationship between the two axes $T^2 = 4l$. That is not one of the answer choices, but the equivalent statement is $T = 2\sqrt{l}$.

8. **(C)**

By inspection, the square of the period at $t = 0.5$ s is 2.0 s^2. Thus, the period is $\sqrt{2} \approx 1.4$ s.

9. **(B)**

The tension at the lowest point (II) is the point of greatest tension, because the largest value of centripetal acceleration occurs at that point. The net force becomes fairly large at the bottom and must be supplied by the tension growing in magnitude.

10. **(A)**

The penny is not slipping with respect to the turntable; therefore, do not assume that the static frictional force is at its maximum value ($f_s = \mu_s N$). This means the static frictional force is only equivalent to

$$\sum F = ma_c = f_s \Rightarrow f_s = m\frac{v^2}{R}$$

11. **(C)**

The energy in the spring is $\frac{1}{2}kx^2$. The energy of the ball at its maximum height is $U_g = mgh$. The two energies must equal each other and give a maximum height equal to $h = \frac{kx^2}{2mg}$.

12. **(D)**

The net force on the two-mass system is F. This gives an acceleration for both masses of $a = \frac{F}{4\text{ m}}$. Only one force is acting on the top mass: the static frictional force. That force must equal the mass times the acceleration of mass M. Therefore, the static frictional force is

$$f_s = M\left(\frac{F}{4\text{M}}\right) = \frac{F}{4}.$$

13. **(B)**

The buoyant force is equal to the weight of the amount of water displaced by the block. The distance submerged underwater is y. The block's underwater volume is $V_{under} = A \cdot y$. Therefore, the weight of the water displaced is

$$Weight_{water} = \rho_{water} g V_{under} = \rho_w g A \cdot y.$$

That force must equal the actual weight of the block:

$$mg_{block} = mg_{water/displaced}$$

$$\rho_{block} g V_{total} = \rho_{water} g A \cdot y$$

$$\rho_{block} g A \cdot L = \rho_{water} g A \cdot y \Rightarrow y = \frac{\rho_{block}}{\rho_{water}} L = \frac{600}{1000} L = 0.6\,L$$

Thus, 0.6 L is underwater, which leaves 0.4 L above the water line.

14. **(E)**

To determine the maximum height of the block, use the conservation of energy. The total kinetic energy of the block after the collision is

$$KE = \frac{1}{2}(M - m_o + m_o)v'^2 = \frac{1}{2}Mv'^2.$$

To determine v', use conservation of momentum from the collision:

$$p_{before/collision} = p_{after/collision}$$

$$m_o v_o = Mv' \Rightarrow v' = \frac{m_o}{M} v_o$$

Now use that value in the conservation of energy statement:

$$KE = \frac{1}{2} M\left(\frac{m_o}{M} v_o\right)^2 = \frac{1}{2}\frac{m_o^2}{M} v_o^2$$

That kinetic energy must equal the gravitational potential energy of the block at its maximum height:

$$\frac{1}{2} \cdot \frac{m_o^2}{M} v_o^2 = Mgh \Rightarrow h = \frac{m_o^2}{M^2} \cdot \frac{v_o^2}{2g}$$

15. **(A)**

To determine the loss of energy in the collision, compare the initial kinetic energy of the bullet to the final energy of the system.

$$KE_o = \frac{1}{2} m_o v_o^2 \quad KE_f = \frac{1}{2} M \left(\frac{m_o}{M} v_o \right)^2$$

$$\Delta KE = \frac{1}{2} M \left(\frac{m_o}{M} v_o \right)^2 - \frac{1}{2} m_o v_o^2 = \frac{1}{2} m_o v_o^2 \left(\frac{m_o}{M} - 1 \right) = KE_o \left(\frac{M - m_o}{M} \right)$$

The "loss" is indicated by a negative value for the change in kinetic energy.

16. **(C)**

The combination circuit needs to be reduced. The two $3\mu F$ capacitors in parallel behave as one $6\mu F$ capacitor. That $6\mu F$ capacitor is in series with the first $6\mu F$ capacitor:

$$\frac{1}{C_E} = \frac{1}{6} + \frac{1}{6} = \frac{2}{6} = \frac{1}{3} \Rightarrow C_E = 3\ \mu\text{F}$$

This gives a total charge from the battery of $Q = CV = (3\mu F)(12V) = 36\mu C$.

17. **(A)**

The electric field inside any conductor with charge on its surface is always 0.

18. **(D)**

The electric field at point P is

$$E = \frac{kQ}{(4R)^2} = \frac{kQ}{16R^2}$$

19. **(B)**

The electric potential at the center of the sphere is the same as the potential at the surface of the sphere. This is because the entire sphere is an equipotential surface. Therefore, the potential of the sphere is

$$V = \frac{kQ}{R}.$$

20. **(C)**

A satellite in orbit around a planet has only the gravitational force acting on it. Setting up Newton's second law looks like this:

$$\sum F = M_s a_c = \frac{GM_s M_p}{(4R_p)^2} \Rightarrow a_c = \frac{GM_p}{16R_p^2}$$

21. **(A)**

Gravitational acceleration at the surface of the planet depends only on the planet's mass and the radius of the planet.

$$g_p = \frac{GM_p}{R_p^2}$$

22. **(C)**

The period of simple harmonic motion is $T_o = 2\pi\sqrt{\frac{m}{k}}$. The spring is unchanged, so k remains the same value. The mass is doubled, which gives the new period expression

$$T' = 2\pi\sqrt{\frac{2m}{k}} = 2\pi\sqrt{\frac{m}{k}} \cdot \sqrt{2} = \sqrt{2}T_o.$$

23. **(D)**

The tube with one end open and one end closed exhibits the lowest frequency standing wave with a pattern of $\frac{\lambda}{4} = L$. Thus, the wavelength of the 110-Hz sound is $4L = 4(0.80 \text{ m}) = 3.2 \text{ m}$. Computing the speed of sound of this wave gives

$$v = f\lambda = (110 \text{ Hz})(3.2 \text{ m}) = 352 \text{ m/s}.$$

24. **(A)**

The energy of a photon is related to wavelength through the relationship $E = hf = \frac{hc}{\lambda}$. This gives $\lambda = \frac{hc}{E}$. If we use Planck's constant in the units of eV· s, this becomes an easy computation:

$\lambda = \frac{hc}{E} = \frac{(4.14 \times 10^{-15}\ \text{eV} \cdot \text{s})\,(3 \times 10^{8}\ \text{m/s})}{3\ \text{eV}} = 4.14 \times 10^{-7}\ \text{m}$, which is 414 nanometers.

25. **(B)**

When the experiment is placed underwater, the wavelength of the laser will become shorter by $\frac{\lambda}{n_{water}}$. The path difference that produces interference will be shorter by the same amount. This will show up in the maximums being spaced closer together: $\sin\theta = \frac{m\lambda}{d}$. If the wavelength is smaller, the sine of the angle will be smaller as well, and the maximums will be closer together.

26. **(E)**

When an electron returns to the ground state from an excited state, it can do so from all possible energy levels. The electron can go from $n = 2$ to $n = 1$ and then from $n = 1$ to $n = 0$. It can also go directly from $n = 2$ to $n = 0$. These three possible transitions give three possible energies: 4 eV, 2.5 eV, and 1.5 eV.

27. **(A)**

The field caused by the wire is coming out of the page at point P. Applying the left-hand rule for force on a moving electron gives a force directed outward, the electron moving to the left, and the force upward (toward the top of the page).

28. **(C)**

Region III would have an upward field due to the $4I$ current and a downward field due to the I wire. Because the $4I$ wire is further away and the field depends on $1/r$, the only possible location for these two fields to cancel is in region III.

29. **(A)**

The original circuit (with the switch open) is composed of two resistors in series. The original current is $I_o = \frac{\varepsilon}{2R}$. When the switch is closed, the circuit becomes the resistor R in series with a parallel branch. The parallel branch has an effective resistance of $\frac{R}{2}$. The equivalent resistance of the entire circuit is now $R_E = \frac{3R}{2}$. The new current is $I' = \frac{\varepsilon}{\frac{3R}{2}} = \frac{2\varepsilon}{3R}$. Comparing the two currents: $\frac{I'}{I_o} = \frac{\frac{2\varepsilon}{3R}}{\frac{\varepsilon}{2R}} = \frac{4}{3} = 133\%$. Thus, the new current increases by 33%.

30. **(B)**

The parallel part of the circuit has an effective resistance of

$$\frac{1}{R_e} = \frac{1}{2R} + \frac{1}{R} = \frac{3}{2R} \Rightarrow R_e = \frac{2R}{3}.$$

This parallel part is in series with one resistor R, giving a total effective resistance of $R_E = \frac{5R}{3}$. The parallel branch is $\frac{\frac{2R}{3}}{\frac{5R}{3}} = \frac{2}{5} = 40\%$ of the entire resistance.

Therefore, it consumes 40% of the total voltage, which is $\frac{2\varepsilon}{5}$.

31. **(B)**

The net force on the electron is supplied by the magnetic force on a moving charge. Equating Newton's second law to the magnetic force, solve for the mass of the electron:

$$m\frac{v_o^2}{r} = F_B = Bv_o e \Rightarrow m = \frac{Ber}{v_o}.$$

32. **(B)**

An isothermal line is the process in which the temperature is a constant on the line. This "curve" would look like a typical inverse curve $\left(y = \frac{k}{x}\right)$. The Gas Law at constant temperature yields the expression $P_1V_1 = P_2V_2$. Graphically, that becomes $P = \frac{k}{V}$. This means that the curve from $B \rightarrow C$ is the correct choice. This curve certainly has the look of the inverse curve. Also, the product of $P \cdot V$ values at point B is equal to the product of the $P \cdot V$ values at point C. This fact proves that this curve is an inverse, and the other curve $(B \rightarrow D)$ is not an inverse curve.

33. **(C)**

The adiabatic curve is the BD curve. The adiabatic curve should end up short of where the isothermal ends up. An adiabatic yields $PV^{\gamma} = constant$. That curve on the pressure-versus-volume graph would look more like the BD curve. An adiabatic curve has a steeper downward drop than the standard inverse curve.

34. **(C)**

Here is the free-body diagram of the situation:

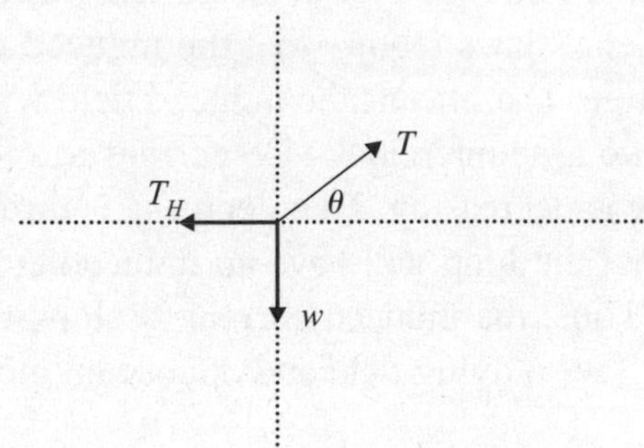

$$\sum F_x = 0 = T\cos\theta - T_H \Rightarrow T_H = T\cos\theta$$

$$\sum F_y = 0 = T\sin\theta - w \Rightarrow T = \frac{w}{\sin\theta}$$

$$\therefore T_H = T\cos\theta = \left(\frac{w}{\sin\theta}\right)\cos\theta = w\cot\theta$$

35. **(E)**

Applying the work–energy theorem, the initial kinetic energy of the book equals the work done by the frictional force:

$KE_o = \frac{1}{2}mv_o^2$ and the work done by friction is:

$$W_f = -f \cdot d = -\mu Nd = -\mu mgd$$

$$W_f = \Delta KE$$

$$-\mu mgd = -\frac{1}{2}mv_o^2 \Rightarrow \mu = \frac{v_o^2}{2gd}$$

36. **(A)**

If the image is one-quarter the size of the object, then $\frac{d_i}{d_o} = \frac{1}{4} \Rightarrow d_o = 4d_i$. Also, for a virtual image, the image distance is negative:

$$\frac{1}{f} = \frac{1}{60} + -\frac{1}{15} \Rightarrow \frac{1}{f} = \frac{-3}{60} \Rightarrow f = -20 \text{ cm}$$

37. **(A)**

As the loop enters the field, the flux is increasing through the loop into the page. Faraday's and Lenz's laws require that the induced current create a field opposing the flux change. That means the induced field will be out of the page, and the loop must have a counterclockwise current to create the field. When the loop exits, the flux is decreasing. That decrease is directed out of the page. Lenz's law requires that the loop will have an induced current creating a field that is into the page. Thus, the induced current is clockwise. A phrase that is easy to remember is "Save a dying field and oppose an increasing field."

38. **(D)**

The induced EMF can be computed using Faraday's law for a moving conductor: $\varepsilon = Bv_o w$. The length of the conductor used in this law is the length that is perpendicular to the field. That length is w. Apply Ohm's law to get the current: $i = \frac{Bv_o w}{R}$.

39. **(E)**

When the loop is completely in the region of field, the flux changes to 0. Therefore, the force acting on the loop is 0.

40. **(C)**

The capacitor has a potential difference between its plates of $\Delta V = \frac{Q_o}{C_o}$. The energy that an electron would gain from that potential difference is $\Delta U_E = \Delta Ve = \frac{Q_o}{C_o} \cdot e$. The potential energy will convert into kinetic energy as it hits the positive plate:

$$\frac{1}{2}m_e v^2 = \frac{Q_o}{C_o}e \Rightarrow v = \sqrt{\frac{2Q_o e}{C_o m_e}}$$

41. **(D)**

In the circuit, the 6-ohm resistor is 75% of the total resistance, which means it will consume 75% of the total voltage. Thus, the capacitor has 7.5 V across its plates, and $Q = CV = (4\mu F)(7.5V) = 30\mu C$.

42. **(B)**

Efficiency is the amount of work derived from the engine divided by the amount of heat used to generate that work. Because 500 J of heat went into the engine and 300 J of heat was discarded, 200 J is available to do the work:

$$e = \frac{W_{out}}{Q_{in}} = \frac{200\text{ J}}{500\text{ J}} = 40\%$$

43. **(B)**

The photoelectric effect relationship is $E = \varphi + KE_{max}$. First, calculate the energy of a 300-nm photon of UV light:

$$E = hf = \frac{hc}{\lambda} = \frac{(4.14 \times 10^{-15}\text{ eV} \cdot \text{s})(3 \times 10^{8}\text{ m/s})}{300 \times 10^{-9}} = 4.14\text{ eV} \approx 4\text{ eV}$$

Then insert that into the photoelectric effect relationship:

$$E = \varphi + KE \Rightarrow 4\text{ eV} = 3\text{ eV} + KE \Rightarrow KE = 1\text{ eV}$$

44. **(D)**

Temperature is proportional to the average kinetic energy of the gas molecules. Kinetic energy is proportional to the square of the speed. If the speed is tripled, the kinetic energy is larger by a factor of 9, and the temperature would also increase by a factor of 9.

45. **(C)**

The farthest from the starting point will be the graph that has the greatest displacement without respect to direction. Determine the displacement of each object by computing the area under the velocity-versus-time graph. By inspection, the greatest area under the curve is represented in graph III.

46. **(E)**

Graph V shows an object that has a constantly increasing slope. Slope is the acceleration of each object.

47. **(C)**

The objects in graph I and graph IV return to their starting points. This is indicated by a net displacement of 0. The cumulative area under each curve is equal to 0.

48. **(C)**

$$KE = \frac{p^2}{2\text{ m}} = \frac{10^2}{2 \cdot (0.5\text{ kg})} = 100\text{ J}$$

49. **(B)**

The energy of a photon is related to its momentum by the following relationship:

$$E = pc = \left(2.21 \times 10^{-21}\text{ kg} \cdot \text{m/s}\right)\left(3 \times 10^{8}\text{ m/s}\right) \cdot \frac{1\text{ eV}}{1.6 \times 10^{-19}\text{ J}}$$
$$= 4.14 \times 10^{6}\text{ eV} = 4.14\text{ MeV}$$

50. **(C)**

The Doppler effect is the apparent change in frequency that an observer hears when a source of sound is moving relative to the observer.

51. **(C)**

The relationship for diffraction from a grating is $\sin\theta = \frac{m\lambda}{d}$, where d is the distance between each diffraction slit. For a 1,200-mm slit, $d = \frac{1 \times 10^{-3}\text{ m}}{1200\text{ lines}} = 8.33 \times 10^{-7}\text{ m}$. Changing to 1,600 lines per millimeter results in d getting smaller. When d gets smaller, $\sin\theta$ gets larger. This shows up in the pattern as the maximums being farther apart.

52. **(D)**

All the answer choices other than (D) are versions of the actual rays that can be drawn in a ray diagram.

53. **(C)**

The image distance is negative for a virtual image. If the image is twice the size, then the image distance is twice the object distance:

$$\frac{1}{f} = \frac{1}{d_o} + \frac{-1}{2d_o} \Rightarrow \frac{1}{f} = \frac{1}{2d_o} \Rightarrow d_o = \frac{f}{2}$$

54. **(E)**

An alpha particle is He^4_2. Two successive decays of an alpha would reduce the mass number of tungsten by 8 and its atomic number by 4. This would result in Yb^{158}_{70}.

55. **(B)**

The object's density is greater than water, which means the object will sink. The upward force on the object is the weight of the water displaced. When the object is completely underwater, the amount of water displaced equals the volume of the object. Therefore, the buoyant force is $F_B = \rho_w V_o g$.

56. **(E)**

$P = VI \Rightarrow I = \dfrac{P}{V} = \dfrac{60\text{ W}}{120\text{ V}} = 0.5\text{ A}$. The current is operating for one minute:

$$\Delta Q = I\Delta t = (0.5\text{ A})(60\text{ s}) = 30\text{ C} \cdot \frac{e}{1.6 \times 10^{-19}\text{ C}} = 1.875 \times 10^{20}\text{ e}$$

An alternative calculation that is easy to perform without a calculator is

$$30\text{ C} \cdot 6.25 \times 10^{18}\frac{e}{C} = 187.5 \times 10^{18} = 1.875 \times 10^{20}.$$

57. **(C)**

The standing wave has three antinodes that make three half wavelengths between the endpoints, giving $3\dfrac{\lambda}{2} = L_o \Rightarrow \lambda = \dfrac{2}{3}L_o$. The speed of a wave is $v = f\lambda = f_o\dfrac{2}{3}L_o = \dfrac{2}{3}f_oL_o$.

58. **(C)**

Rutherford's experiment was the first to identify that the nucleus has all its positive charge located in a very small volume in the center of the atom.

59. **(A)**

Dispersion occurs because light has slightly different indices of refraction for different wavelengths of light. At larger angles of refraction, the slight difference becomes more pronounced, and each color of white light bends at slightly different angles of refraction, causing a beautiful "rainbow" effect, or dispersion of light.

60. **(D)**

Applying the right-hand rule for force on a current-carrying conductor, the current is your right thumb, the field is your fingers, and the direction of the force is indicated by your palm. In this case, the force is down. As shown in the following vector drawing, the current crossed with B gives the force direction:

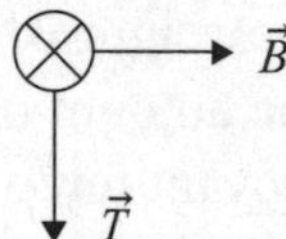

61. **(B)**

The induced current follows from Faraday's law:

$$\varepsilon_i = Bv_o b \Rightarrow I = \frac{\varepsilon}{R} = \frac{Bv_o b}{R}$$

62. **(A)**

The direction of the magnetic force must follow Lenz's law and will be opposite to the direction of motion of the rod: left.

63. **(B)**

As the flux of the loop increases into the page, the wire loop will induce an outwardly directed magnetic field to oppose the change that is occurring in the loop.

64. **(C)**

The acceleration of the pendulum at the instant shown is center directed.

65. **(A)**

The pendulum bob is still in equilibrium in the vertical direction. So draw the forces and equate them in the vertical direction:

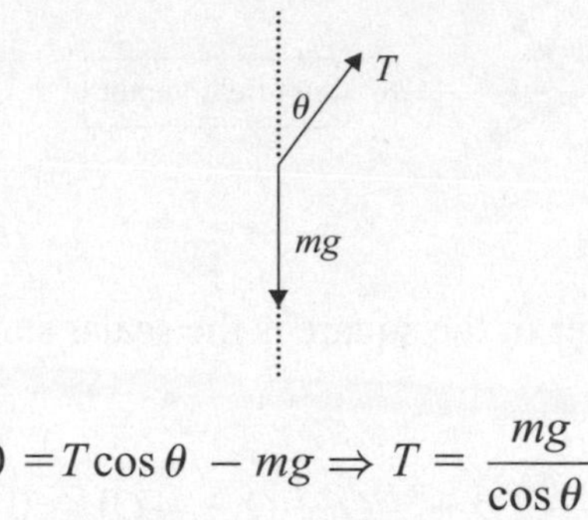

$$\sum F_y = 0 = T\cos\theta - mg \Rightarrow T = \frac{mg}{\cos\theta}$$

66. **(C)**

To get the period of the pendulum, determine the speed of the pendulum bob. The net force on the bob is equal to the following:

$$\sum F_c = m\frac{v^2}{R} = T\sin\theta \Rightarrow m\frac{v^2}{R} = \left(\frac{mg}{\cos\theta}\right)\sin\theta = mg\tan\theta$$

$$\Rightarrow \frac{v^2}{R} = g\tan\theta \Rightarrow v = \sqrt{gR\tan\theta}$$

$$v = \frac{2\pi R}{T} \Rightarrow T = \frac{2\pi R}{v} = \frac{2\pi R}{\sqrt{gR\tan\theta}}$$

Square both sides, to simplify the expression: $T^2 = \dfrac{4\pi^2 R^2}{gR\tan\theta}$

$$T = 2\pi\sqrt{\frac{R}{g\tan\theta}}$$

But this expression is not an answer choice. Thus, further simplification is required. Notice that the radius of revolution $R = L\sin\theta$. Using this in the previous expression to replace R gives the final expression:

$$T = 2\pi\sqrt{\frac{R}{g\tan\theta}} = 2\pi\sqrt{\frac{L\sin\theta}{g\left(\frac{\sin\theta}{\cos\theta}\right)}} = 2\pi\sqrt{\frac{L}{g}\cos\theta}$$

67. **(C)**

The field at the center of the square is the sum of four individual field vectors. Here is the vector drawing:

net field vector

68. **(E)**

The potential at the center of the square is the scalar sum of all four potentials of each point charge:

$$V = \sum \frac{kQ_i}{r_i} = \frac{k}{r}[Q + -Q + Q + -Q] = 0$$

All the charges are the same distance away from the center of the square, and the two positive Q's cancel the two negative Q's.

69. **(B)**

The diagonal distance between the two charges is $\sqrt{2}a$. Use this distance in Coulomb's law:

$$\|F\| = k\frac{Q \cdot Q}{\left(\sqrt{2}a\right)^2} = \frac{kQ^2}{2a^2}$$

70. **(D)**

$$h = \frac{1}{2}gt_o^2 \Rightarrow t_o = \sqrt{\frac{2h}{g}} \quad \text{and}$$

$$2h = \frac{1}{2}gt^2 \Rightarrow t = \sqrt{\frac{4h}{g}} = \sqrt{2} \cdot \sqrt{\frac{2h}{g}} = \sqrt{2} \cdot t_o$$

Section II

1. (a) The acceleration of the car at $t = 10$ seconds is the slope of the velocity-versus-time graph at 10 seconds. The slope is $m = -3$ m/s^2. Therefore, the magnitude of the acceleration at 10 seconds is 3 m/s^2.

(b) The distance traveled in this interval of time is equal to the absolute value of the area enclosed by the graph and the time axis. The area of each segment is equal to the area of the rectangle: $A = \frac{1}{2}(6\text{ m/s})(2\text{ s}) = 6\text{ m}$. The area above the time axis is $+6$ m, and the area below the time axis is -6 m. The displacement of the object during this interval is 0 meters. The distance traveled is $|+6\text{ m}| + |-6\text{ m}| = 12\text{ m}$.

(c) Because the graph is symmetrical when inverted about $t = 10$ seconds, the area above the axis between $t = 0$ and $t = 10$ seconds is the same magnitude as the area below the axes and between $t = 10$ and $t = 20$ seconds. Thus, there is no need to compute the area because the areas cancel each other out and leave the final position of the object back at its starting point, for a displacement of 0.

(d) A position-versus-time graph of the object's motion looks like this:

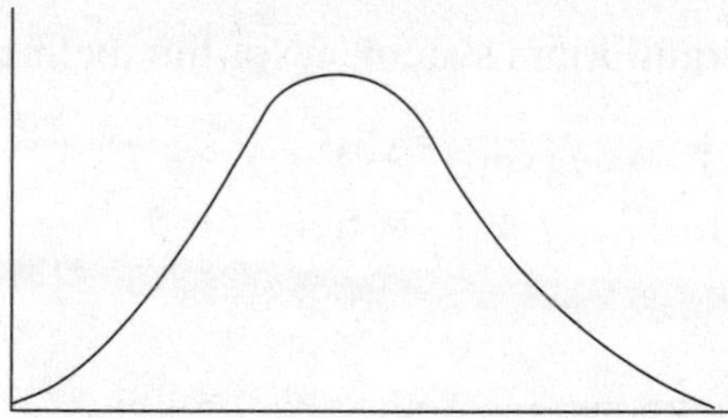

2. (a) Here is a free-body diagram of mass M_1 at the point of slipping:

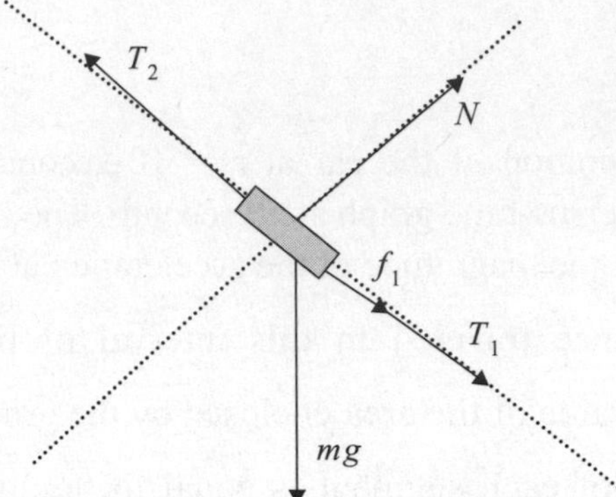

(b) The maximum static frictional force on M_1 occurs when $f_s \leq \mu_s N$ at the point of equality. Therefore,

$$N = mg\cos 37 = (1\text{ kg})(10\text{ m/s}^2)(0.8) = 8\text{ N}$$

$$f_{smax} = \mu_s N = (0.5)(8\text{ N}) = 4\text{ N}$$

(c) To determine the unknown mass, realize that all three masses are in equilibrium at this slipping point. The frictional force on M_1 is 4 N. The tension between M_1 and M_2 (T_1) is equal to the maximum static friction between M_2 and the horizontal surface. Computing this force gives

$$f_{smax} = \mu_s N = (0.5)(1\text{ kg})(10\text{ m/s}^2) = 5\text{ N}.$$

Set up an equilibrium statement for the inclined block:

$$\Sigma F = 0 = T_2 - mg\sin 37 - f - T_1 \Rightarrow T_2$$
$$= mg\sin 37 + f + T_1 = 6 + 4 + 5$$
$$\therefore T_2 = 15\text{ N}$$

Thus, the unknown mass must be 1.5 kg:

$$m_{unknown}g = 15\text{ N} \Rightarrow m_u = \frac{15\text{ N}}{10\text{ m/s}^2} = 1.5\text{ kg}$$

(d) If a mass greater than 1.5 kg is placed hung from the cord, the frictional forces will become kinetic friction and will lower by about 20%. This will create a much bigger unbalanced force on all the masses, and the whole system will accelerate.

3. (a) The completed ray diagram looks like this:

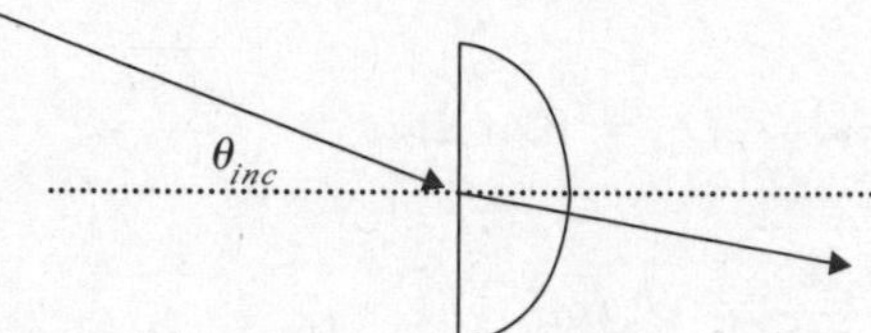

The ray bends at the air–glass interface, but not at the glass–air interface because the circular shape is perpendicular to the ray. The angle of refraction is less than the angle of incidence. Therefore, it bends toward the normal line.

(b) The index of refraction for the glass block is determined as follows:

$$n_{air} \sin \theta_1 = n_{glass} \sin \theta_2$$

$$(1) \sin 45^\circ = n \cdot \sin 30 \Rightarrow n = \frac{\sqrt{2}}{2} \cdot 2 = \sqrt{2} \approx 1.4$$

(c) At this large angle, the difference in indices of refraction begin to show. The indices for the different colors are of slightly different values. For instance, n for red = 1.40, and n for blue = 1.43. This results in the light separating at higher angles of incidence. The student will see this on the white screen as the colors starting to separate.

(d) The picture is an example of total internal reflection. The light cannot refract out of the glass into air. Therefore, all the light reflects on the glass–air interface as shown.

4. (a) The electric field lines are as follows:

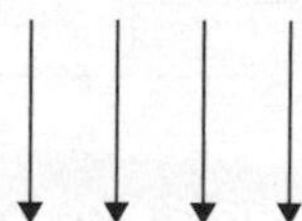

(b) The sign on the ion is negative. The weight of the particle is downward. The electric force on the ion must be upward to allow for the suspension of the particle. A negative charge will have a force opposite the field lines.

(c) The electric field is determined as follows:

$$E = \frac{\Delta V}{d} \Rightarrow F_e = qE = e\frac{V}{d}$$

$$mg = F_e \Rightarrow mg = e\frac{V}{d}$$

$$m = \frac{eV}{gd}$$

(d) The kinetic energy of the ion will equal the electric potential energy lost during the acceleration of the ion.

$$KE = \frac{1}{2}mv^2 = U_e = V2e \Rightarrow v = \sqrt{\frac{4\ Ve}{m}}$$

$$v = \sqrt{\frac{4\ Ve}{\left(\frac{\text{eV}}{gd}\right)}} = 2\sqrt{gd}$$

5. (a) With the switch open, the circuit is three resistors in series. Therefore,

$$R_E = 3\ \Omega + 4\ \Omega + 3\ \Omega$$

$$I_t = \frac{V_t}{R_e} = \frac{40\text{ V}}{10\ \Omega} = 4\text{ A}$$

(b) The voltmeter reading is $V_4 = I_4R_4 = 4 \cdot 4 = 16V$.

(c) With the switch closed, the circuit becomes two 3-ohm resistors in series with the two 4-ohm resistors in parallel. The two 4-ohm resistors in parallel act effectively as 2 ohms. This makes the total resistance in the new circuit 8 ohms. Thus, the new voltmeter reading is $\frac{2\ \Omega}{8\ \Omega} \cdot 40\text{ V} = 10\text{ V}$

(d)

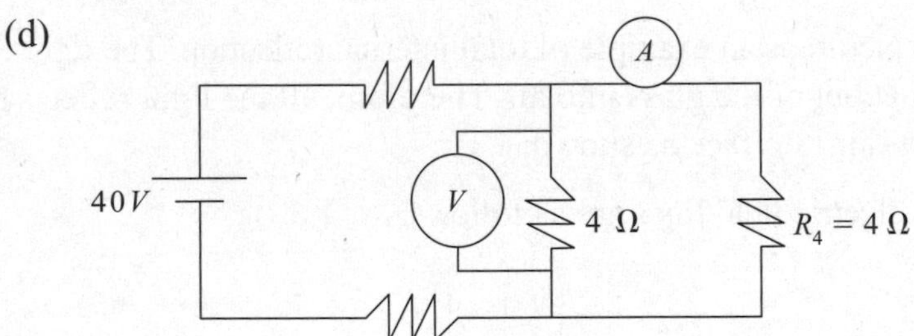

6. (a) Using the left-hand rule for a moving negative charge, the left thumb is the velocity vector, palm is facing down for the initial force, and fingers are pointing inward. The magnetic field is directed into the page, which is the *z*-axis.

(b) The magnetic force is directed inward (radially) at point P. The magnitude is $F_B = Bv_oe$.

(c) $\sum F_{electron} = \frac{mv^2}{R} = Bve \Rightarrow R = \frac{mv_o}{Be}$

(d) A doubly charged ion will have half the radius. Look at the expression for *R* shown in the solution to part (c).

PRACTICE EXAMS

AP Physics C

PRACTICE EXAM 3

AP Physics C Mechanics

Section I

Time: 45 Minutes
35 Questions

DIRECTIONS: Each of the questions or incomplete statements below is followed by five answer choices. Select the one that is best in each case and fill in the oval on the corresponding answer sheet.

NOTE: Units associated with numerical quantities are abbreviated, using the abbreviations listed in the Table of Information found at the back of this book. To simplify calculations, you may use $g = 10$ m/s^2 for all problems.

1. A baseball is projected at an angle of 45 degrees with a speed of v_o. The projectile reaches a maximum height of h_o. The same ball is then projected with the same launch speed but completely in the vertical direction. What is the maximum height of the second projectile launched?

   (A) h_o

   (B) $\frac{\sqrt{2}}{2}h_o$

   (C) $\sqrt{2}h_o$

   (D) $2h_o$

   (E) $4h_o$

2. A ball is freely falling, with air drag acting on it. The air drag force follows the relationship $F_d = mbv$, where b is a constant with units s^{-1}. What is an expression for the terminal velocity of the ball as it is freely falling through the air?

   (A) $v_{terminal} = \frac{mg}{b}$

   (B) $v_{terminal} = \frac{g}{b}$

   (C) $v_{terminal} = \frac{b}{mg}$

   (D) $v_{terminal} = \frac{b}{g}$

   (E) $v_{terminal} = \frac{b}{m}$

Use the following situation to answer questions 3 and 4. A car accelerates with an acceleration described by the expression $a = 3t + 2$. The car begins its motion from rest.

3. Determine the instantaneous speed of the car at $t = 2.0$ seconds.

(A) 3 m/s
(B) 6 m/s
(C) 8 m/s
(D) 10 m/s
(E) 28 m/s

4. Determine the average velocity of the car over the time interval of $t = 0$ to $t = 2.0$ seconds.

(A) 4 m/s
(B) 5 m/s
(C) 10 m/s
(D) 12 m/s
(E) 14 m/s

Use the following situation to answer questions 5 and 6. An Atwood machine, like that shown in the diagram, is completely frictionless, and the moment of inertia of the pulley can be ignored. Mass m_2 > mass m_1. Mass m_2 falls a distance h to the floor.

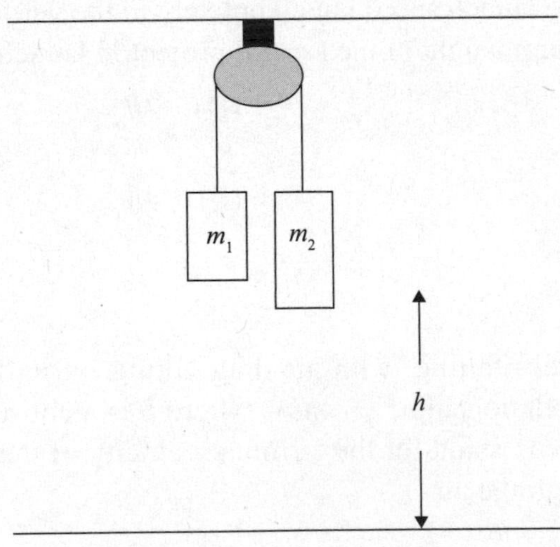

5. Which is the correct expression for the acceleration of the masses?

(A) $a = \frac{m_2}{m_1} g$

(B) $a = \frac{(m_2 - m_1)}{(m_1 + m_2)} g$

(C) $a = \frac{m_2}{(m_1 + m_2)} g$

(D) $a = \frac{(m_1 + m_2)}{(m_2 - m_1)} g$

(E) $a = \frac{g}{2}$

6. Which is the correct expression for the speed of m_2 as it hits the floor?

(A) $v = \sqrt{2gh}$

(B) $v = \sqrt{2gh(m_2 - m_1)}$

(C) $v = \sqrt{\frac{2(m_2 - m_1)}{(m_1 + m_2)} gh}$

(D) $v = \sqrt{2m_2gh}$

(E) $v = \sqrt{2(m_1 + m_2)gh}$

7. A block (mass m) is held in equilibrium by the smallest applied force F_{min} that will allow this to occur, as shown in the following diagram. What is the correct expression for the maximum coefficient of static friction?

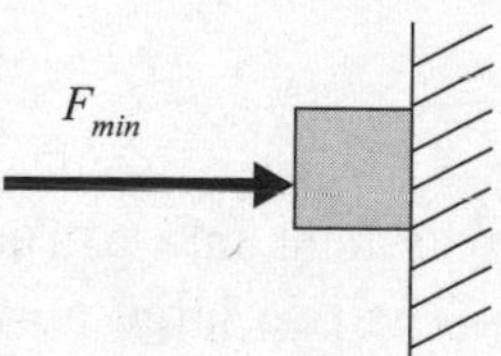

(A) $\mu_s = \frac{F_{min}}{mg}$

(B) $\mu_s = \frac{mg}{F_{min}}$

(C) $\mu_s = \frac{F_{min}}{g}$

(D) $\mu_s = F_{min}$

(E) $\mu_s = mg$

8. A nonlinear spring has a force function of $F_s = -2x + \frac{3}{2}\sqrt{x}$, where x is the variable for spring displacement. How much work is done by the spring in stretching from $x = 0$ m to $x = 4.0$ m?

(A) $\frac{13}{8}$ J

(B) $-\frac{13}{8}$ J

(C) 8 J

(D) -8 J

(E) 24 J

9. A bullet of mass M_o is shot into a block of mass $200M_o$. The bullet was shot into the block with a speed of v_o. The block completely absorbs the bullet and moves off with a speed consistent with the conservation of momentum. What is the loss of energy from this totally inelastic collision?

(A) $\frac{18}{200}KE_o$

(B) $\frac{180}{200}KE_o$

(C) $\frac{199}{200}KE_o$

(D) $\frac{200}{201}KE_o$

(E) $\frac{1}{201}KE_o$

10. A large piece of metal is bent into a truncated U shape, as shown in the following diagram. The two large portions of the U shape are both of length L. The short portion is $L/4$. Determine the center of mass for the shape.

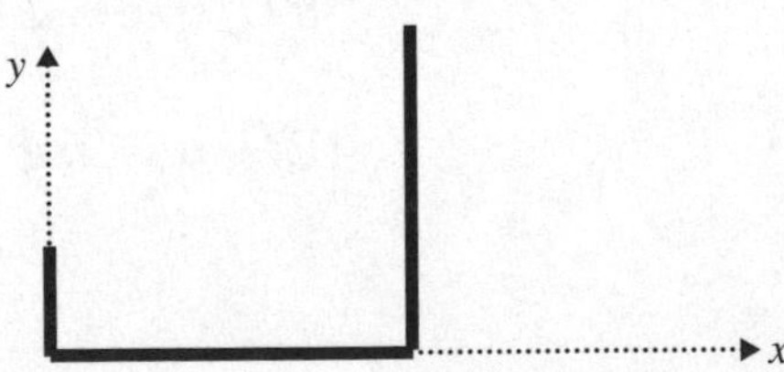

(A) $\left(\frac{L}{3}, \frac{17L}{72}\right)$

(B) $\left(\frac{2L}{3}, \frac{17L}{72}\right)$

(C) $\left(\frac{25L}{36}, \frac{5L}{8}\right)$

(D) $\left(\frac{2L}{3}, \frac{17L}{36}\right)$

(E) $\left(\frac{L}{3}, \frac{17L}{72}\right)$

11. A car of mass $m = 1{,}000$ kg is making a turn on a wet, level road. The coefficient of static friction between the road and tires is $\mu s = 0.4$. The turn the car is making has a radius of curvature of $r = 25\,\text{m}$. What is the maximum speed the car can have in making this turn without skidding?

(A) 10 m/s
(B) 100 m/s
(C) 32 m/s
(D) 20 m/s
(E) 16 m/s

12. Two stars of equal mass M orbit a common center of mass, as shown in the following diagram. What is the correct expression for the orbital speed of each star?

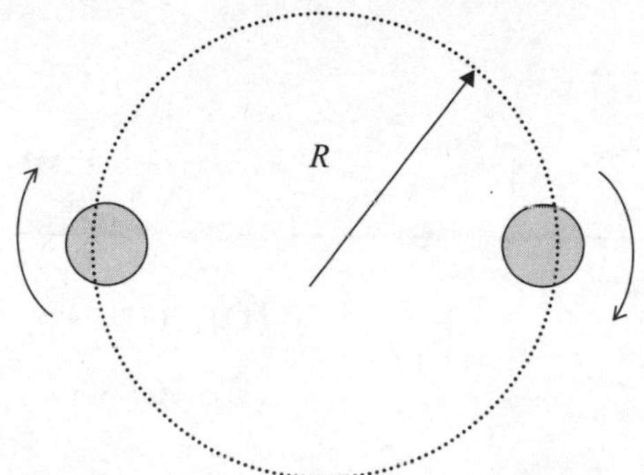

(A) $v = \sqrt{\dfrac{GM}{R}}$

(B) $v = \sqrt{\dfrac{GM^2}{R}}$

(C) $v = \sqrt{\dfrac{GM}{2R}}$

(D) $v = \sqrt{\dfrac{GM^2}{2R}}$

(E) $v = \dfrac{1}{2}\sqrt{\dfrac{GM}{R}}$

13. A pendulum on Earth has a period of 1.5 seconds. The same pendulum is taken to a different planet with an unknown gravity and is tested. The new period on this unknown planet is 1.0 second. The gravitational acceleration on this new planet is most nearly

(A) 22.5 m/s^2
(B) 4.4 m/s^2
(C) 15 m/s^2
(D) 6.7 m/s^2
(E) 10 m/s^2

14. An object is acted on only by a linear restoring force of a spring. The object is set into motion by an initial outside force. This motion is best explained by which of the following differential equations?

(A) $\frac{dv}{dt} = -kv$

(B) $\frac{dv}{dt} = \omega kx$

(C) $\frac{dv}{dt} = -\omega kv$

(D) $\frac{dv}{dt} = -\omega^2 x$

(E) $\frac{dv}{dt} = -\omega^2 v$

15. A hoop of mass M, radius R, and moment of inertia $I = MR^2$ rolls down an incline, as shown in the diagram below. When the hoop reaches the bottom of the incline, how much of the hoop's kinetic energy is rotational kinetic energy?

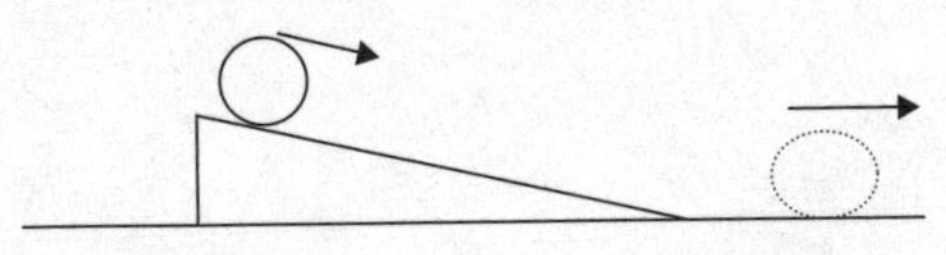

(A) 25%

(B) 40%

(C) 50%

(D) 60%

(E) 67%

16. An object slides down a frictionless track beginning from rest, as shown in the following diagram. The object is then launched at a 60-degree angle and is set into projectile motion. What is the maximum height of the projectile?

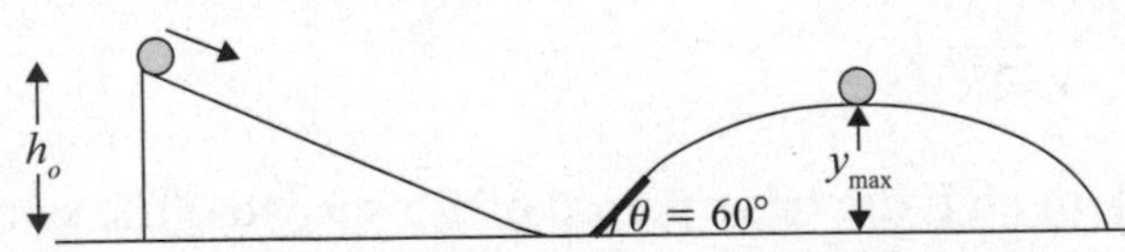

(A) $y_{max} = \frac{h_o}{4}$

(B) $y_{max} = \frac{h_o}{3}$

(C) $y_{max} = \frac{h_o}{2}$

(D) $y_{max} = \frac{2h_o}{3}$

(E) $y_{max} = \frac{3h_o}{4}$

17. A satellite of mass m_s is orbiting the Earth (m_e) with an orbital distance from the center of the Earth of $r = 3R$. Which of the following expressions represents the total energy of the satellite?

(A) $TE = \frac{Gm_s m_e}{3R}$

(B) $TE = -\frac{Gm_s m_e}{3R}$

(C) $TE = \frac{Gm_s m_e}{6R}$

(D) $TE = -\frac{Gm_s m_e}{6R}$

(E) $TE = -\frac{Gm_s m_e}{2R}$

18. Which of the following three types of motion have a changing acceleration?

I. A ball falling with air resistance, with $v < v_{terminal}$

II. A pendulum bob in motion

III. A mass attached to a vertical spring and undergoing oscillations

(A) II only

(B) II and III only

(C) I and II only

(D) III only

(E) I, II, and III

19. A spring with spring constant k is attached to a mass m and set into vertical simple harmonic motion (SHM), as shown in case I in the following diagram. The spring is then cut in half, and the resulting two springs are reattached as shown in case II. The period of SHM in case I is T_o. What is the period of SHM in case II?

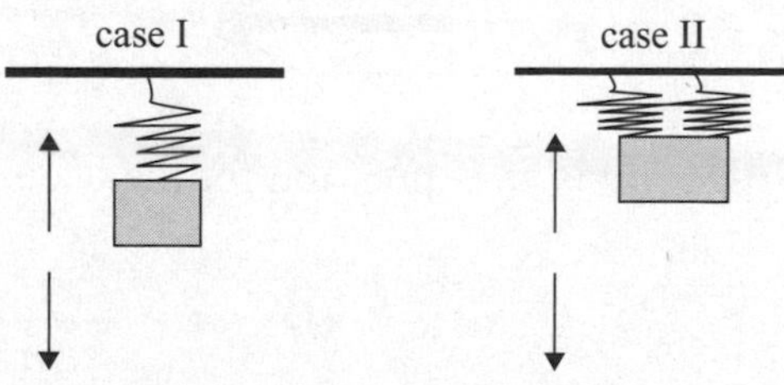

(A) $\frac{T_o}{4}$

(B) $\frac{\sqrt{2}T_o}{2}$

(C) $\frac{T_o}{2}$

(D) T_o

(E) $2T_o$

20. A CD player angularly accelerates a CD from rest at a rate of $\alpha = 5\pi\frac{\text{rad}}{\text{s}^2}$. The CD player accelerates the CD up to its top angular speed of 1,800 RPMs. What is the angular displacement of the CD during this motion?

(A) 180 πrad
(B) 360 πrad
(C) 720 πrad
(D) 540 πrad
(E) 144 πrad

21. A ball is being swung in a vertical circle on the end of a light string. The radius of this circular motion is 0.8 m. The mass of the ball is 2.0 kg. At the very bottom of the circular motion, the tension in the string is exactly three times the weight of the ball (3 mg). Which of the following is most nearly the speed of the ball at this bottom point?

(A) 2.8 m/s
(B) 4 m/s
(C) 5 m/s
(D) 5.7 m/s
(E) 7.7 m/s

22. Two blocks are interacting as shown in the following diagram. Both blocks move relative to each other. The kinetic frictional force between block 1 and 2 is $2f$. The kinetic frictional force between block 2 and the horizontal surface is f. The mass of each block is m. An applied force F_a is applied to block 2.

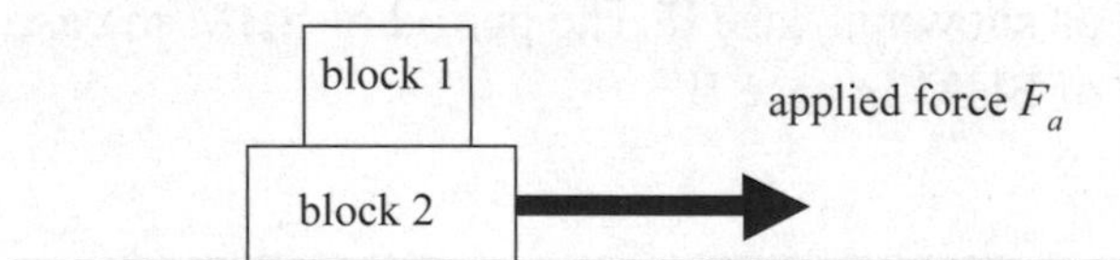

Which of the following is an expression for the acceleration of block 2?

(A) $a = \frac{F_a}{2m}$
(B) $a = \frac{F_a - f}{2m}$
(C) $a = \frac{F_a - 2f}{m}$
(D) $a = \frac{F_a - 3f}{m}$
(E) $a = \frac{F_a - 2f}{2m}$

Use the following situation to answer questions 23 and 24. A block of mass m slides down a frictionless incline of height h_o, as shown in the diagram. The block then slides on a horizontal surface with friction. After sliding a distance d, the block comes completely to rest.

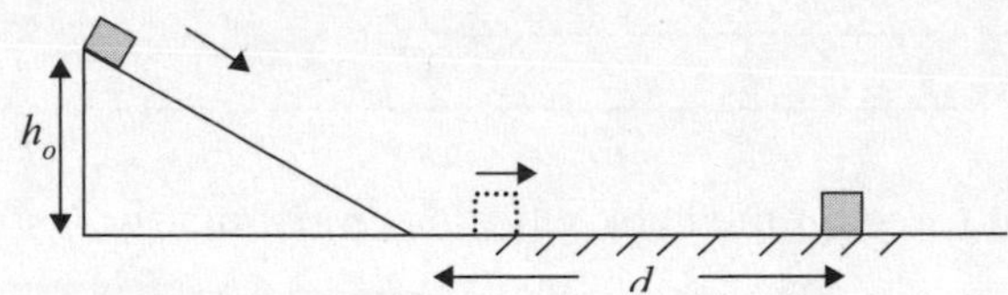

23. Which expression is the amount of work done by friction?

(A) $-mgh_o$
(B) mgh_o
(C) $-mgd$
(D) mgd
(E) 0

24. Which of the following expressions is the coefficient of kinetic friction for the horizontal surface/block?

(A) $\mu = \frac{d}{2}$
(B) $\mu = \frac{d}{h_o}$
(C) $\mu = \frac{h_o}{d}$
(D) $\mu = \frac{h_o}{2d}$
(E) $\mu = \frac{2h_o}{d}$

25. A car's center of mass (CM) is located as shown in the diagram. The CM is located a distance $\frac{d}{3}$ from the back wheels. The distance between the wheels is d.

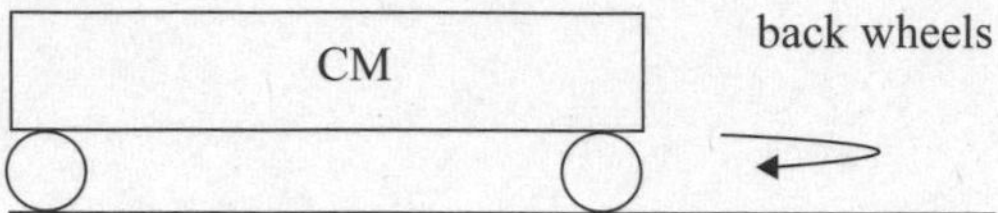

The normal force on the back wheels is most nearly

(A) $\frac{1}{3}mg$

(B) $\frac{1}{2}mg$

(C) $\frac{2}{3}mg$

(D) $\frac{4}{3}mg$

(E) mg

Use the following situation to answer questions 26 and 27. A merry-go-round is a large disk of mass M, radius R, and moment of inertia $I = 0.5MR^2$. It is rotating with an angular velocity of ω_o. Two sandbags, each of mass $M/5$, are dropped at different spots on the edge of the merry-go-round. The two sandbags have no initial angular momentum when they are dropped.

26. What is the new angular velocity of the merry-go-round after the two sandbags are dropped onto the edge?

(A) $\omega' = \frac{1}{2}\omega_o$

(B) $\omega' = \frac{5}{7}\omega_o$

(C) $\omega' = \frac{2}{9}\omega_o$

(D) $\omega' = \frac{1}{3}\omega_o$

(E) $\omega' = \frac{5}{9}\omega_o$

27. How much of the original energy is lost in this collision?

(A) None

(B) $\frac{1}{4}E_o$

(C) $\frac{5}{36}E_o$

(D) $\frac{4}{9}E_o$

(E) $\frac{1}{9}E_o$

28. A physical pendulum consists of a uniform rod of length L and mass M. The rod has a hole drilled through it at a distance $L/4$ from the top edge, as shown in the diagram. An axle is put through the hole, and the rod is put into small-angle oscillations.

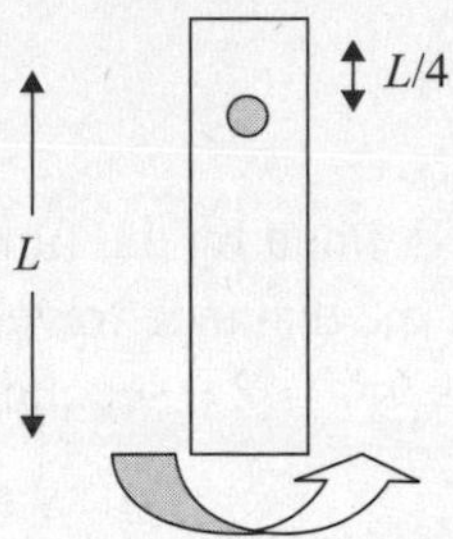

The period of this physical pendulum is most nearly

(A) $T = 2\pi\sqrt{\dfrac{L}{3g}}$

(B) $T = 2\pi\sqrt{\dfrac{2L}{3g}}$

(C) $T = 2\pi\sqrt{\dfrac{4L}{3g}}$

(D) $T = 2\pi\sqrt{\dfrac{7L}{12g}}$

(E) $T = 2\pi\sqrt{\dfrac{5L}{12g}}$

Use the following situation to answer questions 29 and 30. A mass is resting in static equilibrium on an incline with friction, as shown in the diagram. The mass is 3 kg. The incline is set at 37 degrees.

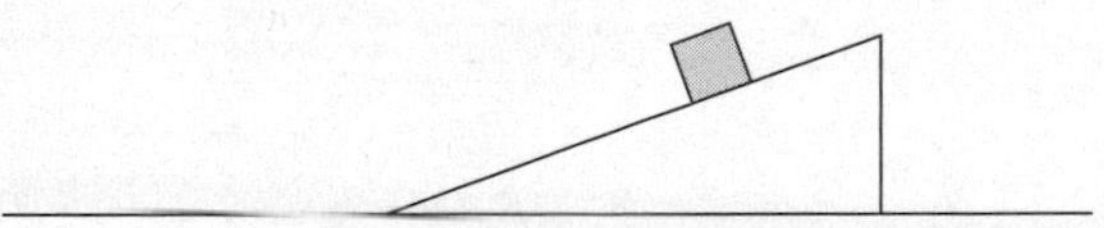

29. The magnitude of the normal force is most nearly

(A) 12 N

(B) 16 N

(C) 20 N

(D) 24 N

(E) 30 N

30. The minimum possible coefficient of static friction between the incline and the mass is most nearly

(A) $\mu_s = 0.25$
(B) $\mu_s = 0.5$
(C) $\mu_s = 0.6$
(D) $\mu_s = 0.67$
(E) $\mu_s = 0.75$

31. An object's acceleration is defined by the function $a = 2t + 5$. The object starts from rest. Determine the distance traveled by this object in the time interval from $t = 0$ seconds to $t = 2.0$ seconds.

(A) 18 m
(B) 36 m
(C) $\frac{38}{3}$ m
(D) 9 m
(E) $\frac{9}{2}$ m

32. A projectile is launched from a gun at an angle of 30 degrees. The range of the projectile is R. The same gun launches the same projectile at a new angle of 60 degrees. The range of the second launch is most nearly

(A) $\frac{R}{2}$
(B) R
(C) $2R$
(D) $\frac{\sqrt{3}}{2}R$
(E) $\frac{\sqrt{2}}{2}R$

Use the following situation to answer questions 33 and 34. The pendulum shown in the diagram is pulled out to angle θ_o (< 10 degrees) and released from rest. The length of the pendulum is L. The period of the pendulum is T_o.

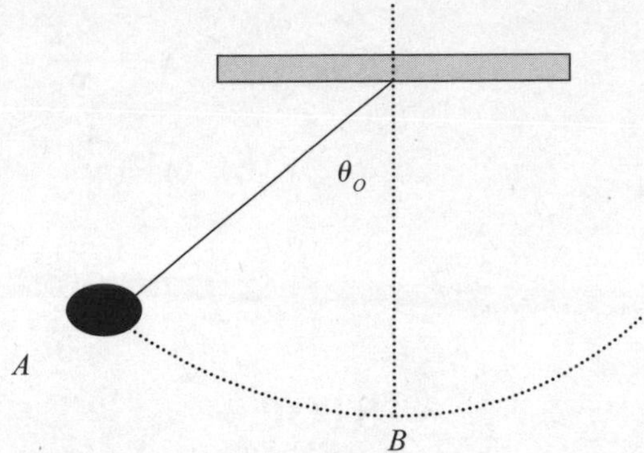

33. Which of the following is equivalent to the magnitude of the tension in the cord at the instant it is released?

(A) $T = mg\tan\theta_o$

(B) $T = mg\sin\theta_o$

(C) $T = \dfrac{mg}{\sin\theta_o}$

(D) $T = \dfrac{mg}{\cos\theta_o}$

(E) $T = mg\cos\theta_o$

34. Which of the following vectors represents the direction of the acceleration of the pendulum at point B?

(A) →

(B) ↑

(C) ↓

(D) ←

(E) 0

35. A conservative force acting on a particle in one dimension has the following potential energy function: $U(x) = \frac{2}{3}x^2 + 3x + 2$. There is a point of stable equilibrium on the x-axis. Find that point of stable equilibrium.

(A) $x = 0$

(B) $x = \frac{-9}{4}$

(C) $x = \frac{9}{4}$

(D) $x = \frac{-4}{9}$

(E) $x = \frac{4}{9}$

STOP

This is the end of Section I.

If time still remains, you may check your work only in this section.

Do not begin Section II until instructed to do so.

Section II

Time: 45 Minutes
3 Free-Response Questions

DIRECTIONS: Carefully read each question and be sure to answer *each part* of the question. Each question is worth 15 points, but the parts within a question may not have equal weight. Show all your work. Crossed-out work will not be graded. For this section of the exam, you may use your calculator and the equation tables for Physics C found at the back of this book.

1. Two blocks are interacting with an incline, as shown in the following diagram. The top block is attached to the incline system with a cord. The bottom block is free to move on the incline and begins to accelerate downward when released from rest. The top block has a mass of M, and the bottom block has a mass of $4M$. The coefficients of kinetic friction between all surfaces is $\mu = 0.4$. Use $g = 10\ \text{m/s}^2$, $\sin 37° = 0.6$, and $\cos 37° = 0.8$.

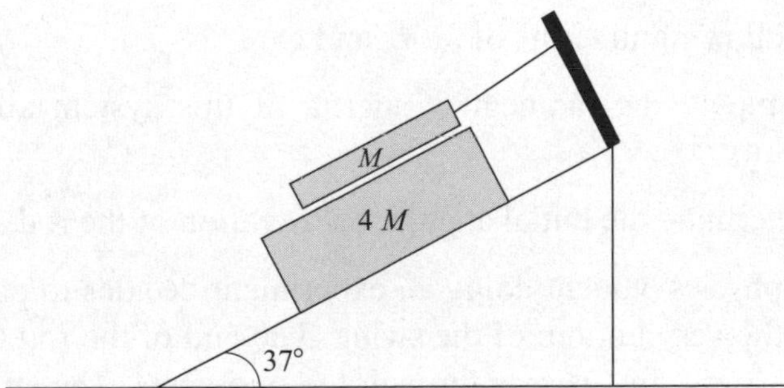

(a) Draw a free-body diagram of the bottom block.

(b) Determine the acceleration of the bottom block as it slides down the incline.

(c) Determine the tension in the cord during the time that the bottom block is in contact with the top block.

2. A uniform rod of mass 3 M and length L has a slotted lab mass attached to the end, as shown in the following diagram. The slotted mass has a mass of M and is attached exactly at the end of the rod. This system is then pivoted through the end of the rod and allowed to freely rotate, starting from the horizontal position shown.

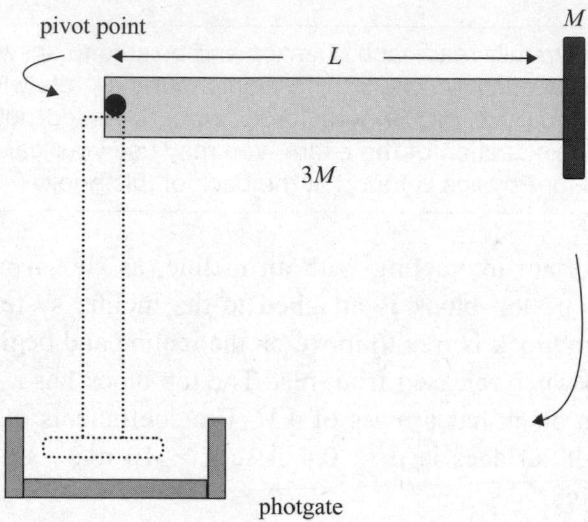

Do the following in terms of M, L, and g:

(a) Compute the moment of inertia of this system about the pivot point.

(b) Determine the initial angular acceleration of the rod/system.

(c) A physics student doing an experiment decides to put a photogate at the very bottom of the swing. The end of the rod (with the slotted mass) just passes through the photogate. The student uses the photogate to measure the linear velocity of the system at that point. What is the linear velocity of the rod at that point?

3. Two stars orbit each other around a common center of mass (CM), as shown in the following diagram. The smaller mass has a mass of M, and the larger mass has a mass of $3M$. d is the distance between the two stars.

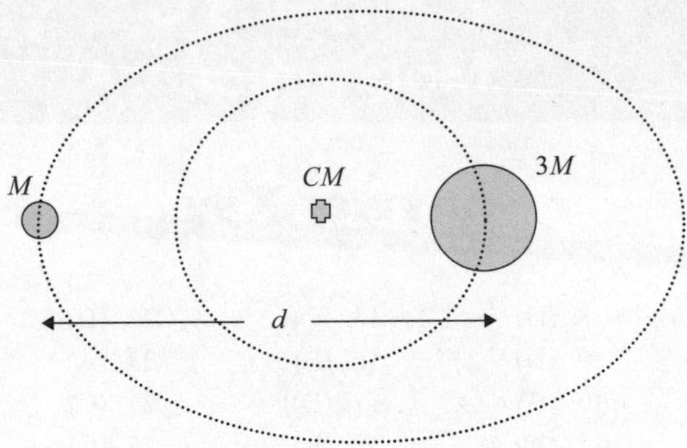

In terms of M, G, and d, determine the following:

(a) The CM of the system in terms of d

(b) The period of orbit of mass $3M$

(c) The total energy of the two-star system

END OF EXAM

PRACTICE EXAM 3

AP Physics C
Mechanics

Answer Key

1. (D)	8. (D)	15. (C)	22. (D)	29. (D)
2. (B)	9. (D)	16. (E)	23. (A)	30. (E)
3. (D)	10. (B)	17. (D)	24. (C)	31. (C)
4. (A)	11. (A)	18. (E)	25. (C)	32. (B)
5. (B)	12. (E)	19. (C)	26. (E)	33. (E)
6. (C)	13. (A)	20. (B)	27. (D)	34. (B)
7. (B)	14. (D)	21. (B)	28. (D)	35. (B)

PRACTICE EXAM 3

AP Physics C
Mechanics

Detailed Explanations of Answers

Section I

1. **(D)**

The maximum height for the projectile projected at 45 degrees is

$$y_{max} = \frac{v_o^2 \sin^2(\theta)}{2g} = \frac{v_o^2 \sin^2(45)}{2g} = \frac{v_o^2\left(\frac{\sqrt{2}}{2}\right)^2}{2g} = \frac{v_o^2}{4g} = h_o.$$

For a projectile launched vertically upward, the maximum height is determined using the kinematic relationship $v_f^2 = v_o^2 + 2gy_{max}$. At the maximum height of this projectile, the speed is instantaneously 0. Substitute this value into the equation and solve for the maximum height:

$$-v_o^2 = 2(-g)y_{max}$$

$$v_o^2 = 2gy_{max}$$

$$\Rightarrow y_{max} = \frac{v_o^2}{2g} = 2x\left(\frac{v_o^2}{4g}\right) = 2h_o$$

The other answer choices are based on common mathematical errors.

2. **(B)**

The solution to this question involves setting the two forces equal to each other. This occurs because the acceleration is equal to 0 when the object reaches terminal velocity.

$$\Sigma F = 0 = mg - bmv$$

$$\Rightarrow v_{terminal} = \frac{mg}{bm} = \frac{g}{b}$$

There is also a way to analyze all the incorrect answer choices. None of those choices has the correct units for velocity. A very useful way to find correct answers in multiple-choice tests is to check the units of the answer choices. At a minimum, it usually eliminates two or three choices from consideration.

3. **(D)**

Using the acceleration function $a = 3t + 2$, determine the velocity and displacement functions:

$$v = \int a dt = \int (3t + 2)dt = \frac{3}{2}t^2 + 2t + C$$

Remember that the car started its motion from rest, so $C = 0$ (or initial speed $= 0$ m/s)

$$\therefore v(2\text{ s}) = \frac{3}{2}(2)^2 + 2(2) = 6 + 4 = 10\text{ m/s}$$

4. **(A)**

The answer to this question is based on the definition of average velocity:

$$v_{avg} = \frac{\Delta x}{\Delta t}$$

So the displacement function must be found from the original acceleration function. This is used to find the displacement over the 2-second period:

$$\Delta x = \int vdt = \int (\frac{3}{2}t^2 + 2t)dt = \frac{t^3}{2} + t^2$$

$$\Rightarrow \Delta x \text{ (from } t = 0 \text{ to } t = 2\text{ s}) = \int_0^2 vdt$$

$$\Delta x = \frac{(2)^3}{2} + (2)^2 = 8$$

$$\text{so, } v_{avg} = \frac{\Delta x}{\Delta t} = \frac{8}{2 - 0} = 4\text{ m/s}$$

The most common wrong answer choice would be an average velocity of 5 m/s. This choice comes from taking the instantaneous velocity at 2 seconds (the answer to question 3) and dividing it by the time interval. Make sure that you understand why this is not the "average velocity" over the 2-second period.

5. **(B)**

The quickest way to solve for the acceleration of the Atwood machine is to use the idea that there is "net gravitational force" acting on the system:

$$\sum F_{system} = (m_2 - m_1)g$$

This is essentially the difference between the gravitational forces of the two masses. Take this net force and divide by the total mass of the system:

$$a = \frac{\sum F_{system}}{m_{system}} = \frac{(m_2 - m_1)}{(m_1 + m_2)}g$$

6. **(C)**

The quickest way to get the speed of the block when it hits the ground is to use energy concepts. The speed of the block is the same as the speed of the entire system, because both masses move in unison as one system:

$$\Delta U_g = \Delta KE$$

$$(m_2 - m_1)gh = \frac{1}{2}(m_1 + m_2)v^2$$

$$\Rightarrow v = \sqrt{\frac{2(m_2 - m_1)}{(m_1 + m_2)}gh}$$

7. **(B)**

The free-body diagram for the mass is

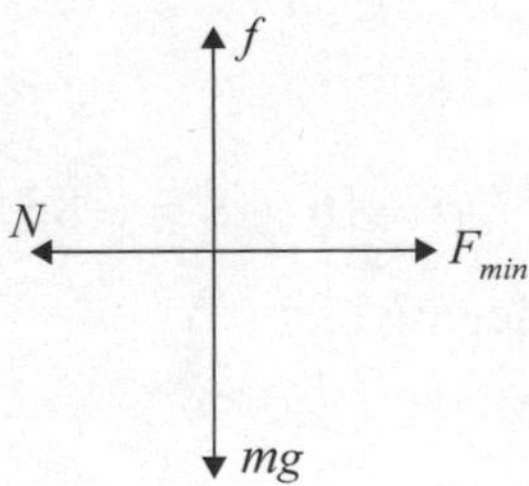

$$\sum F_x = 0 = F_a - N$$
$$\sum F_y = 0 = f_s - mg$$
$$F_a = N$$
$$f_s = mg$$
$$f_s \leq \mu_s N = mg$$

so, the minimum coefficient of static friction is when this frictional force is equal to *mg*.

$$\mu_s = \frac{mg}{N}$$

and, $N = F_{min}$

$$mg = \frac{mg}{F_{min}}$$

$$\Rightarrow \mu_s = \frac{mg}{F_a}$$

Taking a look at some of the incorrect answer choices, again look at the units for the coefficient of friction. The units of the coefficient are dimensionless. Thus, the only possible answer choices are those with a ratio of two of the same physical quantities. This leaves choices (D) and (E) impossible.

8. **(D)**

The work done by the spring should be negative, because any positive work causes the spring to stretch. Therefore, three of the answer choices are incorrect because of the sign. To determine which of the remaining two answer choices is correct, use the integral of the force function to find the potential energy function:

$$W_{spring} = \int F dx = \int \left(-2x + \frac{3}{2}\sqrt{x}\right)$$
$$= -\frac{2x^2}{2} + \frac{2}{3} \cdot \frac{3}{2} x^{3/2}$$

Now, evalluate

$$W = -(4)^2 + (4)^{3/2} = -16 + 8 = -8\,\text{J}$$

Notice that the answer is negative.

9. **(D)**

A quick solution to the totally inelastic collision fractional energy expression is

$$\frac{\Delta KE}{KE_o} = \frac{m_2}{m_1 + m_2}.$$

This is a typical homework question on momentum. It was referenced in Chapter 7 of this book. Solving for the change in kinetic energy results in

$$\Delta KE = \frac{200}{200 + 1} \cdot KE_o = 0.995KE_o.$$

A totally inelastic collision typically loses much of its initial energy.

10. **(B)**

This question is an application of the center of mass (CM) definition. There are many possible math mistakes that can be made in computing the CM. Realize that the short portion of the U-shaped wire ($L/4$) is also one-fourth of the mass (M) of one of the longer portions of the U shape (L). The CM of the short portion lies on the coordinate (0, $L/8$). The CM of the longer portion that is horizontal on the x-axis is at the coordinate ($L/2$, 0). The CM of the portion of U-shaped wire that is vertical is (L, $L/2$).

$$x_{cm} = \frac{\left(\frac{M}{4}\right) \cdot (0) + (M) \cdot \left(\frac{L}{2}\right) + (M) \cdot (L)}{M_{total}}$$

The lengths of each portion of the U shape are proportional to the masses of each portion of the U shape:

$$M_{total} = \frac{M}{4} + M + M = \frac{9M}{4}$$

$$x_{cm} = \frac{\left(\frac{M}{4}\right) \cdot (0) + (M) \cdot \left(\frac{L}{2}\right) + (M) \cdot (L)}{M_{total}} = \frac{\frac{3ML}{2}}{\frac{9M}{4}} = \frac{2L}{3}$$

$$y_{cm} = \frac{\left(\frac{M}{4}\right) \cdot \left(\frac{L}{8}\right) + (M) \cdot (0) + (M) \cdot \left(\frac{L}{2}\right)}{\frac{9M}{4}} = \frac{\frac{17ML}{32}}{\frac{9M}{4}} = \frac{17L}{72}$$

$$\therefore CM = \left(\frac{2L}{3}, \frac{17L}{72}\right)$$

11. **(A)**

The critical velocity for a car traveling around a circular track is

$$v_c = \sqrt{\mu_s rg} = \sqrt{(0.4)(25)(10 \text{ m/s}^2)} = 10 \text{ m/s}.$$

The expression comes from the fact that the static frictional force is the only force acting in the centripetal direction.

$$\sum F_c = ma_c = f_s \leq \mu_s N$$

$$\Rightarrow ma_c = \mu_s mg$$

$$\Rightarrow a_c = \mu_s g$$

$$\Rightarrow \frac{v^2}{r} = \mu_s g \Rightarrow v = \sqrt{\mu_s rg}$$

12. **(E)**

Both masses travel in circular motion with the same speed around a common center of mass: the center of mass of the two masses. The net force acting on any one of the masses is equal to the gravitational force of attraction between the two masses:

$$\sum F_c = Ma_c = F_g$$

$$\Rightarrow M\frac{v^2}{r} = \frac{GM^2}{(2R)^2}$$

and the radius of the circular motion is only R.

$$\therefore \frac{v^2}{R} = \frac{Gm}{4R^2} \Rightarrow v = \frac{1}{2}\sqrt{\frac{Gm}{R}}.$$

Answer choices (B) and (D) have incorrect units for velocity. The other two incorrect choices are based on flawed mathematics in computing the velocity.

13. **(A)**

The period of a pendulum depends on two quantities: gravitational acceleration and the length of the pendulum. Because the length of the pendulum is the same on both planets, only the gravity of each planet affects the period:

$$T = 2\pi\sqrt{\frac{l}{g}}$$

$$T^2 = \frac{4\pi^2 l}{g} \Rightarrow T_o^2 = \frac{4\pi^2 l}{g}$$

$$T_1^2 = \frac{4\pi^2 l}{g_1} \Rightarrow \frac{T_o^2}{T_1^2} = \frac{g_1}{g_o} \Rightarrow g_1 = g_o\left(\frac{T_o^2}{T_1^2}\right)$$

$$= g_{earth}\left(\frac{\left(\frac{3}{2}\right)^2}{(1)^2}\right) = \frac{9}{4}g_{earth} \approx 22.5\,\text{m/s}^2$$

A common incorrect answer choice is (B). This is the inverse of the answer. Just be very careful with your algebra, and take your time!

14. **(D)**

This is simply the definition of simple harmonic motion.

15. **(C)**

The hoop has a moment of inertia of MR^2. The hoop also has linear translational kinetic energy and rotational kinetic energy. The total potential energy of the hoop at the top of the incline turns into total kinetic energy at the bottom of the incline.

$$\Delta U = \Delta KE$$

$$mgh = KE_{rotation} + KE_{translational}$$

$$mgh = \frac{1}{2}I\omega^2 + \frac{1}{2}mv^2$$

$$\omega = \frac{v}{R}, \text{and, } I = mR^2$$

$$mgh = \frac{1}{2}(mR^2)\left(\frac{v}{R}\right)^2 + \frac{1}{2}mv^2 = \frac{1}{2}mv^2 + \frac{1}{2}mv^2 = mv^2$$

This algebra shows that the kinetic energy of rotation and the kinetic energy of translation are equivalent, and each is equal to one-half of the total energy.

16. **(E)**

An efficient way to solve this question is to use the conservation of total mechanical energy. The potential energy at the beginning of the launch (*mgh*) is equal to the potential energy and the kinetic energy at the top of the projectile's trajectory. The speed of the projectile at the top of the trajectory is equivalent to the initial *x*-component of the velocity:

$$v_x = v_{ox} = v_o \cos 60 = v_o \cdot \frac{1}{2}$$

also, $v_o = \sqrt{2gh_o}$

(from conservation of energy)

So, $\text{TME}_{top\,of\,incline} = TME_{top\,of\,trajectory}$

$$mgh_o = mgy_{max} + \frac{1}{2}m\left(\frac{\sqrt{2gh_o}}{2}\right)^2 = mgy_{max} + \frac{mgh_o}{4}$$

$$\Rightarrow mgy_{max} = \frac{3}{4}mgh_o \Rightarrow y_{max} = \frac{3}{4}h_o$$

17. **(D)**

The satellite orbiting the planet has a velocity of

$$v = \sqrt{\frac{Gm_e}{3R}}.$$

Because it is located at a distance of $3R$ from the Earth, the satellite has a potential energy of

$$U_g = -\frac{Gm_s m_e}{3R}$$

This gives a total energy of

$$TE = U_g + KE = \frac{-Gm_s m_e}{3R} + \frac{1}{2}m_s\left(\sqrt{\frac{Gm_e}{3R}}\right)^2$$

$$TE = \frac{-Gm_s m_e}{6R}$$

18. **(E)**

All three types of motion have changing acceleration vectors.

19. **(C)**

This is a tricky question. The cutting of the spring gives each half of the spring a spring constant equal to $2k$. An easy way to think of this is that a full spring of spring constant k is composed of two half springs in series. Each half spring would have a spring constant of $2k$. Springs in series add reciprocally:

$$\frac{1}{k} = \frac{1}{2k} + \frac{1}{2k} = \frac{2}{2k} = \frac{1}{k}$$

Each half spring with a spring constant of $2k$ is in a parallel combination. In parallel, the spring constants are additive. This gives a net spring constant of $4k$. Now incorporate this into the period relationship:

$$T_o = 2\pi\sqrt{\frac{m}{k}},$$

$$\text{new period}\ldots T' = 2\pi\sqrt{\frac{m}{4k}} = \frac{T_o}{2}$$

20. **(B)**

First calculate the final angular velocity of the CD in rad/s:

$$1800 \text{ rpm} \cdot \frac{\text{min}}{60 \text{ s}} \cdot \frac{2\pi \text{ rad}}{1 \text{ rev}} = 60\,\pi \frac{\text{rad}}{\text{s}}$$

$$\omega_f = \omega_o + \alpha t$$

$$60\pi = 0 + (5\pi)t$$

$$t = 12 \text{ s}$$

$$\theta = \frac{1}{2}\alpha t^2 = \frac{1}{2}(5\pi)(12)^2 = 360\,\pi \text{rad}$$

21. **(B)**

The forces acting on the ball at the bottom of the circles are the tension force of $3mg$ acting centripetally (vertically upward) and the weight (mg), as shown in the following diagram:

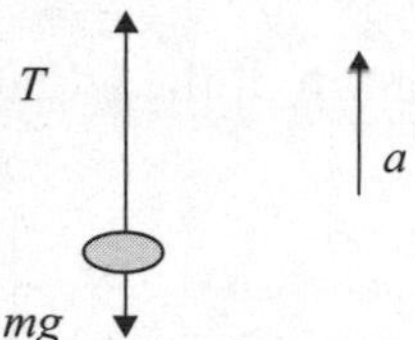

$$\sum F_c = ma_c = T - mg = (3 \text{ mg}) - mg = 2 \text{ mg}$$

$$m\frac{v^2}{R} = 2 \text{ mg} \Rightarrow v = \sqrt{2gR} = \sqrt{2(10)(0.8)} = \sqrt{16} = 4 \text{ m/s}$$

22. **(D)**

Here is the free-body diagram of block 2:

$$\sum F = ma = F_a - 3f \Rightarrow a = \frac{F_a - 3f}{m}$$

23. **(A)**

The work done by friction is the same as the entire loss of initial energy. The work done by friction is negative because it took energy from the system. Therefore, the answer is $W_f = -mgh_o$.

24. **(C)**

The work done by friction is also equal to force times distance:

$$W_f = -(\mu mg)(d) = -mgh_o$$
$$\Rightarrow \mu = \frac{h_o}{d}$$

All the answer choices have the correct units of the coefficient of friction. So it is difficult to eliminate any wrong answer choices by inspection.

25. **(C)**

The sum of the torques must add to 0 about any pivot point. Choosing the pivot point of the front tires results in the following:

$$\sum \Gamma_{fronttire} = mg\left(\frac{2}{3}d\right) - N_{backtire}d = 0$$
$$\Rightarrow N = \frac{2}{3}mg$$

Following is a free-body diagram of the situation:

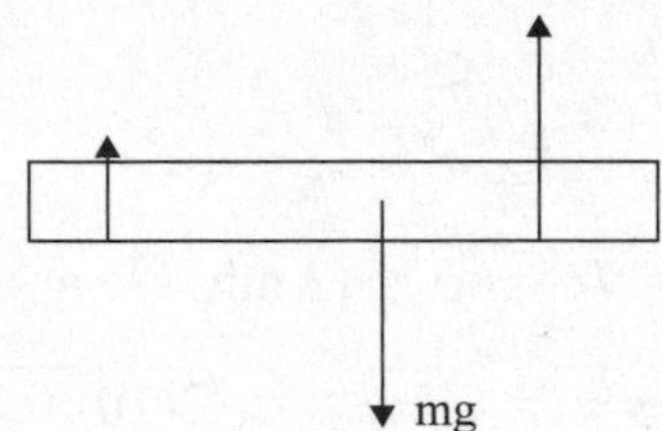

26. **(E)**

The solution involves applying the conservation of angular momentum. No outside torques act on the merry-go-round. The two masses did not contribute to the initial momentum because they had no velocity or momentum to begin with.

$$L_o = L_f$$
$$I_{disk}\omega_o = I_{disk/men}\omega'$$
$$\frac{1}{2}MR^2\omega_o = (I_o + I_{2m})\omega' = \left(I_o + \left[2m_{men}R^2\right]\right)\omega'$$
$$\frac{1}{2}MR^2\omega_o = \left(\frac{1}{2}MR^2 + 2\left(\frac{M}{5}\right)R^2\right)\omega'$$
$$\frac{1}{2}MR^2\omega = \frac{9}{10}MR^2\omega'$$
$$\omega' = \frac{5}{9}\omega_o$$

Choice (C) is a common wrong answer choice. It results when the fractions are added incorrectly in simplifying the moment of inertia term of the new system.

27. **(D)**

$$E_o = \frac{1}{2}I_o\omega_o^2 = \frac{1}{2}\left(\frac{1}{2}MR^2\right)\omega_o^2 = \frac{1}{4}MR^2\omega_o^2$$

$$E' = \frac{1}{2}I'\omega'^2 = \frac{1}{2}\left(\frac{9}{10}MR^2\right)\left(\frac{5}{9}\omega_o\right)^2 = \frac{5}{36}MR^2\omega_o^2$$

$$\therefore \Delta E = E' - E_o = \frac{5}{36}MR^2\omega_o^2 - \frac{1}{4}MR^2\omega_o^2$$

$$= -\frac{4}{36}MR^2\omega_o^2 = -\frac{1}{9}MR^2\omega_o^2$$

$$\frac{\Delta E}{E_o} = \frac{-\frac{1}{9}MR^2\omega_o^2}{\frac{1}{4}MR^2\omega_o^2} = \frac{4}{9} \rightarrow \Delta E = \frac{4}{9}E_o$$

28. **(D)**

To compute the period of this physical pendulum, the moment of inertia needs to be calculated for the pivot point:

$$I' = I_o + Md^2 = \frac{1}{12}ML^2 + M\left(\frac{L}{4}\right)^2 = \frac{7}{48}ML^2$$

$$T = 2\pi\sqrt{\frac{I}{mgd'}}$$

where I is the moment of inertia calculated above and d is the distance from CM to the pivot (L/4).

$$T = 2\pi\sqrt{\frac{\frac{7}{48}ML^2}{Mg\left(\frac{L}{4}\right)}} = 2\pi\sqrt{\frac{7L}{12g}}$$

A common error is failing to compute the new moment of inertia and using the moment of inertia through the CM of the rod, leading to the wrong answer choice of (B). Be careful!

29. **(D)**

The normal force is equivalent to $N = mg\cos 37° \approx (30)(0.8) \approx 24\,\text{N}$.

30. **(E)**

The slip angle occurs when

$$\tan\theta_{slip} = \mu_s$$

$$\mu_{slip} = \tan 37° = \frac{3}{4} = 0.75$$

31. **(C)**

Compute the velocity function by integrating

$$v = \int a dt = \int (2t + 5)dt = t^2 + 5t + C, C = 0$$

Integrate again to get the displacement function:

$$\Delta x = \int (t^2 + 5\,t)dt = \left(\frac{t^3}{3} + \frac{5}{2}t^2\right]_o^2 = \frac{2^3}{3} + \frac{5}{2}2^2 = \frac{8}{3} + 10 = \frac{38}{3}$$

32. **(B)**

The range equation for a projectile launch states

$$R = \frac{v_o^2 \sin(2\,\theta)}{g}$$

and $\sin(2 \cdot 30) = \sin(2 \cdot 60)$. Thus, the ranges are equal.

33. **(E)**

This is a tricky question. The pendulum at the point of maximum amplitude is instantaneously at rest. Thus, for that instant, the centripetal acceleration of the system is 0. This means that the system is momentarily in equilibrium at that one instant, as illustrated in the following free-body diagram:

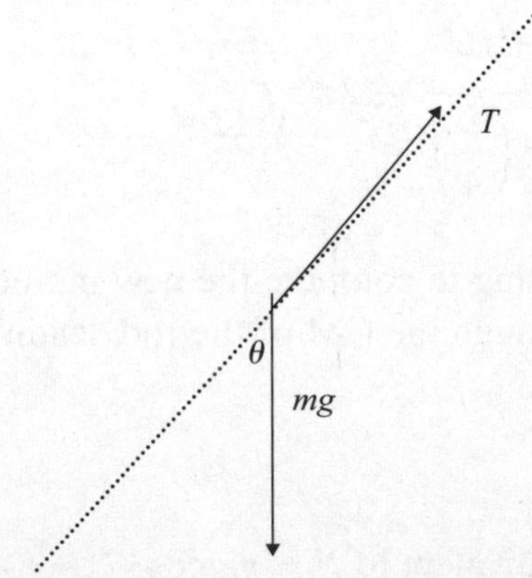

Along the frame of reference of the dashed line (centripetal direction), the net force is momentarily 0:

$$\sum F_c = 0 = T - mg\cos\theta_o \Rightarrow T = mg\cos\theta_o$$

Choice (D) is incorrect because it assumes that the pendulum is in equilibrium in the vertical and horizontal directions. This is a common approach in standard equilibrium problems but does not work in this problem. The pendulum is only in equilibrium along the centripetal direction. It is in an accelerated state in the tangential direction. The only frame of reference that can be used is the one used in the solution.

34. **(B)**

The pendulum's acceleration at the bottom-most point of its trajectory is completely in the centripetal direction.

35. **(B)**

The point of equilibrium will occur when the conservative force function is 0:

$$F = -\frac{dU}{dx} = -\frac{d}{dx}\left(\frac{2}{3}x^2 + 3x + 2\right) = -\left(\frac{4}{3}x + 3\right)$$

$$F = 0 = \frac{-4}{3}x - 3 \Rightarrow x = -\frac{9}{4}$$

Section II

1. First, draw a free-body diagram of each mass:

   (a) Forces on $4M$ (bottom block):

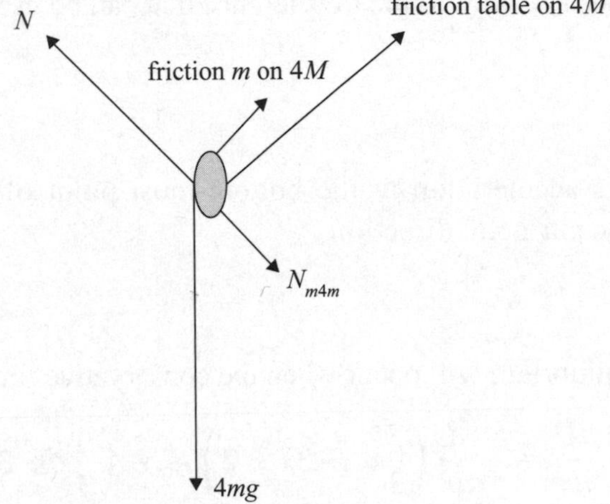

This diagram is needed to solve other parts of the problem:

Forces on M:

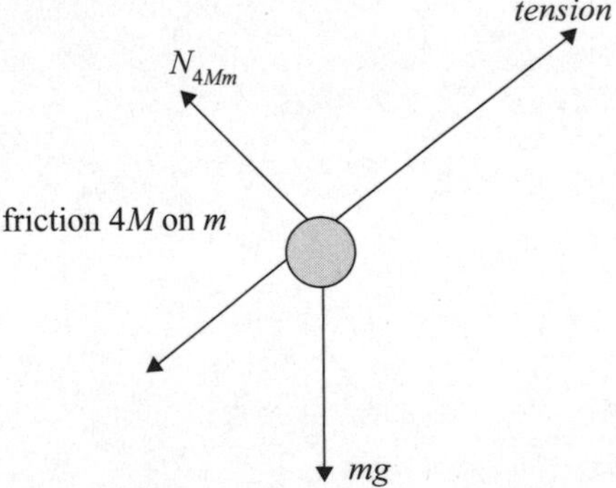

   (b) Set up the statements of Newton's second law for each mass:

For $4M$:

$$\sum F_x = 4Ma_{4m} = 4Mg \sin 37 - f_{m/4m} - f_{incline/4m}$$

$$\sum F_y = 0 = N_{incline/4M} - 4Mg \cos 37 - N_{M/4M}$$

For M:

$$\sum F_{Mx} = 0 = T - Mg\sin 37 - f_{4M/M}$$
$$\sum F_{My} = 0 = N_{4M/M} - Mg\cos 37$$

and

$$\|N_{4M/M}\| = \|N_{M/4M}\|$$
$$\|f_{M/4M}\| = \|f_{4M/M}\| = \mu N_{4M/M}$$
$$N_{4M/M} = Mg\cos 37$$
$$\therefore \|f_{M/4M}\| = \|f_{4M/M}\| = \mu(Mg\cos 37)$$
$$f_{incline/4M} = \mu N_{incline/4m} = \mu(5\text{Mg}\cos 37)$$

Solving for a:

$$\sum F_x = 4\,Ma_{4m} = 4\,Mg\sin 37 - f_{m/4m} - f_{incline/4m}$$
$$\Rightarrow 4\,Ma = 4\,Mg(\sin 37) - \mu(Mg\cos 37) - \mu(5Mg\cos 37)$$
$$\Rightarrow 4\,Ma = 4\,Mg(0.6) - \mu(6\,Mg\cdot(0.8))$$
$$\mu = 0.4$$
$$\Rightarrow 4\,Ma = 2.4\,Mg - 1.92\,Mg = 0.48\,Mg$$
$$\Rightarrow a = 0.12\,g \approx 1.2\text{ m/s}^2$$

(c) Set up net force on M, taken from above:

$$\sum F_{Mx} = 0 = T - Mg\sin 37 - f_{4M/M}$$
$$\sum F_{My} = 0 = N_{4M/M} - Mg\cos 37$$
$$T = Mg\sin 37 + m(Mg\cos 37)$$
$$T = (0.6\text{Mg}) + (0.4)(Mg\cdot 0.8) = 0.92Mg$$
$$T = 0.92\text{Mg}$$

2. (a) The moment of inertia of this rod and mass combination is the sum of the rod's inertia about the pivot plus the inertia of the mass about the pivot. Consider the slotted mass to be a point mass:

$$I_{rod-about-end} = I_{cm} + Md^2 = \frac{1}{12}(3\text{ M})L^2 + (3\text{ M})\left(\frac{L}{2}\right)^2$$
$$I_{rod-about-end} = ML^2$$
$$I_{pointmass} = MR^2 = ML^2$$
$$I_{total} = I_{rod-about-end} + I_{pointmass} = 2\,ML^2$$

(b) To determine the torque, draw a rigid-body diagram of the rod in its initial state:

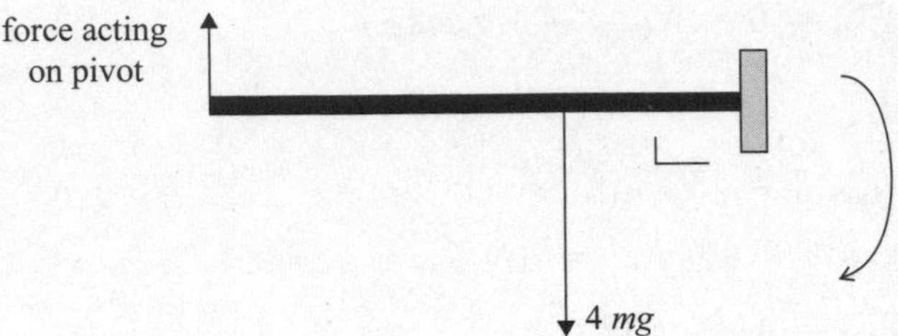

The force acting on the pivot contributes no torque to the system about that point. Only the weight vector contributes to the torque about the pivot. The weight is acting from the CM, and the CM must be computed first.

$$x_{cm} = \frac{\sum m_i x_i}{M_{total}} = \frac{\left(3\,M \cdot \frac{L}{2}\right) + (M \cdot L)}{4\,M} = \frac{5}{8}\,\mathrm{L}$$

So the net torque on the system is as follows:

$$\sum \Gamma_{pivot} = I_{total}\alpha = (4\ \mathrm{mg})\left(\frac{5}{8}L\right)$$

$$\Rightarrow \alpha = \frac{20\ \mathrm{mgL}}{8 I_{total}} = \frac{20\ \mathrm{mgL}}{8 \cdot (2\ \mathrm{mL}^2)} = \frac{5g}{4L}$$

(c) The most efficient way to find the speed of the slotted mass passing through the photogate is to use conservation of energy. The change in the gravitational potential energy is equal to the gain in the rotational kinetic energy of the system. Once the angular velocity of the system is known, compute the linear velocity of the rotating system at the end of the rod. The rod's CM will fall from the horizontal position to the vertical position. This is a total drop of $5/8L$:

$$\Delta U_g = (4\ \mathrm{m})g\Delta y_{cm} = 4\ \mathrm{mg}\left(\frac{5}{8}L\right)$$

$$\Delta KE_{rot} = \frac{1}{2}I\omega^2 = \frac{1}{2}\left(2\ \mathrm{mL}^2\right)\omega^2 = mL^2\omega^2$$

Solving for angular velocity results in the following:

$$\Delta U_g = \Delta KE_{rot}$$

$$\frac{20\ \mathrm{mgL}}{8} = mL^2\omega^2$$

$$\Rightarrow \omega = \sqrt{\frac{20g}{8L}} = \sqrt{\frac{5g}{2L}}$$

Since the photogate is set to measure the speed at the end of the rod, the linear speed of the rod at that point on the rod is

$$v = \omega r = \sqrt{\frac{5\ \mathrm{g}}{2\ \mathrm{L}}} \cdot L = \sqrt{\frac{5\ \mathrm{gL}}{2}}$$

3. (a) The center of mass of the system as measured from mass M:

$$x_{cm} = \frac{\sum m_i x_i}{M_t} = \frac{(M)\cdot(0) + (3\ \mathrm{M})\cdot d}{4\ \mathrm{M}} = \frac{3}{4}d$$

(b) The period of orbit is the same for both masses, so it does not matter which one you focus on. However, you need to know the velocity of each star for part (c) anyway. Therefore, get both stars' orbital velocities. Both stars orbit around the common CM and are locked into this orbit with a common period. The star of mass M is moving faster because of the longer orbital distance it covers. The radius of orbit for mass M is $\frac{3}{4}d$. The distance of separation between the two masses to compute the gravitational force is d:

$$\sum F_M = M\frac{v^2}{\left(\frac{3}{4}d\right)} = \frac{G(M)(3\mathrm{M})}{d^2}$$

$$\Rightarrow v^2 = \frac{G(9\mathrm{M})}{4d} \Rightarrow v = \sqrt{\frac{9GM}{4d}}$$

Now to get the period.... $v = \frac{2\pi r}{\mathrm{T}} \Rightarrow T = \frac{2\pi r}{v} = \frac{2\pi\left(\frac{3}{4}d\right)}{\sqrt{\frac{9GM}{4d}}}$

Squaring both sides: $\Rightarrow T^2 = \frac{4\pi^2\frac{9}{16}d^2}{\frac{9GM}{4d}} = \frac{\pi^2 d^3}{GM}$

$$T = \pi\sqrt{\frac{d^3}{GM}}$$

c. The total energy of the system is equal to the kinetic energy of both stars plus the gravitational potential energy of the two-star system. The orbital speed of 3 M is needed to compute its kinetic energy:

$$\sum F_{3\text{ M}} = 3\text{M}\frac{v^2}{\left(\frac{d}{4}\right)} = \frac{G(\text{M})(3\text{ M})}{d^2}$$

$$\Rightarrow v^2 = \frac{GM}{4d} \Rightarrow v = \sqrt{\frac{GM}{4d}}$$

$$KE_{\text{M}} = \frac{1}{2}Mv_m^2 = \frac{1}{2}M\left(\frac{9GM}{4d}\right) = \frac{9GM^2}{8d}$$

$$KE_{3\text{M}} = \frac{1}{2}Mv_{3\text{M}}^2 = \frac{1}{2}(3M)\left(\frac{GM}{4d}\right) = \frac{3GM^2}{8d}$$

$$KE_{total} = \frac{9GM^2}{8d} + \frac{3GM^2}{8d} = \frac{12GM^2}{8d} = \frac{3GM^2}{2d}$$

$$U_{M3\text{M}} = \frac{-G(3\text{M})(M)}{d} = -\frac{3\ GM^2}{d}$$

$$TotalEnergy = KE_{total} + U_{3mm} = \frac{3GM^2}{2d} + -\frac{3GM^2}{d} = \frac{-3GM^2}{2d}$$

PRACTICE EXAM 4

AP Physics C
Electricity and Magnetism

Section I

Time: 45 Minutes
35 Questions

DIRECTIONS: Each of the questions or incomplete statements below is followed by five answer choices. Select the one that is best in each case and fill in the oval on the corresponding answer sheet.

NOTE: Units associated with numerical quantities are abbreviated, using the abbreviations listed in the Table of Information and Equations found at the back of this book. To simplify calculations, you may use $g = 10 \text{ m/s}^2$ for all problems.

1. Two conductive electrically isolated spheres are sitting a distance d apart, as shown in the following diagram. One sphere has a $+4Q$ charge on its surface and the other sphere has a $-2Q$ charge on its surface. The force that the two spheres experience is $\vec{F_1}$.

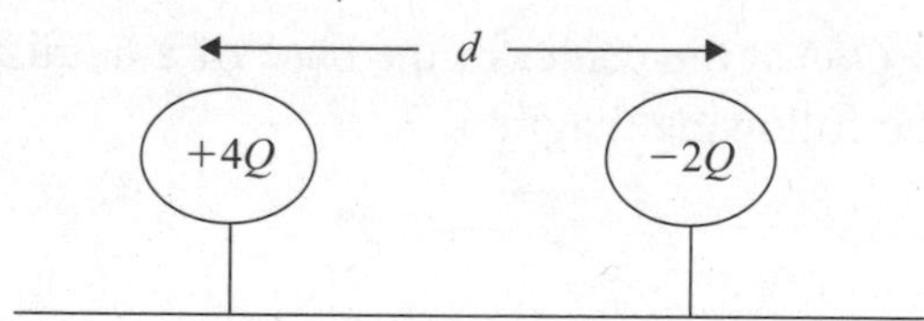

The two spheres are brought together so that they touch each other. Then the spheres are again separated by the same distance d. The new force that the two spheres experience is $\vec{F_2}$. What is the relationship between $\vec{F_1}$ and $\vec{F_2}$?

(A) $\vec{F_1} = 2\vec{F_2}$

(B) $\vec{F_1} = 4\vec{F_2}$

(C) $\vec{F_1} = -4\vec{F_2}$

(D) $\vec{F_1} = 8\vec{F_2}$

(E) $\vec{F_1} = -8\vec{F_2}$

Use the following situation to answer questions 2 and 3. Three charges, Q_1, Q_2, and Q_3, are fixed and stationary on a line marked with three points, A, B, and C, as shown in the diagram. Point A is the midpoint charge between Q_1 and Q_2. Point B is a distance *d* from Q_2. Point C is a distance *d* from Q_3. The magnitudes of the three charges are $Q_1 = +Q$, $Q_2 = +Q$, and $Q_3 = +5Q$.

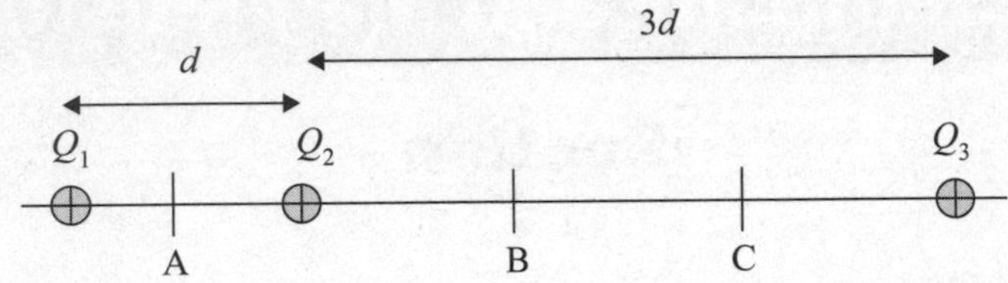

2. At which of the three points is the net electric field 0?
   (A) A only
   (B) B only
   (C) C only
   (D) A and B only
   (E) None of the points

3. At which of the points is the electric potential 0?
   (A) A only
   (B) B only
   (C) C only
   (D) A and B only
   (E) None of the points

4. A charge of $+Q$ is at the center of the base of a hemisphere of radius R, as shown in the following diagram.

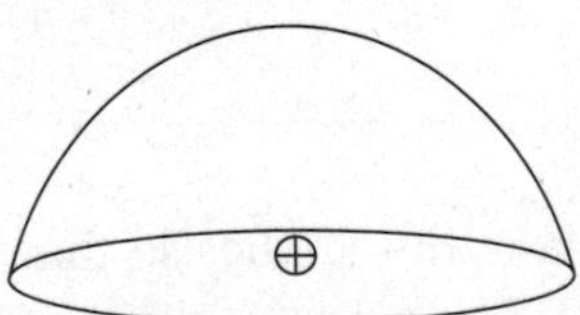

What is the net electric flux through the hemisphere?

(A) $\frac{Q}{\varepsilon_o}$

(B) $\frac{Q}{2\varepsilon_o}$

(C) $\frac{\sigma}{2\pi R^2 \varepsilon_o}$

(D) $\frac{\sigma}{4\pi R^2 \varepsilon_o}$

(E) 0

5. A microscopic definition for a current is $I = neAv_{drift}$. A typical value for the drift velocity of a typical charge carrier in a conductor is

(A) 10^{-4} m/s

(B) 10^{1} m/s

(C) 10^{4} m/s

(D) 10^{7} m/s

(E) 10^{8} m/s

6. A parallel-plate capacitor has a plate area of A and a plate separation of a. The capacitance is C_o. A metal slab of thickness b ($b < a$) is placed between the capacitor plates, as shown in the following diagram:

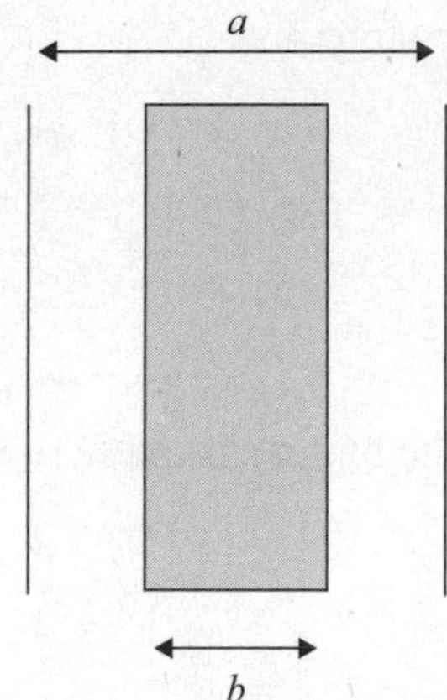

The ratio of the new capacitance C' to the original capacitance C_o is

(A) $\frac{C'}{C_o} = \frac{1}{1}$

(B) $\frac{C'}{C_o} = \frac{a-b}{a}$

(C) $\frac{C'}{C_o} = \frac{a}{a-b}$

(D) $\frac{C'}{C_o} = \frac{a}{b}$

(E) $\frac{C'}{C_o} = \frac{b}{a}$

Use the following situation to answer questions 7 and 8. Three 3-μF capacitors are arranged in series and attached to a 10-volt battery, as shown in the diagram. The battery is connected to the capacitors for a long time.

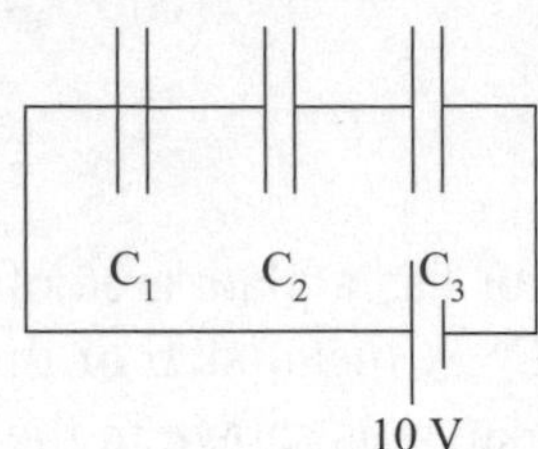

7. What is the amount of charge on C_1?

(A) 3 μC
(B) 9 μC
(C) 10 μC
(D) 4.5 μC
(E) 1.5 μC

8. How much charge did the battery provide to the three-capacitor system?

(A) 30 μC
(B) 9 μC
(C) 10 μC
(D) 27 μC
(E) 4.5 μC

9. As shown in the following diagram, two point charges of magnitude $+Q$ lie on a line that is bisected by the x-axis. Point P is on the x-axis.

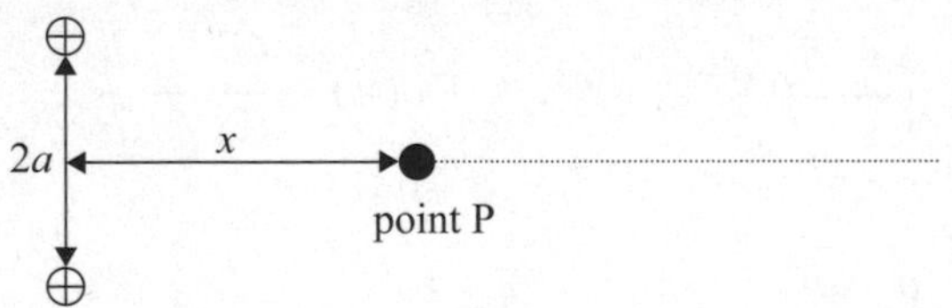

What is the correct expression for the electric field at point P?

(A) $\dfrac{Qx}{2\pi\varepsilon_o(x^2 + a^2)^{\frac{3}{2}}}$

(B) $\dfrac{Q}{2\pi\varepsilon_o(x^2 + a^2)}$

(C) $\dfrac{Qx}{4\pi\varepsilon_o(x^2 + a^2)^{\frac{3}{2}}}$

(D) $\dfrac{Q}{4\pi\varepsilon_o(x^2 + a^2)}$

(E) $\dfrac{Q}{2\pi\varepsilon_o(x^2 + a^2)^{\frac{3}{2}}}$

10. The following diagram shows the electric field in the region surrounding two concentric spheres. The inner sphere has a charge of $+Q$ on the shell.

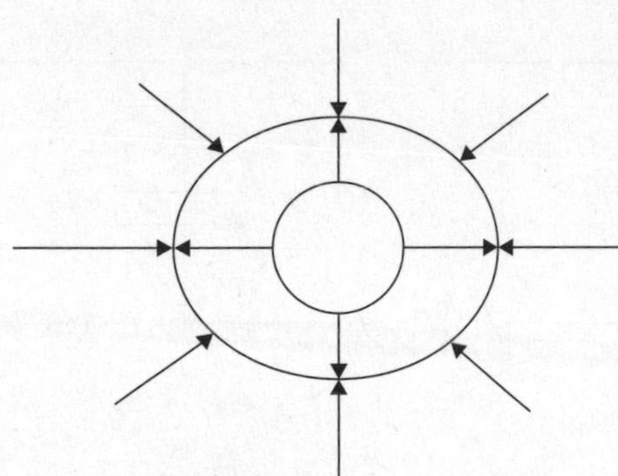

What is the magnitude and sign of the charge on the outer shell?

(A) $-2Q$

(B) $-3Q$

(C) $-4Q$

(D) $+2Q$

(E) $+3Q$

11. A conductive semicircle is placed as shown in the diagram. Charge is uniformly placed on the semicircle with a linear charge density of λ. The point C is at the center of the semicircle. The radius of the semicircle is R.

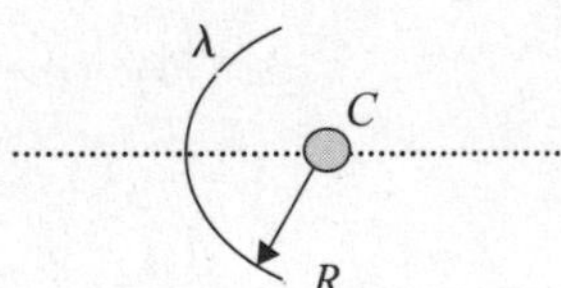

Determine the electric potential at point C.

(A) $\dfrac{\lambda}{2\pi R\varepsilon_o}$

(B) $\dfrac{\lambda}{4\pi R\varepsilon_o}$

(C) $\dfrac{\lambda}{4\varepsilon_o}$

(D) $\dfrac{\lambda}{R\varepsilon_o}$

(E) $\dfrac{\lambda}{\varepsilon_o}$

Use the following diagram to answer questions 12 through 14.

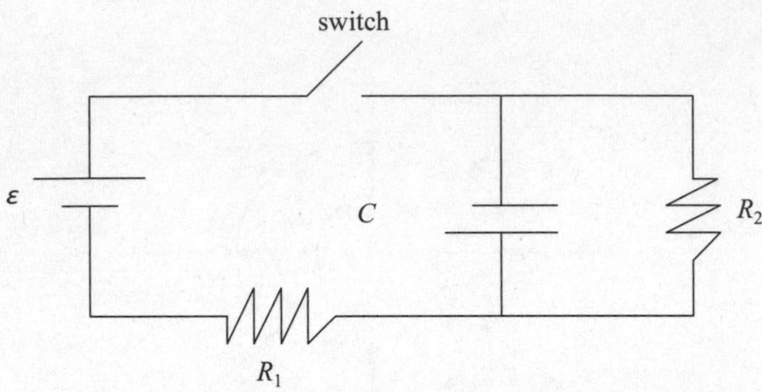

12. Determine the current in the battery at the instant the switch is closed.

(A) $\frac{\varepsilon}{R_2}$

(B) $\frac{\varepsilon}{R_1}$

(C) $\frac{\varepsilon}{R_1 + R_2}$

(D) $\varepsilon \cdot \frac{R_1 + R_2}{R_1 R_2}$

(E) 0

13. Determine the current in the battery a long time after the switch is closed.

(A) $\frac{\varepsilon}{R_2}$

(B) $\frac{\varepsilon}{R_1}$

(C) $\frac{\varepsilon}{R_1 + R_2}$

(D) $\varepsilon \cdot \frac{R_1 + R_2}{R_1 R_2}$

(E) 0

14. Determine the charge on the capacitor a long time after the switch is closed.

(A) εC

(B) $\varepsilon C \frac{R_1}{R_1 + R_2}$

(C) $\varepsilon C \frac{R_2}{R_1 + R_2}$

(D) $\varepsilon C \frac{R_1}{R_2}$

(E) $\varepsilon C \frac{R_1 + R_2}{R_1}$

15. An electron is shot into the B field horizontally, as shown in the following diagram. Three possible paths for the electron's trajectory are paths A, B, and C.

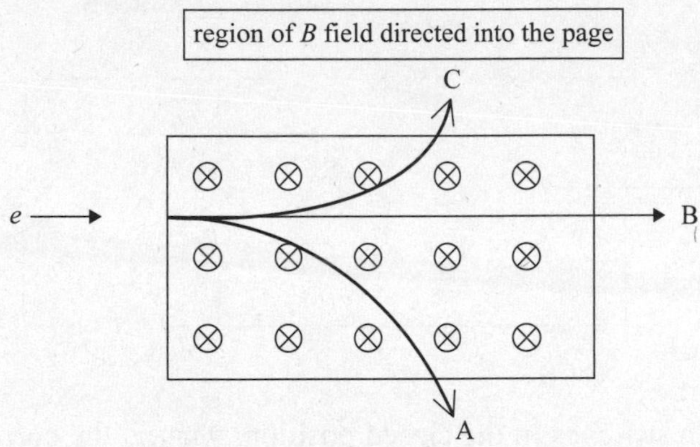

Which is the most likely path of the electron?

(A) A

(B) B

(C) C

(D) All the paths are equally likely.

(E) None of the paths are correct.

16. A wire with positive conventional current is next to an electron moving parallel to the wire, as shown in the diagram.

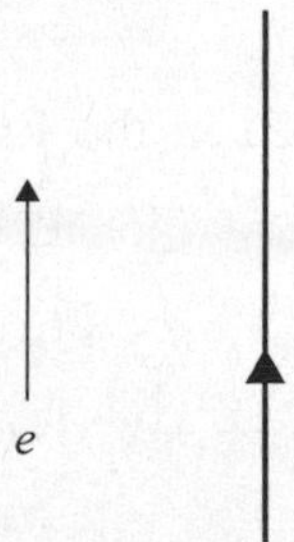

What is the direction of the force on the electron due to the wire's magnetic field?

(A) Left

(B) Right

(C) Up

(D) Down

(E) No force exists.

Use the following diagram to answer questions 17 and 18. The battery has no internal resistance.

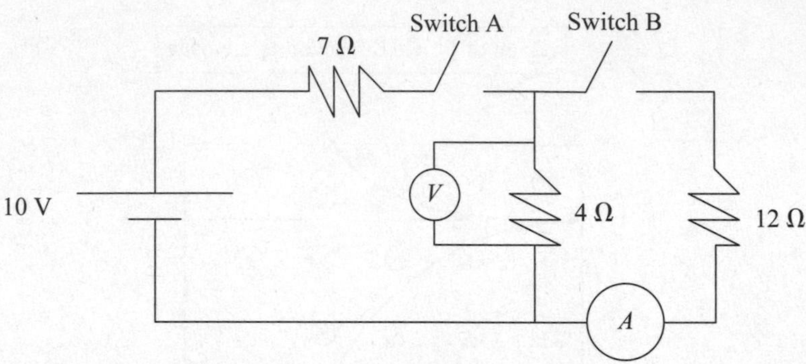

17. With both switches in the closed position, what is the current reading in the ammeter?

(A) 0.83 A
(B) 0.53A
(C) 0.25 A
(D) 1.0 A
(E) 0.43 A

18. If switch B is open and switch A is closed, what is the reading on the voltmeter?

(A) 10.0 volts
(B) 4.0 volts
(C) 0.57 volt
(D) 2.0 volts
(E) 3.63 volts

19. A capacitor is being charged in the RC circuit shown in the following diagram:

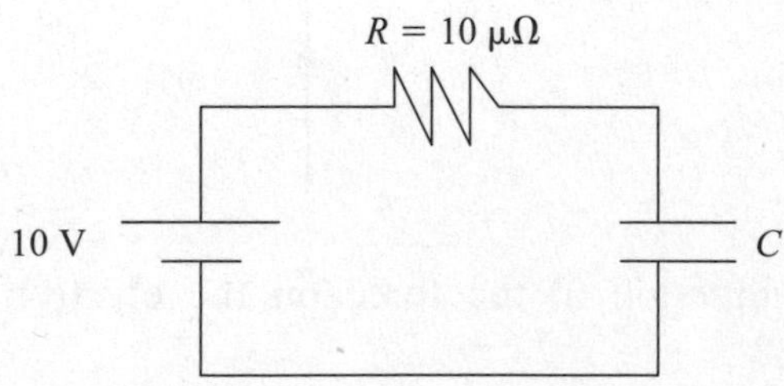

The following graph shows current versus time for the circuit. Note that the current at time $t = 0$ seconds is 1.0 microampere.

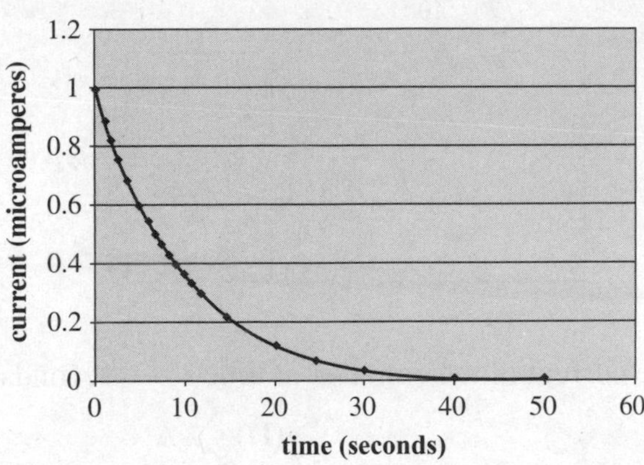

From the graph and the circuit diagram, determine the value of the capacitor.

(A) $C = 1\ \mu F$

(B) $C = 10\ \mu F$

(C) $C = 100\ \mu F$

(D) $C = 1\ nF$

(E) $C = 100\ nF$

20. The region shown in the following diagram comprises an electric field that is vertically downward and a magnetic field directed out of the page. An electron is shot into this region at a speed of 1.0×10^6 m/s. The electric field has a magnitude of 1×10^5 N/C. The electron moves through the region undeflected.

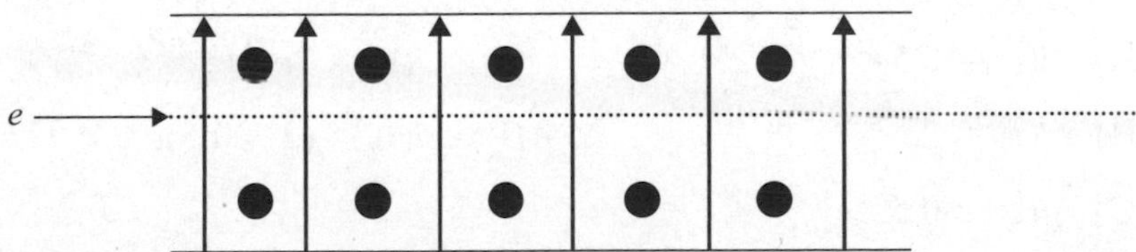

Determine the magnitude of the magnetic field that will allow the electron to move through the region undeflected.

(A) 0.001 tesla

(B) 0.01 tesla

(C) 0.1 tesla

(D) 1.0 tesla

(E) 10 tesla

Use the following diagram to answer questions 21 through 23. The switch begins in the open positions. At time $t = 0$, the switch is closed.

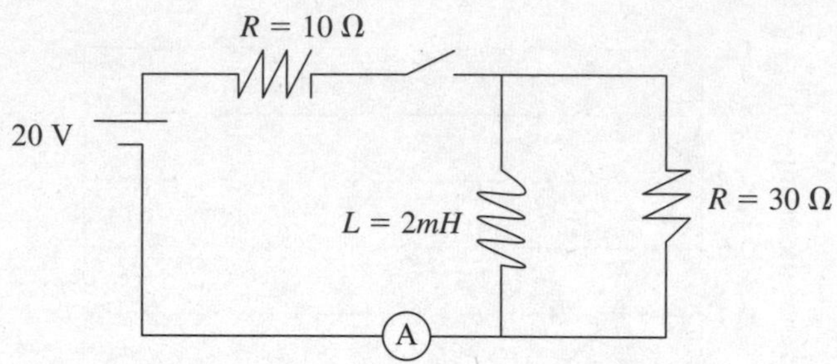

21. What is the current in the ammeter at time $t = 0$ seconds?

(A) 0 A
(B) 0.5 A
(C) 1 A
(D) 2 A
(E) 4 A

22. What is the current in the ammeter after the switch has been closed for a long time?

(A) 0 A
(B) 0.5 A
(C) 2 A
(D) 4 A
(E) 10 A

23. After the circuit has reached steady state, the switch is pulled open at time $t = t_1$. Which of the following expressions correctly expresses how the current in the inductor will behave after $t = t_1$?

(A) $i(t) = 0.5e^{-6.6 \times 10^{-5}t}$
(B) $i(t) = 2e^{-6.66 \times 10^{-5}t}$
(C) $i(t) = 0.5e^{-15 \times 10^{3}t}$
(D) $i(t) = 2e^{-15 \times 10^{3}t}$
(E) $i(t) = (2 - 0.5)e^{-15 \times 10^{3}t}$

24. A conductive loop of wire of resistance $R = 8$ ohms is placed in a time-varying magnetic field, as shown in the following diagram. The wire is initially directed out of the page.

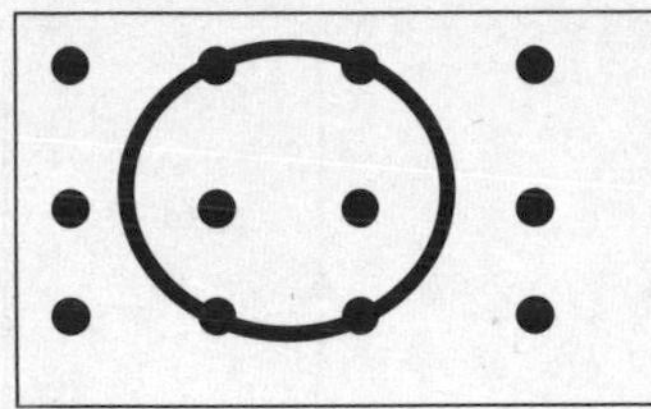

The magnetic field changes with the relationship $B = 2e^{-2t}$ tesla. The area of the loop is $A = 2\pi \text{m}^2$. Determine the magnitude and direction of the current in the loop at $t = 1.0$ second.

(A) $i = \dfrac{8\pi}{e^2}$, clockwise

(B) $i = \dfrac{8\pi}{e^2}$, counterclockwise

(C) $i = \dfrac{\pi}{e^2}$, clockwise

(D) $i = \dfrac{\pi}{e^2}$, counterclockwise

(E) $i = 8\pi$, clockwise

25. Two concentric conducting metal spheres have charges on their surfaces. The inner sphere of radius R has $+3Q$ charge on its surface, and the outer sphere of radius $2R$ has $-3Q$ charge on its surface.

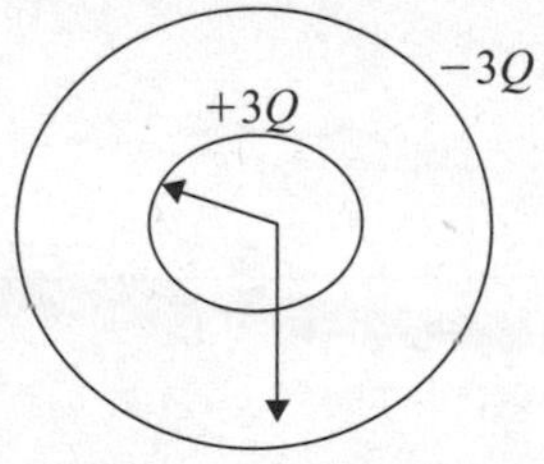

What is the difference in potential between the two spheres?

(A) $\Delta V = \dfrac{9Q}{8\pi\varepsilon_o R}$

(B) $\Delta V = \dfrac{3Q}{8\pi\varepsilon_o R}$

(C) $\Delta V = \dfrac{9Q}{4\pi\varepsilon_o R}$

(D) $\Delta V = \dfrac{3Q}{4\pi\varepsilon_o R}$

(E) $\Delta V = \dfrac{9Q}{16\pi\varepsilon_o R}$

26. Three wires carrying conventional current are arranged as shown in the following diagram. Point P is at the midpoint between wire 2 and wire 3. Wire 1 has a current of I, wire 2 has a current of $2I$, and wire 3 has a current of $2I$.

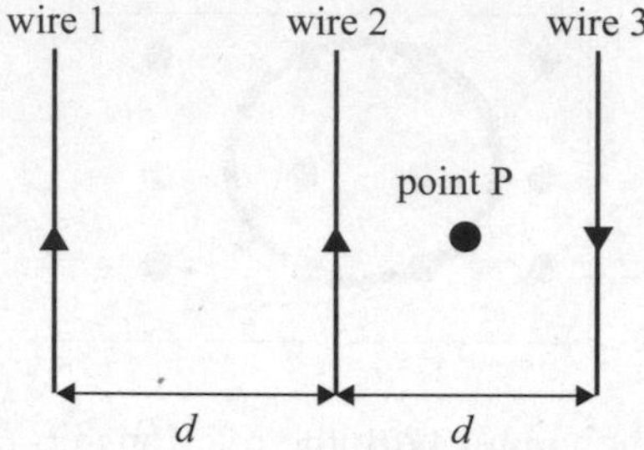

The magnitude of the magnetic field at point P is best expressed by which expression?

(A) $B = \frac{\mu_o I}{3\pi d}$

(B) $B = \frac{4\mu_o I}{3\pi d}$

(C) $B = \frac{13\mu_o I}{3\pi d}$

(D) $B = \frac{2\mu_o I}{3\pi d}$

(E) $B = \frac{2\mu_o I}{\pi d}$

27. A loop of wire with a radius R and a current I is centered on the x-y-z origin as shown in the following diagram.

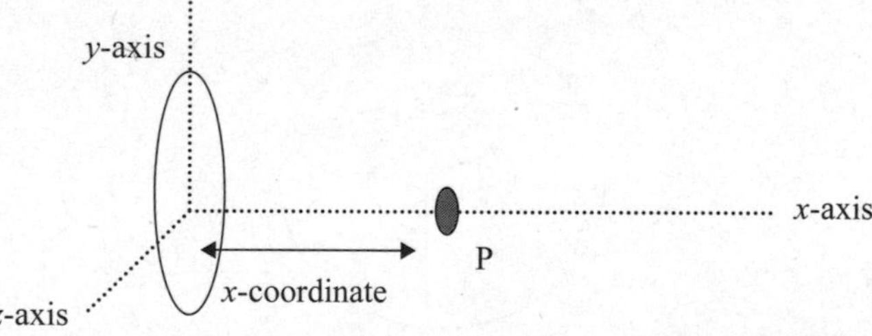

What is the magnitude of the magnetic field at point P?

(A) $B = \frac{\mu_o I}{2R}$

(B) $B = \frac{\mu_o I R^2}{2(x^2 + R^2)^{\frac{3}{2}}}$

(C) $B = \frac{\mu_o I R^2}{2\sqrt{(x^2 + R^2)}}$

(D) $B = \frac{\mu_o I R}{2(x^2 + R^2)}$

(E) $B = \frac{\mu_o I}{2(x^2 + R^2)^{\frac{3}{2}}}$

28. What type of shape would be required to use Ampere's law to determine the magnetic field due to a long straight wire carrying current?

(A) Rectangle
(B) Square
(C) Ellipse
(D) Circle
(E) Helix

Use the following situation to answer questions 29 and 30. The diagram represents a circulating charged particle in a magnetic field. An electron of mass *m* and charge *e* is moving in a complete circular path of radius *R* within a magnetic field of strength *B*.

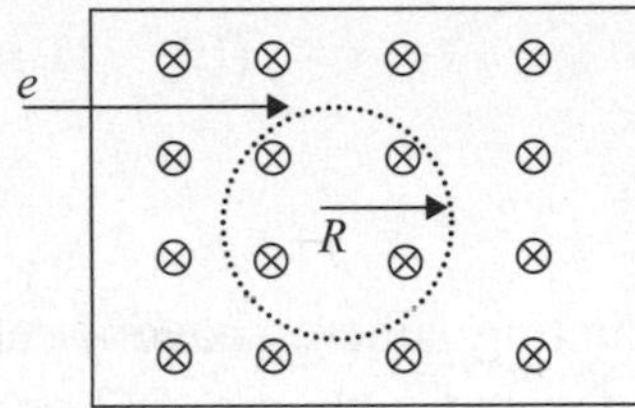

29. Which of the following is the correct expression for the period of the electron's circular motion?

(A) $T = \dfrac{m}{Be}$

(B) $T = \dfrac{Be}{m}$

(C) $T = \dfrac{BeR}{m}$

(D) $T = 2\pi\dfrac{BeR}{m}$

(E) $T = 2\pi\dfrac{m}{Be}$

30. The speed of the electron is increased, and the electron enters the field. Which of the following correctly describes the changes in the period of the orbit and the radius of the orbit?

(A) Period and radius both remained unchanged
(B) Period is unchanged, radius is increased
(C) Period is increased, radius is unchanged
(D) Period is unchanged, radius is decreased
(E) Period and radius both increase

31. Three capacitors are arranged as shown in the following diagram and attached to a 12-volt source:

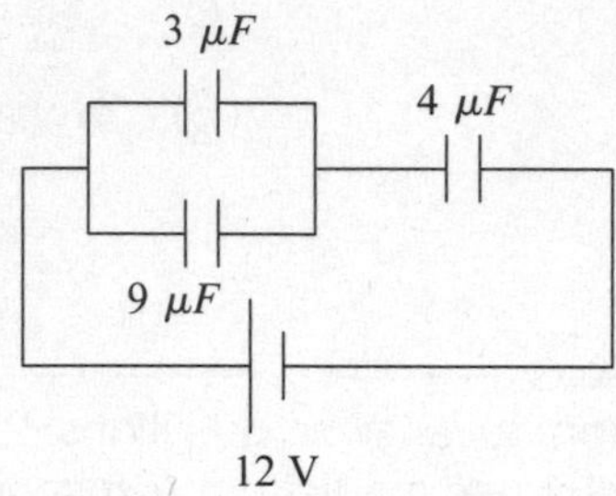

What is the final charge on the 3-μF capacitor?

(A) 27 μC

(B) 36 μC

(C) 9 μC

(D) 3 μC

(E) 21 μC

32. Two concentric conducting spheres have a capacitance of C. The inner sphere has a radius of a and a charge $+Q$ on the surface of the sphere. The outer sphere has a radius b and a charge of $-Q$ on its surface. Which is the correct expression for the capacitance of the two spheres?

(A) $C = \dfrac{4\pi\varepsilon_o ab}{b - a}$

(B) $C = \dfrac{4\pi\varepsilon_o a^2}{b}$

(C) $C = 4\pi\varepsilon_o a$

(D) $C = \dfrac{2\pi\varepsilon_o ab}{b - a}$

(E) $C = \dfrac{4\pi\varepsilon_o (b - a)}{ab}$

Use the following diagram to answer questions 33 and 34. Three point charges of $-Q$ are held stationary and placed in an equilateral triangle with sides of length d. Point P is at the midpoint of the base of the equilateral triangle.

P

33. Which of the following correctly identifies the magnitude and direction of the electric field at point P? (Note: Use $k = \frac{1}{4\pi\varepsilon_o}$.)

(A) $E = \frac{8kQ}{d^2}$, up

(B) $E = \frac{8kQ}{d^2}$, down

(C) $E = \frac{4kQ}{3d^2}$, up

(D) $E = \frac{4kQ}{3d^2}$, down

(E) $E = \frac{2kQ}{d^2}$, up

34. What is the electric potential at point P?

(A) $V = \frac{2kQ}{d}\left(\frac{2\sqrt{3}+1}{\sqrt{3}}\right)$

(B) $V = -\frac{2kQ}{d}\left(\frac{2\sqrt{3}+1}{\sqrt{3}}\right)$

(C) $V = \frac{-4kQ}{d}$

(D) $V = \frac{-2\sqrt{3}kQ}{d}$

(E) $V = -\frac{2kQ}{\sqrt{3}d}$

35. The product of Tesla $\cdot$ m^2 is equivalent to which of the following expressions?

(A) $\frac{N}{A \cdot m}$

(B) $\frac{\text{Weber}}{s}$

(C) Volt · second

(D) $\frac{\text{Volt}}{s}$

(E) $\frac{A \cdot m}{N}$

STOP

This is the end of Section I.

If time still remains, you may check your work only in this section.

Do not begin Section II until instructed to do so.

Section II

Time: 45 Minutes
3 Free-Response Questions

DIRECTIONS: Carefully read each question and be sure to answer *each part* of the question. Each question is worth 15 points, but the parts within a question may not have equal weight. Show all your work. Crossed-out work will not be graded. For this section of the exam, you may use your calculator and the equation tables for Physics C found at the back of this book.

1. A long cylindrical insulator is completely filled with negative charge and has a uniform charge density, ρ. The wire has a length of L and a radius of R.

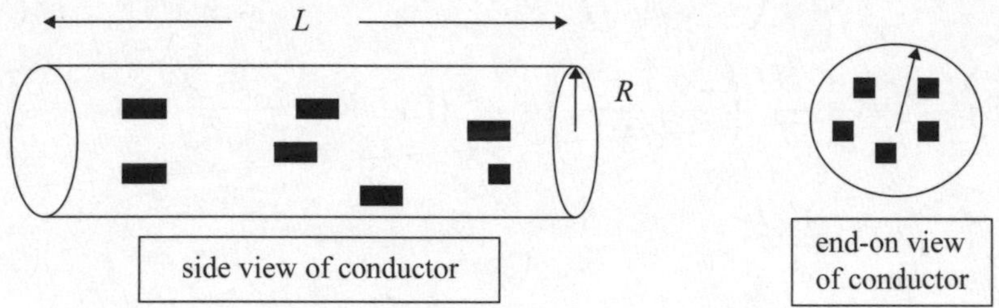

(a) Draw an electric field vector at point P and at point Q in the diagram.

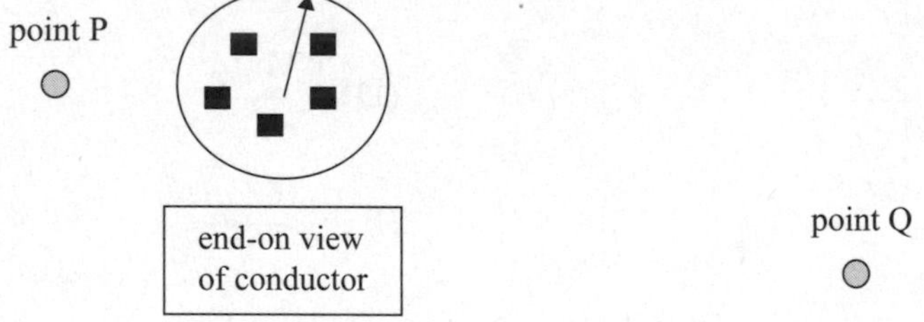

(b) Using Gauss's law, determine an expression for the electric field due to the wire for all distances $r < R$. Use the symbols ρ , r, L, R, and other fundamental constants in your expression.

(c) Using Gauss's law, determine an expression for the electric field due to the wire for all distances $r > R$. Use the symbols ρ , r, L, R, and other fundamental constants in your expression.

(d) Suppose the charge density ρ is no longer a uniform constant. The wire has a new charge density defined by the relationship $\rho = \rho_o \frac{r}{R}$, where

ρ_o is a constant measured in $\frac{coul}{m^3}$, r is the position vector from the center of the cylinder, and R is the radius of the cylinder. Determine the total charge contained in the wire.

2. The circuit shown in the following diagram is used to measure voltage and current. In one section of the circuit, elements are placed. That section is indicated in the diagram by the dark black box. Determine the readings on the voltmeter and the ammeter in each of the three cases. Assume all wires and connectors have negligible resistance. In the case of the capacitor and inductor, assume that both measurements are made in a steady-state situation.

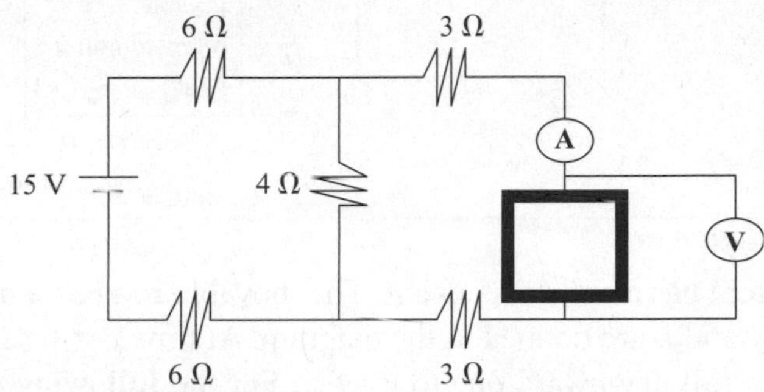

(a) A 6-ohm resistor is placed in the black box. Determine the voltmeter and ammeter readings. Show your work.

Ammeter reading: ________ *amperes*

Voltmeter reading: ________ *volts*

(b) A 2 μF capacitor is placed in the black box. Determine the voltmeter and ammeter readings.

Ammeter reading: ________ *amperes*

Voltmeter reading: ________ *volts*

(c) A 2.0 mH inductor is placed in the black box. Determine the voltmeter and ammeter readings.

Ammeter reading: ________ *amperes*

Voltmeter reading: ________ *volts*

3. A movable wire slides vertically along a wire rail system. Assume there is no friction in any part of the rail system, and assume the movable wire maintains contact with the rail system at all times. The wire system is sitting in a uniform magnetic field B that is directed into the page.

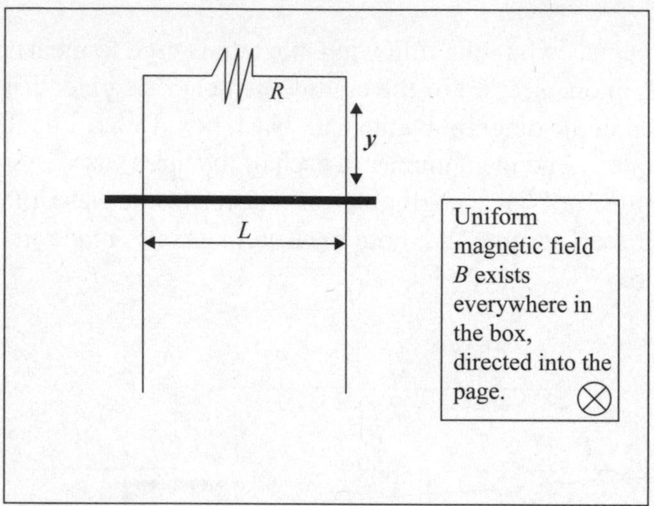

The system has a net resistance R. The movable rod has a mass of m. The lengths y and L are defined in the diagram. At time $t = 0$ seconds, the rod begins to fall downward due to gravity. For the following questions, use the symbols R, y, L, B, and m and any necessary fundamental constants.

(a) Determine the magnetic flux at any time t.

(b) Determine the terminal velocity of the movable rod.

(c) Determine the magnetic force on the movable rod as a function of time.

(d) Determine an expression for the speed of the movable rod at any time $t > 0$ seconds.

END OF EXAM

PRACTICE EXAM 4

AP Physics C
Electricity and Magnetism

Answer Key

1. (E)	8. (C)	15. (A)	22. (C)	29. (E)
2. (B)	9. (A)	16. (A)	23. (D)	30. (B)
3. (E)	10. (B)	17. (C)	24. (D)	31. (C)
4. (B)	11. (C)	18. (E)	25. (B)	32. (A)
5. (A)	12. (B)	19. (A)	26. (C)	33. (C)
6. (C)	13. (C)	20. (C)	27. (B)	34. (B)
7. (C)	14. (C)	21. (B)	28. (D)	35. (C)

PRACTICE EXAM 4

AP Physics C Electricity and Magnetism

Detailed Explanations of Answers

Section I

1. **(E)**

The two spheres touch and share the net charge equally across both surfaces. That means that a net charge of $+2Q$ is shared between the two spheres. Each sphere has a net charge of $+Q$ on it. The force in the first case is

$$\vec{F_1} = \frac{k(+4Q)(-2Q)}{d^2} = -\frac{8kQ^2}{d^2}.$$

The force for the second case is

$$\vec{F_2} = \frac{k(+Q)(+Q)}{d^2} = \frac{kQ^2}{d^2}.$$

Therefore, the relationship between F_1 and F_2 is $\vec{F_1} = -8\vec{F_2}$. The negative sign indicates that the forces are in opposite directions.

2. **(B)**

Be careful with this tricky question! At first it appears that only choice (A) is the logical answer. Because the net E field is due to the effect of all three charges, the field at point A has a net contribution from the third charge. If you analyze point B,

$$\vec{E}_{net} = \left\|\vec{E}\right\|_1 + \left\|\vec{E}\right\|_2 - \left\|\vec{E_3}\right\|$$

$$\left\|\vec{E_1}\right\|_B = \frac{kQ}{(2d)^2}, \left\|\vec{E_2}\right\|_B = \frac{kQ}{d^2} \Rightarrow \left\|\vec{E_1}\right\| + \left\|\vec{E_2}\right\| = \frac{5}{4}\frac{kQ}{d^2}$$

$$\left\|\vec{E_3}\right\| = \frac{k5Q}{(2d)^2} = \frac{5}{4}\frac{kQ}{d^2}$$

This means that the sum of the three fields adds to 0 only at point B.

3. **(E)**

The potential at a point in space due to point charges is equivalent to the following definition:

$$\sum \frac{kQ}{r}.$$

Since all three charges are positive, there is absolutely no way to get a sum that adds to 0 from that expression. So the answer is no point has 0 potential.

4. **(B)**

The flux through one complete sphere is always equal to the net charge enclosed divided by the permittivity of free space (Gauss's law). Because the Gaussian surface is exactly half of a complete sphere, the net flux through the hemisphere is exactly half of the full flux:

$$\oint_{hemisphere} \vec{E} \cdot d\vec{A} = \frac{Q}{2\varepsilon_o}$$

5. **(A)**

The drift velocity of an electron is very slow. It is not close to the speed of light. Here is a quick calculation for this value with some typical values:

$$I = neAv_d \approx (10^{29}\text{ elec/m}^3)(10^{-19}\text{ C})(10^{-4}\text{ m}^2)(10^{-4}\text{ m/s}) \approx 10^2\text{ A}$$

This calculation uses an estimate for the density of electrons and the area of the wire. Notice that the drift velocity has to be as small as possible to get a typical value for current, on the order of 1 A.

6. **(C)**

One way to solve this problem is to treat the capacitor with a metal slab as two capacitors in series. The metal slab has a net field of 0 inside. Thus, it is effectively making the distance over which the field acts a smaller distance, decreasing voltage and thus increasing net capacity for the same amount of charge. To compute the capacitance of the two "new" capacitors, simply apply the definition of parallel plate capacitors. The new distance between the plates is $d' = (a - b)/2$. Thus,

$$C' = \frac{\varepsilon_o A}{\frac{(a-b)}{2}} = \frac{2\varepsilon_o A}{a-b}.$$

There are two of these capacitors in series with each other. So we have to add the capacitors in series:

$$\frac{1}{C_e} = \frac{1}{C'} + \frac{1}{C'} = \frac{1}{\frac{2\varepsilon_o A}{a-b}} + \frac{1}{\frac{2\varepsilon_o A}{a-b}} = \frac{a-b}{\varepsilon_o A} \Rightarrow C_e = \frac{\varepsilon_o A}{a-b}$$

Now compare the two situations:

$$\frac{C'}{C_o} = \frac{\frac{\varepsilon_o A}{a-b}}{\frac{\varepsilon_o A}{a}} = \frac{a}{a-b}$$

7. **(C)**

In a series arrangement, the charge on each capacitor is the same as a result of induction. The voltage drop across each capacitor adds up to the total battery voltage drop. This is why the capacitors add reciprocally in series. Adding the capacitors in series gives the following relationship:

$$\frac{1}{C_E} = \frac{1}{3} + \frac{1}{3} + \frac{1}{3} \Rightarrow C_E = 1\ \mu\text{F}$$

$$Q_{net} = C_E V = (1\ \mu\text{F})(10\ \text{V}) = 10\ \mu\text{C}$$

By induction, the net charge on the capacitor system is the same as the individual charge on each capacitor. Each of the 3-μF capacitors has a 10-μC charge on it.

8. **(C)**

The net charge on the system is also 10 μC.

9. **(A)**

This is a classic E field question. The net field at point P is the vector sum of the two E fields at point P, as shown in the following diagram:

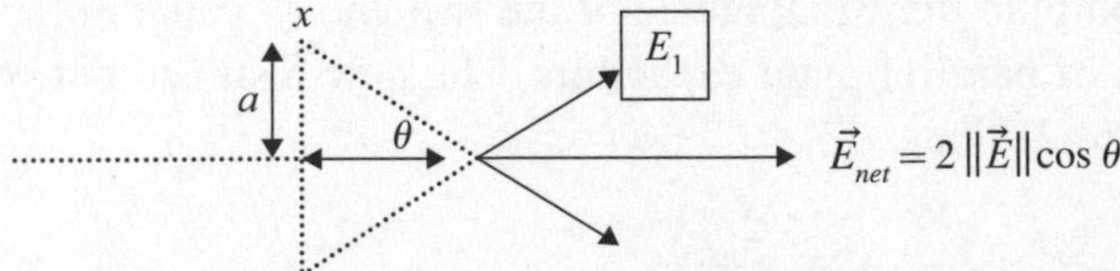

Due to symmetry, E_1 and E_2 have the same magnitude, and E_{net} is simply the sum of these two magnitudes' x-components. Computing the magnitude of the E field gives

$$\left\|\vec{E_1}\right\| = \left\|\vec{E_2}\right\| = \frac{kQ}{\left(\sqrt{x^2 + a^2}\right)^2}$$

Now, consider the cos θ contribution:

$$\cos\theta = \frac{x}{\sqrt{x^2 + a^2}}$$

$$\left\|\vec{E}_{net}\right\| = 2\left\|\vec{E_1}\right\|\cos\theta = 2\frac{kQ}{\left(\sqrt{x^2 + a^2}\right)^2}\cdot\frac{x}{\sqrt{x^2 + a^2}} = \frac{2kQx}{(x^2 + a^2)^{\frac{3}{2}}}$$

$$k = \frac{1}{4\pi\varepsilon_o} \Rightarrow \left\|\vec{E}_{net}\right\| = \frac{Qx}{2\pi\varepsilon_o\,(x^2 + a^2)^{\frac{3}{2}}}$$

10. **(B)**

The net field outside the outer sphere is twice the magnitude of the inner sphere and in the opposite direction. We know that the inner sphere has an electric field proportional to $+Q$. The net charge enclosed from the two spheres has to be twice as large as $+Q$ and the opposite sign. So the net charge enclosed is $-2Q$, and $-2Q = Q_{outer} + Q$. Therefore, $Q_{outer} = -3Q$.

11. **(C)**

Using the calculus definition of potential due to a continuously charged conductor, $V = \int \frac{kdq}{r}$. In this case, the charge is always on the ring, so the differential charge element dq is always a distance R away from the point in question. The definition of dq is $dq = \lambda dl$. The integral of dl around a semicircular ring is $\int_0^{\pi R} dl = L_0^{\pi R} = \pi R$. So apply the entire definition:

$$V_{center} = \int \frac{k\lambda dl}{R} = \frac{k\lambda}{R}\int dl = \frac{k\lambda\pi R}{R} = k\pi\lambda \Rightarrow$$

$$k = \frac{1}{4\pi\varepsilon_o} \Rightarrow V_{center} = \frac{\lambda}{4\varepsilon_o}$$

12. **(B)**

The moment the switch is thrown, the uncharged capacitor branch behaves like a short circuit, and the initial circuit is simply the loop that contains R_1 and C.

The R_2 loop at $t = 0$ is seen as highly resistive compared with its zero-resistance alternative of the uncharged capacitor. That means the initial current is $I = \frac{\varepsilon}{R_1}$.

13. **(C)**

After a long time, the capacitor is completely filled and that branch has an infinite resistance. The loop for the circuit flow is simply through R_1 and R_2 in series. The new steady-state current in the circuit becomes $I_{ss} = \frac{\varepsilon}{R_1 + R_2}$.

14. **(C)**

To determine the charge on the capacitor, determine the voltage across the capacitor. Because the capacitor is in parallel with R_2, then it has the same voltage as R_2. The voltage across R_2 is $V_{R_2} = \varepsilon \cdot \frac{R_2}{R_1 + R_2}$. Therefore, the charge is simply $Q = CV$, or $Q = \varepsilon C \frac{R_2}{R_1 + R_2}$.

15. **(A)**

A moving charge will deflect in a magnetic field and move in circular motion. This deflection is predicted by the left-hand rule, in the case of an electron. Using your left hand, the thumb will point with electron's initial velocity to the left, the fingers will point inward to represent the magnetic field, and the palm of your left hand will point down to represent the initial force on the electron.

16. **(A)**

The field due to the wire at the electron's position is out of the page. Again, using the left-hand rule, the electron's velocity is upward (thumb), the field is out of the page (fingers), and the palm representing the initial force on the electron is facing left.

17. **(C)**

With switches A and B both closed, the circuit becomes a 7-ohm resistor in series with parallel branches of 4 and 12 ohms. The 4- and 12-ohm resistors have an effective resistance of 3 ohms $\left(\frac{1}{R_E} = \frac{1}{12} + \frac{1}{4} = \frac{4}{12} \Rightarrow R_E = 3\ \Omega\right)$. So the net resistance for the total circuit is $7 + 3 = 10$ ohms. The net current in the circuit is $I_{total} = \frac{10\text{ V}}{10\ \Omega} = 1$ A. The voltage drop across the parallel branch is $\frac{3\ \Omega}{10\ \Omega} \cdot 10\text{ V} = 3$ V. So the current in the 12-ohm branch is $I_{12} = \frac{3\text{ V}}{12\ \Omega} = 0.25$ A.

18. **(E)**

With switch B closed, the circuit becomes a simple series circuit of 7 ohms and 4 ohms in series. The total effective resistance of the series circuit is 11 ohms. The 4 ohms will consume 4/11 of the total voltage. Thus,

$$V_{4\Omega} = \frac{4\ \Omega}{11\ \Omega} \cdot 10\ \text{V} = \frac{40}{11}\ \text{V} \approx 3.63\ \text{V}$$

19. **(A)**

The graph shows that at 10 seconds, the current is approximately 37% of the initial value of 1 μA. This is the value at which the exponent in the expression $e^{-\left(\frac{t}{RC}\right)}$ is equal to 1, so

$$\frac{t}{RC} = 1 \Rightarrow RC = 10$$

Therefore,

$$C = \frac{10\ \text{s}}{10 \times 10^6\ \Omega} = 1 \times 10^{-6}\ \text{F} = 1\ \mu\text{F}$$

20. **(C)**

In the crossed-field velocity selector problem, the magnetic force must equal the electric force for the charge to move through undeflected in the crossed-field region:

$$F_B = F_E$$

$$Bve = eE \Rightarrow B = \frac{E}{v} = \frac{1 \times 10^5\ \text{N/C}}{1 \times 10^6\ \text{m/s}} = 0.1\ \text{Tesla}$$

21. **(B)**

At time $t = 0$ seconds, the inductor acts to oppose the change happening to it. So at time $t = 0$, the inductor behaves as an infinite resistance, which leaves the initial circuit as one with a 10-ohm resistor and a 30-ohm resistor in series. Therefore, the initial current is $i = \frac{V}{R} = \frac{20\ \text{V}}{40\ \Omega} = 0.5\ \text{A}$.

22. **(C)**

In a steady-state situation, the inductor is a zero-resistance wire. So the inductor basically short-circuits the 30-ohm resistor, and the circuit becomes one with only a 10-ohm resistor. Therefore, the steady-state current is $i = \frac{20\ \text{V}}{10\ \Omega} = 2\ \text{A}$.

23. **(D)**

This is a tricky question. The opening of the switch leaves a current of 2 A in the inductor at time $t = t_1$. This current will decay exponentially as it goes through the loop created by the inductor and the 30-ohm resistor. The exponent for the exponential decay is

$$\frac{R}{L} = \frac{30\ \Omega}{2 \times 10^{-3} H} = 15 \times 10^{3}\ \text{s}^{-1}.$$

This leaves the expression as

$$i(t) = I_o e^{-\frac{R}{L}t} = 2e^{-15\times10^{3}}.$$

24. **(D)**

To determine the induced current, find the induced voltage. Induced voltage is $\varepsilon = -\frac{d\vartheta_B}{dt}$. The flux in this problem is defined by $\vartheta_B = \int \vec{B} \cdot \vec{dA} = B \int dA = BA$. Remember, the field is uniform across the circular area and is diminishing in time. So the flux expression is $\vartheta_B = BA = (2e^{-2t})(2\pi) = 4\pi e^{-2t}$. Taking the derivative of this expression gives the induced voltage:

$$\varepsilon_i = \frac{d}{dt}\left(4\pi e^{-2t}\right) = -8\pi e^{-2t}$$

$$\therefore i = \frac{\varepsilon_i}{R} = \frac{-8\pi e^{-2t}}{8} = \pi e^{-2t} \Rightarrow i(1\ \text{s}) = \pi e^{-2} = \frac{\pi}{e^2}$$

That is the magnitude of the current. To determine the direction of the current, apply Lenz's law.

The diminishing field is creating a decreasing flux (which is why there is a negative sign). Lenz's law states that the induced current and field will oppose the change that is occurring. That means the induced current will try to create a field that opposes a diminishing field, which is why the saying "save a dying field" works in this case. Thus, the induced current must be counterclockwise so that the induced field is "out of the page," just as the initial decreasing field is directed. In other words, the system is trying to "save the dying field."

25. **(B)**

This problem must be treated as finding the difference in potential between two points in an electric field. The first step in the solution is to determine the electric field between the two spheres. That electric field can be determined by

Gauss's law. The enclosed charge is $+3Q$. This gives an electric field between the spheres of $E = \frac{3kQ}{r^2}$, directed outward.

The difference in potential between the two spheres is

$$\Delta V = -\int_{2R}^{R} \frac{3kQ}{r^2} = -3kQ \int_{2R}^{R} \frac{1}{r^2} = -3kQ\left[-\frac{1}{r}\right]_{2R}^{R}$$

$$= 3kQ\left[\frac{1}{R} - \frac{1}{2R}\right] = 3kQ \cdot \frac{1}{2R} = \frac{3kQ}{2R}$$

$$\text{subink} = \frac{1}{4\pi\varepsilon_o} \Rightarrow \Delta V = \frac{3Q}{8\pi\varepsilon_o R}$$

26. **(C)**

Using the right-hand rule for a field composed of long wire with current, first understand that each wire contributes a magnetic field into the page at point P. Then add each field to determine the net magnetic field. The field of a wire is $B = \frac{\mu_o I}{2\pi r}$.

$$B_1 = \frac{\mu_o I}{2\pi\left(\frac{3d}{2}\right)}, B_2 = \frac{\mu_o(2I)}{2\pi\left(\frac{d}{2}\right)}, B_3 = \frac{\mu_o(2I)}{2\pi\left(\frac{d}{2}\right)}$$

$$B_1 + B_2 + B_3 = \frac{\mu_o I}{3\pi d} + \frac{2\mu_o I}{\pi d} + \frac{2\mu_o I}{\pi d} = \frac{13\mu_o I}{3\pi d}$$

27. **(B)**

This solution involves applying the Biot–Savart law. The two vectors shown in the following diagram come from a circuit element length at the top and the bottom of the ring. The direction of each dB is obtained by using the cross-product definition.

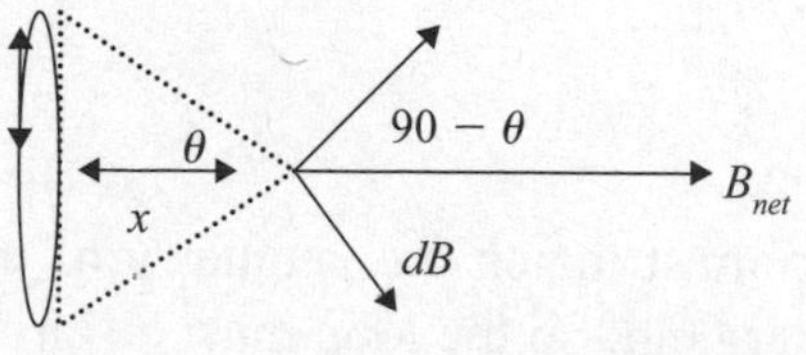

R
θ
x
90 − θ
B_{net}
dB

So each little element of the rings current dl carries current I:

$$B = \frac{\mu_o I}{4\pi} \int \frac{\vec{dl} \times \hat{r}}{r^2}$$

Some things to consider with this calculation: dl and r are at 90 degrees with each other, so the cross-product contribution is 1. Every part of the circular wire is the same distance away from point P. So this makes everything a constant except integrating dl. Here is how it looks now:

$$B = \frac{\mu_o I}{4\pi} \int \frac{d\vec{l} \times \hat{r}}{r^2}, r = \sqrt{R^2 + x^2} \Rightarrow B = \frac{\mu_o I}{4\pi} \cdot \frac{1}{\left(\sqrt{R^2 + x^2}\right)^2} \int dl$$

All that is left is to integrate dl, but consider the vector addition as well. Notice that the net B field results from adding up the x-component of every dB vector created. All these vectors would create a cone, and all the x-components would add up in the direction shown in the diagram as B_{net}. So this makes the final computation the following:

$$B_{net} = \int dB_x = \int dB \cdot \cos(90 - \theta) = \int dB \cdot \sin\theta \Rightarrow$$

$$B_{net} = \frac{\mu_o I}{4\pi} \cdot \frac{1}{\left(\sqrt{R^2 + x^2}\right)^2} \int dl \cdot \sin\theta$$

$$\sin\vartheta = \frac{R}{\sqrt{R^2 + x^2}} \text{ (from the triangle in the picture)}$$

$$\Rightarrow B_{net} = \frac{\mu_o I}{4\pi} \cdot \frac{1}{\left(\sqrt{R^2 + x^2}\right)^2} \cdot \frac{R}{\sqrt{R^2 + x^2}} \int dl$$

$$\int dl = \text{circumference of circle} = 2\pi R$$

$$\Rightarrow B_{net} = \frac{\mu_o I}{4\pi} \cdot \frac{1}{\left(\sqrt{R^2 + x^2}\right)^2} \cdot \frac{R}{\sqrt{R^2 + x^2}} \cdot 2\pi R = \frac{\mu_o I R^2}{2(R^2 + x^2)^{\frac{3}{2}}}$$

A quick way to validate the answer is to check the answers for the field at the center of the circle $x = 0$. This is sometimes a familiar value to physics students: $B = \frac{\mu_o I}{2R}$.

28. **(D)**

The Amperian loop must match the geometry of the magnetic field of the wire, which is a circular field. So the loop must be circular.

29. **(E)**

The electron is in circular motion caused by the magnetic force acting on the moving electron. So the magnetic force is the net force:

$$\sum F_{electron} = ma_c = F_B$$

$$\Rightarrow m\frac{v^2}{R} = Bve \Rightarrow mv = BeR$$

Since the electron is in a circular motion with constant speed, then the speed of the electron, $v = \dfrac{2\pi R}{T} \Rightarrow$

$$m\frac{2\pi R}{T} = BeR \Rightarrow T = 2\pi\frac{m}{Be}$$

30. **(B)**

If v is increased, the period is unchanged. The period is independent of speed. However, the radius will increase. Notice from the work done to solve question 29, $v = \dfrac{BeR}{m}$. B, e, and m are all unchanged, so if the speed increases, the radius of circular motion also increases.

31. **(C)**

The network of capacitors should be reduced. The two capacitors in parallel simply add up to their net capacitance: 9 + 3 = 12 μF. This 12-μF capacitor is in series with the 4-μF capacitor. In series, the two capacitors add reciprocally.

$$\frac{1}{C_E} = \frac{1}{4} + \frac{1}{12} \Rightarrow C_E = 3\ \mu\text{F}$$

The net charge in the system is

$$Q_{\text{net}} = CV = (3\ \mu\text{F})(12\ \text{V}) = 36\ \mu\text{C}.$$

This gives a voltage across the parallel branch of $V = Q/C = 36/12 = 3$ volts. The charge on the 3-μF capacitor is

$$Q = CV = (3\ \mu\text{F})(3\ \text{V}) = 9\ \mu\text{C}.$$

Notice that the 9-μF capacitor will have 27 μC on it, the total of the parallel system being 36 μC, as it should be.

32. **(A)**

The capacitance of two spheres is very similar to the parallel-plate definition of capacitance, which depends only on area and distance of separation. The spherical definition also has that look. The first step is to get the E field between the two spheres, which was done in question 25. Revisiting that solution:

$$E = \frac{kQ}{r^2} \Rightarrow \Delta V = -\int_b^a \frac{kQ}{r^2}dr = \left[\frac{kQ}{r}\right]_b^a = kQ\left[\frac{1}{a} - \frac{1}{b}\right] = kQ\frac{b-a}{ab}$$

Now apply the definition of capacitance:

$$C = \frac{Q}{V} = \frac{Q}{kQ\dfrac{b-a}{ab}} = \frac{ab}{k(b-a)} = \frac{4\pi\varepsilon_0 ab}{b-a}$$

33. **(C)**

The net field at point P turns out to be only the contribution from the top charge. Here is the diagram:

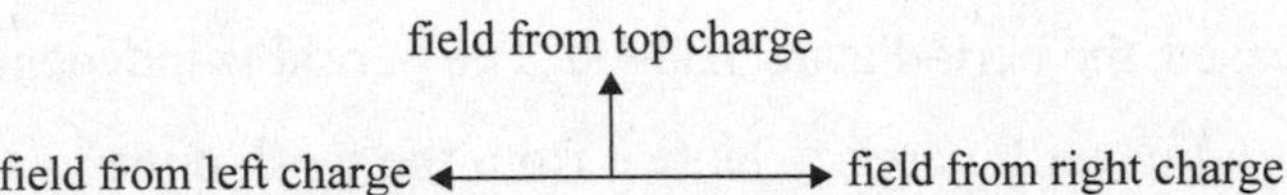

Thus, the net field is only the electric field due to the top-point charge. The distance from the top charge to the bottom of the base is $\frac{\sqrt{3}}{2}d$. So the E field is

$$E = \frac{kQ}{\left(\dfrac{\sqrt{3}}{2}d\right)^2} = \frac{4kQ}{3d^2}.$$

The direction is up.

34. **(B)**

The potential at point P is the sum of all the point charge potential contributions.

$$\sum \frac{kQ}{r} = -kQ\left[\frac{1}{\frac{d}{2}} + \frac{1}{\frac{d}{2}} + \frac{1}{\frac{\sqrt{3}}{2}d}\right] = -kQ\left[\frac{2}{d} + \frac{2}{d} + \frac{2}{\sqrt{3}d}\right] = \frac{-2kQ}{d}\left(\frac{2\sqrt{3}+1}{\sqrt{3}}\right)$$

This solution skips over some steps in the algebra for the sake of simplification. Make sure you get the final answer. It is important that your algebra skills be strong in any physics class. This question certainly tests those skills.

35. **(C)**

Replace the unit Tesla with its equivalent units and then perform some algebra with the units until it is simplified into an expression containing the unit Volt.

$$Tesla = \frac{N}{A \cdot m}$$

$$Tesla \cdot m^2 = \frac{N}{A \cdot m} \cdot m^2 = \frac{N}{A} \cdot m = \frac{N}{\frac{C}{s}} \cdot m = \frac{N \cdot m}{C} \cdot s = \frac{J}{C} \cdot s = V \cdot s$$

Section II

1. (a) The vectors are shown in the following diagram.

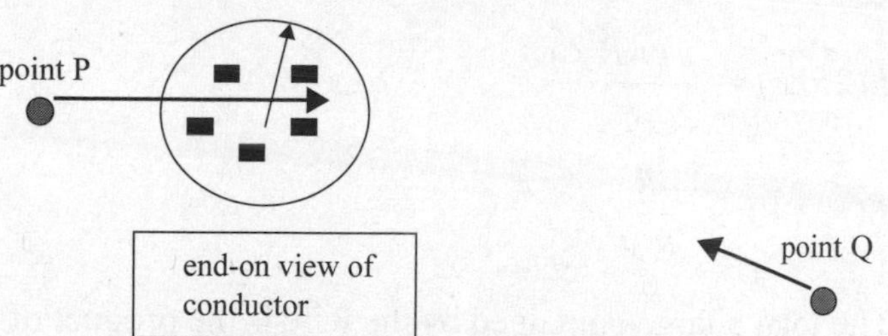

Notice that the magnitude of the vector at point P is greater than the magnitude of the vector at point Q. Both vectors should be inwardly directed and radially directed.

(b) To use Gauss's law, imagine a cylindrical Gaussian surface that partially encloses some of the wire. The radius of this Gaussian surface is $r < R$, and the length of the surface is the entire length of the actual wire L. So the volume of the surface is $V = \pi r^2 L$. The surface area is $A = 2\pi rL$. Because the cylinder is uniformly charged, the net charge enclosed would be $Q_{net} = \rho V_{enclosed} = \rho \pi r^2 L$. Now, applying Gauss's law gives the following:

$$\oint_{SA} \vec{E} \cdot \vec{dA} = \frac{q_{enclosed}}{\varepsilon_o}$$

SA of Gaussian cylinder $= 2\pi rL$

$\vec{E}$, $\vec{dA}$ are parallel to each other at every point on the surface. So the dot product contribution is 1.

Since $\vec{E}$ is radial and dependent on r at every point, then the magnitude of E at ev on the Gaussian cylinder is a constant.

$$\therefore \oint \vec{E} \cdot \vec{dA} = \frac{q_{enclosed}}{\varepsilon_o} \Rightarrow E \oint dA = \frac{q_{enclosed}}{\varepsilon_o} \text{ and the}$$

$\oint dA =$ total surface area of Gaussian surface

$$\Rightarrow E(2\pi rL) = \frac{q_{enclosed}}{\varepsilon_o}$$

$$\Rightarrow E(2\pi rL) = \frac{\rho(\pi r^2 L)}{\varepsilon_o} \Rightarrow E(r < R) = \frac{\rho r}{2\varepsilon_o}$$

(c) To find E for $r > R$, use the same approach as in part (b). The only exception is that the Gaussian cylinder is $r > R$, and it encloses all the charge in the wire. So in this case, $Q_{total} = \rho V_{wire} = \rho(\pi R^2 L)$. Now follow the same steps as in part (b), getting to the following step:

$$E \oint dA = \frac{Q_{total}}{\varepsilon_o}$$

$$E(2\pi rL) = \frac{\rho(\pi R^2 L)}{\varepsilon_o}$$

$$E(r > R) = \frac{\rho R^2}{2\varepsilon_o r}$$

(d) The total charge contained by the wire is the product of the changing charged density times volume: $\int \rho dV$. Determine the proper expression for dV:

$$dV_{cylindricalvolume} = 2\pi rLdr$$

This is basically a thin cylindrical shell of radius r, thickness dr, and length L, as shown here:

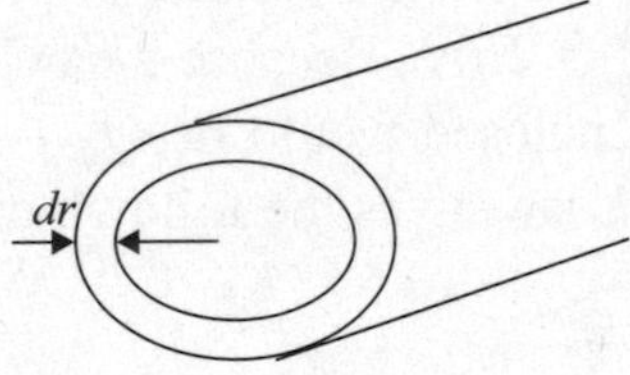

Now integrate the expression from $r = 0$ to $r = R$:

$$Q_{enclosed} = \int_0^R \rho dV = \int_0^R \left(\rho_o \tfrac{r}{R}\right)(2\pi rLdr)$$

$$Q = \frac{2\pi L\rho_o}{R}\int_0^R r^2 dr = \frac{2\pi L\rho_o}{R}\left[\frac{[r^3]}{3}\right]_0^R = 2\pi L\rho_o \frac{R^2}{3}$$

2. (a) With a 6-ohm resistor, the box looks like this:

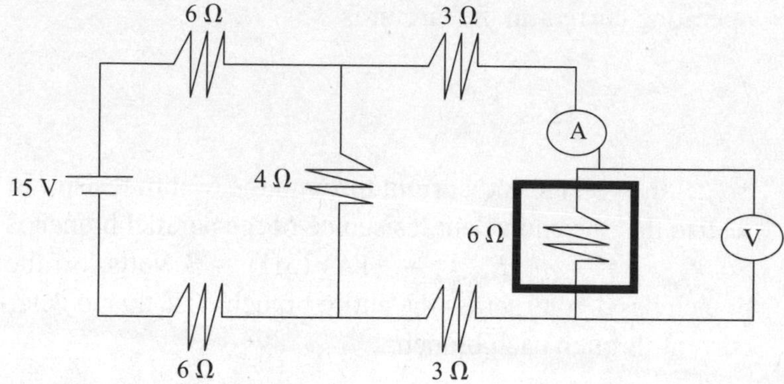

The circuit is reduced to this:

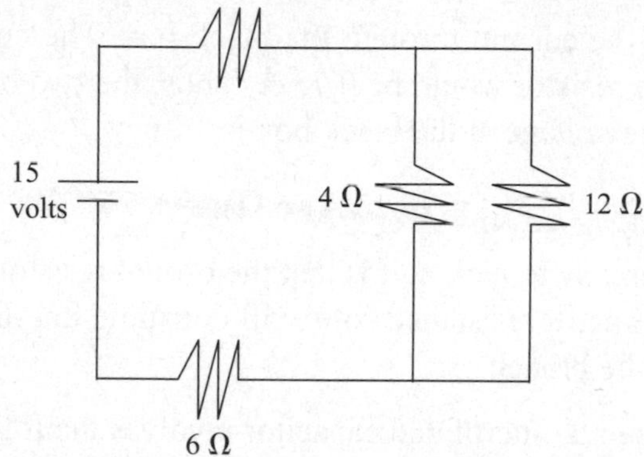

The 4-ohm and 12-ohm resistors are in parallel and further reduce the circuit:

$$\frac{1}{R_e} = \frac{1}{4} + \frac{1}{12} = \frac{1}{3} \Rightarrow R_e = 3\ \Omega$$

So the circuit becomes:

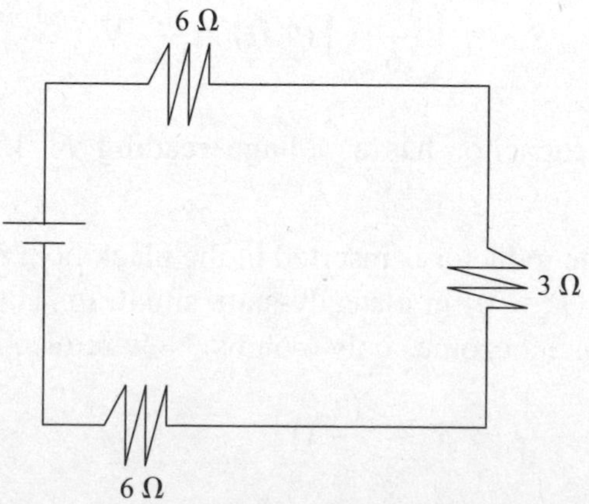

This reduces to a single equivalent resistance of 15 ohms. So the total operating current in the circuit is

$$I = \frac{V}{R_e} = \frac{15\text{ V}}{15\ \Omega} = 1\text{ A}.$$

To get the voltage and current through the 6-ohm resistor in the box, realize that the equivalent resistance of the parallel branch is 3 ohms. So $V_{branch} = I_{branch} R_{branch} = (1\text{A})\ (3\Omega) = 3$ Volts. So the parallel branch has 3 volts across the entire branch. Use this to determine the current through each branch:

$$I_{branch} = \frac{V_{branch}}{R_{branch}} = \frac{3\text{ V}}{12\ \Omega} = 0.25\text{ A}$$

This is the current through the black box. The current through the 12-ohm resistor would be 0.75 A. Thus, the two branches add up to 1 A. The voltage at the black box is

$$V_{6\Omega} = I_{6\Omega} R_{6\Omega} = (0.25\text{ A})(6\ \Omega) = 1.5\text{ V}$$

Another way to look at it is that the 6-ohm resistor is one-half of the total branch's resistance so it will consume one-half of the voltage across the branch.

(b) Inserting a 2-microfarad capacitor involves the following: A charged capacitor in a circuit branch behaves as if it has "infinite resistance." So the current in the ammeter will read 0. Because the branch is effectively knocked out of the circuit, the rest of the circuit becomes a 16-ohm series circuit. The branch with the capacitor is in parallel with the 4-ohm resistor. The voltage across the 4-ohm resistor is the same as the voltage across the branch with the capacitor and ultimately across the capacitor:

$$V_{4\Omega} = I_{total} R_{4\Omega} = \left(\frac{15}{16}\text{ A}\right)(4\ \Omega) = \frac{15}{4}\text{ V}$$

So the capacitor has a voltage reading of 15/4 volts across its plates.

(c) When the inductor is inserted in the black box, it behaves as a piece of wire ($R \approx 0$) in a steady-state situation. Thus, the resistance in that branch becomes only 6 ohms. Now reduce that circuit:

$$\frac{1}{R_e} = \frac{1}{6} + \frac{1}{4} \Rightarrow R_e = \frac{12}{5}\ \Omega$$

This resistance of 12/5 is added in series to the two 6-ohm resistors, giving a total resistance of 72/5 ohms. So the total current is

$$I_t = \frac{V_t}{R_e} = \frac{15\text{ V}}{\frac{72}{5}} = \frac{75}{72}\text{ A.}$$

The parallel branch behaves like 12/5 ohms. Therefore, the total voltage across that branch is

$$V = \left(\frac{75}{72}\text{ A}\right)\left(\frac{12}{5}\ \Omega\right) = \frac{15}{6}\text{ V} \Rightarrow$$

$$I_{6\ ohm\ branch} = \frac{V}{R} = \frac{\frac{15}{6}}{6} = \frac{15}{36}\text{ A}$$

The ammeter reading is thus $\frac{15}{36}$ A. The voltage reading across the inductor is 0. The inductor has zero resistance, so it consumes 0 voltage.

3. (a) The magnetic flux at time $t > 0$ is dependent on the area of the conductive loop that intersects the B field. The area of the loop is y times L. So the flux is $\vartheta_B = \int \vec{B} \cdot \vec{dA}$, where B is uniform and constant and the dot product between B and dA contributes 1.0 to the product. So $\int \vec{B} \cdot \vec{dA} = B \int dA = BA = ByL.$

(b) After some time, the conductive loop gets a large enough current that the magnetic force acting on the movable rod will equal the weight of the rod, as shown in the following diagram.

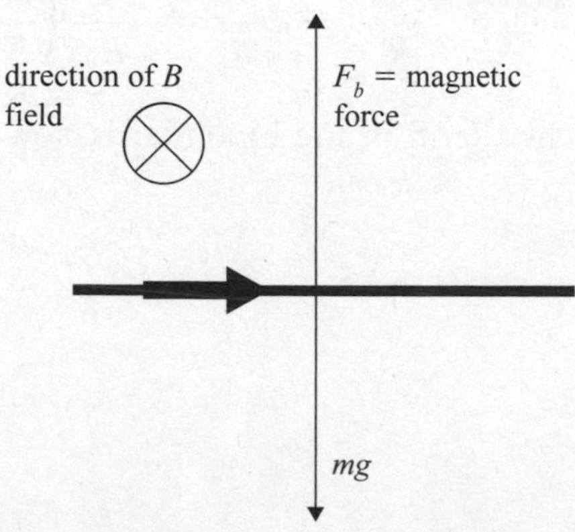

Check the direction of the B force and the current in the rod with the right-hand rule to make sure it makes sense. Because the weight must equal the magnetic force at the terminal velocity point, equate those two relationships:

$$F_B = BIL = mg$$

Obtain the current from the flux change. The flux change when the rod reaches terminal velocity is

$$\frac{d\vartheta_B}{dt} = BvL = Bv_tL$$

This is equivalent to the voltage:

$$\varepsilon = Bv_tL$$

$$\text{so, } I = \frac{\varepsilon}{R} = \frac{Bv_tL}{R}$$

$$\text{Now, } F_B = BIL = mg \Rightarrow B\left[\frac{Bv_tL}{R}\right]L = mg$$

$$v_t = \frac{mgR}{B^2L^2}$$

(c) The magenetic force on the rod as a function of time is as follows (some of the work was done in part (b)):

$$F_B = BIL = B\left[\frac{BvL}{R}\right]L = \frac{B^2L^2}{R}v(t) = \frac{B^2L^2}{R}\cdot\frac{dy}{dt}$$

(d) Setting the net force equal to ma will allow for writing a differential equation in terms of v:

$$\sum F_{rod} = m\frac{dv}{dt} = mg - F_b \Rightarrow m\frac{dv}{dt} = mg - \frac{B^2L^2}{R}v$$

$$\text{Divide through by } \frac{B^2L^2}{R} \Rightarrow m\frac{dv}{dt} = \frac{B^2L^2}{R}\left(\frac{mgR}{B^2L^2} - v\right)$$

Notice the first term in the binomial is now the terminal velocity term:

$$\therefore\ m\frac{dv}{dt} = \frac{B^2L^2}{R}(v_t - v)$$

$$\frac{dv}{(v_t - v)} = \frac{B^2L^2}{mR}dt$$

Integrate both sides $\Rightarrow$

$$\int_0^v \frac{dv}{(v_t - v)} = \int_0^t \frac{B^2L^2}{mR}dt \Rightarrow -\left[\ln(v_t - v)\right]_0^v = \left[\frac{B^2L^2}{mR}t\right]_0^t$$

$$\ln(v_t - v) - \ln v_t = -\left[\frac{B^2L^2}{mR}t\right] \Rightarrow \ln\left[\frac{v_t - v}{v_t}\right] = \left[-\frac{B^2L^2}{mR}t\right]$$

$$\left[\frac{v_t - v}{v_t}\right] = e^{-\frac{B^2L^2}{mR}t} \Rightarrow v = v_t - v_t e^{-\frac{B^2L^2}{mR}t} = v_t\left(1 - e^{-\frac{B^2L^2}{mR}t}\right)$$

$$\therefore\ v = v_t\left(1 - e^{-\frac{B^2L^2}{mR}t}\right)$$

APPENDIX A

AP Physics B & C

APPENDIX A
TABLE OF INFORMATION AND EQUATIONS FOR AP PHYSICS B AND C

The following Table of Information and Equations will be provided to students taking the AP Physics B and C exams. The Table of Information may be used for both the multiple-choice and free-response sections of the exams. However, please note that the equation tables may be used ONLY for the free-response sections.

TABLE OF INFORMATION	
CONSTANTS AND CONVERSION FACTORS	
Proton mass, $m_p = 1.67 \times 10^{-27}$ kg	Electron charge magnitude, $e = 1.60 \times 10^{-19}$ C
Neutron mass, $m_n = 1.67 \times 10^{-27}$ kg	1 electron volt, 1 eV $= 1.60 \times 10^{-19}$ J
Electron mass, $m_e = 9.11 \times 10^{-31}$ kg	Speed of light, $c = 3.00 \times 10^{8}$ m/s
Avogadro's number, $N_0 = 6.02 \times 10^{23}$ mol^{-1}	Universal gravitational constant, $G = 6.67 \times 10^{-11}$ m^3/kg $\cdot$ s^2
Universal gas constant, $R = 8.31$ J/(mol $\cdot$ K)	Acceleration due to gravity at Earth's surface, $g = 9.8$ m/s^2
Boltzmann's constant, $k_B = 1.38 \times 10^{-23}$ J/K	
1 unified atomic mass unit,	$1\text{ u} = 1.66 \times 10^{-27}\text{ kg} = 931\text{ MeV}/c^2$
Planck's constant,	$h = 6.63 \times 10^{-34}\text{ J} \cdot \text{s} = 4.14 \times 10^{-15}\text{ eV} \cdot \text{s}$
	$hc = 1.99 \times 10^{-25}\text{ J} \cdot \text{m} = 1.24 \times 10^{3}\text{ eV} \cdot \text{nm}$
Vacuum permittivity,	$\epsilon_0 = 8.85 \times 10^{-12}\text{ C}^2/\text{N} \cdot \text{m}^2$
Coulomb's law constant,	$k = 1/4\pi\epsilon_0 = 9.0 \times 10^{9}\text{ N} \cdot \text{m}^2/\text{C}^2$
Vacuum permeability,	$\mu_0 = 4\pi \times 10^{-7}\text{ (T} \cdot \text{m)/A}$
Magnetic constant,	$k' = \mu_0/4\pi = 10^{-7}\text{ (T} \cdot \text{m)/A}$
1 atmosphere pressure,	$1\text{ atm} = 1.0 \times 10^{5}\text{ N/m}^2 = 1.0 \times 10^{5}\text{ Pa}$

UNIT SYMBOLS								
	meter,	m	mole,	mol	watt,	W	farad,	F
	kilogram,	kg	hertz,	Hz	coulomb,	C	tesla,	T
	second,	s	newton,	N	volt,	V	degree Celsius,	°C
	ampere,	A	pascal,	Pa	ohm,	Ω	electron-volt,	eV
	kelvin,	K	joule,	J	henry,	H		

PREFIXES		
Factor	Prefix	Symbol
10^9	giga	G
10^6	mega	M
10^3	kilo	k
10^{-2}	centi	c
10^{-3}	milli	m
10^{-6}	micro	μ
10^{-9}	nano	n
10^{-12}	pico	p

VALUES OF TRIGONOMETRIC FUNCTIONS FOR COMMON ANGLES							
θ	0°	30°	37°	45°	53°	60°	90°
$\sin\theta$	0	1/2	3/5	$\sqrt{2}/2$	4/5	$\sqrt{3}/2$	1
$\cos\theta$	1	$\sqrt{3}/2$	4/5	$\sqrt{2}/2$	3/5	1/2	0
$\tan\theta$	0	$\sqrt{3}/3$	3/4	1	4/3	$\sqrt{3}$	∞

The following conventions are used in this exam.

I. Unless otherwise stated, the frame of reference of any problem is assumed to be inertial.

II. The direction of any electric current is the direction of flow of positive charge (conventional current).

III. For any isolated electric charge, the electric potential is defined as 0 at an infinite distance from the charge.

*IV. For mechanics and thermodynamics equations, W represents the work done on a system.

*Not on the Table of Information for Physics C, since Thermodynamics is not a Physics C topic.

Some explanations about notation used in the equation tables:

1. The symbols used for physical constants are the same as those in the Table of Information and are defined in the Table of Information rather than in the right-hand columns of the tables.
2. Symbols in bold face represent vector Quantities.
3. Subscripts on symbols in the equations are used to represent special cases of the variables defined in the right-hand columns.
4. The symbol Δ before a variable in an equation specifically indicates a change in the variable (i.e., final value minus initial value).
5. Several different symbols (e.g., *d*, *r*, *s*, *h*, *l*) are used for linear dimensions such as length. The particular symbol used in an equation is one that is commonly used for that equation in textbooks.

ADVANCED PLACEMENT PHYSICS B EQUATIONS

FLUID MECHANICS AND THERMAL PHYSICS

$$P = P_0 + \rho g h$$

$$F_{buoy} = \rho V g$$

$$A_1 v_1 = A_2 v_2$$

$$P + \rho g y + \frac{1}{2}\rho v^2 = \text{const.}$$

$$\Delta \ell = \alpha \ell_0 \Delta T$$

$$H = \frac{kA\Delta T}{L}$$

$$P = \frac{F}{A}$$

$$PV = nRT = Nk_B T$$

$$K_{avg} = \frac{3}{2}k_B T$$

$$v_{rms} = \sqrt{\frac{3RT}{M}} = \sqrt{\frac{3k_B T}{\mu}}$$

$$W = -P\Delta V$$

$$\Delta U = Q + W$$

$$e = \left|\frac{W}{Q_H}\right|$$

$$e_c = \frac{T_H - T_C}{T_H}$$

A = area
e = efficiency
F = force
h = depth
H = rate of heat transfer
k = thermal conductivity
K_{avg} = average molecular kinetic energy
l = length
L = thickness
M = molar mass
n = number of moles
N = number of molecules
P = pressure
Q = heat transferred to a system
T = temperature
V = volume
v = velocity or speed
v_{rms} = root-mean-square velocity
W = work done on a system
y = height
α = coefficient of linear expansion
μ = mass of molecule
ρ = density

ADVANCED PLACEMENT PHYSICS B EQUATIONS

ATOMIC AND NUCLEAR PHYSICS

$E = hf = pc$

$K_{max} = hf - \phi$

$\lambda = \dfrac{h}{p}$

$\Delta E = (\Delta m)c^2$

E = energy
f = frequency
K = kinetic energy
m = mass
p = momentum
λ = wavelength
ϕ = work function

WAVES AND OPTICS

$v = f\lambda$

$n = \dfrac{c}{v}$

$n_1 \sin \theta_1 = n_2 \sin \theta_2$

$\sin \theta_c = \dfrac{n_2}{n_1}$

$\dfrac{1}{s_i} + \dfrac{1}{s_0} = \dfrac{1}{f}$

$M = \dfrac{h_i}{h_0} = -\dfrac{s_i}{s_0}$

$f = \dfrac{R}{2}$

$d \sin \theta = m\lambda$

$x_m \approx \dfrac{m\lambda L}{d}$

d = separation
f = frequency or focal length
h = height
L = distance
M = magnification
m = an integer
n = index of refraction
R = radius of curvature
s = distance
v = speed
x = position
λ = wavelength
θ = angle

GEOMETRY AND TRIGONOMETRY

Rectangle
$A = bh$

Triangle
$A = \dfrac{1}{2}bh$

Circle
$A = \pi r^2$
$C = 2\pi r$

Parallelepiped
$V = lwh$

Cylinder
$V = \pi r^2 l$
$S = 2\pi r l + 2\pi r^2$

Sphere
$V = \dfrac{4}{3}\pi r^3$
$S = 4\pi r^2$

Right Triangle

$a^2 + b^2 = c^2$

$\sin \theta = \dfrac{a}{c}$

$\cos \theta = \dfrac{b}{c}$

$\tan \theta = \dfrac{a}{b}$

A = area
C = circumference
V = volume
S = surface area
b = base
h = height
l = length
w = width
r = radius

ADVANCED PLACEMENT PHYSICS B EQUATIONS

NEWTONIAN MECHANICS

$v = v_0 + at$

$x = x_0 + v_0 t + \frac{1}{2}at^2$

$v^2 = v_0{}^2 + 2a(x - x_o)$

$\sum \mathbf{F} = \mathbf{F}_{net} = ma$

$F_{fric} \leq \mu N$

$a_c = \frac{v^2}{r}$

$\tau = rF \sin \theta$

$\mathbf{p} = m\mathbf{v}$

$\mathbf{J} = \mathbf{F}\Delta t = \Delta \mathbf{p}$

$k = \frac{1}{2}mv^2$

$\Delta U_g = mgh$

$W = F\Delta r \cos \theta$

$P_{avg} = \frac{W}{\Delta t}$

$P = Fv \cos \theta$

$\mathbf{F}_s = -kx$

$U_s = \frac{1}{2}kx^2$

$T_s = 2\pi\sqrt{\frac{m}{k}}$

$T_p = 2\pi\sqrt{\frac{\ell}{g}}$

$T = \frac{1}{f}$

$F_G = -\frac{Gm_1m_2}{r^2}$

$U_G = -\frac{Gm_1m_2}{r}$

a = acceleration
F = force
f = frequency
h = height
J = impulse
K = kinetic energy
k = spring constant
l = length
m = mass
N = normal force
P = power
p = momentum
r = radius or distance
T = period
t = time
U = potential energy
v = velocity or speed
W = work done on a system
x = position
μ = coefficient of friction
θ = angle
τ = torque

ELECTRICITY AND MAGNETISM

$F = \frac{1}{4\pi\epsilon_0}\frac{q_1q_2}{r^2}$

$\mathbf{E} = \frac{\mathbf{F}}{q}$

$U_E = qV = \frac{1}{4\pi\epsilon_0}\frac{q_1q_2}{r}$

$E_{avg} = -\frac{V}{d}$

$V = \frac{1}{4\pi\epsilon_0}\sum_i \frac{q_i}{r_i}$

$C = \frac{Q}{V}$

$C = \frac{\epsilon_0 A}{d}$

$U_c = \frac{1}{2}QV = \frac{1}{2}CV^2$

$I_{avg} = \frac{\Delta Q}{\Delta t}$

$R = \frac{\rho\ell}{A}$

$V = IR$

$P = IV$

$C_p = \sum_i C_i$

$\frac{1}{C_S} = \sum_i \frac{1}{C_i}$

$R_S = \sum_i R_i$

$\frac{1}{R_p} = \sum_i \frac{1}{R_i}$

$F_B = qv\,B \sin \theta$

$F_B = BIl \sin \theta$

$B = \frac{\mu_0}{2\pi}\frac{I}{r}$

$\phi_m = BA \cos \theta$

$\varepsilon_{avg} = -\frac{\Delta \phi_m}{\Delta t}$

$\varepsilon = Blv$

A = area
B = magnetic field
C = capacitance
d = distance
E = electric field
ε = emf
F = force
I = current
l = length
P = power
Q = charge
q = point change
R = resistance
t = time
U = potential (stored) energy
V = electric potential or potential difference
v = velocity or speed
ρ = resistivity
θ = angle
ϕ_m = magnetic flux

ADVANCED PLACEMENT PHYSICS C EQUATIONS

MECHANICS

$v = v_0 + at$

$x = x_0 + v_0 t + \frac{1}{2}at^2$

$v^2 = v_0^2 + 2a(x - x_0)$

$\sum \mathbf{F} = \mathbf{F}_{net} = ma$

$\mathbf{F} = \frac{d\mathbf{p}}{dt}$

$\mathbf{J} = \int \mathbf{F}dt = \Delta\mathbf{p}$

$\mathbf{p} = m\mathbf{v}$

$F_{fric} \leq \mu N$

$W = \int \mathbf{F} \cdot d\mathbf{r}$

$K = \frac{1}{2}mv^2$

$P = \frac{dW}{dt}$

$p = \mathbf{F} \cdot v$

$\Delta U_g = mgh$

$a_c = \frac{v^2}{r} = \omega^2 r$

$\tau = \mathbf{r} \times \mathbf{F}$

$\sum \tau = \tau_{net} = I\alpha$

$I = \int r^2 dm = \sum mr^2$

$\mathbf{r}_{cm} = \sum m\mathbf{r} / \sum m$

$v = r\omega$

$\mathbf{L} = \mathbf{r} \times \mathbf{p} = I\omega$

$K = \frac{1}{2}I\omega^2$

$\omega = \omega_0 + \alpha t$

$\theta = \theta_0 + \omega_0 t + \frac{1}{2}\alpha t^2$

$\mathbf{F}_s = -k\mathbf{x}$

$U_s = \frac{1}{2}kx^2$

a = acceleration
F = force
f = frequency
h = height
I = rotational inertia
J = impulse
K = kinetic energy
k = spring constant
l = length
L = angular momentum
m = mass
N = normal force
P = power
p = momentum
r = radius or distance
$\mathbf{r}$ = position vector
T = period
t = time
U = potential energy
v = velocity or speed
W = work done on a system
x = position
μ = coefficient of friction
θ = angle
τ = torque
ω = angular speed
α = angular acceleration

$T = \frac{2\pi}{\omega} = \frac{1}{f}$

$T_s = 2\pi\sqrt{\frac{m}{k}}$

$T_p = 2\pi\sqrt{\frac{\ell}{g}}$

$\mathbf{F}_G = -\frac{Gm_1 m_2}{r^2}\hat{\mathbf{r}}$

$U_G = -\frac{Gm_1 m_2}{r}$

ADVANCED PLACEMENT PHYSICS C EQUATIONS

ELECTRICITY AND MAGNETISM

$$F = \frac{1}{4\pi\epsilon_0}\frac{q_1 q_2}{r^2}$$

$$\mathbf{E} = \frac{\mathbf{F}}{q}$$

$$\oint \mathbf{E} \cdot d\mathbf{A} = \frac{Q}{\epsilon_0}$$

$$E = -\frac{dV}{dr}$$

$$V = \frac{1}{4\pi\epsilon_0}\sum_i \frac{q_i}{r_i}$$

$$U_E = qV = \frac{1}{4\pi\epsilon_0}\frac{q_1 q_2}{r}$$

$$C = \frac{Q}{V}$$

$$C = \frac{\kappa\epsilon_0 A}{d}$$

$$C_p = \sum_i C_i$$

$$\frac{1}{C_s} = \sum_i \frac{1}{C_i}$$

$$I = \frac{dQ}{dt}$$

$$U_c = \frac{1}{2}QV = \frac{1}{2}CV^2$$

$$R = \frac{\rho\ell}{A}$$

$$\mathbf{E} = \rho\mathbf{J}$$

$$I = Nev_d A$$

$$V = IR$$

$$R_s = \sum_i R_i$$

$$\frac{1}{R_p} = \sum_i \frac{1}{R_i}$$

$$P = IV$$

$$\mathbf{F}m = q\mathbf{v} \times \mathbf{B}$$

$$\oint \mathbf{B} \cdot d\ell = \mu_0 I$$

A = area
B = magnetic field
C = capacitance
d = distance
E = electric field
ε = emf
F = force
I = current
J = current density
L = inductance
l = length
n = number of loops of wire per unit length
N = number of charge carriers per unit volume
P = power
Q = charge
q = point change
R = resistance
r = distance
t = time
U = potential (stored) energy
V = electric potential
v = velocity or speed
ρ = resistivity
ϕ_m = magnetic flux
κ = dielectric constant

$$d\mathbf{B} = \frac{\mu_0}{4\pi}\frac{Id\ell \times \mathbf{r}}{r^3}$$

$$\mathbf{F} = \int Id\ell \times \mathbf{B}$$

$$B_s = \mu_o nI$$

$$\phi_m = \int \mathbf{B} \cdot d\mathbf{A}$$

$$\varepsilon = -\frac{d\phi_m}{dt}$$

$$\varepsilon = -L\frac{dI}{dt}$$

$$U_L = \frac{1}{2}LI^2$$

ADVANCED PLACEMENT PHYSICS C EQUATIONS

GEOMETRY AND TRIGONOMETRY

Rectangle

$A = bh$

Triangle

$A = \frac{1}{2}bh$

Circle

$A = \pi r^2$

$C = 2\pi r$

Parallelepiped

$V = lwh$

Cylinder

$V = \pi r^2 l$

$S = 2\pi rl + 2\pi r^2$

Sphere

$V = \frac{4}{3}\pi r^3$

$S = 4\pi r^2$

Right Triangle

$a^2 + b^2 = c^2$

$\sin\theta = \frac{a}{c}$

$\cos\theta = \frac{b}{c}$

$\tan\theta = \frac{a}{b}$

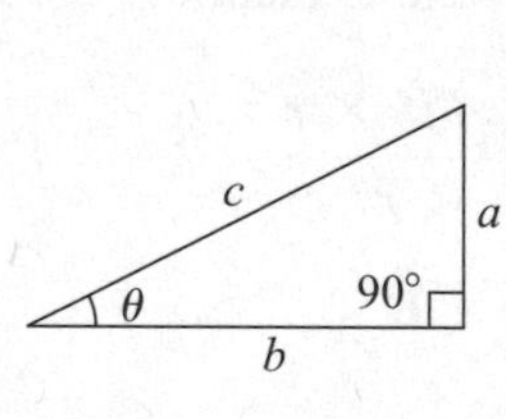

A = area
C = circumference
V = volume
S = surface area
b = base
h = height
l = length
w = width
r = radius

CALCULUS

$$\frac{df}{dx} = \frac{df}{du}\frac{du}{dx}$$

$$\frac{d}{dx}(x^n) = nx^{n-1}$$

$$\frac{d}{dx}(e^x) = e^x$$

$$\frac{d}{dx}(\ln x) = \frac{1}{x}$$

$$\frac{d}{dx}(\sin x) = \cos x$$

$$\frac{d}{dx}(\cos x) = -\sin x$$

$$\int x^n dx = \frac{1}{n+1}x^{n+1},\ n \neq -1$$

$$\int e^x dx = e^x$$

$$\int \frac{dx}{x} = \ln|x|$$

$$\int \cos x\, dx = \sin x$$

$$\int \sin x\, dx = -\cos x$$

ANSWER SHEETS

AP Physics B & C

PRACTICE EXAM 1

AP Physics B

Answer Sheet

1. Ⓐ Ⓑ Ⓒ Ⓓ Ⓔ	28. Ⓐ Ⓑ Ⓒ Ⓓ Ⓔ	55. Ⓐ Ⓑ Ⓒ Ⓓ Ⓔ
2. Ⓐ Ⓑ Ⓒ Ⓓ Ⓔ	29. Ⓐ Ⓑ Ⓒ Ⓓ Ⓔ	56. Ⓐ Ⓑ Ⓒ Ⓓ Ⓔ
3. Ⓐ Ⓑ Ⓒ Ⓓ Ⓔ	30. Ⓐ Ⓑ Ⓒ Ⓓ Ⓔ	57. Ⓐ Ⓑ Ⓒ Ⓓ Ⓔ
4. Ⓐ Ⓑ Ⓒ Ⓓ Ⓔ	31. Ⓐ Ⓑ Ⓒ Ⓓ Ⓔ	58. Ⓐ Ⓑ Ⓒ Ⓓ Ⓔ
5. Ⓐ Ⓑ Ⓒ Ⓓ Ⓔ	32. Ⓐ Ⓑ Ⓒ Ⓓ Ⓔ	59. Ⓐ Ⓑ Ⓒ Ⓓ Ⓔ
6. Ⓐ Ⓑ Ⓒ Ⓓ Ⓔ	33. Ⓐ Ⓑ Ⓒ Ⓓ Ⓔ	60. Ⓐ Ⓑ Ⓒ Ⓓ Ⓔ
7. Ⓐ Ⓑ Ⓒ Ⓓ Ⓔ	34. Ⓐ Ⓑ Ⓒ Ⓓ Ⓔ	61. Ⓐ Ⓑ Ⓒ Ⓓ Ⓔ
8. Ⓐ Ⓑ Ⓒ Ⓓ Ⓔ	35. Ⓐ Ⓑ Ⓒ Ⓓ Ⓔ	62. Ⓐ Ⓑ Ⓒ Ⓓ Ⓔ
9. Ⓐ Ⓑ Ⓒ Ⓓ Ⓔ	36. Ⓐ Ⓑ Ⓒ Ⓓ Ⓔ	63. Ⓐ Ⓑ Ⓒ Ⓓ Ⓔ
10. Ⓐ Ⓑ Ⓒ Ⓓ Ⓔ	37. Ⓐ Ⓑ Ⓒ Ⓓ Ⓔ	64. Ⓐ Ⓑ Ⓒ Ⓓ Ⓔ
11. Ⓐ Ⓑ Ⓒ Ⓓ Ⓔ	38. Ⓐ Ⓑ Ⓒ Ⓓ Ⓔ	65. Ⓐ Ⓑ Ⓒ Ⓓ Ⓔ
12. Ⓐ Ⓑ Ⓒ Ⓓ Ⓔ	39. Ⓐ Ⓑ Ⓒ Ⓓ Ⓔ	66. Ⓐ Ⓑ Ⓒ Ⓓ Ⓔ
13. Ⓐ Ⓑ Ⓒ Ⓓ Ⓔ	40. Ⓐ Ⓑ Ⓒ Ⓓ Ⓔ	67. Ⓐ Ⓑ Ⓒ Ⓓ Ⓔ
14. Ⓐ Ⓑ Ⓒ Ⓓ Ⓔ	41. Ⓐ Ⓑ Ⓒ Ⓓ Ⓔ	68. Ⓐ Ⓑ Ⓒ Ⓓ Ⓔ
15. Ⓐ Ⓑ Ⓒ Ⓓ Ⓔ	42. Ⓐ Ⓑ Ⓒ Ⓓ Ⓔ	69. Ⓐ Ⓑ Ⓒ Ⓓ Ⓔ
16. Ⓐ Ⓑ Ⓒ Ⓓ Ⓔ	43. Ⓐ Ⓑ Ⓒ Ⓓ Ⓔ	70. Ⓐ Ⓑ Ⓒ Ⓓ Ⓔ
17. Ⓐ Ⓑ Ⓒ Ⓓ Ⓔ	44. Ⓐ Ⓑ Ⓒ Ⓓ Ⓔ	
18. Ⓐ Ⓑ Ⓒ Ⓓ Ⓔ	45. Ⓐ Ⓑ Ⓒ Ⓓ Ⓔ	
19. Ⓐ Ⓑ Ⓒ Ⓓ Ⓔ	46. Ⓐ Ⓑ Ⓒ Ⓓ Ⓔ	
20. Ⓐ Ⓑ Ⓒ Ⓓ Ⓔ	47. Ⓐ Ⓑ Ⓒ Ⓓ Ⓔ	
21. Ⓐ Ⓑ Ⓒ Ⓓ Ⓔ	48. Ⓐ Ⓑ Ⓒ Ⓓ Ⓔ	
22. Ⓐ Ⓑ Ⓒ Ⓓ Ⓔ	49. Ⓐ Ⓑ Ⓒ Ⓓ Ⓔ	
23. Ⓐ Ⓑ Ⓒ Ⓓ Ⓔ	50. Ⓐ Ⓑ Ⓒ Ⓓ Ⓔ	
24. Ⓐ Ⓑ Ⓒ Ⓓ Ⓔ	51. Ⓐ Ⓑ Ⓒ Ⓓ Ⓔ	
25. Ⓐ Ⓑ Ⓒ Ⓓ Ⓔ	52. Ⓐ Ⓑ Ⓒ Ⓓ Ⓔ	
26. Ⓐ Ⓑ Ⓒ Ⓓ Ⓔ	53. Ⓐ Ⓑ Ⓒ Ⓓ Ⓔ	
27. Ⓐ Ⓑ Ⓒ Ⓓ Ⓔ	54. Ⓐ Ⓑ Ⓒ Ⓓ Ⓔ	

Free-Response Answer Sheet

For the free-response section, write your answers on sheets of blank paper.

PRACTICE EXAM 2

AP Physics B

Answer Sheet

1. (A) (B) (C) (D) (E)
2. (A) (B) (C) (D) (E)
3. (A) (B) (C) (D) (E)
4. (A) (B) (C) (D) (E)
5. (A) (B) (C) (D) (E)
6. (A) (B) (C) (D) (E)
7. (A) (B) (C) (D) (E)
8. (A) (B) (C) (D) (E)
9. (A) (B) (C) (D) (E)
10. (A) (B) (C) (D) (E)
11. (A) (B) (C) (D) (E)
12. (A) (B) (C) (D) (E)
13. (A) (B) (C) (D) (E)
14. (A) (B) (C) (D) (E)
15. (A) (B) (C) (D) (E)
16. (A) (B) (C) (D) (E)
17. (A) (B) (C) (D) (E)
18. (A) (B) (C) (D) (E)
19. (A) (B) (C) (D) (E)
20. (A) (B) (C) (D) (E)
21. (A) (B) (C) (D) (E)
22. (A) (B) (C) (D) (E)
23. (A) (B) (C) (D) (E)
24. (A) (B) (C) (D) (E)
25. (A) (B) (C) (D) (E)
26. (A) (B) (C) (D) (E)
27. (A) (B) (C) (D) (E)
28. (A) (B) (C) (D) (E)
29. (A) (B) (C) (D) (E)
30. (A) (B) (C) (D) (E)
31. (A) (B) (C) (D) (E)
32. (A) (B) (C) (D) (E)
33. (A) (B) (C) (D) (E)
34. (A) (B) (C) (D) (E)
35. (A) (B) (C) (D) (E)
36. (A) (B) (C) (D) (E)
37. (A) (B) (C) (D) (E)
38. (A) (B) (C) (D) (E)
39. (A) (B) (C) (D) (E)
40. (A) (B) (C) (D) (E)
41. (A) (B) (C) (D) (E)
42. (A) (B) (C) (D) (E)
43. (A) (B) (C) (D) (E)
44. (A) (B) (C) (D) (E)
45. (A) (B) (C) (D) (E)
46. (A) (B) (C) (D) (E)
47. (A) (B) (C) (D) (E)
48. (A) (B) (C) (D) (E)
49. (A) (B) (C) (D) (E)
50. (A) (B) (C) (D) (E)
51. (A) (B) (C) (D) (E)
52. (A) (B) (C) (D) (E)
53. (A) (B) (C) (D) (E)
54. (A) (B) (C) (D) (E)
55. (A) (B) (C) (D) (E)
56. (A) (B) (C) (D) (E)
57. (A) (B) (C) (D) (E)
58. (A) (B) (C) (D) (E)
59. (A) (B) (C) (D) (E)
60. (A) (B) (C) (D) (E)
61. (A) (B) (C) (D) (E)
62. (A) (B) (C) (D) (E)
63. (A) (B) (C) (D) (E)
64. (A) (B) (C) (D) (E)
65. (A) (B) (C) (D) (E)
66. (A) (B) (C) (D) (E)
67. (A) (B) (C) (D) (E)
68. (A) (B) (C) (D) (E)
69. (A) (B) (C) (D) (E)
70. (A) (B) (C) (D) (E)

Free-Response Answer Sheet

For the free-response section, write your answers on sheets of blank paper.

PRACTICE EXAM 3

AP Physics C Mechanics

Answer Sheet

1. Ⓐ Ⓑ Ⓒ Ⓓ Ⓔ
2. Ⓐ Ⓑ Ⓒ Ⓓ Ⓔ
3. Ⓐ Ⓑ Ⓒ Ⓓ Ⓔ
4. Ⓐ Ⓑ Ⓒ Ⓓ Ⓔ
5. Ⓐ Ⓑ Ⓒ Ⓓ Ⓔ
6. Ⓐ Ⓑ Ⓒ Ⓓ Ⓔ
7. Ⓐ Ⓑ Ⓒ Ⓓ Ⓔ
8. Ⓐ Ⓑ Ⓒ Ⓓ Ⓔ
9. Ⓐ Ⓑ Ⓒ Ⓓ Ⓔ
10. Ⓐ Ⓑ Ⓒ Ⓓ Ⓔ
11. Ⓐ Ⓑ Ⓒ Ⓓ Ⓔ
12. Ⓐ Ⓑ Ⓒ Ⓓ Ⓔ
13. Ⓐ Ⓑ Ⓒ Ⓓ Ⓔ
14. Ⓐ Ⓑ Ⓒ Ⓓ Ⓔ
15. Ⓐ Ⓑ Ⓒ Ⓓ Ⓔ
16. Ⓐ Ⓑ Ⓒ Ⓓ Ⓔ
17. Ⓐ Ⓑ Ⓒ Ⓓ Ⓔ
18. Ⓐ Ⓑ Ⓒ Ⓓ Ⓔ
19. Ⓐ Ⓑ Ⓒ Ⓓ Ⓔ
20. Ⓐ Ⓑ Ⓒ Ⓓ Ⓔ
21. Ⓐ Ⓑ Ⓒ Ⓓ Ⓔ
22. Ⓐ Ⓑ Ⓒ Ⓓ Ⓔ
23. Ⓐ Ⓑ Ⓒ Ⓓ Ⓔ
24. Ⓐ Ⓑ Ⓒ Ⓓ Ⓔ
25. Ⓐ Ⓑ Ⓒ Ⓓ Ⓔ
26. Ⓐ Ⓑ Ⓒ Ⓓ Ⓔ
27. Ⓐ Ⓑ Ⓒ Ⓓ Ⓔ
28. Ⓐ Ⓑ Ⓒ Ⓓ Ⓔ
29. Ⓐ Ⓑ Ⓒ Ⓓ Ⓔ
30. Ⓐ Ⓑ Ⓒ Ⓓ Ⓔ
31. Ⓐ Ⓑ Ⓒ Ⓓ Ⓔ
32. Ⓐ Ⓑ Ⓒ Ⓓ Ⓔ
33. Ⓐ Ⓑ Ⓒ Ⓓ Ⓔ
34. Ⓐ Ⓑ Ⓒ Ⓓ Ⓔ
35. Ⓐ Ⓑ Ⓒ Ⓓ Ⓔ

Free-Response Answer Sheet

For the free-response section, write your answers on sheets of blank paper.

PRACTICE EXAM 4

AP Physics C Electricity and Magnetism

Answer Sheet

1. (A) (B) (C) (D) (E)
2. (A) (B) (C) (D) (E)
3. (A) (B) (C) (D) (E)
4. (A) (B) (C) (D) (E)
5. (A) (B) (C) (D) (E)
6. (A) (B) (C) (D) (E)
7. (A) (B) (C) (D) (E)
8. (A) (B) (C) (D) (E)
9. (A) (B) (C) (D) (E)
10. (A) (B) (C) (D) (E)
11. (A) (B) (C) (D) (E)
12. (A) (B) (C) (D) (E)
13. (A) (B) (C) (D) (E)
14. (A) (B) (C) (D) (E)
15. (A) (B) (C) (D) (E)
16. (A) (B) (C) (D) (E)
17. (A) (B) (C) (D) (E)
18. (A) (B) (C) (D) (E)
19. (A) (B) (C) (D) (E)
20. (A) (B) (C) (D) (E)
21. (A) (B) (C) (D) (E)
22. (A) (B) (C) (D) (E)
23. (A) (B) (C) (D) (E)
24. (A) (B) (C) (D) (E)
25. (A) (B) (C) (D) (E)
26. (A) (B) (C) (D) (E)
27. (A) (B) (C) (D) (E)
28. (A) (B) (C) (D) (E)
29. (A) (B) (C) (D) (E)
30. (A) (B) (C) (D) (E)
31. (A) (B) (C) (D) (E)
32. (A) (B) (C) (D) (E)
33. (A) (B) (C) (D) (E)
34. (A) (B) (C) (D) (E)
35. (A) (B) (C) (D) (E)

Free-Response Answer Sheet

For the free-response section, write your answers on sheets of blank paper.

INDEX

AP Physics B & C

Index

D

F

G

H

I

J

K

L

M

N

O

P

U

V

W

INSTALLING REA's TestWare®

SYSTEM REQUIREMENTS

Pentium 75 MHz (300 MHz recommended), or a higher or compatible processor; Microsoft Windows 98 or later; 64 MB Available RAM; Internet Explorer 5.5 or higher.

INSTALLATION

1. Insert the AP Physics TestWare® CD-ROM into the CD-ROM drive.
2. If the installation doesn't begin automatically, from the Start Menu, choose the RUN command. When the RUN dialog box appears, type d:\setup (where D is the letter of your CD-ROM drive) at the prompt and click OK.
3. The installation process will begin. A dialog box proposing the directory "Program Files\REA\AP_PhysicsB" will appear. If the name and location are suitable, click OK. If you wish to specify a different name or location, type it in and click OK.
4. Start the AP Physics TestWare® application by double-clicking on the icon.

REA's AP Physics TestWare® is **EASY** to **LEARN AND USE**. To achieve maximum benefits, we recommend that you take a few minutes to go through the on-screen tutorial on your computer. The "screen buttons" are also explained there to familiarize you with the program.

SSD ACCOMMODATIONS FOR STUDENTS WITH DISABILITIES

Many students qualify for extra time to take the AP Physics exam, and our TestWare® can be adapted to accommodate your time extension. This allows you to practice under the same extended time accommodations that you will receive on the actual test day. To customize your TestWare® to suit the most common extensions, visit our Website at *www.rea.com/ssd*.

TECHNICAL SUPPORT

REA's TestWare® is backed by customer and technical support. For questions about **installation or operation of your software**, contact us at:

Research & Education Association
Phone: (732) 819-8880 (9 a.m. to 5 p.m. ET, Monday–Friday)
Fax: (732) 819-8808
Website: www.rea.com
E-mail: info@rea.com

Note to Windows XP Users: In order for the TestWare® to function properly, please install and run the application under the same computer-administrator level user account. Installing the TestWare® as one user and running it as another could cause file access path conflicts.